50 Events That Shaped American Indian History

50 Events That Shaped American Indian History

An Encyclopedia of the American Mosaic

Volume 2

Donna Martinez and Jennifer L. Williams Bordeaux, Editors

GREENWOOD™

An Imprint of ABC-CLIO, LLC
Santa Barbara, California • Denver, Colorado

Library of Congress Cataloging-in-Publication Data

Names: Martinez, Donna, editor of compilation. | Bordeaux, Jennifer L. Williams, editor of compilation.
Title: 50 events that shaped American Indian history : an encyclopedia of the American mosaic / Donna Martinez and Jennifer L. Williams Bordeaux, editors.
Other titles: Fifty events that shaped American Indian history
Description: Santa Barbara, California : Greenwood, an imprint of ABC-CLIO, LLC, [2017] | Includes bibliographical references and index.
Identifiers: LCCN 2016025425 (print) | LCCN 2016026268 (ebook) | ISBN 9781440835766 (set : hardback : acid-free paper) | ISBN 9781440846496 (volume 1 : hardback : acid-free paper) | ISBN 9781440846502 (volume 2 : hardback : acid-free paper) | ISBN 9781440835773 (ebook (set))
Subjects: LCSH: Indians of North America—History—Encyclopedias. | United States—Ethnic relations—History—Encyclopedias. | BISAC: SOCIAL SCIENCE / Ethnic Studies / Asian American Studies. | SOCIAL SCIENCE / Ethnic Studies / General.
Classification: LCC E77 .A125 2017 (print) | LCC E77 (ebook) | DDC 305.800973—dc23
LC record available at https://lccn.loc.gov/2016025425

ISBN: 978-1-4408-3576-6 (set)
ISBN: 978-1-4408-4649-6 (Volume 1)
ISBN: 978-1-4408-4650-2 (Volume 2)
EISBN: 978-1-4408-3577-3

21 20 19 18 17   1 2 3 4 5

This book is also available as an eBook.

Greenwood
An Imprint of ABC-CLIO, LLC

ABC-CLIO, LLC
130 Cremona Drive, P.O. Box 1911
Santa Barbara, California 93116-1911
www.abc-clio.com

This book is printed on acid-free paper ∞

Manufactured in the United States of America

Contents

6

From the Great Depression to Alcatraz, 1929–1969

National Congress of American Indians, 1944

Katie Kirakosian

Chronology

1944   The NCAI is formed in November.

1946   The NCAI pushes to form the Indian Claims Commission.

1949   The NCAI urges President Harry Truman to veto the Navajo-Hopi Rehabilitation Bill because of the inclusion of a controversial Section 9. This would have created state jurisdiction on the Navajo and Hopi reservations. The bill is passed in 1950, but only after Section 9 is removed.

1950   The NCAI pushes to have an anti-reservation clause put into the Alaska statehood bill.

1954   In opposition to termination and assimilation policies earlier in the decade, the NCAI holds an emergency meeting.

1958   The NCAI sends a delegation to Puerto Rico to see Operation Bootstrap in action. This results in "Operation Bootstrap for the American Indian," which is heard in Congress in 1960. Although it does not become law, it is a victory for those who oppose termination.

1961   NCAI members work with other organizations at the American Indian Chicago Conference in June 1961, which establishes the *Declaration of Indian Purpose: The Voice of the American Indian.*

1967 The NCAI intervenes over an unbalanced portrayal of George Armstrong Custer for an ABC television series. Under threat of FCC hearings, the series if quickly cancelled.

1968 The NCAI starts the Miss NCAI Scholarship Pageant.

1970 President Richard Nixon offers a Special Message on Indian Affairs, which essentially ends the federal government's push for termination.

1975–1978 The NCAI helps advocate for the passage of key legislation, including the Indian Self-Determination and Education Assistance Act (1975), the Indian Health Care Improvement Act (1976), the American Indian Religious Freedom Act (1978), and the Indian Child Welfare Act (1978).

1977 NCAI Executive Director Charles Trimble (Oglala Sioux) steps down to head the United Effort Trust.

1988 The NCAI and other groups support the passage of the Indian Gaming Regulatory Act, which promises economic stability for many tribal nations.

1990 The Native American Graves Protection and Repatriation Act is passed, which establishes a process for museums and Federal agencies to return Native American human remains, funerary objects, sacred objects, and objects of cultural patrimony to federally recognized tribes.

1990 In response to the Supreme Court's decision in *Duro v. Reina*, the Duro fix is passed. It confirms that recognized tribes do have jurisdiction over American Indians.

1994 President Bill Clinton issues a memorandum to all executive departments, explaining the government's responsibility to consult with tribal nations.

1996 The NCAI and other groups push for passage of the Native American Housing Assistance and Self-Determination Act, which ensures control of housing-related funds and resources.

1996 President Bill Clinton signs Executive Order No. 13007, which is aimed at preserving and protecting Indian religious practices on federal lands by allowing the access and use of religious sites.

1997 The NCAI Youth Commission is founded.

2003 The NCAI works to start the Policy Research Center, which remains a key NCAI initiative.

2009 The NCAI works with other groups to ensure that the Embassy of tribal nations opens in Washington, D.C.

2009 The NCAI works with the Native American Rights Fund (NARF) to release *Tribal Principles for Climate Change Legislation*, which argues that climate-change legislation must consider tribal nations as sovereign partners.

2010   Through the support of the NCAI and other groups, the Tribal Law and Order Act and the Indian Health Care Improvement Act become law.

2010   President Barack Obama endorses the *UN Declaration on the Rights of Indigenous Peoples*, although the United States had initially voted against the Declaration in 2007.

2011   The NCAI makes keynote address at the National Congress of Australia's First Peoples and co-hosts a board meeting with Canada's Assembly of First Nations.

2013   The Violence against Women Act becomes law with added provisions to ensure that tribal governments protect Native women.

2015   The NCAI starts the *First Kids 1st* newsletter.

Introduction

The National Congress of American Indians (NCAI) is an intertribal, activist, non-profit organization that seeks to provide a space for its members to voice their concerns about, and offer solutions to, the complex issues in Indian country and, more broadly, faced by American Indians and Alaska Natives. Although not the first organization of its kind, today the NCAI is the "oldest, largest, and most representative American Indian and Alaska Native organization" (National Congress of American Indians). Since its founding in 1944, the NCAI's mission has been focused on protecting treaties and sovereign rights, ensuring continued access to traditional culture for future generations, historicizing tribal governments and their right to nation-to-nation relations with other governments, and improving the overall quality of life for American Indians and Alaska Natives. Five key policy areas help structure the NCAI's efforts: Community & Culture; Economic Development & Commerce; Education, Health, & Human Services; Land & Natural Resources; and Tribal Governance (National Congress of American Indians).

The 1940s

Cornell (1988) paints the 1940s and the decades that followed as a time when "Indians not only have demanded a voice in decision making but they have *appropriated* such a voice for themselves" (Cornell 1988, 5). The founding of the NCAI came at a crucial time because many politicians and Americans wanted full integration of

Representatives of various tribes attending an organizational meeting of the National Congress of American Indians (NCAI), 1944. Their founding conference occurred in Denver, Colorado, due to its central location to the majority of reservations. It stood against federal termination and relocation policies that sought to end the legal status of all tribes. The NCAI remains active on various issues and is the oldest American Indian national organization in the United States. (nsf/Alamy Stock Photo)

American Indians and Alaska Natives. For example, in 1943 Congressman Karl Mundt questioned the need for an Indian Bureau at all, arguing that was "not more necessary than a bureau to handle problems for Italians, French, Irish, Negroes, or any other racial group" (Mundt 1943 as cited in Bernstein 1999, 114). Here the argument for American Indian integration into dominant society fueled others who felt tribal sovereignty was unnecessary and even contradictory.

Despite varied dissent, on November 15, 1944, nearly 80 delegates representing 50 tribes met at the Metropolitan Hotel in Denver, Colorado (National Congress of American Indians). This was an unprecedented gathering of intertribal leaders and included a diverse group of tribal councilors, religious leaders, and members of the BIA. By the time the group dispersed on November 18, 1944, the NCAI was officially formed.

Sidebar 1: The Road to the NCAI's Founding

The founding of the NCAI must be contextualized within a wave of pan-Indianism or supratribalism that emerged in the 20th century, in "response to [the United States government's] termination and assimilation policies" (National Congress of American Indians). In 1933, President Franklin Roosevelt tapped John Collier to serve as the commissioner for the Bureau of Indian Affairs, a position that he held until 1945. Collier was vehemently opposed to forced assimilation and set four new objectives for the BIA, which were "rebuilding Indian tribal societies, enlarging and rehabilitating Indian landholdings, fostering Indian self-government, and preserving and promoting Indian culture" (Blackman 2013, 54). He argued against boarding schools that took children away from their families and communities, which was also a concern noted in the *Meriam Report*. Instead, he pushed for local reservation-based schools that fostered traditional teachings and cultural pride. During his tenure as Indian Commissioner, Collier worked to ensure that the BIA's monopoly on "Indian lives and affairs by the BIA was curbed, at least for a while, and the powers of the agents were checked; cultural preservation was encouraged and the suppression of indigenous religion reduced" (Cornell 1988, 93).

One key piece of legislation during Collier's tenure that helped pave the way for the NCAI was the Indian Reorganization Act (IRA) of 1934. This act set a new course for American Indians and Alaska Natives (Cornell 1988), and the initiative was meant to facilitate Collier's "dream of reviving Indian tribes and customs, thus restoring to Indians a sense of pride in their communities and themselves" (Taylor 1980, 17). Specifically, through this act, Collier and his staff worked to combat many of the devastating effects of colonization while also promoting self-governance, economic stability, and tribal rights. The spirit of the IRA led many to call Collier a communist, while he repeatedly had to dodge congressional attacks that relentlessly pushed for termination and assimilation following the IRA's passage (Wilkinson 2006). None of this deterred Collier and his determination to see his vision realized, although he is still seen of as a controversial figure in Indian country today.

The founding of the NCAI was "a turning point in Indian affairs as Indians emerged as skilled political organizers and lobbyists for their interests at the national level" (Bernstein 1999, 112). Things like the Indian Reorganization Act "convinced a new generation of Indian that they could determine their own destiny" (Bernstein

Sidebar 2: A List of All NCAI Presidents and Executive Directors

Term	President
1944–1952	Napoleon B. Johnson (Cherokee)
1953–1959	Joseph R. Garry (Coeur D'Alene)
1960–1964	Walter Wetzel (Blackfeet)
1965–1966	Clarence Wesley (San Carlos Apache)
1967–1968	Wendell Chino (Mecalero Apache)
1969–1970	Earl Old Person (Blackfeet)
1971–1972	Leon F. Cook (Colville)
1973–1976	Mel Tonasket (Colville)
1977–1978	Veronica L. Murdock (Mohave)
1979–1980	Edward Driving Hawk (Sioux)
1981–1984	Joseph DeLaCruz (Quinault)
1985–1987	Reuben A. Snake, Jr. (Winnebago)
1988–1989	John Gonzales (San Ildefonso Pueblo)
1990–1991	Wayne L. Ducheneaux (Cheyenne River Sioux)
1992–1995	gaiashkibos (Lac Courte Oreilles)
1996–1999	W. Ron Allen (Jamestown S'Klallam)
2000–2001	Susan Masten (Yurok)
2002–2005	Tex Hall (Mandan/Hidatsa/Arikara)
2006–2009	Joe A. Garcia (Ohkay Owingeh)
2010–2013	Jefferson Keel (Chickasaw Nation)
2014–Present	Brian Cladoosby (Swinomish)

Term	Executive Director
1944–1948	Ruth Muskrat Bronson (Cherokee)
1949	Louis R. Bruce (Mohawk/Sioux) Edward Rogers (Chippewa)
1950	John C. Rainer (Taos Pueblo)
1951	Ruth Muskrat Bronson (Cherokee)
1952	Frank George (Colville)
1953–1959	Helen Peterson (Oglala Sioux)
1960–1963	Robert Burnett (Rosebud Sioux)

1964–1967	Vine Deloria, Jr. (Standing Rock Sioux)
1968	John Belindo (Navajo/Kiowa)
1969	Bruce Wilkie (Makah)
1970	Franklin Ducheneaux (Cheyenne River Sioux)
1971	Leo W. Vocu (Oglala Sioux)
1972–1977	Charles Trimble (Oglala Sioux)
1978	Andrew E. Ebona (Tlingit)
1979–1982	Ronald Andrade (Luiseno-Dieguneo)
1983	Silas Whitman (Nez Perce)
1984–1989	Susan Shown Harjo (Cheyenne)
1990–1991	A. Gay Klingman (Cheyenne River Sioux)
1992	Michael J. Anderson (Creek/Choctaw)
1993	Rachel A. Joseph (Shoshone/Paiute/Mono)
1994–2000	JoAnn K. Chase (Mandan/Hidatsa/Arikara)
2001–2014	Jacqueline Johnson Pata (Tlingit)

1999, 112). While the NCAI changed the political landscape, concerns over tribal and BIA factionalism were a real threat during these early years.

The NCAI accomplished a great deal by the close of the decade, such as establishing the Indian Claims Commission (ICC), working against termination legislation, and seeking an end to voting discrimination in states like Arizona and New Mexico (Cowger 2001). The NCAI also directly aided tribes under threat, like the Navajo and Hopi tribes in the late 1940s. To ensure solidarity over these and other issues, the theme of the 1948 convention was "One for All, All for One, United We Endure." A document entitled "Treaty of Peace, Friendship, and Mutual Assistance" was meant to "erase past tribal differences and to unite the tribes in a common future" and was signed by all NCAI member tribes (Cowger 2001). Little did the NCAI know that they would need to be more united then ever on issues soon to come (Cowger 2001, 74).

The 1950s

Although this decade was difficult for the NCAI, it did start with a decided victory. In 1950, the NCAI worked to add an anti-reservation clause in the Alaska Statehood bill, which allowed Alaska Natives to form reservations. However, a dire situation took hold of Indian country in this decade because of the efforts of the

Commissioner of Indian Affairs from 1950 to 1953, Dillon S. Myer, who relocated and "integrated" thousands of American Indian adults from reservations to nearby cities (Fixico 2000). Myer had experience with relocations, as he was in charge of the War Relocation Authority (WRA), which oversaw the forced removal and relocation of Japanese Americans during World War II. In 1952, the federal government started the Urban Indian Relocation Program, which pushed for the assimilation of American Indians into dominant society. This initiative was continued by the next commissioner as well, Glenn Emmons (1953–1960). In 1953, Congress introduced House Concurrence Resolution 108 (HCR 108), which required that "the end of reservations and federal services and protections be completed 'as rapidly as possible'" (Wilkinson 2006, 57). Coupled with this was Public Law 280, which gave states criminal jurisdiction in over half of the Indian reservations (Champagne and Goldberg 2012). The 1953 conference became a critical meeting for the NCAI. Yellowtail spoke at the convention, referring to termination as "a conspiracy." He was clear that "The job of the Indians everywhere is to arrest and defeat these bills. . . . There is no time for bickering among tribal leaders; it is instead time for the united action against the common enemy" (Yellowtail as cited by Hoxie 2012). Also during this conference, the membership elected Joseph Garry (Coeur d'Alene) as the group's third president. A master organizer and politician at heart, he worked tirelessly visiting numerous tribes across the country to explain what termination would mean for them (Fahey 2012). His efforts were also supported by the NCAI's Executive Director, Helen Peterson (Oglala Sioux), who served alongside Garry. Together they worked to thwart federal assimilation and termination efforts and to ensure that self-determination was just that. Three things supported their vision for self-determination: honoring treaty rights, self-governance, and economic self-sufficiency (Tomblin 2009, 226).

In February 1954, Garry called an emergency conference in Washington, D.C., which was covered by thousands of media outlets (National Congress of American Indians). By the close of the conference, the group had proposed a Point IX program that argued for long-term self-sufficiency and had also approved a "Declaration of Indian Rights." Although the Point IX program was never implemented, it proved that American Indians could advocate for themselves. Another victory later that year included voting down Public Law 280. Here Yellowtail's words from the year before had come to fruition as the NCAI membership worked together, more united then ever before, to speak out against termination and relocation.

In 1958, the NCAI put together a 14-member delegation to visit Puerto Rico and learn more about "Operation Bootstrap" (Goldstein 2012). More specifically, they wanted to see how Puerto Rico had successfully positioned itself as "foreign in a domestic sense" while also ensuring "political autonomy" (Goldstein 2012, 85).

Upon their return, they helped put together a proposal entitled "Operation Bootstrap for the American Indian," which resulted in congressional hearings starting in 1960 (U.S. Government Printing Office 1960). While this did not become law, the push for termination quieted somewhat.

The 1960s

According to Cowger (2001), the NCAI has always been seen as a moderate group. This was in extreme contrast to more militant groups like the National Indian Youth Council (NIYC) and the American Indian Movement (AIM), which were both founded in the 1960s and saw the NCAI as a "paper tiger." While the moderate road forged by the NCAI may have led to its survival, it likely also led to some growing pains during this decade.

The NCAI worked off of the momentum of its earlier "Operation Bootstrap" initiative to write the "Declaration of Indian Purpose: The Voice of the American Indian" in 1961, which focused on the importance of tribal sovereignty and pre-serving American Indian and Alaska Native identity. Many elements of this declaration were later implemented in President Lyndon Johnson's "Great Society" (National Congress of American Indians). Later in his administration, Johnson began the Office for Economic Opportunity (OEO), which was often at odds with the BIA, which they saw as "anti-Indian." OEO's efforts were focused on "not only economic development but expertise development," which led to numerous reservations starting programs that were not dependent on the BIA (Tomblin 2009, 229).

This decade saw troubles in Indian country as well. As the executive director of the NCAI from 1964 to 1967, Deloria is credited with returning "the organization back to financial and organizational stability" (Cowger 2001, 4). Unfortunately, these were difficult years internally for the NCAI for other reasons, with issues still boiling over in regard to termination as well as the complex identities and histories of various reservation and urban American Indian groups, who had strong communities in Los Angeles, Oakland, Chicago, and Minneapolis, for example (Deloria, Jr. 2014). In 1964, the NCAI and the Affiliated tribes of Northwest Indians revoked membership from the Menominee Indians of Wisconsin over their internal push for termination, which the NCAI vehemently opposed. By 1968, however, tribal leadership had changed, and termination was off the table, leading the NCAI to reverse several membership decisions (Wilkinson 2006, 182).

As mentioned, early in the decade another Indian organization, the National Indian Youth Council (NIYC), was formed and had a rather different vision for American Indians' future as well as methods to attain this vision. Many leaders in the NIYC had been born on reservations and represented a new group of Indian activists who were tired of the tactics of earlier generations. The NIYC supported various initiatives and protests in the decade, like the 1964 fish-ins in Washington State. The NCAI focused its efforts in different ways. For example, the first Miss NCAI Scholarship Pageant was held in 1968, which was intended to empower and celebrate young Native women for their many gifts. Also in 1968, the Indian Civil Rights Act (ICRA) was passed and was aimed at ensuring civil rights in Indian country. When applying the ICRA, the courts have ensured that tribal customs and traditions are considered and that federal courts are only involved after tribal processes and courts have been involved.

The 1970s

During this time, the NCAI continued its moderate path. This lies in contrast to three groups founded in the previous decade: the American Indian Movement (AIM), the Indians of All Tribes (IOAT), and the United Native Americans (UNA). These groups were more militant in focus and took part in numerous occupations throughout the country to bring attention to their cause. Instead, the NCAI focused its efforts on working within Washington to push for change. According to Charles Trimble (Oglala Sioux), who served as executive director from 1972 until 1977, the NCAI almost collapsed in 1970 due to financial mismanagement the year before.

This decade bore witness to many positive changes for American Indians and Alaska Natives. Although such policies had waned by this time, in 1970, President Nixon officially ended the federal government's push for tribal termination. Instead, he endorsed self-determination, which was a huge victory supported by the NCAI. In part, Nixon and his staff argued, "We have concluded that the Indians will get better programs and that public monies will be more effectively expended if the people who are most affected by these programs are responsible for operating them" (Nixon 1970).

Congress passed several key pieces of legislation with the support of groups like the NCAI, including the Indian Self-Determination and Education Assistance Act (1975), the Indian Health Care Improvement Act (1976), and finally, the American Indian Religious Freedom Act and the Indian Child Welfare Act (1978). Ironically, this also came at a time when there was a "white backlash" from 1976 to 1977 that "saw the rise of state-level anti-tribal groups," which sent over a dozen pieces of legislation to Congress "calling for reversing Indian hunting and fishing rights court victories, terminating federal-tribal relations, and abrogating the Indian treaties" (Trimble 2009). The NCAI was able to push through, with the help of other groups like the American Indian Law Center, NARF, AIM, and the NTCA under the name "United Effort Trust."

The 1980s

The early 1980s were difficult years in terms of securing strong NCAI leadership. By 1984, Susan Shown Harjo (Cheyenne) became the executive director. Being well connected in Washington and around the country, Harjo ensured that the NCAI had a strong presence on Capitol Hill. She helped push for the Tribal Government Tax Status Act of 1983, various programs aimed at economic development, and the establishment of the National Museum of the American Indian.

In 1983, President Ronald Reagan issued a statement on Indian Policy, which pushed for local control of tribal affairs. Reagan was clear that he saw the federal government's role with Indian nations as a government-to-government relationship. Partly in response to this, the NCAI published an extensive report that same year, entitled *Tribal Governments at the Crossroads of History*. Environmental protection, especially the impacts of nuclear waste, was an increasing concern that led to the 1988 publication of *Environmental Protection in Indian Country: A Handbook for Tribal Leaders and Resource Managers*. As with each earlier decade, the NCAI continued its work with other groups to ensure the passage of important legislation. The most important piece of legislation to come out of this was the passage of the Indian Gaming Regulatory Act of 1988, which set the state for economic security for federally recognized tribal nations.

The 1990s

This decade began with the passage of two key pieces of legislation supported by many groups, including the NCAI. These were the Native American Graves Protection and Repatriation Act (NAGPRA) and the Indian Arts and Crafts Act. Since that time, the NCAI has been critical of the actual achievements of both laws by the federal government. In 1990, the Supreme Court also heard *Duro v. Reina* and ruled that Indian tribes could not prosecute nonmember Indians on their lands. In other words, Indian tribes only have jurisdiction over their own tribal members. This came as a blow to American Indians and Alaska Natives, but it was soon corrected with the Congressional "Duro fix" the following year, which determined that due to the powers of self-government, Indian tribes indeed have jurisdiction over all Indians (both members and non-members). In 1994, President Bill Clinton issued a memorandum to all executive departments, explaining the government's responsibility to consult with tribal nations. In 1996, Clinton also issued Executive Order 13007, which was aimed at protecting and preserving Indian religious practices and sacred sites located on federal lands. Finally, in 1996, the Native American Housing Assistance and Self-Determination Act was passed, which sought to address the housing crisis in Indian country. This bill has been amended and reauthorized numerous times since its initial passage. In 1997, the NCAI started the Youth Commission, which brings together youth aged 16 to 23 to consider issues facing their communities, and unique ways to met those challenges.

The New Millennium

The new millennium has seen many new NCAI initiatives and programs. In 2003, the Policy Research Center was formed, which is a "think tank" focused on unique issues faced by tribal communities across the United States. In 2009, the Embassy of tribal nations was opened in Washington, D.C. According to then NCAI president Jefferson Keel, "For the first time since settlement, tribal nations will have a permanent home in Washington, D.C., where they can more effectively assert their sovereign status and facilitate a much stronger nation-to-nation relationship with the federal government" (National Congress of American Indians). Since 2010, the NCAI has worked with other groups to support the passage of the Tribal Law & Order Act (2010), the Indian Health Care Improvement Act (2010), and the Violence Against Women Act (2013) with added provisions to ensure that tribal governments protect Native women.

The NCAI has also focused on larger global issues as well as making connections to other indigenous populations in the new millennium. For example, the NCAI partnered with the Native American Relief Fund (NARF), which now represents the NCAI on matters related to climate change. In 2009, the two groups proposed Tribal Principles for Climate Change legislation, which brought attention to the fact that American Indians and Alaska Natives are incredibly vulnerable when it comes to climate change and should, therefore, be closely consulted about climate change legislation. In 2010, President Barack Obama endorsed the United Nations Declaration on the Rights of Indigenous Peoples. This was a symbolic victory for indigenous groups, as the United States had initially voted against the declaration in 2007 (along with Australia, Canada, and New Zealand). In 2011, the NCAI was invited to give the keynote address at the National Congress of Australia's First People, and they held the first-ever joint meeting with Canada's Assembly of First Nations (National Congress of American Indians).

The NCAI has focused its energies on many new initiatives to involve Native youth. Successful programs include the NCAI's National Native Youth Cabinet (NNYC), which was established to support the growth of tomorrow's tribal leaders (aged 16 to 25). In 2012, it also formed an online community for Native youth called NDN Spark. The NCAI also offers internships and fellowship, including two specifically focused on tribal policy and governance and health disparities.

In his 2015 State of Indian Nations address, current NCAI president Brian Cladoosby (Swinomish) urged the NCAI to consider its part in a larger story "of pride and resilience book-ended by self-determination on either end" (Cladoosby 2015). Cladoosby is optimistic that today, American Indians and Alaska Natives are living in a time "that our ancestors prayed for" (Cladoosby 2015). If it were not for the determination of groups like the NCAI, the future of American Indians and Alaska Natives would be less certain. Over more than seven decades, the NCAI has served as a voice, although never *the* voice, for Indian country. The NCAI is keenly aware that its members come from an incredibly diverse group of nations, and it sees the value in bringing various perspectives together to consider issues that affect every corner of Indian country.

Biographies of Notable Figures

Joseph Garry (Coeur d'Alene) and Helen Peterson (Oglala Sioux)

One notable duo who can be credited with saving the NCAI as well as countless Indian nations are Joseph Garry (Coeur d'Alene) and Helen Peterson (Oglala Sioux), by working together to push against federal assimilation and termination efforts during their tenure. Garry was elected NCAI President in 1953, with Peterson named executive director that same year. They served together through the end of that tumultuous decade. As leaders and organizers, they were able to bring together diverse Native and non-Native groups around issues of mutual concern.

Garry was born in 1910 and grew up on the Coeur d'Alene reservation in Idaho. He served in the U.S. Marines in World War II and the Korean War and was elected to his tribal council. He was also the president of the Affiliated tribes of the Northwest Indians. Garry set his sights on becoming NCAI's President in 1953 and, according to Peterson, "ran a very dignified and sophisticated campaign to become president" (Peterson as cited in Fahey 2012, 30). Garry ensured the support of many in that year's elections, especially when Clarence Wesley officially nominated him. Peterson was born in 1915 on the Pine Ridge Reservation in South Dakota. She grew up in Nebraska, in the house of her Cheyenne grandmother, who was Black Kettle's niece (Varnell and Hanson 1999). She went to the NCAI after working in Denver's Department of Health and Welfare, getting minority voters registered.

Upon being elected, Garry and Peterson inherited a troubling situation. They were faced with the impending demise of all tribal nations through a series of congressional bills, and the NCAI was nearly bankrupt. There were also a series of congressional committees at that time, focused on the effectiveness of tribal governance and law enforcement on reservations and possible land taxation. Congress also wanted to allow the sale of liquor and firearms to American Indians, explaining that their efforts were aimed at equal rights for all. Garry and Peterson, however, sensed ulterior motives (Fahey 2012). Together they traveled the country asking for donations and soliciting new members to help fund the NCAI's much-needed presence in Washington, D.C. During that time, Arrow was of little help, although established as a fundraising arm for the NCAI. Garry and Peterson were unimpressed with Arrow's efforts and urged the closure of its New York office. They also worked tirelessly against McCarthyism during that time, as the NCAI was at times labeled a Communist group.

In early 1954, Garry and Peterson called an emergency conference focused on these issues. In his press release, Garry explained that the meeting was to "develop constructive programs which will serve Indian values and serve the best interests of the nation by protecting its national honor" (Rosier, 175). Amazingly, they were able to organize this meeting in less than three weeks, given the urgency of the situation. In a letter from Peterson to Garry, Peterson was clear that "The convention this year may very well be the most critical for Indians in this century . . . There can be no doubt that the accumulated bills in the last session were the gravest threat to Indian property and rights since the Allotment Act of 1887 . . . To consolidate the gains of this year and to plan for the future may never be more important than now" (Peterson as cited in Fahey 2012). Garry and Peterson were careful to enlist the support of other groups as well, including the Association of American Indian Affairs. At the time, this meeting was the largest inter-tribal demonstration, with representatives from 42 tribes. The conference also included individuals from 19 non-Indian organizations who were equally concerned with the current situation (Fahey 2012). Garry and Peterson also worked to show that Indians could solve their own problems, as outlined by Congress.

By 1955, the threat of termination had lessened, as supportive Democrats gained control of Congress, with increased power in 1957 as well. The challenges experiences during these years helped strengthen the NCAI and also made American Indian and Alaska Natives more politically savvy. In 1956, the NCAI helped support a program called "Register, Inform Yourself and Vote." Politicians took note of these important changes during this time as well and recognized Native Americans and Alaska Natives as viable constituents with unique needs and challenges (Cowger 2001). Peterson collaborated with McNickle to start a summer workshop series for Native American students at Colorado College, which began in 1956 and ended in 1970. These workshops set the stage for countless collegiate ethnic studies departments across the country. Peterson was the NCAI's first female director, and when she left office, she had been the longest-serving executive director as well.

By the end of Garry's and Peterson's tenure, the NCAI "had become a sophisticated organization formulating policies reflecting the opinions and views of Indian Country, as well as organizing lobbying skills that battered the US government's termination policy, protected Indian land rights and promoted Indian civil rights" (Ryser 2012, 58). Together, they are credited with getting the NCAI back on solid ground during one of the organization's most challenging times.

Vine Deloria, Jr.

Another important figure in the NCAI in the 1960s was Vine Deloria, Jr. (Standing Rock Sioux). Born in 1933 and raised partly on the Pine Ridge Indian Reservation, he came of age during a crucial time in American Indian history. Deloria, Jr. came from a prominent family, with his great-grandfather a noted medicine man, his grandfather an Episcopal priest, his aunt an anthropologist and linguist, and his father also an Episcopal priest. After serving in the U.S. Marines, he earned a B.A from Iowa State University and a B.D. in theology from Augustana Lutheran Seminary in 1963. Shortly thereafter, he worked for a time in Denver in the United Scholarship Service, which helped American Indians get scholarships to attend college.

By the time he ran for executive director in 1964, Deloria, Jr. was utterly discouraged with the state of Indian activism. The NCAI had shrunk significantly and only represented 19 tribes, although, by the end of his tenure, membership had swelled to 156 tribes (Lawrence 2010). The group was also yet again in financial straights, which he corrected during his time as executive director. In that role, he often testified before Congress on civil rights and other issues related to American Indians. For example, he testified before the Senate Subcommittee on Constitutional Rights of the Committee on the Judiciary on a bill that later became the Indian Civil Rights Act of 1968 (Deloria and Wildcat 2006). In that testimony, he argued that tribes would need funding to train Indian trial judges. His suggestion is credited with leading to the establishment of the National American Indian Court Judges Association in 1969 (Deloria, Jr. and Wildcat 2006).

Deloria, Jr. found that American Indians themselves, who were very focused on internal squabbles, stymied many of his efforts. There were also many other American Indian groups forming at the time, and they had visions different from the more moderate NCAI, which required his attention as well. Deloria, Jr. was always careful to downplay the many occupations of key locations across the country by more militant American Indian groups as chance happenings, for fear that it would undue his and the NCAI's hard work in Washington, D.C. In the end, his vision for activism was much different from that of many at the time. It was more in line with the NCAI's in that he saw the need for change from within the federal government. He wrote about his NCAI experiences in part in *Custer Died for Your Sins: An Indian Manifesto* (Deloria 1969).

Concerned about the general public's understanding of Native American history, Deloria, Jr. and the NCAI worked during this period to ensure that American Indians and Alaska Natives were fairly portrayed and equally represented in the media. In 1967, for example, the NCAI learned that ABC was airing a television series on Custer. The group protested the series because of its unbalanced portrayal of Custer, and they sued for equal airtime. Although the general public was largely unaware of the struggles occurring behind the scenes over this series, the NCAI was able to have the series cancelled after only nine episodes when FCC hearings became imminent (Deloria, Jr. 2014).

His time in the NCAI had a profound effect on Deloria, Jr. Most directly, his time as NCAI's executive director increased his national stature. As he recalls, he began writing during that time because "I wanted to give good briefings before Congress. I got to love old documents and learning how to root around in them" (Deloria, Jr. as cited in Lawrence 2010). Ultimately, Deloria, Jr.'s belief that there needed to be more trained Indian lawyers led to his resignation in 1967 and his enrollment in the University of Colorado Law School (Lawrence 2010). Deloria, Jr. still consulted with the NCAI during that time and also published many short columns in the *Sentinel*, the NCAI's quarterly newsletter (Lawrence 2010). Deloria, Jr. was a prolific writer, publishing a book every few years—20 books throughout his life, many of which were bestsellers.

Deloria, Jr. worked to support fishing rights, starting in the 1960s. For most of the 1970s, he served as the chairman of the Institute for the Development of Indian Law and on the board for the National Museum of the American Indian. He also came to the assistance of the Iroquois Six Nations in their wampum belt recovery. In 1974, he was called as a witness for the defense in the Wounded Knee Trials, where he collaborated with attorney John Thorne. In the 1990s, he continued his activism and spoke out against federal acknowledgment. While testifying before Congress, he argued, "It is certainly unjust to require Indian nations to perform documentary acrobatics for a slothful bureaucracy." For three decades (until his retirement in 2000), he taught at various universities, and he helped to establish a master's program in American Indian studies at the University of Arizona.

Further Reading

Bernstein, Alison R. *American Indians and World War II: Toward a New Era in Indian Affairs*. Norman: University of Oklahoma Press, 1999.

Champagne, Duane and Carole E. Goldberg. *Captured Justice: Native Nations and Public Law 280*. Durham, NC: Carolina Academic Press, 2012.

Cladoosby, Brian. State of Indian Nations address. http://www.ncai.org/about-ncai/state-of-indian-nations (accessed September 24, 2015).

Cornell, Stephen. *The Return of the Native: American Indian Political Resurgence*. Oxford, UK: Oxford University Press, 1988.

Cowger, Thomas W. *The National Congress of American Indians: The Founding Years*. Lincoln: University of Nebraska Press, 2001.

Deloria, Vine, Jr. *Custer Died for Your Sins: An Indian Manifesto*. Norman: The University of Oklahoma Press, 2014 [1969].

Deloria, Vine, Jr. and Daniel R. Wildcat. *Destroying Dogma: Vine Deloria, Jr. and His Influence on American Society*. Golden, CO: Fulcrum Publishing, 2006.

Fahey, John. *Saving the Reservation: Joe Garry and the Battle to Be Indian*. Seattle: The University of Washington Press, 2012.

Fixico, Donald Lee. *The Urban Indian Experience in America*. Albuquerque: The University of New Mexico Press, 2000.

Goldstein, Alyosha. *Poverty in Common: The Politics of Community Acton During the American Century*. Durham, NC: Duke University Press. 2012.

Hoxie, Frederick E. *This Indian Country: American Indian Political Activists and the Place They Made*. New York: The Penguin Press. 2012.

Lawrence, Michael Anthony. *Radicals in their Own Time: Four Hundred Years of Struggle for Liberty and Equal Justice in America*. Cambridge: Cambridge University Press. 2010.

National Congress of American Indians. www.ncai.org (accessed September 24, 2015).

Nixon, Richard. *President Nixon, Special Message on Indian Affairs, July 8, 1970*. http://www.ncai.org/resources/consultations/nixon-special-message-on-indian-affairs (accessed on September 25, 2015).

Ryser, Rudolph C. *Indigenous Nations and Modern States: The Political Emergence of Nations Challenging State Power*. New York: Routledge. 2012.

Tomblin, David C. *Managing Boundaries, Healing the Homeland: Ecological Restoration and the Revitalization of the White Mountain Apache Tribe, 1933–2000*. Dissertation, Virginia Polytechnic Institute and State University. 2009.

Truman, Harry S. *233. Veto of Bill Establishing a Program in Aid of the Navajo and Hopi Indians*. http://trumanlibrary.org/publicpapers/viewpapers.php?pid=1251 (accessed September 24, 2015).

Varnell, Jeanne and M.L. Hanson. *Women of Consequence: The Colorado Women's Hall of Fame*. Boulder: Big Earth Publishing. 1999.

Wilkinson, Charles F. *Blood Struggle: The Rise of Modern Indian Nations*. New York: W.W. Norton & Company. 2006.

The Anti-Discrimination Act, Alaska Natives, 1945

Caskey Russell

Chronology

1741   The first recorded contact Europeans had with Tlingits comes on July 17, 1741, when Russian Captain Chirikov anchors his ship, the *St. Paul*, near Sitka. The *St. Paul* stayed over a week in Tlingit territory, during which time Chirikov sent two longboats with armed Russian sailors to shore in order to replenish fresh water casks. Neither longboat returned. Toward the end of their stay, the crew of the *St. Paul* saw Tlingits in canoes paddling close to shore and attempting to communicate with the Russians (of course, the Russians couldn't understand Tlingit language), but the canoes did not come near the *St. Paul,* which departed without ever learning the fate of the missing sailors. European and Tlingit accounts of what happened to those Russian sailors differ greatly. The European version assumes the crews were killed by hostile Natives. The Tlingit oral account tells the local Tlingits welcomed the Russian sailors. The sailors had made known to the Tlingits that they feared the trip back to Russia in the coming winter, and wished to defect. The sailors eventually married Tlingit women and became prominent members of the Tlingit village of Klawock.

1830– Smallpox epidemics. The first major smallpox epidemic struck Alaska in
1860   the 1830s. Tlingit villages across the southeast were devastated. Another smallpox epidemic would strike in the 1860s. That epidemic directly affected Roy Peratrovich: his grandmother was one of the few survivors of the destruction of the Kuiu K̲waan (village on Kuiu Island). She fled Kuiu and relocated to Klawock, where Roy's mother would later be born.

1867   Sale of Alaska. The Treaty of Purchase between American and Russia stated that the Czar would sell to the United States the territory and dominion—on the continent and on islands—that he possessed at the time. Many Tlingit activists and scholars, along with historians both Native and non-Native, have pointed out that Russia "possessed" very little Tlingit territory at the time (a military stockade and a few small forts). The same situation applies with much of the Native territory in Alaska and thus calls into question what exactly was sold.

1885   William Paul is born.

1908   Roy Peratrovich is born.

1911   Elizabeth Wanamaker is born.

1912   Founding of the Alaskan Native Brotherhood (ANB).

1915   Founding of the Alaskan Native Sisterhood (ANS).

1920   William Paul is admitted to the Alaska Bar, becoming the first Alaskan Native lawyer.

1923   William Paul is elected to Alaskan Territorial Legislature, becoming the first Alaskan Native legislator.

1924   Indian Citizenship Act declares that all non-citizen Indians born within U.S. territory would be considered U.S. citizens.

1925   William Paul is re-elected to the Alaskan Territorial Legislature. Also in 1925, Alaska's Territorial Legislature enacts a law requiring voters to be able to read and write English. Paul adds a provision to the law to allow anyone who had previously voted, to continue voting regardless of literacy in English, which enables many Alaskan Natives to keep voting in important elections.

1931   Roy Peratrovich marries Elizabeth Wanamaker in Bellingham, Washington, where both attend Western College of Education.

1935   U.S. Congress authorizes the U.S. Court of Claims to adjudicate lawsuits against the U.S. government brought by Tlingit and Haida tribes.

1937   The ANB organizes Tlingit and Haida Central Council in order to sue the U.S. government for land and property theft.

1940   Roy Peratrovich becomes Grand President of the ANB.

1941   Roy and Elizabeth Peratrovich move to Juneau, where they encounter firsthand the legalized segregation and discrimination that Alaskan Natives had faced for decades in cities across Alaska.

1943   Roy and Elizabeth's first Alaska Anti-Discrimination Bill is introduced and subsequently defeated in the Alaskan Territorial Legislature.

1945   Roy and Elizabeth's second Alaska Anti-Discrimination Bill is introduced in the Alaskan Territorial Legislature on February 8. It is passed after a two-hour debate. Elizabeth and Roy Peratrovich are the only Natives who speak on the floor of the Senate during the debate. The bill is signed into law on February 16, becoming the first comprehensive anti-discrimination legislation in America.

1958   Elizabeth Peratrovich dies.

1959   Alaska becomes the 49th state.

1977   William Paul dies.

1988   Alaska's State Legislature establishes February 16 as Elizabeth Peratrovich Day—an official state holiday in memory of Elizabeth Peratrovich and her advocacy for civil rights.

1989   Roy Peratrovich dies.

Alaska Natives and the Fight against Discrimination

The gallant fight that Alaska Natives are waging today for the defense of their rights is a fight against racist principles that threaten all Americans. For the rights of each of us in a democracy can be no stronger that the rights of our weakest minority.

Felix Cohen, 1948

In Juneau, Alaska, on February 8, 1945, the Alaskan Territorial Legislature was in session debating a bill designed to put an end to legalized racial discrimination and segregation in Alaska's public buildings and privately owned businesses. Sitting in the packed public gallery amid a host of Alaskan Natives during the 1945 legislative session were the architects of the anti-discrimination bill: Elizabeth and Roy Peratrovich, both Tlingit Indians. Roy and Elizabeth had introduced a similar anti-discrimination bill before the legislature two years earlier, in 1943, but it had been defeated, in part because of a clause that would have desegregated public schools. That clause had been removed when the bill came up again before the legislature in 1945. Desegregating public schools would have to wait.

Alaskan legislative procedure at the time allowed for the public to address the legislature during open debate, so both Roy and Elizabeth were able to speak directly to any legislators who opposed their bill. The bill passed the House by a large margin, but was held up in the Senate, culminating in a two-hour debate, where racist senators lashed out against the idea of legally prohibiting segregation. Senator Allen Shattuck represented the feelings of many non-Indians when he told Roy during the debate, "Mr. Peratrovich, as I mentioned to you before, this bill will aggravate, rather than allay, the little feeling that now exists. Our Native cultures have ten centuries of white civilization to encompass in a few decades" (Dauenhauer 1994, 537).

Roy replied, "Only an Indian can know how it feels to be discriminated against. Either you are for discrimination or you are against it, accordingly as you vote on this bill" (Dauenhauer 1994, 537). This was not the first time Senator Shattuck and Roy Peratrovich disputed the myth of white superiority. Several years earlier, in response to comments made by Shattuck regarding Indians' low level of civilization, Roy had written, "I am wondering just what they [white people] call civilization. Looking over the court record in Alaska, one wonders if the white man is really civilized" (Dauenhauer 1994, 534).

Elizabeth Peratrovich's debate with Senator Shattuck during the 1945 session is best remembered by history. Elizabeth sat calmly knitting during much of the debate. When her turn to speak came, Elizabeth stood before the all-white male Senate and ripped apart the pro-segregation senators. The following excerpt, taken from the Senate Record, is a small part of that confrontation:

> **Senator Shattuck**: This legislation is wrong. Rather than being brought together, the races should be kept further apart. Who are these people, barely out of savagery, who want to associate with us whites, with 5,000 years of recorded civilization behind us?
>
> **Elizabeth Peratrovich**: I would not have expected that I, who am barely out of savagery, would have to remind the gentlemen with 5,000 years of recorded history behind them of our Bill of Rights. . . .
>
> **Senator Shattuck**: Will this law eliminate discrimination?
>
> **Elizabeth Peratrovich**: Do your laws against larceny, rape and murder prevent those crimes? No law will eliminate crimes, but at least you, as legislators, can assert to the world that you recognize the evil of the present situation and speak of your intent to help us overcome discrimination. . . . This super race attitude is wrong and forces our fine Native People to be associated with less than desirable circumstances. (Dauenhauer 1994, 537–38)

After her speech, the gallery exploded with applause. The anti-discrimination bill passed the Senate, eleven to five. The bill became law on February 16, 1945. A famous picture from that day shows a smiling Elizabeth standing next to the Alaskan Territorial Governor Ernest Gruening as he signed the bill into law. Later that evening, Elizabeth and Roy danced the night away at the Baranof Hotel in downtown Juneau. The "No Natives" sign that once adorned the hotel had been taken down. February 16 is now an official state holiday in Alaska in honor of Elizabeth and her civil rights work—in particular, to the memory of her speech in support of her anti-discrimination bill.

To understand how this bill became law nearly 20 years before the civil rights movements of the 1960s and the Civil Rights Act of 1964, it is helpful to examine the background of the Peratroviches, the Native political organizations to which they belonged, and the situation that Alaskan Natives found themselves in at the turn of the 20th century. Alaska in the 1800s and early 1900s was seen by non-Natives as a frontier of potential wealth. In American mythology, Alaska symbolized the Horatio Alger narrative writ large onto a new "frontier": poor, white, American men could travel to the gold fields of the Alaskan interior or to the Alaskan shores and forests, which teemed with fish, furs, and timber, and with enough tenacity, masculinity, and a bit of luck they could become wealthy. In reality, the profits from the vast resources of Alaska, taken from lands, forests, and seas stolen from Alaskan Natives, usually ended up in the coffers of wealthy businessmen, mine owners, cannery owners, and lumber barons who often resided outside Alaska.

In both the mythology and the reality, Alaskan Native communities mattered little. For the Native People who had lived in Alaska from time immemorial, the late 1800s up through 1950s was a prolonged period of colonization, cultural loss and destruction, racism and segregation, and sustained erosion of tribal sovereignty. Jim Crow policies similar to those in the American South were common across Alaska during this era. If one were to walk through the major towns of early 20-century Alaska, one would find signs on restaurants, theaters, businesses, and public buildings that read, "All White Help," "No Dogs, No Natives," and "No Natives Allowed." Alaskan Native families, to this day, share stories of family members of that era being forced out of businesses and buildings, or being refused housing, jobs, or school admission because they were Indian. "We don't want you stinking siwashes in here," one Alaskan drugstore owner yelled at the author's great grandmother when she and young her daughter tried to enter his store in Ketchikan. At the time, the term "*siwash*, which was derived from the word for *savage* in Chinook Jargon, was the most opprobrious slur a non-Native could use against an Alaskan Native. Alaskan Native Elders still associate that word with virulent racism.

Alaskan Natives had no legal redress in the courts for such discrimination. The legal status of Alaskan Natives was tenuous. When Russia sold Alaska to the Unites States, Alaskan Natives were not considered American citizens. Moreover, in Alaska until the 1930s, ". . . with the exception of the Tsimshians on Annette Island, Congress had not formally recognized any tribes" (Metcalfe 2014, 1). Yet, Alaskan Natives were subject to state taxation (including the five-dollar yearly public school tax, even though they were banned from attending public schools), state laws, and, subsequently, the Alaskan criminal justice system. Robbed of their lands and resources, and lacking the legal standing needed for redress within the U.S. legal system, early Alaskan Native leaders focused their efforts on gaining citizenship and voting rights, which would provide the legal footing needed to fight for civil and political rights. Citizenship was conferred to all American Indians in 1924 with the passage of the Indian Citizenship Act, which also secured voting rights for American Indians. Shortly thereafter, in 1925, the Alaskan Territorial Legislature, in a blatant attempt to prevent Alaskan Natives from voting, passed a law making literacy in English a perquisite. This was Alaskan Native reality that Elizabeth and Roy were born into during the early 20th century.

After graduating from Chemawa, an Indian boarding school in Oregon, Roy attended Western College of Education (now Western Washington University). Elizabeth was attending the same college. Though Roy and Elizabeth had known each other before college, their relationship blossomed at Western, and the two married in Bellingham, Washington, in December 1931. Roy and Elizabeth eventually moved to the Tlingit village of Klawock on the west coast of the Prince of Wales Island in the early 1930s. Klawock was a natural choice: Roy had been born in Klawock, and Elizabeth had lived there for a short period of time in her youth. In Klawock, they involved themselves in local politics—Roy served as mayor of the village for four terms—and in the two main political organizations for Alaskan Natives that, at that time, were dedicated to political and social change in Alaska: the Alaskan Native Brotherhood (ANB) and the Alaskan Native Sisterhood (ANS).

When it was founded in 1912, the ANB encouraged Natives to become educated and assimilated, and to adopt Western customs in order that they might become active members of the larger Alaskan and American community. By the time the Peratroviches became leaders of the ANB in 1940, however, the ANB had become an activist organization involved in protecting Native lands, ending segregation, and pursuing legal action against the U.S. government. The ANB also became a watchdog group that kept an eye on the political machinations of non-Natives. According to Richard and Nora Dauenhauer:

> When Indian school children were denied admission to the public school in Juneau, the ANB sued the district and forced the school to integrate. The ANB and ANS monitored federal legislation, assuring that Natives and all minority groups in the territory were treated equitably. (Daunehauer 1994, 532)

The ANB was also instrumental in electing the first Native Alaskan Territorial Legislator, William Paul, in 1923. Paul is one of the most important figures in 20th century Tlingit history. He attended Carlisle Indian School in Pennsylvania, graduated from Whitworth College in Washington State, and worked on a law degree through a correspondence/extension program at LaSalle University. By 1920, he had passed the Alaskan bar exam and become the first Native lawyer in Alaska and shortly thereafter was elected to the Alaskan Territorial Legislature. Paul had

Sidebar 1: The Alaskan Native Brotherhood (ANB): From Assimilation to Activism

The ANB was founded in 1912 by a group of Russian Orthodox and Presbyterian Alaskan Natives who had been educated in western religious institutions. The ANB was derivative of certain groups, or "societies," founded by Russian Orthodox priests in Alaska, all of whom were assimilationist in nature. Donald Mitchell, in his book *Sold American*, credits the initial idea of a Native political organization to Joseph McAfee, secretary of the Presbyterian Board of Missions, who suggested the idea after listening to Native grievances regarding turn-of-the-century U.S. policy in Alaska (194). As originally founded, the ANB had overtly assimilationist goals and attempted to promote "civilization" among Alaskan Natives. Two of the ANB's tenets were an English-only requirement for membership, and a belief in Christian theology. The First Article of ANB's constitution states, "The purpose of this organization shall be to assist and encourage the Native in his advancement from his Native state to his place among the cultivated races of the world" (Mitchell 1997, 274).

A basis in Christian theology was due to the fact that the ANB founders were all products of Native education programs based on religious models of education (such as missions or boarding schools). Regarding the English-only aims of the ANB, it has been pointed out that, at the founding of the ANB, the Tlingit language was in no apparent danger of being lost. Tlingit was still the first language for most tribal members. The Tlingit people themselves, however, were of a generation that remembered the danger of simply being Indian. At such times, survival is more important than any language concern.

Under the leadership of William Paul, beginning in the 1920s, the ANB became a political organization aimed at promoting voting rights, citizenship for Alaskan Natives, and desegregating public schools. With the leadership of William Paul, and later the Peratroviches (Roy, Elizabeth, and Frank), the ANB turned into an activist organization to attack segregation and discrimination.

joined the ANB soon after its founding. He would become a major figure in the ANB throughout the early 20th century. Paul served as Grand President of the ANB five times between 1920 and 1940. As a legislator and attorney familiar with the legal aspects of politics, his influence was immense. Paul must be given credit for turning the ANB into a politically active organization whose concern was protection of Alaskan Native rights and resources. He refocused the ANB toward issues of citizenship, property rights, ending school segregation, and redress for stolen tribal land and resources.

In 1920, Paul pushed the ANB to adopt a resolution against school segregation in Alaskan public schools (Dauenhauer 1994, 508). Paul was also a strong advocate for Native suffrage. The Native voting presence in Alaska was considerable—roughly one-quarter of the population of Alaska—and elections could be lost if prospective candidates failed to court the Native vote. If one wanted the Native vote, one had to court the ANB, or more precisely, the leaders of the ANB who could rally Native People behind a candidate. Paul created an ingenious voting device to help Alaskan Natives who could not read English: cardboard templates that could be placed atop voting ballot sheets. Holes were cut out of the cardboard templates that allowed Natives to make a mark next to the ANB-supported candidate (Metcalfe 2014, 102). With Paul's ability through the authority of the ANB to influence a large voting demographic, Alaskan Natives influenced the outcome of elections during the first half of the 20th century.

The Paul-controlled ANB era eventually came to an end when the Peratroviches wrested the reins of power in the late 1930s, which caused a division within ANB that was devastating and long-lasting. William Paul and the Peratroviches would remain enemies until the end of their lives. Yet, the ANB that the Peratroviches inherited from Paul had become a powerful organization in Alaskan politics with a history of fighting for progressive, pro-Indian causes. Paul's role in the fight against segregation is often forgotten due to the growing political and tribal recognition of the Peratroviches—Elizabeth in particular. However, Paul should rightly be remembered as an advocate whose struggles on behalf of Alaskan Native rights set an example for the Peratroviches to follow.

In time, the Peratrovich family wielded immense power in Alaskan Native politics: Roy served as Grand President of the ANB; Elizabeth served as Grand President of the ANS; and, Frank Peratrovich, Roy's older brother, served as an Alaskan Territorial Senator (he would eventually serve as president of the Alaska State Senate after statehood) and ANB Grand President. The ANB, under the Peratroviches, set its sights on land claims, rejecting the imposition of reservations in Alaska, and constant vigilance over the federal government's various pushes toward termination, statehood, and extinction of aboriginal title. The Peratrovich-led ANB also set its sights on ending Jim Crow segregation in Alaska.

There is no doubt the impetus behind the Peratroviches' anti-discrimination bill came from Roy and Elizabeth's lived experiences of segregation and discrimination, which they shared with thousands of Alaskan Natives across the territory. Shortly after Roy became the ANB Grand President in 1940, he took a job with the Bureau of Indian Affairs (BIA) in Juneau. Upon arrival, the Peratroviches were denied housing in what was considered the "white" part of Juneau. The move from the small, mostly Tlingit village of Klawock, to the large city exposed Roy and Elizabeth to other forms of blatant discrimination and racism:

> Signs in businesses and stores read "No Natives Allowed", "We Cater to white trade only", or advertised "Meals at all hours—All white help." Natives in Juneau could only buy a home in certain parts of town, could only attend Indian schools. (CCTHITA 1991, 13)

Faced with such discrimination, Elizabeth organized lobbying efforts with other Tlingit women to confront Alaskan senators about the realities of discrimination and racism in the lives of Alaskan Natives. As Grand Presidents of the ANB and ANS, in December of 1941, Roy and Elizabeth wrote a letter to Governor Gruening, in which they denounced the hypocrisy behind Alaska's legalized segregation: "In the present emergency [WWII]," they wrote, "our Native boys are being called upon to defend our beloved country, just as White boys. There is no distinction being made there" (CCTHITA 1991, 16). Roy and Elizabeth also attacked the hypocrisy of whites who expressed concern over the Jewish situation in Europe while turning a blind eye to what was happening in their own backyards:

> We were shocked when the Jews were discriminated against in Germany. Stories were told of public places having signs, "No Jews Allowed." All freedom loving people in our country were horrified at these reports yet it is being practiced in our country. We as Indians consider this an outrage because we are the real Natives of Alaska by reason of our ancestors who have guarded these shores and woods for years past. We will still be here to guard our beloved country while hordes of uninterested whites will be fleeing South. (CCTHITA 1991, 16)

That last sentence is especially interesting in that it was written just days after the Japanese bombing of Pearl Harbor. Roy and Elizabeth were insinuating that, should an Axis invasion of Alaska take place (as indeed it did when the Japanese captured islands in the Aleutian chain), Alaskan Natives would stay and fight for their country while, in their estimation, "hordes of whites" would make a mass exodus to the lower 48.

Roy and Elizabeth found in Governor Gruening a sympathetic listener who urged them to draft legislation prohibiting such discrimination in Alaska. With sample bills given them by Anthony Dimond (Alaska's U.S. Congressman at the time), Roy and Elizabeth drafted their first anti-discrimination bill, which outlawed segregation and discrimination in public buildings, schools, housing, and private businesses. The bill was sent before the territorial legislature in 1943 and defeated by a vote of nine to seven after an intense and heated debate on the floor of the legislature. The dissenting legislators particularly disliked the fact that the bill would force local public schools to integrate.

Since the Alaskan Territorial Legislature met every two years, Roy and Elizabeth used the interim between 1943 and 1945 to garner support for their bill, both within and outside the Native community. On February 8, 1945, the anti-discrimination bill was once again before the legislature, but this time without the provision about public school integration. Governor Gruening had encouraged the Peratroviches to leave that out of the bill. He thought school integration too unrealistic a goal at the time and that it could come through later legislation.

Alaskan Natives won the day. The Peratroviches took on and defeated the pro-segregation contingent of senators and garnered enough votes to pass the bill. It became the first comprehensive anti-discrimination law of its kind in America. Governor Gruening would later reminisce, "Had it not been for that beautiful Tlingit woman, Elizabeth Peratrovich, being on hand every day in the hallways, it (the anti-discrimination bill) never would have passed" (CCTHITA 1991, 23). Governor Gruening signed the bill into law on February 16, 1945. Article One states:

> All citizens within the jurisdiction of the Territory of Alaska shall be entitled to the full and equal enjoyment of accommodations, advantages, facilities and privileges of public inns, restaurants, eating houses, hotels, soda fountains, soft drink parlors, taverns, roadhouses, barber shops, beauty parlors, bathrooms, resthouses, theaters, skating rinks, cafes, ice cream parlors, transportation companies, and all other conveyances and amusements, subject only to the conditions and limitations established by law and applicable alike to all citizens.

Article Two of the bill delineates the punishment for those persons or businesses guilty of practicing or inciting discrimination and/or segregation.

In reality, there is large difference between the ideal of a law as expressed in a legal document, and the actual application of that law in everyday life. As Elizabeth stated in her debate with Senator Shattuck, having a law on the books never precludes the crime. Discrimination against Alaskan Natives remains a major problem. However, the anti-discrimination bill was an attempt to demand equality within American society that was not ready for complete equality; as such, the bill was ultimately ahead of its time.

As Alaskan Native leaders actively changing the status quo of Alaska and permanently altering the trajectory of Alaskan Native history, the Peratroviches were an integral part of American Indian history in the 20th century. The seeds of leadership were instilled in Peratroviches by previous Tlingit leaders, including grandmothers and grandfathers and clan leaders and warriors who had always been willing to organize in order to fight for their rights and properties. The Peratroviches, William Paul, and the ANB actively worked to change the future of Alaskan Natives and, in doing so, changed American history.

Biographies of Notable Figures

Elizabeth Peratrovich (née Wanamaker), whose Tlingit name was Ḵaaxgal.aat, was born on July 4, 1911, in Petersburg, Alaska. Elizabeth was a raven (the Tlingit tribe is divided into two halves or moieties—Raven and Eagle/Wolf—determined by matrilineal descent) of the Lukaax̱.adi clan. She was adopted when very young by Andrew Wanamaker and his wife Mary, both of whom were Tlingit. Wanamaker was a Presbyterian minister who worked across southeast Alaska. The village of Klawock was one of Andrew's precincts, and thus the Wanamakers were familiar with the Peratrovich family. Elizabeth graduated from high school in Ketchikan, and attended Sheldon Jackson Junior College, a Native school in Alaska named after a minister who started the Alaskan Native education system. Eventually, Elizabeth would go on to attend Western College of Education (now Western Washington University) in Bellingham, Washington. She married Roy Peratrovich in 1931 and moved to Klawock, where she became actively involved in the Alaskan Native Sisterhood (ANS). Elizabeth would go on to become the Grand President of the ANS and to play an instrumental role in the passage of the 1945 Anti-Discrimination Act, which banned legal segregation in Alaska. Elizabeth also served as the ANB's liaison to the National Congress of American Indians (NCAI) in Washington, D.C. Elizabeth passed away on December 1, 1958, and was buried in Evergreen Cemetery in Juneau. In 1988, the Alaskan State Legislature established February 16 as Elizabeth Peratrovich Day, a state holiday in honor of her groundbreaking civil rights work.

    Roy Peratrovich, whose Tlingit name was Lk'uteen, was born on May 1, 1908, in Klawock, Alaska. Klawock is a small Tlingit village located on the west side of Prince of Wales Island in Southeast Alaska. Roy was an Eagle whose ancestors were originally from Kuiu Ḵwaan. Roy had ties to the Flicker House (Ḵóon Hít) of the Naasteidi clan through his grandmother Ḵaatx̱weich (whose English name was Kitty Collins). Ḵaatx̱weich was a survivor of the 1860s smallpox epidemic. Originally hailing from Kuiu Island, as a young girl Ḵaatx̱weich escaped the utter devastation of her home village (Kuiu Ḵwaan) and made it to Klawock in one of several canoes laden with a small group of survivors who were mostly children. Eventually, Ḵaatx̱weich would become a powerful matriarch in Klawock and would live well beyond 100 years. Roy and his brothers and sisters learned much about leadership from K̲aatx̲weich. Roy was sent to Chemawa Indian School in Oregon and attended Western College of Education (now Western Washington University) in Bellingham, Washington, where he married Elizabeth Wanamaker in 1931. Roy moved back to Klawock and served four terms as mayor of the village and five consecutive terms as Grand President of the Alaskan Native Brotherhood (ANB). He moved to Juneau in 1940 and spent the rest of his life actively involved in Alaskan Native politics. Roy passed away in 1989 and was buried next to Elizabeth in Evergreen Cemetery in Juneau.

William Paul, whose Tlingit name was Shgúndi, was born into the Teeyhittaan clan in 1885 in Tongass Village, Alaska. He was a Raven through his mother. His father disappeared during a canoe trip when he was one year old. William's mother was left with two young boys (William and his brother Samuel) and pregnant with a third child. The Pauls eventually moved to Sitka, where William's mother held a variety of jobs at the Sitka Industrial and Training School. When William was 14, he was sent to Carlisle Indian School in Pennsylvania. William graduated from Whitworth College, which at the time was a Presbyterian school in Tacoma, Washington. He attended seminary for a year in San Francisco and eventually settled on law for his graduate education. He took a correspondence course from Lesalle University of Philadelphia. He passed the bar exam in 1920, becoming the first Alaskan Native lawyer, and in 1923 he became the first Alaskan Native elected to the Alaska Territorial Legislature. William Paul was a key figure in the Alaskan Native Brotherhood; he was elected President of ANB, served as the organization's attorney, and was instrumental in the getting the U.S. Court of Claims to hear a lawsuit brought by the Tlingit and Haida tribes against the United States government. After being pushed aside in preparation for that case, Paul took another lawsuit to the Court of Claims and, ultimately, to the U.S. Supreme Court (Tee-Hit-Ton Indians v. United States) in 1955. Though he lost, the case did establish the key fact that Alaskan Natives had aboriginal title to the land, which would give Alaska Natives a basis for later land claims. Alaskan Native land holding might be vastly less today if it had not been for Paul's Tee-Hit-Ton case. In the 1950s and 1960s, Paul would become a legal and political advisor to younger Alaskan Native leaders. Paul passed away in 1977.

DOCUMENT EXCERPTS

Testimony in the Senate on the Alaska Anti-Discrimination Bill

The Testimony from the Senate floor during the February 8, 1945, debate on the Alaska Anti-Discrimination Bill. Roy and Elizabeth Peratrovich, the architects behind the bill, were the only Indians who spoke during the debate.

Senator Tolber Scott: Mixed breeds are the source of trouble. It is only they who wish to associate with the whites. It would have been better if the Eskimos had put up signs "No Whites Allowed." This issue is simply an effort to create political capital for some legislators. Certainly white women have done their part in keeping the races distinct. If white men had done as well, there would be no racial feeling in Alaska.

Senator Grenold Collins: I'd like to speak in support of Senator Scott. The Eskimos of St. Lawrence Island have not suffered from the White Man's evil, and they are well off. Eskimos are not an inferior race, but they are an individual race. The pure Eskimos are proud of their origin and are aware that harm comes to them from mixing with whites. It is the mixed breed who is not accepted by either race who causes trouble. I believe in racial pride and do not think this bill will do other than arouse bitterness. Why, we should prohibit the sale of liquor to these Natives—that's the real root of our troubles.

Senator Frank Whaley: I am also against the Equal Rights Bill. I personally would prefer not to have to sit next to these Natives in a theater. Why, they smell bad. As a bush pilot, I believe from my experiences that this legislation is a lawyer's dream and a "natural" in creating hard feelings between whites and Natives. However, I will vote for this bill if we amend it by striking Section II which reads: "any person who shall violate or aid or incite such violation shall be deemed guilty of a misdemeanor punishable by imprisonment in jail for not more than one month or fined not more than $50 or both."

Senator O.D. Cochran: I am personally assailed by Senator Whaley's remarks. I stand in support of the Equal Rights Bill. Discrimination does exist. In Nome, an Eskimo woman was forcibly removed from a theater when she dared sit in the "white section." And I have a list of similar occurrences based solely on my own experiences that would occupy the full afternoon to relate.

Senator Walker: I too would like to state my support for the legislation. I know of no instance where a Native died of a broken heart, but I do know of situations where discrimination has forced Indian women into lives "worse than death."

Roy Peratrovich: I would like to remind the legislature that the Honorable Ernest Gruening, in his report to the Secretary of the Interior, as well as his message to the legislature, has recognized the existence of discrimination. Even the plank adopted by the Democratic Party at its Fairbanks convention favors the Equal Rights Bill. In fact, members of that committee are present in this Senate body.

Senator Allen Shattuck: Mr. Peratrovich, as I mentioned to you before, this bill will aggravate, rather than allay the little feeling that now exists. Our Native cultures have ten centuries of white civilization to encompass in a few decades. I believe that considerable progress has already been made, particularly in the last fifty years, but still much progress needs to be made.

Roy Peratrovich: Only an Indian can know how it feels to be discriminated against. Either you are for discrimination or you are against it, accordingly as you vote on this bill.

Senator Allen Shattuck: This legislation is wrong. Rather than being brought together, the races should be kept further apart. Who are these people, barely out of savagery, who want to associate with us whites, with 5,000 years of recorded civilization behind us?

Elizabeth Peratrovich: I would not have expected that I, who am barely out of savagery, would have to remind the gentlemen with 5,000 years of recorded history behind them of our Bill of Rights. When my husband and I came to Juneau and sought a home in a nice neighborhood where our children could play happily with our neighbor's children, we found such a house and arranged to lease it. When the owners learned that we were Indians, they said no. Would we be compelled to live in the slums?

Senator Shattuck: Will this law eliminate discrimination?

Elizabeth Peratrovich: Do your laws against larceny, rape and murder prevent those crimes? No law will eliminate crimes, but at least you, as legislators, can assert to the world that you recognize the evil of the present situation and speak of your intent to help us overcome discrimination. There are three kinds of persons who practice discrimination: First, the politician who wants to maintain an inferior minority group so that he can always promise them something; second, the "Mr. and Mrs. Jones" who aren't quite sure of their social position, and who are nice to you on one occasion and can't see you on others, depending whom they are with; and third, the great superman, who believes in the superiority of the white race. This super race attitude is wrong and forces our fine Native People to be associated with less than desirable circumstances.

Senator Joe Green: Thank you, Mrs. Peratrovich. You may be seated.

Senator Walker: I move to close debate.

Source: Congressional Record, February 8, 1945.

The Anti-Discrimination Bill

The 1945 Anti-Discrimination Bill drafted and written by Roy and Elizabeth Peratrovich. It passed on February 8 and signed into law on February 16.

An Act

To provide for full and equal accommodations, facilities and privileges to all citizens in places of public accommodation within the jurisdiction of the Territory of Alaska; to provide penalties to violations.

Be it enacted by the Legislature of the Territory of Alaska:

Section 1: All citizens within the jurisdiction of the Territory of Alaska shall be entitled to the full and equal enjoyment of accommodations, advantages, facilities and privileges of public inns, restaurants, eating houses, hotels, soda fountains, soft drink parlors, taverns, roadhouses, barber shops, beauty parlors, bathrooms, resthouses, theaters, skating rinks, cafes, ice cream parlors, transportation companies, and all other conveyances and amusements, subject only to the conditions and limitations established by law and applicable alike to all citizens.

Section 2: Any person who shall violate or aid or incite a violation of said full and equal enjoyment; or any person who shall display any printed or written sign indicating a discrimination on racial grounds of said full and equal enjoyment, for each day for which said sign is displayed shall be deemed guilty of a misdemeanor and upon conviction thereof shall be punished by imprisonment in jail for not more than thirty (30) days or fined no more than two hundred fifty ($250.00) dollars, or both. Approved February 16, 1945.

Source: Anti-Discrimination Act, House Bill 14. Session Laws of Alaska, 1945, 35–36.

Further Reading

CCTHITA. *A Recollection of Civil Rights Leader Elizabeth Peratrovich, 1911–1958*. Juneau: Central Council of Tlingit and Haida Indian Tribes of Alaska, 1991.

Cohen, Felix. "Alaska's Nuremberg Laws/Congress Sanctions Racial Discrimination." *Commentary*, 143, 1948.

Dauenhauer, Nora Marks and Richard Dauenhauer, eds. *Haa Shuká, Our Ancestors: Tlingit Oral Narratives*. Seattle: University of Washington Press, 1987.

Dauenhauer, Nora Marks and Richard Dauenhauer. *Haa Tuwuunaagu Yís, for Healing Our Spirit: Tlingit Oratory*. Seattle: University of Washington Press, 1990.

Dauenhauer, Nora Marks and Richard Dauenhauer. *Haa Kusteeyí, Our Culture: Tlingit Life Stories*. Seattle: University of Washington Press, 1994.

Dombrowski, Kirk. *Against Culture: Development, Politics, and Religion in Indian Alaska*. Lincoln: University of Nebraska Press, 2001.

For the Rights of All: Ending Jim Crow in Alaska. Directed by Jeffry Silverman. Blueberry Productions, 2009 (DVD).

Haycox, Stephen. *Alaska: An American Colony*. Seattle: University of Washington Press, 2006.

Haycox, Stephen. "William Paul, Sr., and the Alaska Voters' Literacy Act of 1925." *Alaska History* 2:1 (Winter 1986/87): 17–38. Accessed 7/14/2015 http://www.alaskool.org/native _ed/articles/literacy_act/LiteracyTxt.html

Hope, Andrew and Thomas Thornton, eds. *Will the Time Ever Come?: A Tlingit Source Book*. Fairbanks: Alaskan Native Knowledge Network, 2000.

Kan, Sergei *Symbolic Immortality: The Tlingit Potlatch of the Nineteenth Century*. Washington, D.C.: Smithsonian Institution Press, 1998.

Laguna, Frederica de. *Under Mt. St. Elias: The History and Culture of the Yakutat Tlingit*. Washington, D.C.: Smithsonian Institution Press, 1972.

Metcalfe, Peter. *A Dangerous Idea: The Alaska Native Brotherhood and the Struggle for Indigenous Rights*. Fairbanks: University of Alaska Press, 2014.

Mitchell, Donald. *Sold American: The Story of Alaska Native and Their Land, 1867–1959*. Hanover: University Press of New England, 1997.

Paul, Fred. *Then Fight For It! The Largest Peaceful Redistribution of Wealth in the History of Mankind and the Creation of the North Slope Borough*. Victoria, Canada: Trafford Publishing, 2003.

Skinner, Ramona Ellen. *Alaska Native Policy in the Twentieth Century*. New York: Garland Publishing, Inc., 1997.

Williams, Mary Shaa Tlaa, ed. *The Alaska Native Reader: History, Culture, Politics*. Durham, NC: Duke University Press, 2009.

Termination Policy, Mid-1940s to Mid-1960s

Megan Tusler

Chronology

1934 The Indian Reorganization Act ("Indian New Deal") allows tribes increased management of their own assets. Termination effectively reversed this policy.

1953 House Concurrent Resolution 108 calls for the termination of a number of tribes, some of which are designated by tribal affiliation, and others by the state in which the reservation is located.

1953 Public Law 280 extends criminal and civil jurisdiction to some states with respect to the Indian nations housed within their borders.

1954 Individual termination acts begin application. This ends the trust relationship between the federal government and 110 tribes and bands in eight states.

1962   The final termination act is passed.

1975   The passage of the Indian Self-Determination and Education Assistance Act (Public Law 93–638) ends termination policy by producing relationships between government agencies and tribes. These include the Department of Health, Education, and Welfare and the Department of the Interior.

The Termination of Federal Supervision and Control of American Indians

Termination, as a dynamic of federal American Indian policy, is generally referred to as the "termination era," because the decisions to end federal trust relationships with American Indian nations spread out over a number of years. The primary act, however, was House Concurrent Resolution 108, passed in 1953. It reads, in part: "That it is declared to be the sense of Congress that, at the earliest possible time, all of the Indian tribes and the individual members thereof located within the states of California, Florida, New York, and Texas, and all of the following named Indian tribes and individual members thereof, should be freed from Federal supervision and control and from all disabilities and limitations specially applicable to Indians: The Flathead tribe of Montana, the Klamath tribe of Oregon, the Menominee tribe of Wisconsin, the Potowatamie tribe of Kansas and Nebraska, and those members of the Chippewa [Ojibwe] tribe who are on the Turtle Mountain Reservation, North Dakota." "Freed from Federal supervision" is the telling phrase of this act. In practice, this "freedom" meant that the nations named were to be effectively unrecognized by the federal government and the institutions under it that served Indians, particularly the Department of the Interior and the Bureau of Indian Affairs.

In addition to the 1953 act, further policy decisions terminated or named other tribes for termination. In a memo dated January 21, 1954, the office of the secretary of the interior called for the termination of specific tribes that were previously named under the portion of HCR 108 that described members within the states of California, Florida, New York, and Texas. The Iroquois Confederation of New York was one of the groups chosen for termination in this memo; the tribes under the confederation are the Cayuga, Mohawk, Oneida, Onandaga, Seneca, and Tuscarora. The Texas nation under particular scrutiny was the Alabama-Coushatta nation; for Florida, the Seminole nation was targeted. An earlier act of law, Title 25 U.S. Code § 217a ch. 276, 54 Stat. 249 in Kansas (1940) had effectively terminated Indian relations because its effect was to enforce state law upon the nations that were fully or partially within the Kansas borders: the Sac and Fox, Kickapoo,

Potawatomi, and Iowa. The termination of California tribes is one of the most complex elements of federal Indian policy because California frequently uses rancherias to define tribal location. In 1958, Public Law 85–671 was passed and affected California nations, a number of which have yet to be re-recognized as nations. This bill reads, in part, *"Be it enacted by the Senate and House of Representatives of the United States of America in Congress assembled*, That the lands, including minerals, water rights, and improvements located on the lands, and other assets of the following rancherias and reservations in the State of California shall be distributed in accordance with the provisions of this Act: Alexander Valley, Auburn, Big Sandy, Big Valley, Blue Lake, Buena Vista, Cache Creek, Chicken Ranch, Chico, Cloverdale, Cold Springs, Elk Valley, Guidiville, Graton, Greenville, Hopland, Indian Ranch, Lytton, Mark West, Middletown, Montgomery Creek, Mooretown, Nevada City, North Fork, Paskenta, Picayune, Finoleville, Potter Valley, Quartz Valley, Redding, Redwood Valley, Robinson, Rohnerville, Ruffeys, Scotts Valley, Smith River, Strawberry Valley, Table Bluff, Table Mountain, Upper Lake, Wilton."

The nations terminated in the 1940s, 1950s, and 1960s have had a number of challenges toward their being re-recognized. A number of California tribes, again, are still not under federal recognition. Among the challenges that tribes have had to face in their efforts to be recognized under federal law is the instatement or reinstatement of formally organized tribal courts. The lack of tribal courts for the four nations of Kansas was seen as the reason for termination in 1940—the state wanted jurisdiction over tribal members who committed crimes that would fall under state law. In response, tribal nations have sometimes had to demonstrate the efficacy of tribal courts. In other cases, members of nations tagged for termination were able to halt the process through congressional testimony. The Turtle Mountain Chippewa were able to avoid termination because tribal chairman Patrick Gourneau and other tribal members traveled to Washington and argued that termination would have a profoundly negative affect on the tribe, which was still struggling to be economically self-sufficient and had so small a land base that development would prove difficult. They were successful in the efforts to end their termination. The Potowatomie were also able to persuade congress not to follow through with their termination.

Since the termination era, activists, tribal governments, and politicians have been mostly successful in having tribal governments and tribal enrollment criteria reinstated. Again, however, there continue to be nations whose recognition and tribal sovereignty the federal government denies.

Termination can be said to have a longer historical reach than the particular period called the "termination era." Acts of the 18th and 19th centuries that forcibly relocated tribal members, such as the Trail of Tears, were intended as forms of "termination," given that they had the effect of the mass deaths of tribal members. Treaty law has also been under constant revision since contact, and the recognition of nations (and the termination of that recognition) is contingent upon the extent to which treaties have been followed.

In the most direct sense, however, termination has its origins in the federal jurisprudence of the late 19th century, particularly the Dawes Act, also called the General Allotment Act: "An Act to Provide for the Allotment of Lands in Severalty to Indians on the Various Reservations, and to Extend the Protection of the Laws of the United States and the Territories over the Indians, and for Other Purposes. Be it enacted by the Senate and House of Representatives of the United States of America in Congress assembled, That in all cases where any tribe or band of Indians has been, or shall hereafter be, located upon any reservation created for their use, either by treaty stipulation or by virtue of an act of Congress or executive order setting apart the same for their use, the President of the United States be, and he hereby is, authorized, whenever in his opinion any reservation or any part thereof of such Indians is advantageous for agricultural and grazing purposes, to cause said reservation, or any part thereof, to be surveyed, or resurveyed if necessary, and to allot the lands in said reservation in severalty to any Indian located thereon."

There were a small number of tribes considered exempt from allotment: Section 8 notes that "the provisions of this act shall not extend to the territory occupied by the Cherokees, Creeks, Choctaws, Chickasaws, Seminoles, and Osage, Miamies and Peorias, and Sacs and Foxes, in the Indian Territory, nor to any of the reservations of the Seneca Nation of New York Indians in the State of New York, nor to that strip of territory in the State of Nebraska adjoining the Sioux Nation on the south added by executive order." The Dawes Act was intended to portion Indian lands into individual plots, which scholars agree was an effort to move away from collectively held lands to individually controlled lands, thus discouraging collective interests for tribes. Furthermore, when lands were redistributed to individuals, a great deal of "surplus" land was returned to the federal government, at which point it was often purchased by white individuals. Indians who received allotments were also frequently in the financial position where they had no choice but to sell the land for the small profit. These variables led to a significant loss of land for tribes; according to Sharon O'Brien, "of the ninety million acres lost after 1890, only three million have been restored to Indian ownership" (79).

Other legal decisions had major impacts on Indian sovereign status as well. The Indian Citizenship Act of 1924 declared American Indians to be United States citizens, a provision to which they had not been previously entitled. This act had the ameliorative effect of allowing Indian citizens to vote and participate in federal lawmaking, but it also reinforced the notion that the primary identity for the Native person was in his or her national (U.S.) citizenship and not his or her tribal citizenship.

The allotment process was to end in 1934, with the passage of the Indian Reorganization Act (IRA), sometimes called the "Indian New Deal." This was intended to support the reinstatement of tribal governments, and supported the production of tribal constitutions. The IRA was one of the few legal actions in the first half of the 20th century that intended to extend and reinstate sovereignty; it was with the termination legislation beginning in the 1940s that this well-intentioned political act was effectively overturned.

In the state of Kansas in 1940, legislators passed the "Kansas Act," 18 U.S. Code § 3243. This act allowed the state of Kansas jurisdiction over the four tribes that were fully or partially contained within its boundaries. It reads, "Jurisdiction is conferred on the State of Kansas over offenses committed by or against Indians on Indian reservations, including trust or restricted allotments, within the State of Kansas, to the same extent as its courts have jurisdiction over offenses committed elsewhere within the State in accordance with the laws of the State.

"This section shall not deprive the courts of the United States of jurisdiction over offenses defined by the laws of the United States committed by or against Indians on Indian reservations."

This is a highly significant provision because it set a major precedent for the later acts of termination. Where the state of Kansas is capable of exercising jurisdiction over the Indian nations contained within it, it radically changes the way that tribal sovereignty functions within state borders. Previously, and particularly as a result of the IRA, tribal nations dealt with criminal matters that would otherwise be under state jurisdiction; after the Kansas Act, Native individuals were to be held responsible by tribal, state, *and* federal government.

In 1946, the Indian Claims Commission (ICC) was established. According to Thomas Clarkin, this allowed Native People to make claims upon the federal government and receive settlements. On its face, this seems like an effort to ameliorate Native poverty and to serve as a kind of very small reparation. In practice, however, the ICC was intended to give *individual* Indian people—not tribes—enough money that they might "assimilate" into "mainstream" American culture (Clarkin 7).

As mentioned, the 1953 passage of HCR 108 was the most striking legislation of the termination era. Each of the nations selected for termination had its own methods for coping with the end of federal recognition. Furthermore, states had their own notions of what to do about the "Indian problem."

Called the "Flathead tribe" in the text of HCR 108, The Confederated Salish and Kootenai tribes, in fact, comprise the Bitterroot Salish, the Pend d'Oreille, and the Kootenai tribes. Many of the tribal members reside on the Flathead reservation in Montana. The Flathead reservation is one of many reservation spaces on which there are more non-Indian residents than Indian residents; it was profoundly affected by the Dawes Act and as such is "checkerboarded" with white landholdings. The federal legislators perceived this "mixing" as one of the reasons for termination, given that the reservation was not wholly "Indian" in the first place and that inter-marriage was common. Furthermore, the Salish-Kootenai had some degree of eco-nomic security in the 1950s because of a successful timber program (Confederated Salish and Kootenai tribes 2015). Termination would make Indian residents sub-ject to state taxes and would end the federal trust relationship as well as voiding any treaties that would entitle them to particular land rights. The Confederated tribes successfully fought termination. According to Little Shell tribe history, "Flathead leaders confronted their termination bill, which the Bureau of Indian Affairs had hurriedly drafted. On February 27, 1954, Flathead spokesperson Ste-phen DeMers testified before a joint congressional hearing that the tribe would 'need a minimum period of ten years in which to fully prepare its people to take over full management responsibility, including a complete analysis and survey of all assets.' That spring the combined opposition of Mansfield and Metcalf, the Montana Inter-tribal Policy board, and other vocal non-Indian citizens forced committee leaders to drop the proposed legislation" (Bishop 1993).

The Klamath tribe of Oregon was selected very early for termination, as it was in the unusual position of being quite self-sufficient by the early 1950s. The termi-nation was suggested by Senator Arthur Watkins (R-Utah) and Congressman Ellis Berry (R-South Dakota). According to the Klamath tribe's history of termina-tion, "termination came by pronouncement from Sen. Watkins. The tribe never requested it and when speaking through elected tribal official consistently opposed it. The majority of the tribal members did not want termination." Furthermore, at the time of the termination legislation, the Klamath tribe had filed suit against the U.S. government for reappropriation of moneys for the taking of tribal lands. Again, according to their own history, "when the elected representatives of the tribes traveled to Washington, D.C. to seek appropriations legislation to pay the tribes the debt owed by the United States, Sen. Watkins treated the representatives of the tribes with great disdain, seizing on the opportunity to withhold approval of the payment until the elected leaders agreed to termination. Intimidated by their surroundings and sensitive to the need to obtain the goals they had been sent to Washington to accomplish, they nonetheless refused to support termination" (Klam-ath tribes 2012).

Termination was particularly devastating for the Klamaths, because the action broke the practice of collective holding of land and resources. The tribal estate was broken up, and 1,659 tribal members were given individual checks of $43,000. This practice had a major negative impact on the tribal economy—because they no longer held previously treaty-protected lands, tribal members were no longer able to sustain their lumber economy. The tribal profile changed dramatically—termination had severe negative effects on livelihood, lifespan, and use of federal welfare programs. It was only after the tireless work of tribal members to restore protection to their nation that they were finally reinstated as a tribe: the Klamath Restoration Act was signed into law in 1986.

The Menominees, like the Klamaths, had had a relative degree of economic independence in the first half of the 20th century. They, too, were picked for relocation by Senator Watkins, and also argued vociferously against their termination. The federal government "set 1958 as the year the Menominee would be terminated. In the intervening four years, the tribe had to address a spate of issues such as what to do with its tribal assets and federally protected reservation lands. They drew up a plan for termination, but when it became clear that four years was insufficient preparation, the federal government gave the tribe a year's extension. Termination proved to be such a huge task that the Menominee eventually requested two additional one-year extensions. All tribal property was transferred to a corporation, Menominee Enterprises, Inc. (MEI), and the reservation became a new Wisconsin county, Menominee County" (Milwaukee Public Museum website). The tribe was "terminated" in 1961. As in the case of other tribes, the Menominees were considered "shareholders" in the MEI, and this individuation of tribal assets had a poor outcome. Again, according to the Milwaukee Public Museum, "When Congress passed the Menominee termination act in 1954, the tribe's cash assets had been valued at over $10 million. The pressing needs that followed termination in 1961 drained this sum to $300,000 by 1964."

The tribe eventually organized to respond to termination. Members James White and Ada Deer founded the Determination of Rights and Unity for Menominee Stockholders (DRUMS) in 1970. DRUMS fought to reverse termination and to regain federal recognition. Tribal members appealed to Congress, and the restoration of their tribal status was signed by then-president Richard M. Nixon on December 22, 1973.

The California passage of Public Law 85–671 in 1958 affected a great number of tribes and their reservations and rancherias. Section 9 reads, "Prior to the termination of the Federal trust relationship in accordance with the provisions of this Act, the Secretary of the Interior is authorized to undertake, within the limits of available appropriations, a special program of education and training designed to help the Indians to earn a livelihood, to conduct their own affairs, and to assume their responsibilities as citizens without special services because of their status as Indians. . . . For the purposes of such program, the Secretary is authorized to enter into contracts or agreements with any Federal, State, or local governmental agency, corporation, association, or person. Nothing in this section shall preclude any

Federal agency from undertaking any other program for the education and training of Indians with funds appropriated to it" (Indian Affairs Laws and Treaties, okstate .edu). This section introduces into legal language significant terms and phrases. The use of the word "termination" is significant, as it had generally been avoided in previous legal provisions. The act does, however, go on to frame its efforts as being intended to train Indians as "citizens," such that they could "assume their responsibilities." This is the language that characterized termination more generally, in that it was consistently framed as a matter of ending a "dependency" relationship when, in fact, it was an effort to renege on treaties and to terminate federal trust laws.

Biographies

U.S. Senator Arthur Vivian Watkins (R-Utah)

Senator Arthur Vivian Watkins was a Republican U.S. senator from Utah who orchestrated much of termination policy. Watkins was born in Midway, Utah, in 1886. His training was primarily in the law, having studied first at New York University and then at Columbia University, from which he earned an LL.B. in 1912. He returned to his Native Utah, taking up residence in Vernal, where he joined a colleague in a law practice. The town was not significant enough to support their practice, so Watkins took up an interest in political office, which was to characterize the rest of his life (American National Biography). He first ran for county attorney, an election which he was to lose, although he was later named assistant county attorney of Salt Lake City, where he also launched a private practice before moving to Centerville in 1916. "In the early 1920s he resumed law practice in American Fork and then in 1925 went on to practice in Orem, where he also leased a fruit farm, and in Provo. With other berry growers Watkins organized in the late 1920s the Utah Coldpack Fruit Corporation, but the depression hampered the enterprise. In 1928 Watkins was elected a judge of the Fourth Judicial District. The judicial salary proved more dependable than his law practice, to which he returned after the Republicans' 1932 election defeat. He unsuccessfully ran for Congress in 1936" (American National Biography).

After leaving law practice, Watkins took on more bureaucratic and civic roles, serving in the Mormon church as president of the newly created Sharon Stake, a geographic subdivision of the church that included the city of Provo. He had been raised in the church, completing his mission before going to college, and retained his faith through his life. Much of the literature on Watkins emphasizes this Mormon upbringing and faith. Contemporaneous with the termination policy of which he was an advocate, Watkins also served on the Select Committee to Study Censure Charges Against the Senator from Wisconsin, Mr. McCarthy (King and King

41). The *Journal of Mormon History* recalls this action as one that exemplifies Watkins's religiously inflected "courage," characterized by standing against what he saw as McCarthy's excessiveness.

King and King quote McCarthy's biographer: "A leader in the Mormon Church, [Watkins] was respected for his scrupulous ethics, cold objectivity, and personal courage.' Another described Watkins as 'a thin and ascetic Mormon from Utah with an unbending devotion to order and propriety.' . . . Watkins thus played a critical role in ending McCarthy's anti-communist excesses and gross violation of civil liberties." Further, the American National Biography describes his role in the McCarthy Affair: "One wit likened the pitting of McCarthy against Watkins and five colleagues, most of them lightly regarded, to 'throwing a lion into a den of lambs.' Yet meet the challenge they did. Holding McCarthy to strict rules and tight standards of relevance, Watkins gaveled down his outbursts. The committee recommended censure, and Watkins withstood McCarthy and his allies' pummeling. The frail-looking Watkins showed what one observer termed 'steel under [his] almost parsonical mien.' Braving recurrent stomach pain as he spoke, Watkins challenged fellow Republicans to uphold senatorial dignity, moving some listeners to tears. McCarthy was censured not for anticommunist excesses but for behavior contemptuous of the Senate and abusive of colleagues. He soon vanished from the public eye."

Watkins's term in the Senate began in 1946, and he was re-elected in 1952. He was an Eisenhower-supporting Republican, anti-New Deal, and conservative with respect to domestic policy. However, he supported civil rights legislation, and despite termination as a misguided and unsuccessful endeavor, Watkins and others like him considered it an effort at American Indian assimilation (and, therefore, an end to the domestic dependent relationship.) Among his domestic policy endeavors were the aforementioned committee investigating Joseph McCarthy, water policy, the Refugee Act of 1953, and the civil rights legislation of the mid-1950s. Among his water policy actions were sponsorships of both the $760 million Colorado River Storage Act and the $70 million Weber Basin Project Act ("Utah History to go," Utah.gov).

Watkins's support for the Termination Act was in part because of his previous work on Indian affairs. He was the co-chairman of the Joint Committee on Navaho-Hopi Indian Administration (Eighty-Third Congress) and the Joint Committee on Immigration and Naturalization Policy (Eighty-Third Congress) and a member of the Indian Claims Commission, Washington, D.C., from August 1959, until his retirement in September 1967 ("Biographical Directory of the United States Congress: Arthur Vivian Watkins," Congress.gov). Senators from the American west were more likely than others to support termination, in part because of the ongoing resource battles over land, timber, and water between state and Indian governments, but also because of the large land mass that reservations took up in the mountain, plains, and western states. According to David Gene Lewis and R. Warren Metcalf, Watkins's own family had expanded their farm by purchasing surplus reservation lands. Watkins's interest was initially local, again because western states had larger reservation bodies, but also because those, like Watkins, whose families had "bought" land from tribes, felt that in some cases tribes were not taking full advantage of their resources such as land, timber, oil, and water.

In 1958, he was defeated for re-election and succeeded by Democrat Frank Moss. According to the American National Biography, "After his defeat Watkins served briefly as a consultant to the secretary of the interior. He was named to the Indian Claims Commission in 1959, becoming its chair in 1960. Watkins retired from the commission in 1967 and moved back to Salt Lake City. His wife died in 1971, and in 1972 he married Dorothy Watkins (no relation). He died in Orem, Utah."

DOCUMENT EXCERPTS

Of the many legal developments that impacted the termination and relocation era, Public Law (PL) 280 is one that is still in effect. As of 2016, PL 280 is operative in Alaska, Arizona, California, Florida, Idaho, Iowa, Minnesota (except for the Red Lake Nation), Montana, Nebraska, Nevada, Oregon (except the Warm Springs Reservation), North Dakota, South Dakota, Utah, Washington, and Wisconsin (except for the Menominee Reservation). It is significant because the transfer of state jurisdiction to include tribal members is one of the many steps undertaken to reframe Native People as "citizens" and "tribal members," and as such subject to the same state, tribal, and federal laws as non-tribal members. The final selection from the act allows for revision of tribal law by Indian vote.

Public Law 83–280

18 U.S.C. § 1162. State Jurisdiction over offenses committed by or against Indians in the Indian country

(a) Each of the States or Territories listed in the following table shall have jurisdiction over offenses committed by or against Indians in the areas of Indian country listed opposite the name of the State or Territory to the same extent that such State or Territory has jurisdiction over offenses committed elsewhere within the State or Territory, and the criminal laws of such State or Territory shall have the same force and effect within such Indian country as they have elsewhere within the State or Territory:

State of	Indian Country Affected
Alaska	All Indian country within the State, except that on Annette Islands, the Metlakatla Indian community may exercise jurisdiction over offenses committed by Indians in the same manner in which such jurisdiction may be exercised by Indian tribes in Indian country over which State jurisdiction has not been extended.
California	All Indian country within the State.
Minnesota	All Indian country within the State, except the Red Lake Reservation.
Nebraska	All Indian country within the State.
Oregon	All Indian country within the State, except the Warm Springs Reservation.
Wisconsin	All Indian country within the State.

(b) Nothing in this section shall authorize the alienation, encumbrance, or taxation of any real or personal property, including water rights, belonging to any Indian or any Indian tribe, band, or community that is held in trust by the United States or is subject to a restriction against alienation imposed by the United States; or shall authorize regulation of the use of such property in a manner inconsistent with any Federal treaty, agreement, or statute or with any regulation made pursuant thereto; or shall deprive any Indian or any Indian tribe, band, or community of any right, privilege, or immunity afforded under Federal treaty, agreement, or statute with respect to hunting, trapping, or fishing or the control, licensing, or regulation thereof.

(c) The provisions of sections 1152 and 1153 of this chapter shall not be applicable within the areas of Indian country listed in subsection (a) of this section as areas over which the several States have exclusive jurisdiction.

28 U.S.C. § 1360. State civil jurisdiction in actions to which Indians are parties

(a) Each of the States listed in the following table shall have jurisdiction over civil causes of action between Indians or to which Indians are parties which arise in the areas of Indian country listed opposite the name of the State to the same extent that such State has jurisdiction over other civil causes of action, and those civil laws of such State that are of general application to private persons or private property shall have the same force and effect within such Indian country as they have elsewhere within the State:

[Same as above, except for Alaska, where the law affects all Indian country within the State.]

(b) Nothing in this section shall authorize the alienation, encumbrance, or taxation of any real or personal property, including water rights, belonging to any Indian or any Indian tribe, band, or community that is held in trust by the United States or is subject to a restriction against alienation imposed by the United States; or shall authorize regulation of the use of such property in a manner inconsistent with any Federal treaty, agreement, or statute or with any regulation made pursuant thereto; or shall confer jurisdiction upon the State to adjudicate, in probate proceedings or otherwise, the ownership or right to possession of such property or any interest therein.

(c) Any tribal ordinance or custom heretofore or hereafter adopted by an Indian tribe, band, or community in the exercise of any authority which it may possess shall, if not inconsistent with any applicable civil law of the State, be given full force and effect in the determination of civil causes of action pursuant to this section.

25 U.S.C. § 1321. Assumption by State of criminal jurisdiction

(a) Consent of United States; force and effect of criminal laws
The consent of the United States is hereby given to any State not having jurisdiction over criminal offenses committed by or against Indians in the areas of Indian country situated within such State to assume, with the consent of the Indian tribe occupying the particular Indian country or part thereof which could be affected by such assumption, such measure of jurisdiction over any or all of such offenses committed within such Indian country or any part thereof as may be determined by such State to the same extent that such State has jurisdiction over any such offense committed elsewhere within the State, and the criminal laws of such State shall have the same force and effect within such Indian country or part thereof as they have elsewhere within that State.

(b) Alienation, encumbrance, taxation, and use of property; hunting, trapping, or fishing
Nothing in this section shall authorize the alienation, encumbrance, or taxation of any real or personal property, including water rights, belonging to any Indian or any Indian tribe, band, or community that is held in trust by the United States or is subject to a restriction against alienation imposed by the United States; or shall authorize regulation of the use of such property in a manner inconsistent with any Federal treaty, agreement, or statute or with any regulation made pursuant thereto; or shall deprive any Indian or any Indian tribe, band, or community of any right, privilege, or immunity

afforded under Federal treaty, agreement, or statute with respect to hunting, trapping, or fishing or the control, licensing, or regulation thereof.

25 U.S.C. § 1322. Assumption by State of civil jurisdiction

(a) Consent of United States; force and effect of civil laws
The consent of the United States is hereby given to any State not having jurisdiction over civil causes of action between Indians or to which Indians are parties which arise in the areas of Indian country situated within such State to assume, with the consent of the tribe occupying the particular Indian country or part thereof which would be affected by such assumption, such measure of jurisdiction over any or all such civil causes of action arising within such Indian country or any part thereof as may be determined by such State to the same extent that such State has jurisdiction over other civil causes of action, and those civil laws of such State that are of general application to private persons or private property shall have the same force and effect within such Indian country or part thereof as they have elsewhere within that State.

(b) Alienation, encumbrance, taxation, use, and probate of property
Nothing in this section shall authorize the alienation, encumbrance, or taxation of any real or personal property, including water rights, belonging to any Indian or any Indian tribe, band, or community that is held in trust by the United States or is subject to a restriction against alienation imposed by the United States; or shall authorize regulation of the use of such property in a manner inconsistent with any Federal treaty, agreement, or statute, or with any regulation made pursuant thereto; or shall confer jurisdiction upon the State to adjudicate, in probate proceedings or otherwise, the ownership or right to possession of such property or any interest therein.

(c) Force and effect of tribal ordinances or customs
Any tribal ordinance or custom heretofore or hereafter adopted by an Indian tribe, band, or community in the exercise of any authority which it may possess shall, if not inconsistent with any applicable civil law of the State, be given full force and effect in the determination of civil causes of action pursuant to this section.

25 U.S.C. § 1323. Retrocession of jurisdiction by State

(a) Acceptance by United States
The United States is authorized to accept a retrocession by any State of all or any measure of the criminal or civil jurisdiction, or both, acquired by such State pursuant to the provisions of section 1162 of title 18, section

1360 of title 28, or section 7 of the Act of August 15, 1953 (67 Stat. 588), as it was in effect prior to its repeal by subsection (b) of this section.

(b) Repeal of statutory provisions
Section 7 of the Act of August 15, 1953 (67 Stat. 588), is hereby repealed, but such repeal shall not affect any cession of jurisdiction made pursuant to such section prior to its repeal.

25 U.S.C. § 1324. Amendment of State constitutions or statutes to remove legal impediment; effective date

Notwithstanding the provisions of any enabling Act for the admission of a State, the consent of the United States is hereby given to the people of any State to amend, where necessary, their State constitution or existing statutes, as the case may be, to remove any legal impediment to the assumption of civil or criminal jurisdiction in accordance with the provisions of this subchapter. The provisions of this subchapter shall not become effective with respect to such assumption of jurisdiction by any such State until the people thereof have appropriately amended their State constitution or statutes, as the case may be.

25 U.S.C. § 1325. Abatement of actions

(a) Pending actions or proceedings; effect of cession
No action or proceeding pending before any court or agency of the United States immediately prior to any cession of jurisdiction by the United States pursuant to this subchapter shall abate by reason of that cession. For the purposes of any such action or proceeding, such cession shall take effect on the day following the date of final determination of such action or proceeding.

(b) Criminal actions; effect of cession
No cession made by the United States under this subchapter shall deprive any court of the United States of jurisdiction to hear, determine, render judgment, or impose sentence in any criminal action instituted against any person for any offense committed before the effective date of such cession, if the offense charged in such action was cognizable under any law of the United States at the time of the commission of such offense. For the purposes of any such criminal action, such cession shall take effect on the day following the date of final determination of such action.

Source: 18 U.S.C. § 1162, 28 U.S.C. § 1360.

See also: Meriam Report

Further Reading

Bishop, Joan. "From Hill 57 to Capitol Hill: 'Making the Sparks Fly'," *Montana The Magazine of Western History*. Vol. 43 (Summer Issue-3) 1993: pp. 16–29.

Brookings Institution. *The problem of Indian administration report of a survey made at the request of Hubert Work, Secretary of the Interior, and submitted to him, February 21, 1928* / survey staff: Lewis Meriam et al. Baltimore: Johns Hopkins Press, 1928, and Buffalo, NY: William S. Hein & Co., 2012. Accessed via HeinOnline American Indian Law Collection April 29, 2015.

Clarkin, Thomas. *Federal Indian Policy in the Kennedy and Johnson Administrations, 1961–1969*. Albuquerque: University of New Mexico Press, 2001.

"Confederated Salish and Kootenai Tribes." 2015. Montana Governor's Office of Indian Affairs. http://tribalnations.mt.gov/cskt Accessed April 29th, 2015.

Fixico, Donald L. *Termination and Relocation: Federal Indian Policy, 1945–1960*. Albuquerque: University of New Mexico Press, 1990.

King, Robert R. and Kay Atkinson King. "Mormons in Congress, 1851–2000." *Journal of Mormon History* Vol. 26, No. 2 (Fall 2000), pp. 1–50.

"Klamath tribes History." 2012. http://klamathtribes.org/tribal-court Accessed April 29, 2015.

O'Brien, Sharon. *American Indian Tribal Governments*. Tulsa: University of Oklahoma Press, 1993.

Oklahoma State University archive of tribal laws and treaties. http://digital.library.okstate.edu/kappler/Vol6/html_files/v6p0614.html

Philp, Kenneth R. "Termination: A Legacy of the Indian New Deal." *The Western Historical Quarterly* Vol. 14, No. 2 (April 1983), pp. 165–80.

Walch, Michael C. "Terminating the Indian Termination Policy." *Stanford Law Review* Vol. 35, No. 6 (July 1983), pp. 1181–15.

Election of Annie Dodge Wauneka to Navajo Tribal Council, 1951

Claudia J. Ford

Chronology

1910   Annie Dodge born April 10, 1910, in Arizona to parents K'eehabah, the third wife of Henry Chee Dodge, of the Navajo Tse Níjikíní Clan. Her childhood is spent at her father's house in Crystal, New Mexico, with five brothers and one sister.

1917–1927   Annie attends Bureau of Indian Affairs boarding schools in Ft. Defiance, Arizona, and Albuquerque, New Mexico.

1921	The U.S. government creates the Navajo Tribal Council to make it easier to negotiate leases and mineral rights on Navajo land.
1927	The chapter system of governance is established on the Navajo reservation as a locus of community life. Later in life, Annie serves important roles in chapter governance before being elected to the Tribal Council.
1923–1928	Henry Chee Dodge is elected to his first term as the first Navajo Tribal Chairman of the Navajo Tribal Council.
1929	Annie marries George Wauneka in a traditional Navajo ceremony.
1933	The U.S. government Commissioner of Indian Affairs, John Collier, advocates a system of livestock reductions for the Navajo, in order to alleviate soil erosion and overgrazing on the reservation.
1934	The Indian Reorganization Act, or Wheeler-Howard Act, is rejected by the Navajo.
1940–1942	Wauneka is elected chair of the chapter Grazing Committee and eventually chapter Secretary.
1944–1947	Henry Chee Dodge elected and serves second term as Tribal Chairman.
1947	Henry Chee Dodge dies January 7, 1947.
1951	Wauneka is elected, the second woman to win a council delegate seat, to the Navajo Tribal Council from District 17 of the Klagetoh and Wide Ruins Precincts, and serves on the Council Health and Welfare Committee. This begins 27 years of Wauneka's continuous service to the Navajo Tribal Council, usually as the only woman delegate.
1954–1978	Wauneka is re-elected to the Navajo Tribal Council.
1956	Wauneka advocates for the education of Navajo attorneys and the establishment of legal aid services to protect the reservation from corporate leases for gas, oil, and mineral exploitation.
1956	Wauneka becomes a member of the government Advisory Committee on Indian Health at the invitation of the Surgeon General of the United States.
1958–1960	Wauneka receives numerous medals and awards: the Arizona Woman of Achievement for the Year, the Josephine B. Hughes Memorial Award, the All Arizona All Indian Basketball Organization Award, the Public Health Educators Will Ross Medal, and the prestigious

Indian Council Fire Annual Indian Achievement Award—previously received by her father in 1945.

1960   Wauneka serves on New Mexico Governor's Committee on the Aging.

1960   Wauneka hosts a daily Navajo language radio show on KGAK in Gallup, New Mexico, covering general and health issues.

1961   Wauneka testifies in Washington, D.C., before the Indian Claims Committee on behalf of the Navajo Nation.

1963   President John F. Kennedy nominates Wauneka for the Presidential Medal of Freedom, which is awarded to her after his assassination on December 6, 1963, by President Lyndon B. Johnson.

1968   Wauneka testifies before the Senate Subcommittee on Indian Education at the request of Robert F. Kennedy.

1974   Wauneka receives the Navajo Nation Medal of Honor.

1976   Wauneka receives an honorary doctorate in public health from the University of Arizona.

1984   The Navajo Tribal Council honors Wauneka as Legendary Mother of the Navajo people.

1996   Wauneka receives an honorary Doctor of Law from the University of Arizona.

1997   Annie Dodge Wauneka dies, November 10, 1997, at 87 years old.

Annie Dodge Wauneka's Election to the Navajo Tribal Council

Annie Dodge Wauneka (1910–1997) was the second woman to be elected as a delegate to the Navajo Tribal Council. In this historic achievement, Wauneka was preceded on the Council by Lilly J. Neil, who had served for four years before Wauneka's first term. During nearly three decades on the Council, Wauneka was known as an outspoken politician and cultural leader who worked to connect the Bureau of Indian Affairs (BIA), which controlled the council during her tenure, with the pressing health and social needs of the Navajo community.

Annie Dodge was born in Arizona on April 10, 1910, to parents K'eehabah and Henry Chee Dodge of the Navajo Tse Níjikíní Clan. Anna was the youngest of Chee Dodge's children. K'eehabah lived in relative poverty, and Anna was born in a traditional Navajo hogan. Henry Chee Dodge was an influential member of the community and a wealthy rancher and businessman. Anna spent her childhood at her father's house in Crystal, New Mexico, where she was raised by her father's

Native American activist and educator Annie Dodge Wauneka (1910–1997) holds up a Zuni doll that she presented to President Kennedy's daughter Caroline,1963. She was an influential member of the Navajo Nation Council for 27 years beginning in 195l, awarded the Navajo Medal of Honor, and the Presidential Medal of Freedom in 1963 by Lyndon Johnson. (Carl Iwasaki/The LIFE Images Collection/ Getty Images)

first wives and her aunts, alongside his other children. On her father's ranch she learned the skills and business of livestock herding. Anna was educated in government boarding schools in Arizona and New Mexico, beginning at the Ft. Defiance Indian School as a boarder at age eight. During her first year at the school, there was a serious outbreak of tuberculosis, and Anna became known for offering her assistance to the school nurses to take care of her sick classmates. She attended secondary school at the Indian School in Albuquerque, where she met her husband, George Wauneka. In October 1929, Annie Dodge married George Wauneka in a traditional Navajo ceremony. Between 1929 and 1950, Wauneka gave birth to nine children. Due to poor maternal health services in the remote areas in which Wauneka lived, several of her children were born with significant birth trauma, resulting in long-term disabilities. Wauneka and her husband cared for some of their children at home through adulthood. In the 1950s, Wauneka earned a BA in Public Health from the University of Arizona, Tucson, and eventually was awarded two honorary doctorates from her alma mater.

Wauneka was heavily influenced in her career as a politician and community advocate by her powerful father, who took a singular interest in her development as an activist. Chee Dodge was a role model for Wauneka, and she would often accompany him to his council meetings or community visits, bringing her children with her. Wauneka's father tutored her in the cultural and political issues facing the Navajo community, and Wauneka honed her skills in public service and community development through observation of her father's authority and example. Through her father's influence, and with well-developed bilingual Navajo and English language fluency, Wauneka understood the importance of serving as a bridge between the dominant culture and the Diné community.

Since 1824, white male government caretakers from the Bureau of Indian Affairs directed the transactions of the Navajo community, as with all Native reservations, resulting in complex and often contentious tribal politics. However, the Navajo Tribal Councils were convened by, and presided over, by Diné men, and the chapter system and council eventually established strong governance structures for the Navajo. While the custom of women's leadership had always been part of matrilineal Diné history and tradition, increasingly Western and patriarchal models of governance were imposed on the Diné community by the U.S. government, beginning in the early 1800s. These models of community leadership were influential in the establishment of the Council, and largely relegated Navajo women to roles in the domestic sphere. Wauneka's election to the Navajo Tribal Council in 1951 was, therefore, a significant event. Following in her father's legacy of service, Wauneka worked tirelessly within Navajo governance structures and found a way to fit into the male culture of the Navajo Tribal Council.

Wauneka was installed on the Navajo Tribal Council on March 20, 1951, two weeks after the elections. Lilakai Neil, the first woman delegate, who served on the Navajo Tribal Council from 1948 to 1950, had just begun a new term in 1951, when she was involved in a very serious car accident that left her in a coma for more than a month, and with long-term disabilities. Because Neil was no longer able to serve, Wauneka was at that time the only woman on the council. Two of her brothers, Ben Dodge and Justin Shirley, were elected and sworn in with Wauneka in 1951.

One of the first public issues that Wauneka tackled, as a member of her local Grazing Committee, was the protection of Navajo land and herding rights. In the 1930s, the traditional herding and pastoral lifestyle of the Diné was threatened by forced, drastic reductions of livestock numbers. Overgrazing was a longstanding issue on the reservation, intensified by increasing population pressures, significant migration of non-Indians into the reservation areas, and an extended period of drought. "Long before John Collier became commissioner in 1933 . . . the Diné were being scolded for having too many sheep, too many horses, too many goats, and too many cattle" (Iverson 2002, 101). Wauneka's father was a successful rancher, and so the government policies equally affected her family through reductions in grazing areas and imposed livestock rules. In a seven-year period, from 1937 to 1944, the Dodge family's sheep herd was reduced by 3,295 animals. On one morning, government agents shot 1,000 head of Chee Dodge's cattle and let their carcasses rot in the fields (Niethammer 2001). These stock-reduction regulations were

Sidebar 1: Navajo Culture and Governance

Diné clan life is matrilineal, starting with the original Mother, Changing Woman, who formed the first four clans and from whom all Diné are descended. Clan names reflect the abiding relationship that the Diné have with their natural environment. Clans are often named after places of significant migration, trading posts, or gathering spots where communal labor was traditionally organized among the semi-nomadic Diné. The clan remains the locus of relationships of kinship and marriage. By 1920, there were 64 clans among the Navajos.

The Diné Bikeyah are the traditional lands of the Navajo. Currently, the Diné live on the largest Indian reservation in the United States, comprising 17.5 million acres of arid, mostly desert land in the Four Corners region of Arizona, New Mexico, Utah, and Colorado. Ranging in elevation from four to 10,000 feet, this location is the spiritual and physical homeland of the Diné, given to them by Changing Woman and protected by the four sacred mountains. The Diné culture is marked by devotion to the Diné language, storytelling and sacred singing, and attentiveness to traditional ceremonies and medicines. The Diné, especially women, are renowned weavers and silversmiths. The traditional Navajo home is called a "hogan" and is made in a conical shape from wooden poles covered by tree bark and mud. The Diné come from a custom of surviving as semi-nomadic pastoralists. The relationship of the Diné to livestock is one of caretaker, with women being the primary owners of the herds. The Diné are sheepherders but also own goats, cattle, and horses. Livestock is wealth in Diné culture, and the herds are used for transportation, food, fiber, and ceremony.

An important part of Diné history is The Navajo Long Walk, which took place between 1864 and 1868, when more than 8,500 Diné men, women, and children were forced off their traditional lands and marched at gunpoint in the middle of winter into a barren and desolate camp in eastern New Mexico at Bosque Redondo, Ft. Sumner. This brutal relocation was imposed to allow non-Indian Americans to expand their land holdings in Navajo areas. As a result of the failure and suffering of The Long Walk, as it was called, the U.S. government was persuaded to sign an 1868 treaty that established the Navajos as a sovereign nation.

particularly difficult for the Diné community, as they went against deeply held cultural traditions around the size and worth of a family's livestock, and forced the Navajo out of herding and into the wage economy. Smaller herds meant that Diné families could no longer maintain themselves on a lifestyle of subsistence pastoralism. For more than a decade before and after she was elected to the Navajo Tribal Council, Wauneka worked on this issue alongside her father, as a language and cultural interpreter of the regulations of the government and on behalf of the needs of her community.

Wauneka called for accountability in the issuing of long-term land leases to non-Navajo corporations and ranchers as there was increasing pressure on the Navajo to open their land to the exploration and exploitation of natural resources including gas, oil, coal, minerals, and timber. Wauneka opposed these land grabs and exposed the duplicitous tactics of corporations, developers, and attorneys. "One of the most important voices for Navajo rights belonged to Annie Wauneka. She played a central role in the campaign for improved health care, tirelessly toiling for this vital cause. But her interests were not limited to this one issue. The tribal council delegate from Klagetoh spoke out, again and again, about the need for Navajos to be vigilant in safeguarding and demanding their rights" (Iverson 2002b, 121).

Wauneka was especially well known as a public health activist for the Navajo community, where she was considered a compassionate patient advocate and ran numerous effective community health education promotions. She served as the Chair of the Health and Welfare Committee of the Navajo Tribal Council and could be found going door-to-door in Navajo communities to educate families and, if needed, offer transport to Indian Health Service facilities. Wauneka designed and managed critical, successful preventative health programs for tuberculosis, polio, alcoholism, nutrition, water and sanitation, and maternal and child health. She produced public health films in the Navajo language on childcare, diarrhea prevention, and the treatment and prevention of tuberculosis. Wauneka created the first Navajo–English medical dictionary. Wauneka advocated for better health services and more doctors, nurses, and dentists to be brought to the reservation as promised by government treaties. Improvements in health outcomes in the Diné community could be directly attributed to Wauneka's advocacy and educational campaigns. "Wauneka sought to continue the work of her father and her brother, both of whom had pushed the Tribal Council to become more involved in the attempt to gain better health care for the Diné" (Iverson 2002a, 208). Wauneka also worked on issues of education, land and livestock rights, women's rights, and language and cultural preservation. In her service as a delegate to the Navajo Tribal Council, Wauneka travelled widely and was often found lobbying for her community in state capitols, and she was well known in Washington, D.C. In 1956, Wauneka was honored to become a member of the government Advisory Committee on Indian Health at the invitation of the Surgeon General of the United States.

As an elected delegate to the Navajo Tribal Council, Wauneka was a persuasive and passionate speaker who used her considerable energy and skill to serve as a bridge between dominant institutions in health and education and the needs and cultural traditions of her community. Wauneka's tireless contributions to the fields of Navajo and Indian health and education created tangible improvements in the lives of her community members. Wauneka earned well-deserved recognition for continuing her family's legacy of public service. In addition to many other awards, medals, and two honorary doctorates, Wauneka was awarded the Indian Council Fire Achievement Award in 1959 and the Navajo Nation Medal of Honor in 1974. In recognition of the importance of her work and the quality of her service to the Diné community Wauneka, was awarded the Presidential Medal of Freedom by President Lyndon Johnson, on behalf of President John Kennedy, on December 6, 1963.

When Annie Dodge Wauneka died in November 1997, 87 years old, she was ceremonially recognized as a strong willed, confident, and intelligent champion for Native rights and community development, an honored and Legendary Mother, especially for the Diné people.

Biographies of Notable Figures

Henry Chee Dodge (185?–1947)

Chee Dodge was born in Ft. Defiance, Arizona. His father was Juan Cocinas, a Mexican translator for Army Captain Henry Linn Dodge who was related to Senator Dodge of Wisconsin. His mother was Bisnayanchi, a member of the Coyote Pass clan. Juan Cocinas died when Chee Dodge was only a few months old, and his mother disappeared during the beginning of the Navajo Long Walk, leaving Chee Dodge an orphan by the age of four or five. Chee Dodge was taken in by strangers and became caught up in the 1864 Navajo Long Walk. As a young child, Chee Dodge walked over 300 miles to Bosque Redondo and only returned to his homeland in 1868, when the Ft. Sumner internment camp was disbanded. Upon his return to Ft. Defiance, Chee Dodge moved in with an aunt and her white husband, Perry Williams. He went to the Ft. Defiance Indian School and learned to read and write in English, with exposure to the language and customs of white Americans in his new home. Chee Dodge quickly put his skills in Navajo–English translation to use between the Navajo community and government officials. It is understood that both U.S. government officials and Navajo leaders identified Chee Dodge as an intelligent and clever young man, and he was provided with additional schooling. It also seemed possible that he could be the half-Navajo offspring of the famous American Army Captain Henry Linn Dodge, who was known to have a Navajo wife, and for whom Chee Dodge had been named.

Because Chee Dodge was identified by the government as a promising candidate for education and had an early immersion in English language in school and at home, his skills gave him prominence, influence, and reach within the tribe and the American government. Chee Dodge's Diné name is Hastiin Adiits'a'ti, which means "Man Who Interprets" or "Man Who Understands Languages" (Iverson 2002a). It was his role as translator and interpreter between white and Navajo cultures that earned Chee Dodge his reputation as a cunning politician.

Chee Dodge was also very good with money and became a successful rancher and a wealthy member of his clan and Navajo society. In 1921, Chee Dodge was made chair of the business council that was authorized to sign leases and provide mineral exploration rights. This business council eventually became the Navajo Tribal Council, with Chee Dodge as its first Chairman. The U.S. government originally established the Navajo Tribal Council to provide a legal entity with which U.S. corporations could negotiate long-term leases and the rights to explore and exploit minerals, especially oil, on Navajo land. The Navajo Tribal Council was set up to have a delegate and alternate from each of six districts, plus an elected chair and vice-chair. Chee Dodge served as Tribal Council chair from 1923 to 1928 and was re-elected for another term from 1942 to 1946. Two of Chee Dodge's children— Ben and Anna—went into tribal politics, undoubtedly influenced by his masterful style and intercultural practices.

Chee Dodge held multiple positions in Navajo public service. In 1884, he was selected as head of the Navajo Police force. He was named Navajo head chief even though the Navajo had no tradition of a chieftaincy. Chee Dodge opened a trading post in Round Rock, Arizona, and was known as a powerful, skilled, perceptive, and financially prudent businessperson and rancher. In some ways, the story of Chee Dodge was an iconic American rags-to-riches narrative. His power and influence were legendary. "By the 1930s, Chee Dodge and the other Navajos had been back in their homeland for sixty-five years. Chee, a homeless orphan when he returned, had become the richest Navajo ever and the leader of his tribe. His livestock numbered in the thousands—sheep, cattle, horses" (Niethammer 2001, 46). Chee Dodge was a shrewd businessperson who enjoyed the perks of his wealth and influence. It is reported that he had a love of alcohol, cars, diamonds, and beautiful women, and Chee Dodge had eight wives, as was customary in earlier times in traditional Navajo culture.

Chee Dodge died from pneumonia on January 7, 1947, approximately 90 years old. His legacy of service was matched only by that of his youngest daughter, Annie Dodge Wauneka.

Lilakai (Lilly) Julian Neil (1900–)

Lilly Neil was born on January 1, 1900, near Crown Point, New Mexico. Little is known about her childhood, which was spent in the Farmington/Nageezi area of New Mexico. Neil was the first Diné woman to serve on the Navajo Tribal Council. He served on the Navajo Tribal Council from 1948 to 1950 as the delegate from District 19. She had just begun a new term in 1951 when she was involved in a serious car accident on her way to a council meeting that left her in a coma for more than a month, and with long-term disabilities. During her time on the Council, Neil advocated for better educational facilities and social services for Indian children and families. Neil served on the council during the immediate post-WWII period, and she reproached the U.S. government for spending considerable money and resources helping European and Asian countries through the Marshall Plan while Native nations, like the Navajo, continued to suffer critical levels of poverty and neglect. Neil pointed out that the active role of Navajo men and women veterans in WWII made the government neglect more intolerable (Iverson 2002b). Neil was also active in her church community and a cofounder of the La Vida Mission in Farmington, New Mexico. While it is believed that Lilly Neil is about to turn 116 years at the time of writing, as her death has not been reported, there is no definitive information on her current health or her living situation.

DOCUMENT EXCERPTS

Excerpts from Letter from Chee Dodge to Commissioner to the Navajo Tribe, H. J. Hagerman, April 1925

Chee Dodge was a persuasive writer and speaker. In this letter, he advocates for the educational services that were promised to the Navajos in the 1868 treaty. The important issue of mineral rights is briefly raised.

April 20, 1925

My dear Mr. Hagerman:

As I understand superintendents of various agencies among our tribe have orders from the Indian Office to use force in putting children into some Indian Schools, not only on but also off the reservation. The reservation schools are practically all filled and therefore this refers to taking children away from the reservation particularly. Attempts are being made to take children of all ages even up to 20 years to school, but I am afraid this idea of forcing children will not work out satisfactorily. You know well enough how many children have run away from Ft. Apache in the past and further I believe you will realize that by taking these older children the sheep industry of the Navajos will suffer greatly. I therefore think it is very wrong for the government to deprive the Indians of the help of their older children who would not do well in school anyway.

Regarding the forcing of younger children, why not have the children put in the Fort Wingate school where they are not so far away from home and relatives? I am not opposing the education of our children; our tribe has always responded when called upon to send children to reservation schools, but it appears that the government is never satisfied . . . By our treaty of 1868 we promised and kept the promise to put all our children in schools, but the government has failed to keep its side of the agreement by not providing schools on the reserve as specified in said treaty. I am of the impression that the government is playing up a game on us by which they might eventually take our oil interest away from us, if we should happen to make any kind of a bad break . . .

Very sincerely yours, Chee Dodge

Source: Peter Iverson and Monty Roessel, ed. *For Our Navajo People: Diné Letters, Speeches, and Petitions, 1900-1960.* Albuquerque: University of New Mexico Press, 2002, 90–91. Copyright © 2002 University of New Mexico Press. Used by permission.

Excerpts from Reports Written by Annie Wauneka to the Navajo Tribal Council, 1953–1955

It appears that Annie Dodge Wauneka inherited her father's persuasiveness as a writer and speaker. In these reports, Wauneka is clearly advocating for promised medical care, providing examples of the ways that the BIA controlled health services were failing the Navajo community. Wauneka's calling as a health educator is compelling, as she uses the opportunity of the report to the Council to provide critical health education information.

November 2, 1953: Our people are not getting the kind of medical service we were promised under the Long Range Program. We have less health services now than we had four years ago . . . we were promised health centers, field clinics, traveling doctors, nurses, dentists and a large number of public health nurses. Instead of giving us more and better medical service, we see the Fort Defiance hospital almost closed. Every day, sick Navajos are turned away because the hospital people cannot take care of them. We do not understand how a new two million dollar hospital can be built and operated at Tuba City when the Fort Defiance Hospital is almost out of business for lack of money. We approve most of the Public Health doctors who have been loaned to use, but we have reports from Winslow and other places that people have died on the operating table because certain doctors do not know their business. We have reports that many more babies are dying in the hospitals due to poor care. We see that there is a shortage of nurses, but why can't our Navajo girls be trained to be practical nurses? Why must we suffer because registered nurses will not come to the reservation? We see these and many other things that are wrong, but we are not experts, so we must depend on the white leaders. We think that there is no real health program. It there is, we haven't heard about it or seen it. And our sick people are paying for it.

October 12, 1955: Another point I would like to present here on which I would like to ask specifically that the Councilmen participate more. We have three films which we have made. One is on child care, diarrhea prevention, and it is given as it should take place. There is another one on Tuberculosis. One part of this same picture is on treatment of out-patients who have been afflicted with T.B., and the last film is on sanitation which the Doctor presented to you as a preventative measure, how to maintain yourself to prevent disease. These films are available and we would like the backing of every Councilman in getting these films out and getting an understanding on why these films are made—to teach, to train the Navajos to take care of their health. That is why we need your help. It is true that what you do at home in taking preventative measures to maintain your health, is the first step toward prevention from taking an illness which will cause you to go to a hospital. Previous to the transfer of the Indian health service, a Navajo who got sick went to a hospital, got treatment, and went home. That is as far as the health services went. You get your training at home, in your community, how to take that work home and what to do so that your children and you will not get contagious disease and come down with it and be admitted to a hospital. We have an immunization program by use of vaccines. If the Navajo knows how to take advantage of that program they will not have to be subject to any of these contagious diseases. That is your prevention, the preservation of your health.

Excerpts from Annie Wauneka's Speech on Legal Services and Mineral Leases

In this speech about mineral rights on the reservation, Wauneka is clearly advocating for the training of Navajo attorneys while she is also cautioning the Council on the intentions behind the 99-year leases.

We all have opinions regarding different subjects of course, but, under this 99 year lease authority you are requesting, I have my opinion. If Congress gives us the power to give 99 year leases, it means in my thinking that we are opening up the whole Navajo area, the whole Reservation, to anyone who might have other intentions than those which might be best for the tribe. . . . There are many people who are interested in opening up the Reservation in the first place. If we give them one chance to get their foot in, we are through as far as the Reservation is concerned. . . . Now, I would like to come to the tribal attorney. . . . Our attorney is a white man. If we have an attorney from our own tribe to tell us these things which we have had told us by this white man, we would give it our hearty support but there is a doubt about the present attorney's ability, or lack of it, to help us. . . . In the last Council session we agreed with two men to do prospecting for oil and minerals over the Reservation. Without them telling us about what they had found, they turned around and gave it to another group and this group comes before us asking for an agreement with time to develop the oil and gas on the Reservation. . . . The fact is that 99 years is a long time and I would like you to keep that in mind. That is a lot of time and here we are, just getting our children started off in schools. Why cannot we defer this matter until such time as we can get help from our own members of the tribe?

Source: Peter Iverson and Monty Roessel, ed. *For Our Navajo People: Diné Letters, Speeches, and Petitions, 1900–1960.* Albuquerque: University of New Mexico Press, 2002, 200–201. Copyright © 2002 University of New Mexico Press. Used by permission.

Further Reading

Brugge, David M. "Henry Chee Dodge: From the Long Walk to Self-Determination." In *Indian lives: Essays on Nineteenth- and Twentieth-Century Native American Leaders*, edited by L.G. Moses and Raymond Wilson, 91–112. Albuquerque: University of New Mexico Press, 1985.

Caravantes, Peggy. *Daughters of Two Nations.* Missoula, MT: Mountain Press Publishing Company, 2013.

Denetdale, Jennifer Nez. "Chairmen, Presidents, and Princesses: The Navajo Nation, Gender, and the Politics of Tradition." *Wicazo Sa Review* 21, No. 1 (2006): 9–28.

Frisbie, Charlotte J. "Traditional Navajo Women: Ethnographic and Life History Portrayals." *American Indian Quarterly* 6, No. 1/2 (1982): 11–33.

Iverson, Peter. *Diné: A History of the Navajos*. Albuquerque: University of New Mexico Press, 2002a.

Iverson, Peter, ed. *For Our Navajo People: Diné Letters, Speeches, and Petitions, 1900–1960*. Albuquerque: University of New Mexico Press, 2002b.

Lee, Lloyd L. "Reclaiming Indigenous Intellectual, Political, and Geographic Space: A Path for Navajo Nationhood." *American Indian Quarterly* 32, No. 1 (2008): 96–110.

Lee, Lloyd Lance, ed. *Diné Perspectives: Revitalizing and Reclaiming Navajo Thought*. Tucson: University of Arizona Press, 2014.

McPherson, Robert S. *Dinéjí Na'nitin: Navajo Traditional Teachings and History*. Boulder: University Press of Colorado, 2012.

Niethammer, Carolyn. *I'll Go and Do More: Annie Dodge Wauneka, Navajo Leader and Activist*. Lincoln: University of Nebraska Press, 2001.

Niethammer, Carolyn. *Keeping the Rope Straight: Annie Dodge Wauneka's Life of Service to the Navajo*. Flagstaff, AZ: Salina Bookshelf, Inc., 2006.

Shepardson, Mary. "The Status of Navajo Women." *American Indian Quarterly* 6, no. 1/2 (1982): 149–169.

Weisiger, Marsha. *Dreaming of Sheep in Navajo Country*. Seattle: University of Washington Press, 2011.

Witt, Shirley Hill. "An Interview with Dr. Annie Dodge Wauneka." *Frontiers: A Journal of Women's Studies* 6, No. 3 (1981): 64–67.

Bureau of Indian Affairs American Indian Relocation, 1952

Megan Tusler

Chronology

1947 Secretary of the Interior Julius King proposes an American Indian "betterment plan."

1951 The BIA begins moving agents to relocation centers on reservations and in cities.

1952 Relocation officially begins.

1957 Public Law 959, also called the "Indian Relocation Act," provides $3.5 million to the BIA to aid in the relocation process.

Federal Funds for American Indians to Relocate

American Indian relocation was the result of the Bureau of Indian Affairs (BIA) passing a series of laws that provided funds for moving Native individuals and families from rural reservations to urban centers. Relocation offices were set up in Chicago, Denver, Los Angeles, San Francisco, San Jose, St. Louis, Cincinnati, Cleveland, and Dallas; there were also relocation centers on reservations themselves that encouraged families and single adults to move for perceived increased opportunity. A set of political and legal changes spurred relocation—in 1947, Secretary of the Interior Julius Krug proposed a ten-year plan for aiding Native People in "bettering" themselves. In 1951, the Bureau of Indian Affairs assigned agents to work on reservations and in urban relocation centers with the hope of encouraging Native People to move. The relocation program itself began in 1952.

According to Donald L. Fixico, by 1954, 6,200 Native People had been relocated from reservations to cities ("Dislocated," in Philip Weeks 196). The "relocatees," as they were called, were encouraged to work in factories and at other kinds of industrial labor. They were moved into living quarters that denoted a sense of typical urban living, such as small apartments in neighborhoods like Chicago's Uptown. In general, members of one tribe were physically placed apart from each other in the interest of encouraging assimilation. Inter-tribal friendships, however, were common, with Navajo and Hopi tribal members (for example) placed in proximity in Los Angeles. In 1956, the federal government passed a funding initiative, Public Law 959, that provided $3.5 million to the Bureau of Indian Affairs to aid in the process. The law reads, in part:

> *Be it enacted by the Senate and House of Representatives of the United States of America in Congress assembled,* That in order to help adult Indians who reside on or near Indian reservations to obtain reasonable and satisfactory employment, the Secretary of the Interior is authorized to undertake a program of vocational training that provides for vocational counseling or guidance, institutional training in any recognized vocation or trade, apprenticeship, and on the job training, for periods that do not exceed twenty-four months, transportation to the place of training, and subsistence during the course of training. (Accessed via Oklahoma State University Library)

This law had the effect of the BIA opening training centers both on reservations and in cities. The jobs open to Native People tended to be gender-selective—women were trained for secretarial work, while men trained for factory or mechanical jobs. Furthermore, this legislative decision provided for training at the secondary educational level—vocational schools were opened on reservations that provided technical training. There was, for example, a training program at Taos Pueblo Junior High that taught boys industrial labor.

The "success" or "failure" of the relocation process is the subject of debate among scholars of American Indian history. Given that a significant number of the original relocatees moved back to reservations, the program might be considered a failure. For others, the fact that many Native People considered the city their permanent home might also be considered a major issue as it implies ongoing culture loss and increasing assimilation. For yet others, the fact that intertribal coalitions were forged as a result of relocation suggests that the program was a success in some ways and a failure in others. In Chicago, the American Indian Center was founded in 1953; members of the Oneida, Ojibwa, Menominee, Sac and Fox, and other nations were represented among the original participants in this intertribal organization. In Oakland, California the Intertribal Friendship House was established in 1955 as a community center and evolved into a social service provider as well. The American Indian Movement (AIM) began its political action in an urban center as well—among its first actions was the creation of the Minneapolis AIM Patrol to combat police brutality against American Indian people in that urban center. In this sense, and for this third category of scholars, relocation had severe effects—it removed reservation dwellers from their traditional homelands and repositioned them in urban locations, where they continued to be ill-served by the United States government. It also had some unexpected positive consequences—when Native People were relocated to urban centers, it facilitated intertribal organizing and the creation of coalitions that persist to this day.

Relocation can be seen to have its origins in the Indian Reorganization Act, or what is called the "Indian New Deal." After the Meriam report of 1928 found Native reservation dwellers to be disproportionately impoverished and living in substandard circumstances, the Director of the BIA, John Collier, proposed legislation that would allow tribes more economic and governmental independence. The IRA slowed the allotment practice that had been breaking reservation lands into individual holdings since the General Allotment Act of 1887. Furthermore, it encouraged tribal governments to enact constitutions, a practice that would encourage tribal sovereignty and independence.

After Collier left the Bureau of Indian Affairs, other "reformers" added to the IRA. In 1954, the Indian Reorganization Act was amended to exclude certain tribes from exercising their rights of sovereignty; while this is not necessarily obvious from the act itself, the removal of sovereign status from such nations as the Klamath of Oregon effectively "terminated" that tribe. The early 1950s are considered among scholars of Indian history to be the "relocation and termination era"—the two governmental practices should be thought of as conjoined. When the government began to terminate sovereign nations, it simultaneously began its program of relocating Native People in an effort to "desegregate" Indian populations and encourage assimilation.

Dillon Myer was the Commissioner of Indian Affairs from 1950 to 1953 and coined the term "relocation" to refer to the practice of moving Native People from reservations to cities. Scholars such as Stan Steiner have noted that the term "relocation" is a loaded one in the context of Dillon Myer; prior to his appointment at the BIA, he led the War Relocation Authority from 1942 to 1946. The War Relocation Authority was responsible, during the Second World War, for the incarceration of Japanese and Japanese Americans in "relocation" camps. It was under his leadership as well as a number of senators and other lawmakers that House Concurrent Resolution 108 was passed in 1953. It reads, in part,

> Whereas it is the policy of Congress, as rapidly as possible, to make the Indians within the territorial limits of the United States subject to the same laws and entitled to the same privileges and responsibilities as are applicable to other citizens of the United States, to end their status as wards of the United States, and to grant them all of the rights and prerogatives pertaining to American citizenship; and Whereas the Indians within the territorial limits of the United States should assume their full responsibilities as American citizens.

This coded language, which implies that "full citizenship" should be extended to Native Peoples, had the effect of spurring both termination and relocation policies. When Indians are asked to "assume their full responsibilities as American citizens," the act attempts to end the special "domestic dependent" relationship that tribes have had with the United States government since the Marshall Trilogy of the 1820s and 1830s.

After HCR 108, agents from the Bureau of Indian Affairs began the process of building relocation centers on reservations and in major cities. They used a number of methods for encouraging Native People to relocate: promises of steady work; opportunities for city living that were assumed to be particularly exciting for the young and single; demonstrations of apparent "equal economic opportunity." To do this, the agents produced bulletins, posters, and scrapbooks that they showed reservation-dwellers to encourage them to move. The agents produced small studies to demonstrate to the Bureau that their efforts were effective and could be more effective: an agent at the Sisseton branch constructed a pie chart showing that, of the 464 people he had interviewed on the reservation, 312 were "fully employable," 35 were "unemployable," and 117 were "handicapped" (United States, Bureau of Indian Affairs. Bureau of Indian Affairs Indian relocation records [manuscript]

1936–1975). They also took a massive archive of photographs, the prints of which are now housed in various institutions, such as the Newberry Library in Chicago.

As mentioned, 1956 saw the passage of Public Law 959, which earmarked $3.5 million for employing and relocating reservation dwellers. The finding guide for the Newberry Library's archive demonstrates that PL 959 stepped up the relocation effort. "Participants, mostly between the ages of eighteen and thirty-five, received two years of benefits for either on-the-job experience or vocational classes. Typically, Indians working in factories on the reservation received apprenticeship provisions, and relocated individuals received vocational training. The 1956 legislation also increased counseling services" (Newberry finding guide: http://mms.newberry.org/xml/xml_files/relocation.xml). The Bureau of Indian Affairs worked with factories, corporations, and private offices to encourage the hiring of tribal members. Brief narratives of relocatees' journeys are included in the archive: a photograph of a young Winnebago woman and her white supervisor bears the caption, "Miss Irene Snowball, Winnebago, from Black River Falls, Wisconsin, came to Chicago, April 19, 1955. Irene is working for Nelson-Eismann as a typist at $60.00 a week. There are many schools for typing, stenography and business machine operation. Girls can go to these schools while working on a job to earn living" [sic]. Another picture, of an Ojibwe man, has this text attached: "Mr. LaRoy Miller, Jr., Chippewa, from Shawano, Wisconsin. He came to Chicago April 18, 1955. He is working at the Teletype Corporation as a machine operator trainee at $1.72 an hour [about $610.00 a week U.S. 2016]. LaRoy came to Chicago upon the advice of his brother, Roger" (United States, Bureau of Indian Affairs. Bureau of Indian Affairs Indian relocation records [manuscript] 1936–1975).

The bulletins and letters that circulated between relocation officers show the importance of the industrial work that greets Indians in their new city homes; the following is excerpted from a letter between Jack Womeldorf, the relocation officer at Intermountain School, and Rudolph Russell, a Chicago relocation agent in Joliet. Intermountain School in Brigham City, Utah, was a boarding/vocational school primarily for Navajo (Diné) children.

> Intermountain School is the largest off-reservation school operated by the Bureau of Indian Affairs. Under separate cover we are mailing you an information album to better acquaint you with our program. Since the first graduating class four years ago [1953], approximately 714 young men and women have been placed in employment off the reservation. . . .
>
> Because of the limited time these young people are in school it becomes necessary to give them specialized training. This, in simple language, means to train them to do one job (or trade) rather than a general course of

doing many things. We find that our most successful graduates are those who have been placed in jobs for which they have been trained.

We will have approximately 57 boys this year seeking employment and a start through Relocation Services. If it is at all possible, I would like to see each one of them have an opportunity to work in his field of training . . . (United States, Bureau of Indian Affairs. Bureau of Indian Affairs Indian relocation records [manuscript], 1936–1975)

When Womeldorf repeatedly requests that the Native students be placed in their "fields of training," he is referring to the exclusively industrial trades in which Intermountain School provided training, including driving (trucks and other manufacturing vehicles), equipment maintenance, cabinet and millwork, electrical engineering, etc. Intermountain strongly emphasized the importance of off-reservation employment; at an assembly in 1959 four students stand on a stage holding a massive banner that reads "Remember our words: Finish your education! Be on the bus next August!" (Utah State University, Merrill-Cazier Library, Special Collections and Archives, Compton Photograph Collection).

Once Native People arrived in their new urban homes, they pursued not just industrial labor but also connections with other Indian people. It is in part as a result of the desire for tribal and intertribal connection that institutions like the American Indian Center in Chicago and Intertribal Friendship House in Oakland were founded. Again, as a result of these connections, urban Indians redrew the lines of "cultural belonging," arguing in favor of an intertribal community in addition to the tribal communities that theretofore had been located on reservations. A great number of relocatees became more involved in organized social movements after relocation. Indian relocatees did not simply move from reservations and passively accept the demands of the Bureau of Indian Affairs, as demonstrated in interviews with relocatees. In the series of interviews conducted by the Chicago American Indian Oral History Project, transcripts of which are also owned by the Newberry, a number of commentators describe their early efforts at meeting other Native People. Phyllis Fastwolf notes that when she moved to Chicago in the 1950s with her family, "at the time we met at the Two Crow [a bar frequented by relocatees], there were quite a few families that were here on relocation. There were some from South Dakota. We had met a lot of families. It didn't take that long. In fact, we met quite a few Indians." The unidentified manuscript author describes the intertribal alliance that formed: "The relocation program attempted to scatter the Indian relocatees throughout the city, but as soon as families learned about the various neighborhoods and could afford to move, they sought to rent apartments close together to form their own ethnic enclave. Uptown became a popular Indian neighborhood, where the Indian population has gravitated" (88). Indeed, Inez Running

Bear Dennison, an early relocatee, notes the intertribal connections, and shows how belonging could be about racial solidarity and not tribal status alone: "I don't think I'd ever want to move out of Uptown because that is where the Indians are. I said I don't care what tribe they are, if they are Indian—they are Indians. I love all Indians" (14).

Additionally, the reliance of some Natives on social services (a lifestyle shared with many other members of the working class) exposed many of the problems between the institutions of federal aid and the people enjoined to take advantage of that aid. For example, the House Subcommittee on Indian Affairs' Indian Relocation and Industrial Development Programs noted that in Los Angeles, "Relocatees are advised that the relocation office cannot be used as a crutch indefinitely and that they must learn to utilize the same community resources as do other residents of the city" (Quoted in Neils 61), despite the fact that social services were being cut for all poor urbanites during the 1950s and 1960s. This push to cut Indian "reliance" shows the particular concern with the federal government on purported Indian "dependence."

Although Native People were often able to adapt—if not "assimilate"—to their urban surroundings, it is important to note that the campaign to "desegregate" Indian people into industrial labor was in some ways based on a faulty premise: that American industrial might was growing. In her article "Historical Background" from *The American Indian Today*, Nancy Oestrich Lurie accounts for many of the complicated outcomes of relocation and termination:

> Because Indian people showed a marked aptitude for industrial work during the war, and it was obvious they would not succeed as farmers, the solution was simple. Relocate them in urban centers, preferably in each case as far from the home reservation as possible, and legislate the reservation out of existence so that Indian people could not run home when things got tough or share their good fortune periodically with kinsmen who lacked the gumption to get out on their own.
>
> Like the grand scheme of 1887 to solve the Indians' problems by the simple expedient of allotment in severality [she refers to the Dawes Act, which in many cases carved reservation land into individual "allotments" with the hope of turning communally-held land into family plots], *the relocation-reservation termination plan of the 1950s was out of date for its time in terms of national social and economic trends.* If the ideal of the Allotment Act [Dawes Act] was to ensconce Indian people in a kind of average, small farm middle-class, which was actually disappearing, the ideal of the policy of the 1950s was primarily to get the government out of the Indian business and scant attention was paid to where Indian people might be able to fit in American life. . . .

At the very time that suburbs were burgeoning, commuting was a way of life for much of the nation, and far-sighted people were anticipating greater segmentation of industrial operations and dispersing them to where the people live, Indian policy was based on models of concentrating population in large urban centers.

Lurie notes that one of the problems with relocation was the way that it deposited Indian people into an urban environment that had already demonstrated the beginning of its collapse from a 19th century ideal. Scholars of urban history have argued since the 1980s that the "urban crisis" of the 1970s was a problem that actually had its origins in the late 1940s and 1950s, with the increase in the United States' global hegemony. As a result of this decline in industrial power, relocation makes it difficult for Native People to assimilate in the way the Bureau assumes they will—into being particular kinds of workers.

As a result of the relocation and termination policies, governmental and non-profit organizations issued reports on the "success" of the policy. The Commission on the Rights, Liberties, and Responsibilities of the American Indian issued *A Program for Indian Citizens: A Summary Report*, which eventually became the 1966 book *The Indian, America's Unfinished Business*, by William A. Brophy and Sophie D. Aberle. By that point, mainstream scholars of American Indians had taken a new tack, arguing that Native persons with "a foot in both worlds" were the most beneficial to society at large.

The Indian himself should be the focus of all public policy affecting him. Money, land, education, and technical assistance should be considered as only means to an end—making the Indian a self-respecting and useful American citizen. This policy involves restoring his pride of origin and faith in himself after years of crippling dependence on the federal government and arousing his desire to share in the advantages of modern civilization. These are deeply human considerations. If disregarded, they will defeat the best-intentioned government plans.

To encourage pride in Indianness is not to turn back the clock. On the contrary, it is to recognize that the United States policy has hitherto neglected this vital factor as a force for assimilation, with a corresponding loss to our national culture. As a result, Indians who have already entered our greater society have tended to disdain their historical background, drawing away from it as though ashamed. Instead of seeing it as a bridge to enable others to follow in their footsteps, they have too often misinterpreted their heritage to the dominant race and misrepresented their adopted culture to their own people. Yet men who have a foot in each world with an appreciation of both can effectively lessen the gap that divides the two and thus cross-fertilize both. (3)

This line of argumentation demonstrates that the program of relocation intended a version of assimilation that is congruent with the dominant political and cultural mode of the 1950s. For example, that the transition to "useful American citizenship" is characterized as a "deeply human consideration" outlines the purported universality of the desegregation project. Aligned here is also the problem of how to produce productive citizens while enabling Indians in particular to retain something like cultural pride; the authors insist that the U.S. government must encourage, simultaneously, "pride of origin" and an end to "crippling dependence." As most of the commentary on the "unfinished business" of "The Indian" notes in the midcentury, the loss of "cultural pride" or "pride of origin" is considered a fundamentally *national* problem. The authors do not refer to a nuanced vision of the nation that might accommodate Indian nations or nationalisms; when they assert that a loss of Indian "pride of origin" is a loss to "our national culture," they are asserting that "the Indian" is a fundamentally—and irrevocably—American construction.

For relocatees themselves, the program had a multitude of effects, some positive and some negative. American Indian urban communities have benefitted greatly from intertribal organizations and a renewed pan-Indian collectivism that grew out of the urban communities. However, the drive for assimilation removed many Native People from their reservation homes, producing increased reservation isolation.

Biographies of Notable Figures

John Collier, 1884–1968

John Collier, who was the commissioner of Indian Affairs from 1933 to 1945, was educated as a sociologist and taught in the discipline before his work in Indian country. His work with Indian communities was inspired by field work, in which he watched traditional dances. During the 1920s, the study of sociology and anthropology were dominated by an ethnographic method that had been pioneered by figures such as Franz Boas, and Collier's interest in preserving traditional Native ways of life while simultaneously expanding Indian integration was in keeping with the perspectives of early 20th-century social scientists. "After teaching sociology at San Francisco State College in 1921–1922, he was appointed research agent for the Indian Welfare Committee of the General Federation of Women's Clubs. He gained national recognition as an Indian reformer by blocking the U.S. Senate Bursum Bill, which would have ended Pueblo land and water rights without adequate compensation" (American National Biography 2004).

Before his work on the Indian Reorganization Act, Collier worked primarily with the American Indian Defense Association. Legal scholar Jay Daniels notes, "He had intended to reverse some of the worst government policies and provide ways for American Indians to re-establish sovereignty and self-government, to reduce the losses of reservation lands, and establish ways for Indians to build economic self-sufficiency" (Daniels 2013). For Collier, Indian self-governance was a value that should be preserved in national policy, and he worked on such issues as religious freedom, water rights, and land preservation. He published his own bulletin, *American Indian Life*, which documented many of the failures of the Indian Bureau to fully provide for the people to whom it should have been accountable. Furthermore, he lobbied for the Indian Oil Act of 1927, which was intended to shift policy such that tribal members were able to receive royalties from oil and mineral deposits that had recently been found on some reservations.

In part due to Collier's continuing objections to Indian policy, the Department of the Interior commissioned an intensive study of the Native population. In 1928, the Meriam Report detailed the quality of life for Native People in the United States. "The Brookings Institution published the results of this review in *The Problem of Indian Administration*, which advocated increased federal appropriations for Indians, limited tribal self-rule, and the end of land allotment. Between 1929 and 1932, Collier constantly criticized federal officials for not following the Brookings recommendations; he also joined members of the Senate Indian Investigating Committee who traveled the country to publicize substandard living conditions on western reservations" (American National Biography).

To quote the report itself, it was:

A survey of the economic and social conditions of the American Indians during the 1920s. Data was collected by field work for approximately 7 months. One or more members of the investigating staff visited 95 different jurisdictions, either reservations, Indian agencies, hospitals, or schools and also communities where Indians have migrated. Practically all western states with any considerable Indian population were included in the field work. Because of the diversity and complexity of Indian affairs this document is necessarily voluminous. The detailed report contains the following sections: (1) a general policy for Indian Affairs, (2) health, (3) education, (4) general economic conditions, (5) family and community life and the activities of women, (6) migrated Indians, (7) legal aspects of the Indian problem, and (8) missionary activities among Indians. Findings and recommendations are listed in detail in the front of this report. Findings cover such areas as health, living conditions, the causes of poverty, and the work of the government in behalf of the Indians. Recommendations include adequate statistics and records, better living and working conditions, and improving general economic conditions. (Wisconsin Historical Society records http://files.eric.ed.gov/fulltext/ED087573.pdf)

In part due to his unflagging support of the Brookings Institute (Meriam) report and his advocacy in Indian country, Collier was made Commissioner of Indian Affairs in 1933, appointed by Franklin D. Roosevelt. Among his significant policy decisions was the Indian Reorganization Act (IRA, also called the "Indian New Deal"). It was passed by Congress in 1934. "This legislation authorized tribal self-rule under federal supervision, discontinued land allotment, and permitted the consolidation, restoration, and purchase of tribal land for Indian reservations. The act set up a federal revolving credit fund to stimulate reservation economic development, and it provided tuition and scholarships to encourage Indian education" (American National Biography).

Despite the good intentions of the IRA, its policies proved difficult to fund and maintain. Collier found it consistently difficult to get Congress to allocate enough funds to continue the programs that the Meriam report advocated. He also raised a number of suggestions for Indian "self-betterment" that proved challenging to institute in practice. For example, "in 1940 Secretary of War Henry Stimson rejected his suggestion that the government form separate Indian military units. Instead, Stimson endorsed compulsory integrated military service, which rapidly accelerated the process of tribal assimilation" (American National Biography). The war years were generally difficult for those who advocated domestic policy funds allocation, in no small part because of the need for war funding.

Collier resigned as commissioner in 1945, although his work continued on the part of subaltern peoples. He worked for the Institute of Ethnic Affairs and advocated for improved livelihoods for people under colonial control in Southeast Asia and Micronesia. He eventually took up a teaching position at the City College of New York. "For the next six years he taught classes, published research on Indian life in the New World, and worked at the Institute of Ethnic Affairs. After his retirement in 1954, he taught classes for one semester at Columbia University and a summer seminar at the Merrill-Palmer School for social workers in Detroit" (American National Biography). He died in 1968.

Dillon S. Myer, 1891–1982

Dillon S. Myer was Commissioner of Indian Affairs from 1950 to 1953. In this role, he was the architect of relocation, and has been widely criticized by those like John

Collier and other policy-makers active in the passage of the IRA (Indian Reorganization Act). Furthermore, Myer's work during the war years with Japanese and Japanese-American internment contributes to the criticism that continues to surround his actions.

Myer's political career began in the Agricultural Adjustment Administration in 1934. It continued in a number of domestic policy departments, including the War Relocation Authority and the Public Housing Authority. Myer's government tenure, however, is primarily remembered in relation to his supervision of the internment of Japanese and Japanese Americans during the Second World War. According to his obituary, published October 25, 1982, in the *New York Times,*

> In 1942, Mr. Myer was appointed director of the War Relocation Authority and put in charge of Japanese aliens and Japanese-Americans who were ordered from their West Coast homes because of fears of an invasion by the Japanese after the attack on Pearl Harbor. Ten austere evacuation centers, patterned after army camps, were established around the country.

> Before the war ended, Mr. Myer began to move individuals and families from the centers to jobs and homes outside the exclusion area, an effort that, he said, encountered resistance and racial prejudice in some areas. When the war in the Pacific ended, the exclusion order was revoked, and Mr. Myer began a major drive to empty the relocation centers.

> Mr. Myer remained in charge of the agency until it was dissolved in 1946. He said he considered the evacuation order a regrettable mistake, but felt that the relocation effort had done something to correct it. ("Dillon S. Myer, Who Headed War Relocation Agency, Dies," accessed via nytimes .com.)

Despite Myer's ambivalence about the effects of internment and "relocation," he designed American Indian relocation in some ways based on the model of the relocation of Japanese and Japanese Americans after the end of internment. Relocation is contemporaneous with, and in many ways dependent upon, the federal termination policy for which Myer was also responsible. "Termination" refers to a group of policies that intended to end the federal trust relationship between tribes and the United States government. Donald L. Fixico points to how Myer, unlike his predecessor John Collier, advocated an assimilationist policy that would end the federal trust relationship by ending the federal recognition of some tribes (Fixico in Weeks 198).

Myer's assimilationist policies were, however, in keeping with much popular opinion toward American Indians. Eleanor Roosevelt voiced her support for ending the "paternalistic" relationship between Native People and the federal government (Philp 45). The rhetoric that Myer used that was taken up by other policy-makers emphasized an end to "dependence," "paternalism," and "reliance" on federal programs. Furthermore, Myer's emphasis on assimilation opened the possibility for increased Indian citizenship participation: seeing the 1924 Indian Citizenship Act as an opportunity for better Indian education, Myer reallocated funds to emphasize better schooling for Indian children (Philp 48).

Among Indian scholars as well as policy-makers like Myer, education policies are often viewed as efforts at assimilation. The distinction between these positions is how they are viewed as aspirational—for indigenous scholars, increased education is potentially both positive *and* negative, whereas for bureaucrats like Myer it was seen as unilaterally positive. These different points of view demonstrate the ongoing problem of how the federal government relates to its Indian citizens—the Bureau of Indian Affairs, which Myer hoped would quickly become unnecessary as Indian people assimilated to the "mainstream," continues to encounter problems with the relationship between the tribal-national trust arrangement and the state form of U.S. governance.

Myer's legacy is still controversial. This is because of his domestic actions with internment and Indian policy but also because of the way he responded to critique over his political life. According to the American National Biography, "In the last months of his life he was again involved in public controversy. The establishment of the Commission on the Wartime Relocation and Internment of Civilians (CWRIC) in late 1980 refocused public attention on the wartime incarceration of Japanese Americans. Too ill to appear at the CWRIC's Washington hearings, he authorized the commission's most vociferous critic, Lillian Baker, to read a statement opposing the idea of an apology. He died in Silver Spring, Maryland, just months before the CWRIC's report denounced both the decision to incarcerate and the process by which the WRA kept Japanese Americans imprisoned" (American National Biography online.) This opposition to apology will continue to make Myer a notorious figure in the history of the 20th century.

DOCUMENT EXCERPTS

An archive of images collected by the Bureau of Indian Affairs in the 1950s is housed at the Newberry Library, having been collected from the Chicago office of the BIA. The collection houses several hundred images taken between 1953 and 1958, many taken from scrapbooks curated by BIA agents, others taken by anonymous agents in order to convince reservation-dwellers to relocate to Chicago, Los Angeles, Minneapolis, Seattle, or another major American city with a BIA office. According to the government office website for the Department of the Interior, "Indian Affairs (IA) is the oldest bureau of the United States Department of the Interior. Established in 1824, IA currently provides services (directly or through contracts, grants, or compacts) to approximately 1.9 million American Indians and Alaska Natives. There are 566 federally recognized American Indian tribes and Alaska Natives in the United States. Bureau of Indian Affairs (BIA) is responsible for the administration and management of 55 million surface acres and 57 million acres of subsurface minerals estates held in trust by the United States for American Indian, Indian tribes, and Alaska Natives. "The Bureau of Indian Affairs (BIA) mission is to: '. . . enhance the quality of life, to promote economic opportunity, and to carry out the responsibility to protect and improve the trust assets of American Indians, Indian tribes, and Alaska Natives'" (BIA website, accessed 27 January 2015).

The archive records a major moment in American Indian history and in the cultural and aesthetic history of American urbanization more generally. The Newberry Library's archive provides a primary textual way to see images of Native People in relocation as well as documents that speak to the motives of the project.

Dated February 8, 1957, the letter presents an introduction to the "Menominee people."

To our friends and co-workers in relocation:

It is a pleasure to present this little picture study of the Menominee people and their reservation. We trust it will give you an insight into out problems and help you when our people come to your office for assistance.

Due to limited time and the season we were unable to get a number of pictures we would like for you to see. We expect to supplement this little book from time to time and eventually give you a complete picture of these people.

Sincerely yours,

C.W. McCall

Agency Relocation Officer

Further documents record some of the resources that the reservation holds. For the Menominee at the time, this was primarily in the form of timberland. The following document advertises "the many things" that relocation can be.

Yes, Relocation <u>is</u> many things!

In the first place, no one wants to move <u>unless</u> he can benefit by it.

If a person has a good job and a place to live, he probably would not profit by the services of the Relocation Program.

On the other hand, if an individual or family needs employment, and desires to move to a distant city where he can get steady work, this program can give assistance.

To start the Relocation procedures you must file an application with the Relocation Officer at the agency Headquarters. These papers are then sent to the Field Relocation Office of your choice. The people in the Field Offices are able to assist applicants in the location of jobs, housing and in making the many adjustments that always come up when a person moves from one locality to another.

Financial assistance is also available for those who can not pay their own expenses involved in making the move to their new location.

Field Relocation services are available only in St. Louis, Missouri, Denver, Colorado, Los Angeles, San Francisco and San Jose in California and Chicago, Illinois.

The pie chart that poses the benefits of the program asserts that relocation is: job benefits (skills, security, promotions, company programs), job, housing (temporary, permanent, home ownership), financial aid (travel subsistence en-route and at destination), sound planning, sincerity, community adjustment, and desire to do better. Finally, among the photographs in the "picture study" are primarily pictures of local reservation buildings.

The relocation agents underscore not just the financial benefits to relocatees, they also pose a very particular 1950s ambition for housing, particularly in the form of "home ownership," as well as for "sound planning." These materials also demonstrate that propagandistic forms were deemed necessary to persuade Native reservation dwellers to relocate. It seems that the Bureau of Indian Affairs went to some lengths to convince Indians that they would be "better off" in urban environments—particularly because it was assumed that reservations themselves were not places in which Native People could find good jobs and high-quality housing.

Source: Bureau of Indian Affairs Indian Relocation Records, The Newberry Library, Chicago.

Further Reading

American National Biography 2004.

Bureau of Indian Affairs Indian Relocation Records, The Newberry Library, Chicago. Finding guide: http://mms.newberry.org/xml/xml_files/relocation.xml

Burt, Larry W. "Roots of the Native American Urban Experience: Relocation Policy in the 1950s." *American Indian Quarterly* Vol. 10, No. 2 (Spring, 1986): pp. 85–99.

Daniels, Jay. Why Justice Scalia is Blind to History, July 12, 2013. Indian Country Today Media Network. http://indiancountrytodaymedianetwork.com/2013/07/12/why-justice-scalia-blind-history)

Fixico, Donald L. *Termination and Relocation: Federal Indian Policy, 1945–1960.* Albuquerque: University of New Mexico Press, 1990.

Hoover, Herbert T. and Miller, David Reed Miller, eds. *Chicago American Indian oral history project records,* manuscript.

Neils, Elaine M. "The Urbanization of the American Indian and the Federal Program of Relocation Assistance." Dissertation. Chicago: University of Chicago, 1969.

Oklahoma State University Archive of Tribal Laws and Treaties. http://digital.library.okstate.edu/kappler/Vol6/html_files/v6p0614.html

Philip, Kenneth. *Dillon S. Meyer and the Advent of Termination: 1950–53.* Western Historical Quarterly. Vol. 19, No. 1 (Jan., 1888): pp. 37–59.

Utah State University, Merrill-Cazier Library, Special Collections and Archives, Compton Photograph Collection, PO313, 1959.

Iroquois Tax and Reservoir Protests, 1957

Nikki Dragone

Chronology

1908	A series of dams are proposed as a means of protecting Pittsburgh, Pennsylvania, from floods and pollution, and to provide the region with electric power.
1927	The Seneca Nation of Indians (SNI) begin protesting calls for a dam that would flood their lands.
1936, 1939, and 1941	Congress first approves the Kinzua and Onondaga Creek Dam projects in three successive Flood Control Acts. However, no funds are appropriated, and no real action is taken until the 1950s.
1941	President Roosevelt bypasses Congress to negotiate an agreement with Canada to construct the St. Lawrence Seaway.
1943	New York State attorney general declares that the state has the right to levy income taxes against the Indians. The State chooses to maintain an unofficial policy of not levying income tax so long as New York Indians earn their living solely from subsistence activities.
1948	Congress passes 25 U.S.C. §232, transferring criminal jurisdiction over Indians to New York State.

1949   The Onondaga Flood Control dam and reservoir are constructed on Onondaga Nation lands.

1950   Congress passes 25 U.S.C. §233, transferring civil jurisdiction over Indians to New York State.

1954–1961   Construction of the St. Lawrence Seaway.

1956 to 1961   Construction of the Niagara Dam and reservoir.

1956   Canadian Superior Court rejects the Kahnawá:ke Mohawks' suit over the expropriation of land.

1956   In June, series of gigantic rock falls causes two-thirds of the Schoellkopf Power Plant to tumble into Niagara Gorge, resulting in massive power outages and providing the justification for the construction of the Niagara Power Project.

1956   SNI contracts renowned engineer and former head of the Tennessee Valley Authority, Arthur Morgan, to study the possibility of alternate sites for proposed dam.

1956–1961   SNI engages in intense lobbying of federal and state officials and a letter-writing campaign, which results in support from a wide variety of Native and non-Native sources, including the ACLU, the National Congress of the American Indian, the Quakers, the Cherokee Nation, and even New York State governor, Averell Harriman.

1957   In January, the U.S. District Court for the Western District of New York holds that the Army Corps were within their legal rights to initiate the condemnation and taking of SNI lands.

1957   Congress passes Public Law 85–159, granting directing the Federal Power Commission (FPC) to grant New York's SPA the license to construct and operate a power plant on the Niagara River.

1957–1958   Mohawk chief Frank Thomas (Standing Arrow) leads a group of Mohawks dispossessed by the construction of the St. Lawrence Seaway in the occupation of lands in original Mohawk territories along the Schoharie Creek, near Fort Hunter, New York.

1958   The Tuscarora begin active protest. Tuscarora Resistance Committee posts signs at reservation entries warning the SPA workers to stay out. Survey stakes are pulled up. The people face off against the surveyors and a large police force. Resistance continues until the U.S. Supreme Court decision is rendered in 1960.

1958	New York State levies taxes on Akwesasne Mohawks employed in the construction of the Seaway. Eventually, the Franklin County Court determines that New York State was within its rights to tax income earned and to seek remedies for non-payment of taxes.
1958	In *St. Regis tribe v. New York St*ate, the Court of Appeals affirms a decision against the Mohawks' suit for compensation of their loss of Barnhart Island to the Seaway.
1959	On the grounds that it violated Haudenosaunee sovereignty and treaty rights, Mohawks demonstrate opposition to New York State income tax on January 29th in Massena.
1959	In February, the FPC rules the Tuscarora Nation could not be compelled to sell its lands, and the government could not exercise eminent domain as this would be "inconsistent for the purpose for which the reservation was created or acquired" (Hauptman 151–.73).
1959	The U.S. Supreme Court denies certiorari to the SNI; their legal battle ends.
1960	In March 1960, the U.S. Supreme Court rules that Tuscarora lands were subject to eminent domain because the land was held in fee simple title rather than Indian title and therefore did not fit the federal definition of a "reservation" (Hauptman 1986, 172–73).
1960	U.S. Supreme Court denies the Akwesasne Mohawks' appeal in *St. Regis v. New York State*.
1960	In September, Kahnawa:ke's Grand Chief, Matthew Lazore, petitions the UN Human Rights Commission for protection against Canada's infringement of Mohawk land and sovereignty.
1961	SNI petitions President John F. Kennedy to once again investigate Morgan's alternate suggestions regarding locations for the dam. Pointing to the Supreme Court's decision, JFK says the dam would continue.
1961–1964	Construction of the Kinzua Dam.

Introduction

The Iroquois Tax and Reservoir protests of the 1950s, which occurred between the advent of the Great Depression in 1929 and the occupation of Alcatraz by the Indians of All Tribes in 1969, resulted from actions that New York State took in extending its jurisdiction over Iroquois lands and peoples during that era. Specifi-cally, after the federal government granted New York State civil jurisdiction over Indians residing within its boundaries, the state sought to levy personal income tax on Iroquois wage workers and to the construction of a series of dams/reservoirs on Iroquois reservations. This chapter focuses less on the injustices perpetrated and more on the continued relevance of Iroquois protests against imposition of New York State income tax and the construction of reservoirs on their lands—the Onon-daga Creek Dam (1947–49); the St. Lawrence Seaway (1954–1959); the New York State Thruway (1951–1960); the Kinzua Dam (1957–1964); and the Niagara Dam (1956–1961)—to the development of North American Indian activism in the 1960s and the birth of the Indigenous Rights Movement in the 1970s.

The Iroquois Confederacy

Before exploring the continuing impact of Iroquois protests on American Indian activism and indigenous rights, it is critically important to know where the Iro-quois are located. While the people of the Iroquois Confederacy are also popularly known as Six Nations Confederacy, they call themselves the Haudenosaunee, or the People of the Longhouse. They consist of the following North American Indian nations: Mohawk, Oneida, Onondaga, Cayuga, Seneca, and Tuscarora. In the pre-conquest era, their traditional territories stretched from the Mohawk River Valley in New York State westward into present-day Ohio, and from Southern Ontario and Quebec southward into Pennsylvania. Today, the majority of their reservation territories are found in upstate New York, Southern Ontario, and Southern Quebec. However, there is also one reservation in Wisconsin and one in Oklahoma. The five Haudenosaunee reservations that are the focus of this discussion are the Onon-daga Nation (located near Syracuse, New York); the Kahnawá:ke Mohawk (located near Montreal, Quebec); the Akwesasne/St. Regis Mohawk (straddling the borders of New York State and the provinces of Ontario and Quebec); the Tuscarora Nation (located near Lewiston, New York); and, the Allegany Seneca (located in the south-west corner of New York state, along the Allegheny River).

Federal and New York State Policies Influencing Iroquois Protests (1948–1968)

In post-World War II America, the Truman and Eisenhower administrations sought ways to cut federal government spending, in part by getting out of the "Indian business." Federal termination legislation provided the means to accomplish this goal by abruptly terminating an Indian nation's federally recognized status as a separate and sovereign, albeit dependent, nation to whom the federal government had treaty-based obligations to provide funds and services, including health and education services. The New York State Haudenosaunee reservations were included on Bureau of Indian Affairs (BIA) lists identifying Indian nations that were "ready for termination" and/or would be termination ready within ten years. While no direct action was taken to terminate New York State–based Iroquois, the construction of the Kinzua Dam resulted in the passage of legislation intended, in part, to terminate the Seneca Nation of Indians (SNI). Located in southwestern New York State on the Cattaraugus and Allegheny reservations, the SNI found itself in a protracted battle to prevent more than 8,000 acres of SNI lands from being submerged underneath the Kinzua Dam's reservoir. When the Kinzua became a *fait accompli*, the federal government passed the Seneca Nation Compensation Act (Public Law 88–533). Section 18 of this law required the SNI to submit a plan for its termination to the federal government within a specific period of time. Due to Seneca protests, which took the form of intense lobbying efforts, Section 18 was never implemented (Bilharz 1998, 72).

While Iroquois protests protected the SNI from termination, no amount of protests prevented the federal government from transferring federal criminal and civil jurisdiction over Indians to New York State. Promulgated in 1950, the transfer of civil jurisdiction was subject to the following limitations: New York State did not have the authority to tax Indians lands and property; it could not authorize the taking of Indian lands or property for failure of the Indians to pay debts; and the Indians retained the rights to regulate hunting and fishing within their territories. 25 U.S.C. §233 would become one of the focal points of tax protests by the Akwesasne Mohawks in 1958 and 1959.

Tax Protests

It should come as no surprise to the reader that within a decade of assuming civil jurisdiction over the Iroquois, New York State attempted to impose state and local income taxes on the Haudenosaunee. According to an August 11, 1958, article in *The Massena Observer,* the state attorney general "held in 1943 that the state had the right to levy taxes against the Indians" ("Indians Plan Rally . . ." 1958, 12). However, New York State chose to maintain an unofficial policy of not levying taxes on Haudenosaunee people so long as they earned their living as subsistence farmers. In the 1950s, when the construction of the St. Lawrence Seaway soon provided Akwesasne Mohawks with the opportunity to become "substantial wage earners," New York State chose to levy income tax on these Mohawk wage earners and to subpoena them for non-payment of back taxes ("Indians are not Exempt. . . ." 1958, 28).

Arthur Hart, the Mohawk's attorney, said that because the "power to tax is the power to destroy," the Mohawks considered the state's attempt to collect back taxes as an attempt to destroy the Akwesasne reservation ("Indians Plan Rally . . ." 1958, 12). A few months later, in Franklin County Court, Hart argued that the because the Mohawks were residing in their original territory on treaty-protected lands, and because this same treaty made the Mohawks as wards to the government, "like infants," the Mohawks could not be taxed unless the federal government were to pass special legislation granting New York State the power to tax them. In response to Hart's oral arguments, Judge Lawrence ruled that even the income of New York State's infant residents is taxable. Consequently, as the Mohawks reside on a reservation within the boundaries of New York State, they are liable to pay income tax, and New York State is within its right to seek remedies for non-payment of said taxes [*State Tax Commissioner v. Barnes*, 14 Misc.2d 311 (N.Y. Misc. 1958)].

After the Mohawks appealed this decision and tore up the legal "Notices to Appear" before the State Tax Commission, New York State offered to waive the penalties, reduce the interest due on their unpaid taxes, and help them file their returns. On January 29, 1959, under the leadership of Tuscarora activist Wallace "Mad Bear" Anderson, and Seneca/Grand Council chief Corbett Sundown, nearly 200 Mohawks descended on Massena Town Hall. Acting as their spokesmen, Anderson and Sundown again voiced Mohawk opposition to New York State income tax on the grounds that it violated Haudenosaunee sovereignty, the U.S. Constitution, and international and treaty law ("Indians Continue to Battle . . ." 1959, 29). The Mohawks' income tax protest spread to other reservations and continued unabated until New York State's favorable ruling in the *Matter of Powless v. State Tax Commission* was affirmed by the U.S. Supreme Court's refusal to review the case on appeal in 1965.

Onondaga Flood Control Dam, 1949

The Onondaga Nation's reservation is located five miles south of Syracuse, New York. Onondaga Creek flows northward through the Onondaga Nation's territory and into Syracuse, where it empties into Onondaga Lake. As Syracuse was prone to flooding throughout the 19th and early 20th centuries, Onondaga Creek was included in the federal Flood Control Acts of 1936, 1939, and 1941. Little has been written about the nature of the Onondaga Nation's protests. However, as Onondaga is the seat of the Confederacy's Grand Council and home to the Tadodaho, their spiritual leader, it is important to point out that in 1949, the Onondaga Flood Control Dam and reservoir were constructed on Onondaga Nation lands despite the protests of the Onondaga Nation (OIE).

The Seneca Nation of Indians (SNI) Protests the Kinzua Dam

The Kinzua Dam was proposed in 1908 as a means of protecting Pittsburgh, Pennsylvania, from floods and pollution, and to provide the region with electric power (Hauptman 1986, 90). While no funds were appropriated, and no real action was taken until the 1950s, Congress first approved the Kinzua Damp project in its 1936, 1939, and 1941 Flood Control Acts (Bilharz 1998, 49; Hauptman 1986, 92–93). As early as 1927, the Seneca Nation of Indians (SNI) began protesting.

By the time construction of the dam was initiated in 1961, SNI protests had already assumed many forms, from legal action and the commissioning the study of alternate sites to letter-writing campaigns and intense lobbying of federal and state officials, which resulted in support from a wide variety of Native and non-Native sources, including the ACLU, the National Congress of the American Indian, the Quakers, the Cherokee Nation, and even New York State's governor, Averell Harriman (Hauptman 1986, 113–15). In addition, the SNI contracted renowned engineer and former head of the Tennessee Valley Authority, Arthur Morgan, to study the possibility of alternate sites for proposed dam. Morgan did, indeed, provide Congress with a viable alternate site; however, his plan was ultimately rejected in favor of the dam's current location. Additionally, the SNI pursued legal avenues against the takings of their federal treaty-protected lands by initiating a suit to prevent the Army Corps of Engineers from entering their lands on the grounds that it violated their sovereignty and their treaty rights and would adversely impact their cultural and spiritual life as the Cold Spring Longhouse was located within the proposed take area. Despite their strong legal arguments, in January 1957, after a protracted legal battle, the U.S. District Court for the Western District of New York held that—the 1794 Canandaigua Treaty notwithstanding—the Corps were within their legal rights to initiate the condemnation and take SNI lands. In 1959, when the U.S. Supreme Court refused to hear the case, the SNI's legal battle ended (Hauptman 1986, 105–22; Bilharz 1998, 53).

Despite the failure of the SNI's protests against the taking of Seneca lands, the removal and relocation of Seneca families, and the building of the Kinzua, their resistance went a long way toward creating a new, more unified SNI. Noted historian Laurence Hauptman interprets the SNI's resistance to the Kinzua Dam as helping to instill a "new sense of nationalism, uniting the people of the Haudenosaunee Confederacy across reservation lines, incorporating in even the Indians living off-reservation in urban communities" (Hauptman 1986, 122).

The Tuscarora Nation Protests the Niagara Power Project

After a series of gigantic rock falls caused the Schoellkopf Power Plant to tumble into Niagara Gorge, and in turn the massive power outages of June 1956, Robert

Moses, the chair of New York's State Power Authority (SPA), met with a large group of corporate and utility executives in Massena, New York. Though it was still under construction, Moses successfully used the tour of the St. Lawrence Seaway, together with the loss of the Schoellkopf Power Plant, to unite the meeting participants over the issue of building a massive power plant along the banks of the Niagara River (Hauptman 1986, 153). For the Tuscarora Nation, this unanimity would be but the first step toward the taking of Tuscarora Nation lands to build the Lewiston dam and reservoir. The following year, Congress passed Public Law 85–159, granting directing the Federal Power Commission (FPC) to grant New York's SPA the license to construct and operate a power plant on the Niagara River.

When the license was granted, the FPC failed to issue a decision about whether or not the SPA could exercise eminent domain over Tuscarora Nation lands. This became the lynch pin of the Tuscarora Nation's legal suit against the SPA. Did the SPA have the authority to take Tuscarora lands for the purposes of constructing a reservoir on their lands? Initially, the FPC held a series of hearings in Washington, D.C., and Rochester, New York, to try to determine the answer to this question. Tuscarora representatives from both the Chief's and the People's Councils participated in these hearings. In the FPC's February 1959 ruling, neither could the Tuscarora Nation be compelled to sell its lands, nor could their land be taken through the government's powers of eminent domain because such a taking would be "inconsistent for the purpose for which the reservation was created or acquired" (Hauptman 1986, 153–71). This ruling was a short-lived victory for the Tuscarora as the FPC asked the federal courts to review the decision. In March 1960, the U.S. Supreme Court ruled against the Tuscaroras on the grounds that the lands subject to eminent domain in this case were held by the Tuscaroras in fee simple title, rather than Indian title, and as such did not fit the federal definition of a "reservation" (Hauptman 1986, 172–73).

While their legal battle was being fought in the courts, the people of the Tuscarora Nation engaged in a more confrontational method of protest. During the FPC hearings, the Tuscarora received word that the SPA planned to enter the reservation and survey lands. It was at this point that the young "warriors,", members of the Tuscarora Resistance Committee, joined the fight by placing notices at the all the entrances to the reservation, warning the SPA's surveyors off. In April 1958, the Tuscarora people stood against the Niagara County sheriff's deputies and New York State troopers who had come with the surveyors. Arrests were made, but the charges were eventually dropped. Over the next several months, the Tuscarora Resistance Committee pulled up survey stakes. One woman lay down in the path of the construction vehicles to prevent them from entering her land. Resistance efforts continued until the U.S. Supreme Court ruled against the Tuscarora Nation in March 1960 (Rickard 1973, 138–52; Hauptman 1986, 151–78).

Akwesasne and Kahnawá:ke Mohawks Protest the St. Lawrence Seaway

In 1941, President Franklin Delano Roosevelt bypassed Congress to negotiate an agreement with Canada to make the St. Lawrence River—which extends from the Atlantic Ocean to Lake Ontario, and which acts as a natural boundary between the United States and Canada—completely navigable by big ocean-going vessels. Construction of what would become the St. Lawrence Seaway began in 1954 and concluded in 1961. To facilitate construction, both the United States and Canada exercised their rights of eminent domain to condemn and take Mohawk lands from the Akwesasne and Kahnawá:ke Mohawk reservations. In response to this loss of land, the Mohawks of both reservations initiated court actions—the Akwesasne Mohawks for the loss of Barnhart Island, and the Kahnawá:ke Mohawks for the loss of their riverfront. Both lost their court battles (Hauptman 1986, 123–50; Bonaparte 2010).

Perhaps more important than their court battles was the stand taken during this time by two Mohawk chiefs: Matthew Lazore and Frank "Standing Arrow"

Cargo ship passing through the Iroquois Lock beside the Iroquois Dam, on the St. Lawrence Seaway, 1955. Tribal lands were routinely confiscated for the construction of dams that flooded ancient burial grounds and the towns of Indian communities. (Pictorial Parade/Archive Photos/Getty Images)

Thomas. Thomas was a condoled chief; as such, he was responsible both to the Mohawk people and to the Haudenosaunee Grand Council. His decision to protest the displacement of Mohawks at Kahnawá:ke by occupying lands in the Mohawks' original homelands in New York State's Mohawk Valley was not taken lightly. In fact, his decision resulted in several meetings of the Grand Council—at both Onondaga and Fort Hunter, the site of the Mohawks' occupation. The occupation lasted from spring 1957 through their eviction in February 1958. During that time, the Mohawks built an "Indian village," complete with a longhouse, and established relationships with surrounding non-Native communities. In addition, Thomas was adept at engaging the local, national, and international media in a way that made Mohawk resistance to the Seaway visible to the public and garnered sympathy and support (Doran 2014, 120–57). Perhaps realizing that all domestic remedies to protect Haudenosaunee lands on both sides of the U.S.-Canadian border were quickly being denied by the federal, state, and provincial governments of Canada and the United States, on July 1, 1957, Thomas told reporters that if these two nations were to continue to ignore Haudenosaunee rights to land and sovereignty, the Mohawk people would be prepared to go to the United Nations (UN) for help (Doran 2014, 137). It is not clear whether Thomas reached out to the UN; however, in his September 27, 1960, letter to the UN Human Rights Commission, Kahnawa:ke's Grand Chief, Matthew Lazore, asked for UN protection against Canada's continued infringement of Mohawk land, sovereignty, and self-governance rights (Simpson 2014).

The Continued Relevance of the Iroquois Tax and Reservoir Protests of the 1950s

While the Iroquois' protests over New York State income tax ended in 1965, they both influenced and were influenced by the Haudenosaunees' protests against reservoirs being constructed in Onondaga, Seneca, Tuscarora, and Mohawk territories between 1949 and 1966. In his ruling against the Akwesasne Mohawks, Judge Lawrence recognized the influence of the reservoir issue when he referred to the rulings of both the Mohawk's Barnhart Island case and the Tuscaroras' suit against the State Power Authority. Note that the unfortunate Akwesasne Mohawks who found themselves subject to New York State income tax are the same Mohawks subjected to New York State income tax because they became wage earners in the construction of the St. Lawrence Seaway. It is also important to point out that the participation of Haudenosaunee Confederacy Council Chiefs in these protests—Corbett Sundown (Seneca) and Irving Powless (Onondaga), who both protested New York State levying income taxes on Iroquois people, and Frank Thomas (Mohawk), who initiated the occupation of Fort Hunter—with Mad Bear Anderson

(Tuscarora), Ray Fadden (Mohawk), Ernie Benedict (Mohawk), and scores of other Haudenosaunee people indicates the resurgence of Haudenosaunee nationalism and leadership in American Indian activism on a national and international level. In fact, many of these leaders would work together to establish the Unity Caravans, which crisscrossed North American teaching about the importance of American Indian spiritual, cultural, and political survival in a way that seeded the Red Power Movement of the 1960s and 1970s, the Indigenous Rights Movement, and, one could argue, even the Idle No More Movement. What proof is there of this? Taken together, Standing Arrow's occupation of Fort Hunter, the Tuscaroras' attention-getting protests against SPA surveyors, the SNI's protracted historical battle against the Kinzua Dam, the Onondaga Nation's quieter protests against the damming of Onondaga Creek, and income tax protests in 1958 and 1959 presaged the Puget Sound Fish-ins (1964), the occupations of Alcatraz (1964, 1969–1971), the birth of the American Indian Movement (1969), and the many protests and occupations that followed from the takeover of the BIA (1972) to the occupation of Caledonia (2006), from the occupation of Wounded Knee (1973) to the birth of Idle No More (2012). Likewise, while Chief Lazore's 1960 letter to the UN is not the first time the Haudenosaunee and other indigenous peoples reached out the UN for help, it is clear that by writing to the UN, the Kahnawá:ke Mohawks, and by extension the Haudenosaunee Confederacy, contributed to what has become an International Indigenous Rights Movement culminating in the adoption of the U.N. Declaration on the Rights of Indigenous Peoples on September 13, 2007.

Biographies of Notable Figures

William Rickard (1917–1964)

Though William Rickard died when he was only 47 years old, he is well remembered for his stand against the New York State Power Authority's taking of Tuscarora Nation lands to construct the Niagara dam and reservoir in the 1950s. Rickard was born in 1917 to Clinton and Elizabeth Rickard. Like his mother, he was born into the Tuscarora Nation and the Bear Clan. As such, he was a citizen of both the Tuscarora Nation and the Haudenosaunee Confederacy (the Iroquois Confederacy). Rickard was raised a Tuscarora on his parents' farm. His paternal grandmother was a clan mother, and his father a condoled chief of the Beaver Clan. Rickard's father was well known as the founder of Indian Defense League of America (IDLA), an organization dedicated to protecting the Jay Treaty defined rights of the Haudenosaunee and other Native North Americans to freely cross the U.S.-Canadian Border. With Clinton Rickard as his example, William Rickard became one of the most influential leaders in Indian country in the decade just preceding his untimely death.

Rickard's rise as a nationally known leader in the fight for indigenous sovereignty and self-determination began slowly when he and other Haudenosaunee delegates were sent to Washington, D.C., to testify before Congress about the deleterious effects of pending termination-era legislation. Held in 1948 and 1950, these hearings centered on legislation that ultimately transferred civil and criminal jurisdiction over the Indians of New York State from the federal government to the state. Rickard's participation in these hearings, as well as his work as the secretary of IDLA, likely resulted in his election as the president of the Niagara chapter of IDLA.

Throughout 1957 and 1958, the Tuscaroras waged a pitched battle against New York's State Power Authority (SPA) and to assert the government's right of eminent domain to take up to one-fifth of Tuscarora Nation's lands to harness Niagara Falls for a hydroelectric power project. As a member of the People's Council, William Rickard traveled to Washington, D.C., and to Rochester and Buffalo, New York, to testify at a series of the Federal Power Commission (FPC) hearings on the matter. He also worked with the Tuscarora Resistance Committee to prevent the SPA's surveyors and workers from entering the reservation. The Tuscaroras posted "No trespassing" signs, shot out the SPA night surveyors' lights, and used their cars to block access to the reservation. Tuscarora women used their bodies to block the surveyors' equipment. In addition, they pulled out surveying stakes used to mark condemned lands. In April 1958, after the FPC granted the New York SPA the license necessary to take land for the power project, Rickard was on the front lines of the more than 150 Tuscaroras who faced off against the SPA's surveyors and workmen, and the state and local law enforcement armed with riot gear, tear gas, rifles, and submachine guns. During the face-off, the police arrested Rickard and two other Tuscarora men for disorderly conduct or unlawful assembly. With national and international media attention focused on Tuscaroras' protests, their cases were dismissed. While their protests have been described as some of the most dramatic protests of state power during this era, ultimately, despite their protracted legal battle, media campaigns, and opposition, the Tuscaroras lost 550 acres to the Niagara Power Project (Rosier 2009, 211–12).

In the wake of these protests, William Rickard became one of the most influential men in Indian country. From January to June of 1961, Rickard participated in organizing the American Indian Chicago Conference. He exerted his influence to ensure that the delegates attending the June conference would be representative of all Indian peoples; consequently, the more than 400 delegates came from not just federally recognized tribes, but also non-federally recognized tribes and urban Indian communities. He also made sure the delegates included traditional and spiritual leaders of Indian communities. At the conference, Rickard emerged as a strong supporter of Indian sovereignty and self-determination.

Also in 1961, William Rickard became the president of the League of North American Indians (LONAI), a pan-Indian organization founded 26 years earlier by Lawrence Two Axe (Kahnawá:ke Mohawk). LONAI intended to unite Indian peoples of North America politically and to protect and preserve Indian rights and sovereignty. In June 1963, under Rickard's leadership, LONAI organized and hosted the Grand Spiritual and Temporal Council. Over 500 people from 35 Indian nations attended. This Council drew on Rickard's experiences attending the Meetings of Religious People organized by the Hopi of Hotavella. The first of these meetings had been held nearly a decade earlier, in 1956, and was extremely influential in Rickard's life. Raised as a Christian, after attending the first of the Meetings of Religious People, Rickard became a Longhouse adherent and supporter of traditional Haudensaunee cultural practices. Rickard's close relations with the Hopis led to strong relations between the Haudenosaunee and Hopi peoples.

By 1964, the emphysema and bronchiectasis resulting from a childhood injury had progressed to the point that Rickard's health was failing quickly. Rickard passed away in 1964. On September 18 of that year, William "Fighting Bear" Rickard passed away of acute pulmonary edema. By the end of the 1960s, Haudenosaunee and Hopi activists and spiritual leaders, including Beeman Logan (Seneca), Mad Bear Anderson (Tuscarora), and Thomas Banyacya (Hopi), worked together to organize what became known as the Unity Caravans and Conventions. These conventions, and the caravans that followed, reinvigorated the cultural life of indigenous communities throughout North America. In this way, Rickard's influence was felt long after his passing.

DOCUMENT EXCERPTS

"The Drums Go Bang, Seaway Ugh, Mohawks Plan Move" (1957)

The excerpt below is from a newspaper article authored by Clayton Sinclair and published in the Montreal Gazette *on August 21, 1957. It clearly identifies the 1957 construction of the Mohawk settlement in Fort Hunter, New York, as a civil protest against the taking of Mohawk lands for the construction of the St. Lawrence Seaway.*

The drums are beating again along the Mohawk and in Caughnawaga the first Indian families are heading the call.

If plans go ahead, more than 2000 Indians at Caughnawaga and the reservations at Oka and St. Regis, Que. will pick up stakes and head for a new home in New York State.

Mohawks here, who constitute a good portion of the Indians populating the reservations, say they are moving because the St. Lawrence Seaway interferes with their homes.

Another reason has been found in the fact that New York State Mohawks have decided to claim land on Schoharie Creek, where the stream flows into the Mohawk River, as their own.

Four hundred Mohawks are now settled on the banks of the creek, but New York State leader of the tribe, short muscular Chief Standing Arrow, a 24-year old Indian who spent a term with the United Stats Navy, says that 4000 will be living there by next summer.

Most are expected to come from Canadian reservations, the Chief said here yesterday . . .

The groups settled near the creek and they have no intention of discussing it with the farmer, who thinks he owns some of the land or with the New York Thruway Authority, which thinks it owns the rest. They won't even talk to the sheriff about it, or even the state legislature at Albany.

The Mohawks are a nation they say, and any dealings will have to be carried through Washington, and presumably through John Foster Dulles, secretary of state. In their view, the land is rightfully theirs as is, for that matter, much of the rest of the state of New York.

The white men in New York are somewhat worried. It seems the Indians might have a case.

The settlement at present is a modest, but neat and clean presentation of shacks, tents and teepees just where the Schoharie passes under the thruway.

Chief Standing Arrow was in Caughnawaga yesterday to confer with six Longhouse chiefs on the reservation and to invite them to a Grand Consulate meeting of the Indians' Confederacy of Six Nations. This is scheduled to be held in Fort Hunter, New York on Sunday and will be the first meeting of its scale to be held in the Mohawk Valley in 163 years. Out of it is likely to come a decision of the Indians whether to remain there. If affirmative, the Indians may call for a large scale migration from the reservations.

Claim Pressure from Government

"Quite a few" of the Indians who now live in the valley are those who formerly lived in Canada. "The reason we have settled there is because of political pressure from the Canadian government."

"It has been unfair and has no right to interfere with the sovereignty of the tribe," Chief Standing Arrow said of the St. Lawrence Seaway Authority's decision to send the Seaway through the Caughnawaga reservation.

The Indians will benefit by moving to New York state he said, because "it is their original homeland and by treaty, the Indian has every right to live there. In

Canada, he lives under three laws, the British, French and Canadian." The Indians here have treaties with all three nations.

It is only right, he says, that the United States give them some land. All they want is an area eight miles deep by seven miles wide, stretching along the Schoharie south of the Mohawk.

Chief Standing Arrow contends that his tribe [. . .] is entitled to a great deal more.

The chief has a lot of photostats of old treaties. The most important, he says, was signed on October 22, 1784. It was between the American government and the assembled chiefs of the Six Nations Confederacy.

Under the treaty, the Confederacy—composed of the Mohawk, Oneida, Onondaga, Cayuga, Seneca and Tuscarora Indians—agreed to let the white man roam over the Ohio River Valley. In exchange they got the rights to an area about 30 miles wide from each bank of the Tonawanda, Seneca and Mohawk rivers—a 60-mile wide strip of land stretching through the heart of the state virtually from Buffalo to Albany . . .

Source: Clayton Sinclair, "The Drums Go Bang, Seaway Ugh, Mohawks Plan Move." Montreal Gazette, August 21, 1957. Used by permission.

Sidebar 1: Reservoirs and Taxes

Case Law & Legislation on Reservoirs and Taxes

25 U.S.C. § 233 (1950)

Federal legislation granting New York State (New York States) civil jurisdiction over the Indians within its state borders subject to limitations. New York Stats cannot levy taxes against reservation lands and properties.

Public Law 85–159 (1957)

Congress passed this law directing the Federal Power Commission to grant New York State's Power Authority the license to construct and operate a power plant on the Niagara River.

State Tax Commission v. Barnes, 14 Misc. 2d 311 (Sup. Ct. Frank. Cty. 1958). During the 1950s, a large number of St. Regis Mohawk people earned "significant" wages while employed in the construction of the St. Lawrence Seaway. Consequently, New York State chose to levy income taxes on them. This decision is the result of their refusal to pay New York State income tax. The Franklin County Court held that the New York State Tax Commission was within its rights to require payment of income tax by the St. Regis Mohawks and to seek remedies for their failure to file their taxes.

St. Regis Tribe v. State of New York, 5 N.Y.2d 24 (N.Y. 1958)

This case upheld New York State's right to use Barnhart Island for the construction of the St. Lawrence Seaway, despite the St. Regis Mohawks' claims to the island.

Tuscarora Nation of Indians v. State Power Authority, 257 F.2d 885 (1958)

This case upheld the right of the State Power Authority (SPA) to enter the Tuscarora Nation's lands and to exercise eminent domain to take the lands necessary to construct the Lewistown Reservoir.

Seneca Nation of Indians v. Wilbur M. Brucker et al. 360 U.S. 909 (1959).

This case held that the 1794 Canandaigua Treaty notwithstanding, the Army Corps were within their legal rights to initiate the condemnation proceedings to gain access to SNI lands for survey purposes. In 1958, the U.S. Court of Appeals and U.S. Supreme Court affirmed this decision.

Matter of Powless v. State Tax Commission, 22 A.D.2d 746, (NY 1964), affd. 16 N.Y.2d 946, (1965), cert. den. 383 U.S. 911 (1965).

Chief Irving Powless (Onondaga) sought relief from New York State's imposition of federal income tax. The holding in the case affirms the holding in *State Tax Commission v. Barnes.*

Public Law 88–533 (1964)

Also known as the Seneca Nation Compensation Act, this federal law provides for the compensation of lands lost by the Seneca Nation and its citizens as a result of the construction of the Kinzua Dam.

Pierce v. State Tax Commission, 52 Misc. 10 (Sup. Ct., Onon. Co. 1968); affirmed 29 AD 2d 124 (4th Dept. 1968). The New York State Tax Department tried to collect taxes on a store located on the Onondaga Nation. The Court ruled that the tax department's actions were illegal, invalid, and unconstitutional as applied to the Onondagas.

Further Reading

Bilharz, Joy A. *The Allegany Senecas and Kinzua Dam: Forced Relocation Through Two Generations.* Lincoln & London: University of Nebraska Press, 1998.

Doran, Kwinn H. 2014. *The Cradle of Globalization: The Iroquois, Eisenhower, and Conflicts over New York state Infrastructure Development During the 1950s*

(Order No. 3619628). Available from ProQuest Dissertations & Theses Full Text. (1534382894). Retrieved from http://search.proquest.com/docview/1534382894?accountid=9609

Hauptman, Laurence M. *The Iroquois Struggle for Survival: World War II to Red Power.* Syracuse, NY: Syracuse University Press, 1986.

Hauptman, Laurence M. *Seven Generations of Iroquois Leadership: The Six Nations Since 1800.* Syracuse, NY: Syracuse University Press, 2008.

Hauptman, Laurence M. *In the Shadow of Kinzua: The Seneca Nation of Indians Since World War II.* Syracuse, NY: Syracuse University Press, 2014.

"Indians Are Not Exempt from State Income Tax Judge Lawrence Rules." *The Massena Observer*, October 23, 1958.

"Indians Continue to Battle Against State Income Tax, Tear up Summonses." The Massena Observer, January 29, 1959.

"Indians Plan Rally Tonight on Tax Fight." *The Massena Observer*, August 11, 1958.

OIE | Onondaga Environmental Institute. "Onondaga Creek Fact Sheet, Geography." *Onondaga Nation, the People of the Hills.* Accessed May 28, 2015. http://www.onondaganation.org/mediafiles/pdfs/onondaga_watershed.pdf

Rickard, Clinton and Barbara Graymont. *Fighting Tuscarora: The Autobiography of Chief Clinton Rickard.* Syracuse, NY: Syracuse University Press, 1973.

Rosier, Paul C. *Serving Their Country: American Indian Politics and Patriotism in the Twentieth Century.* Cambridge, MA: Harvard University Press, 2009.

Simpson, Audra. *Mohawk Interruptus: Political Life Across the Borders of Settler States.* Durham, NC: Duke University Press, 2014.

State Tax Commissioner v. Barnes, 14 Misc.2d 311 (N.Y. Misc. 1958). Accessed May 30, 2015. https://casetext.com/case/state-tax-comm-v-barnes

Tuscarora Dispossession and Strategies for Renewal, 1957–Present

Anne A. Garner

Chronology

Pre-contact   The Tuscarora Nation is located in North Carolina. By 1520, they have contact with European settlers.

1711–1713   Tuscarora Wars in North Carolina over settler land theft and kidnapping of Tuscarora women and children for sale into slavery. Tuscarora begin to migrate out of North Carolina and request protection from the Haudenosaunee (Iroquois) Confederacy.

1722–23	The Tuscarora Nation is adopted into the Haudenosaunee Confederacy as the Sixth Nation. From 1714 to 1777, they reside with the Oneida. By 1780, they are settled on Seneca lands near Niagara Falls in their current location.
1794	The Treaty of Canandaigua affirms Tuscarora Nation rights to the lands they occupy.
1797	Tuscarora Nation acquires three-square-mile reservation from Holland Land Company per agreement with Seneca.
1804	Tuscarora Nation purchases an additional nine acres (the Dearborn tract) to add to their reservation near Lewiston, New York
1931	The New York State Power Authority (SPA) is established to develop the St. Lawrence River and Niagara region as a source of hydroelectric power.
1950	The International Niagara River Treaty is signed by the United States and Canada, with the purpose of developing hydroelectric energy in the Niagara River region and promoting conservation of the environs of Niagara Falls as a parkland.
June 7, 1956	The Schoellkopf Power Station at Niagara Falls collapses into the Niagara River gorge resulting in an energy crisis.
1957	Robert Moses requests 960 acres of Tuscarora Nation land as part of a proposed 2,400-acre reservoir. Tuscarora Nation sends objections to President Dwight Eisenhower, citing treaty protections.
March 1957	SPA's request to survey Tuscarora Nation reservation is denied.
August 1957	Congress passes Public Law 89–159 or Ives-Javits-Miller Bill, authorizing the Federal Power Commission to grant a license to the State Power Authority to develop hydroelectric resources in the Niagara Region.
Jan. 30, 1958	SPA receives license to build reservoir from FPC and requests 1,383 acres (–20 percent of the Tuscarora Nation's reservation).
April 15, 1958	SPA begins expropriation proceedings.
April 16, 1958	The Tuscarora Nation denies Robert Moses's second request to survey the reservation. Moses filed a survey map with the Niagara County Clerk in Lockport and offers the Tuscarora Nation $1,000 per acre.

April 16, 1958	The Tuscarora Nation begins non-violent demonstrations, blocking surveyors and armed police. They hire Arthur Lazarus, Jr. and Richard Schifter to file an injunction to stop the SPA from seizing their land for a reservoir.
April 19, 1958	Arthur Lazarus, Esq. brings suit in the United States District Court for the Southern District of New York, requesting a permanent injunction against taking Tuscarora Nation lands without the express consent of the federal government and the Tuscarora Nation (*Tuscarora Nation v. State Power Authority*, 164 F.Supp. 107). A temporary restraining order is granted. The case is transferred to the U.S. District Court for Western District, where it is dismissed.
May, 1958	Lazarus brings a lawsuit against FPC, questioning the legality of the license granted to the SPA claiming protection under the Federal Power Act. The Court of Appeals agrees and remands the issue of the license back to the Federal Power Commission to determine whether license can be issued for building on tribal lands. The Tuscarora Nation claim is transferred to the United States District Court, where it was subsequently dismissed (Tuscarora *Nation v. FPC*, 164 F. Supp. 107).
July 24, 1958	Decision that SPA does not have authority to condemn Tuscarora Nation land.
Nov. 14, 1958	The United States Court of Appeals rules that FPC must submit to the Federal Power Act and its definition of a reservation. The Court of Appeals overturns the SPA seizure of land for monetary compensation.
Feb. 1959	Decision that Tuscarora Nation lands are protected by the Federal Power Act, and the tribe cannot be forced to sell the land. SPA develops new plans to build the reservoir in the town of Lewiston.
March, 1959	The United States Court of Appeals grants permission to the U.S. Department of Justice to intervene on behalf of the FPC (*Federal Power Commission v. Tuscarora Indian Nation*, 362 U.S. 99, 1960).
March 1959	Haudenosaunee delegates seek audience with President Eisenhower to protest Indian policies and violation of treaties of Fort Stanwix and Canandaigua.

March 7, 1960	The United States Supreme Court rules against the Tuscarora Nation in a 4–3 decision, ruling that there was no treaty obligation to protect their reservation lands, since the lands required for the reservoir (the Dearborn tract) were not acquired by treaty but purchased in fee simple, and ruling that their land could be seized by eminent domain.
March 7, 1960	The United States Supreme Court denies the Tuscarora Nation's request for a rehearing.

The Dispossession of the Tuscarora Nation and Their Strategies for Renewal

The appropriation of indigenous lands for profit by industrial nations has been, according to many, an ongoing global strategy of dispossession that threatens the relationship between indigenous communities and their homelands. As a result, many of the original inhabitants of the land who are referred to as indigenous, Native, or aboriginal, lose many of the critical resources that are necessary to function as distinct societies. Fuelled by ideologies of progress through material accumulation, European merchant "discoverers" in pursuit of natural resources and external markets seized indigenous lands throughout the world and justified their actions by the so-called Doctrine of Discovery, a non-legal concept used by colonizing powers to claim ownership of lands where the indigenous inhabitants did not have a European Christian monarch. In North America, European colonization engulfed the continent and, by the 19th century, land was primarily defined as a commodity in the service of

A 4-year-old Tuscarora boy is shown on the picket line as the Tuscarora people block a state survey of their reservation in Niagara Falls, New York, 1958. The Tuscarora land was seized by the state for a power project. Tribal lands were confiscated for the national parks, dams, and other construction projects without community input or compensation. (AP Photo/Paul E. Thomson)

industrialization rather than as a source of survival and community well-being. To the present day, the continued seizure of indigenous lands for industrial progress threatens the survival of millions of people, their communities, their cultures, and their languages.

To accommodate to the economic needs of emerging industrial nations, waterways worldwide were appropriated and redirected for the purpose of developing inexpensive hydro-electric energy sources that promised to increase industrial profits and provide energy for modern domestic use, such as power for refrigerators and televisions. In the twentieth century, hydroelectric power plants such as the Tennessee Valley Authority, the Aswan High Dam in Egypt, the Three Gorges Dam in China, and the Kinzua Dam in New York State were developed ostensibly for the public good while displacing vast indigenous populations from their homelands. Currently, a worldwide movement of indigenous nations has emerged to regain sovereignty and reclaim their ancestral lands (Wallace 2012, 131).

The 20th century witnessed the seizure of indigenous land in one of the largest power projects in the world at the time, the St. Lawrence Seaway and the Niagara Power Project, both of which required the appropriation of significant portions of Mohawk and Tuscarora reservation lands in New York State. Robert Moses, then

Sidebar 1: What Is an Indigenous Nation?

According to the World Council of Indigenous Peoples (WCIP), indigenous nations are "people living in countries which have populations composed of different ethnic or racial groups who are descendants of the earliest populations which survive in the area, and who do not, as a group, control the national government of the countries within which they live" (Bodley 1999, 146; WCIP information leaflet). One common value among indigenous nations is their respect for the land and the belief that it is intended to provide sustenance for everyone rather than profit for the few. Therefore, the land cannot be bought or sold but is shared for the well-being of the community. They are opposed to technologies that destroy the land and create environmental degradation, since this will threaten future survival. As community-based social structures, indigenous societies are considered more egalitarian that the highly structured industrial social hierarchies (Bodley 1999, 146–47). In 2007, the United Nations adopted the United Nations Declaration on the Rights of Indigenous Peoples (http://www.un.org/esa/socdev/unpfii/documents/DRIPS _en.pdf). It was endorsed by 144 nations in 2007, followed by Australia (2009), the United States (2010), New Zealand (2009), and Canada (2010).

director of the New York State Power Authority (SPA), claimed that the current supply of water in New York State "was not sufficient to promote growth in industrial production and power use without interruption and curtailment" (Hauptman 1986, 152), and further stated that by 1965 the production of some 3.8 million kilowatts was necessary for the well-being of the nation.

In 1931, the New York State Power Authority (SPA) was established to specifically address the St. Lawrence River and Niagara River regions as sources of less expensive hydroelectric power that would provide energy to support local and national industrial growth. From 1954 to 1959, the St. Lawrence Seaway, the Moses-Saunders Power House, the Long Sault Spillway Dam, and related canals, locks and dikes were constructed. On April 25, 1959, the Seaway opened to ocean-going vessels, attracting industry with an inexpensive power source and bringing prosperity to non-Indian communities at the expense of some 9,000 Mohawk people who were devastated by the flooding of 40,000 acres of their land, forced relocation, environmental degradation, and related social costs (Johansen and Mann 2000, 261).

To Robert Moses, director of the State Power Authority, the St. Lawrence Seaway and the Niagara Power Project were inextricably linked in his grand plan for an international seaway, inexpensive power, industrial development, and recreational parkland in the region. In 1950, New York State and Canada signed the International Niagara River Treaty (1 U.S. T.694) to promote hydroelectric energy of the Niagara River and to address the conservation of Niagara Falls and its environs as a recreational area. In this treaty, it was agreed that both Canada and the United States would share equally in the water surplus generated by the project. Due to congressional delays, however, the Niagara Power Project did not move forward until, on June 7, 1956, the existing Schoellkopf Power Station collapsed into the Niagara Gorge, resulting in power outages, a loss of some 400,000 kilowatts of power, and damage to six generators. The Schoellkopf power disaster generated widespread support and lobbying for Moses' Niagara Power Project, and the *New York Times* reported the crash as a crisis that required the immediate construction of a new power plant.

Moses' Niagara Power Project required the expropriation of some 960 acres of Tuscarora Nation reservation land near Lewiston, New York to construct a holding reservoir. It was clear from the beginning that the Tuscarora Nation did not intend to give up any part of their small reservation for Moses' Niagara Power Project. They had occupied their reservation since 1777 and, by additional purchases in 1804, it was expanded to 6,249 acres. The Tuscarora had struggled to keep their nation together after experiencing three centuries of settler oppression in North Carolina. From 1711 to 1713, they were at war with European settlers over blatant land theft and the kidnapping of Tuscarora Nation women and children for sale into slavery. Turning to the Haudenosaunee Confederacy for protection, the Tuscarora refugees were welcomed into Oneida and Seneca lands and, in 1722, they were adopted into the Haudenosaunee Confederacy as the Sixth Nation. Finally, they again had a homeland, and their sense of sovereignty and place was reinforced by assurances of their land rights in the Treaty of Fort Stanwix (1784) and the Treaty of Canandaigua (1794). Eventually, with the inclusion of more refugees from war-torn North Carolina, the Tuscarora Nation was reunited in the Niagara region, where they established a thriving, stable community and participated in the settler market economy. Given the very small scale of their reservation, they did not agree to contribute land to the SPA power project. Their reservation was a place of identity and, according to their worldview, a sacred charge.

In January 1957, the Tuscarora General Council denied SPA surveyor William Latham's request to begin a survey on Tuscarora land to determine the depth of the soil in relation to the bedrock on the reservation as a preliminary procedure to planning construction on the reservoir. On August 21, 1957, Congress passed Public Law 89–159, known as the Ives-Javits-Miller Bill, authorizing the Federal Power Commission (FPC) to grant a license to the State Power Authority (SPA) "for the construction and operation of a power project with a capacity to utilize all of the United States' share of the water of the Niagara River permitted by international agreement" (Hauptman 1986, 153). Moses increased his demand for Tuscarora land from 960 acres to 1,220 acres for the planned 2,400 acre reservoir.

On November 9, 1957, public hearings were held before the Federal Power Commission in Washington, D.C., and Buffalo, New York, over the proposed Niagara Power Project. Testimony was taken from the Tuscarora representatives Chief Elton Greene and Chief Harry Patterson, Sr., who cited treaty protections with the federal government that prohibited seizure of reservation land. William Rickard, son of activist Tuscarora leader Clinton Rickard, testified that the intrusion of the reservoir violated Tuscarora spiritual values, stating, ". . . we do not feel that we own the land. It is only loaned to us to be saved for the 'ever coming faces' of the next generation of the Tuscarora. It is not ours to dispose of. We are only its custodians" (Hauptman 1986, 162). Residents from the Town of Lewiston testified that building the reservoir in Lewiston would result in a loss of taxable land. Over the objections of William Rickard, Elton Green, and Harry Patterson, Sr. of the Tuscarora Chiefs' Council, the Federal Power Commission recommended that it was more logical to locate the reservoir on non-taxable Indian land. On January 30, 1958, the Federal Power Commission granted the SPA a license to build the reservoir. Immediately, Moses announced that part of the reservoir would be located on the Tuscarora reservation since, in his erroneous assessment, the Tuscarora Nation had "uncultivated and unused land" (Chevrier 1959, 5), even although the acreage he demanded was in active agricultural use and housed some fifteen families. Moses again increased his demand for Tuscarora land to 1,383 acres,

Three members of the Tuscarora tribe stake up a notice making it plain they want no part of the Niagara Power Project on their reservation in Niagara County, New York, 1958. (AP Photo)

filed a survey map with the Niagara county clerk in Lockport, New York, and offered payment to the Tuscarora of up to one thousand dollars per acre. For the next two years, the Tuscarora Nation resisted Moses's expropriation of their land with non-violent resistance, public demonstrations, and litigation in state and federal courts, initiating the strategies of Red Power protest that emerged in the United States throughout the 1960s and 1970s, such as in the occupation of Alcatraz island, fishing rights demonstrations, and the activism of the American Indian Movement (Deloria 195, 20–21).

On April 16, 1958, Moses attempted to conduct a second survey, resulting in a confrontation with Tuscarora Nation demonstrators led by activists William Rickard and Wallace "Mad Bear" Anderson. The next day, 150 unarmed demonstrators confronted New York State troopers, sheriffs, and workmen, who were armed with tear gas, pistols, and submachine guns. Tuscarora clan mothers blocked the surveyors' sighting equipment, removed markers, and demonstrated with placards stating, "Warning. No Trespassing. Indian Reserve," "Must You Take Everything the Indians Own?" and "United States Help Us. We Helped You in 1776 and 1812, 1918 and 1941." Some 200 Tuscarora Nation demonstrators, including women and children, stood in the way of the surveyors' equipment and lay down in front of bulldozers to stop them moving forward (Johansen and Mann 2000, 319–20; Wilson 1960, 144–45).

Failing to understand that the Tuscarora Nation's value of community and their spiritual relationship to homeland was in conflict with his own belief in the value of unbridled progress at the expense of communities who got in his way, Moses responded to the demonstrations with an SPA report in which he outlined his offer of settlement, claiming that losses to the Tuscarora Nation were minimal and contending that the portion of Tuscarora Nation land he was requesting, the so-called Dearborn tract, was part of a land purchase in fee simple by the

Tuscarora Nation after the Treaty of Canandaigua (1794), and was not protected by treaty as were the previous land gifts from the Seneca and the Holland Land Company. Although there was an appropriate alternative location in the town of Lewiston, Moses maintained that the Lewiston location was unrealistic, given that more residents would have to relocate, and arrogantly claimed that the Tuscarora Nation would not experience any hardship except the removal of fifteen homes on land that he considered to be abandoned. As part of a settlement, Moses offered recognition of fishing rights on the Niagara River, funds for scholarships, and community development.

By April 19, 1958, Tuscarora Nation nonviolent resistance moved into the courts with the purpose of upholding their legal standing as a reservation and seeking the protections offered by the treaty of Fort Stanwix (1784), the treaty of Canandaigua (1794), and the Federal Power Act (1920). They hired attorneys Arthur Lazarus, Jr. and Richard Schifter of the law firm of Strasser, Spiegelberg, Fried, and Frank, who filed a lawsuit in the United States District Court for the Southern District of New York, requesting a permanent injunction against taking Tuscarora Nation lands without the express consent of both the federal government and the Tuscarora Nation (*Tuscarora Nation v. the State Power Authority*, 257 F2d 885, 1958). Their request for an injunction was subsequently denied. On May 16, 1958, the Tuscaroras filed a petition in the Court of Appeals requesting a determination that the license granted to the SPA was not legal, since Tuscarora Nation lands are a legally recognized reservation under the authority of the Federal Power Act and the treaties of Fort Stanwix and Canandaigua. On February 3, 1959, the Court of Appeals ruled in favor of the Tuscarora Nation, stating that the land requested by the State Power Authority is defined and in use as part of a reservation according to the Federal Power Act, Section 4, and that the Tuscarora Nation cannot be forced to sell their lands. With this ruling, SPA surveying on Tuscarora Nation land was halted, and the SPA made plans to locate the reservoir in the town of Lewiston (Hauptman 1986, 171).

It is speculated that Moses used his political connections to finally defeat the Tuscarora Nation when, on March 24, 1959, the United States Court of Appeals granted permission to the Department of Justice to intervene on behalf of the Federal Power Commission (Federal Power *Commission v. Tuscarora Indian Nation*, 362 U.S. 99, 1960) and to review the definition of a reservation under the Federal Power Act. Simultaneously, the Six Nations Confederacy Council sought to present a petition to President Eisenhower objecting to the invasion by the SPA on Tuscarora Nation land, the resulting violation of the Treaty of Canandaigua (1794), lack of protection by the Justice department, escalating legal fees, interference in fishing rights on the Niagara River, and damage to the Tuscarora Nation environment by transmission lines (Hauptman 1986, 172). On March 7, 1960, the United

States Supreme Court ruled against the Tuscarora Nation in a four-to-three vote, stating that there was no treaty obligation to protect their reservation, since the lands required for the reservoir, the Dearborn tract, were not acquired by treaty but were purchased in fee simple, and that therefore the land could be taken by eminent domain. The dissenting voice of Justice Hugo Black maintained that the Court had misinterpreted the Federal Power Act and that the Tuscarora Nation land was indeed protected. He considered the Supreme Court to be the "governmental agency that breaks faith with this dependent people," adding that "Great nations, like great men, should keep their word" (*Federal Power Commission v. Tuscarora Indian Nation*, 362 U.S. 99, 1960). Subsequently, the Court denied the Tuscarora Nation's request for a rehearing. Construction of the reservoir commenced and on February 10, 1961, it was dedicated in a ceremony at Niagara University in Niagara Falls, New York.

Impact and Renewal

The immediate impact of the Tuscarora Nation's dispossession of a portion of their homeland was expressed in a renewed activism that was grounded in the Tuscarora Nation's worldview and their experiences as a colonized nation. Their political activism reaffirmed a Tuscarora Nation presence in the Niagara region. In turn, they inspired indigenous nations throughout the United States to protect their land base and thereby set a precedent to the emerging Red Power Movement of the 1960s and 1970s.

As a result of the Tuscarora Nation's overwhelming community-based activism and resistance, the SPA demand for Tuscarora land was reduced from 1,383 acres to 550 acres. Nevertheless, the loss was substantial: the reservoir consumed 495 acres, and power lines were positioned on the remaining 55 acres on the Tuscarora Nation reservation (Johansen and Mann 2000, 320). The subsequent flooding and forced relocation of part of the community ignited a sense of siege and indignation in the Tuscarora Nation that, in turn, generated increased political activism in the generation that was growing up at the time of the reservoir construction and anti-reservoir demonstrations.

One focus of current activism has been the issue of environmental justice. In 1992, the Haudenosaunee Environmental Task Force (HETF) was established, and, in turn, the Tuscarora Nation developed the Tuscarora Environmental Program (TEP), a plan for land stewardship that is directed toward the preservation and sustainability of "bio-cultural" concerns such as traditional foods, agriculture, fish migration, and energy (http://www7.nau.edu/itep/main/tcc/Tribes/ne_tuscarora). In October 2012, the Tuscarora Nation, under the auspices of the Haudenosaunee Environmental Task Force, developed a Tuscarora Grassland Restoration Proposal to correct damage done by the Niagara Power Project in 1958 when they rerouted waterways and condemned open space on the reservation. Restoration will safeguard traditional plants and nesting areas that were under threat (http://niagara .NYPA.gov/Tuscarora_Grassland-Restoration-Final-Proposal).

Rerouting waterways and building an invasive reservoir violated Tuscarora Nation values by putting economic progress before the rights of the Tuscarora Nation community to occupy their sovereign lands in peace and respect for the environment. William Rickard testified at the FPC hearings in 1958 that the land is a living, nurturing entity that cannot be bought or sold as a commodity for profit. In this context, resisting the reservoir was a spiritual act intended to protect all forms of life, protect the community from loss of food and housing, preserve community relationships, and preserve the sustainability of the earth for future generations, beliefs that are necessary for survival and intrinsic to Haudenosaunee and Tuscarora Nation philosophies. When the FPC imposed its value system on the Tuscarora Nation community by seizing their land for the reservoir, it violated the Haudenosaunee philosophy of the Two-Row Wampum that was foundational to the first Treaty between the Haudenosaunee (Iroquois) and European settlers, in which respectful co-existence is pledged by all parties. These philosophies were central to Tuscarora resistance and were translated into proactive, non-violent action through community demonstrations, media attention, and litigation in the state and federal court systems.

The political relevance of the Tuscarora Nation cosmology becomes immediately apparent in a reading of the Federal Regulatory Energy Commission Environmental Impact Statement of the Niagara Project (2006), a requirement for relicensing,

---

Sidebar 2: The Two-Row Wampum or Kaswentha

The Two-Row Wampum or Kaswentha is an iconographic statement consisting of two parallel purple rows running lengthwise across the wampum, against a white background. The purple rows suggest the principle of separate but equal co-existence and sharing land, and represent two separate cultures or peoples living in peace and respect, side by side. One purple row is the path of indigenous nations, and the other is the path of European settlers in America. Both rows are woven into a white background symbolizing peace. The concept of the Two-Row Wampum was first scripted to reflect the principles of an agreement or treaty between the Haudenosaunee and Dutch settlers in 1613 to remain separate but tolerant peoples and was later embodied in the Treaty of Canandaigua (1794). It can be read as one of the earliest iconic expressions of a pluralistic democracy in America.

that cites contamination of fish and reservoir sediment with mercury and organic compounds (74), reduced vegetation and wildlife habitat due to the weekly changes in water level in the reservoir (100), and curtailment of customary land use, such as agriculture, hunting, and fishing. Further, many families were displaced when their homes were submerged under the reservoir waters. Although those families received new homes, and six homes were moved, the loss of a traditional, multi-generational home base was devastating. Tuscarora Dorothy Crouse refused to leave and was moved along with her home. Further, this loss had economic dimensions for many Tuscaroras. For example, in the *Niagara Falls Gazette*, Bill Branche notes that although "Chief Harry Patterson, Sr. received a new ranch-style home with two large steel-framed cinder block barns and two structures for his chickens and pigs, he had to abandon his family homestead, his extensive outbuildings, and a productive 600 acre fruit farm" (Branche 1960).

When the SPA applied for relicensing in 2005, requiring the Environmental Impact Statement, the SPA also agreed to open up the process of relicensing to the public with the Cooperative Consultation Process (CCP) that considers the goal of low-cost energy for the governmental, industrial, and residential customers as well as provisions for non-profit values, such as balancing environmental concerns and preservation of historical sites. Although the interests of the Tuscarora Nation and other indigenous nations differ from a general public in that they are the First Peoples who made treaties intended to guarantee their rights and do not need the CCP or other committees to set air and water quality standards, the parallel process of the CCP resulted in a separate agreement and settlement between the Tuscarora Nation and the Power Authority of the State of New York (2005) in which the relicensing terms include a payment to the Tuscarora Nation of $21,824,176, allocation of low-cost power, the return of 52 unused acres, funding for Tuscarora Nation cultural initiatives, historic preservation, a customary use plan for land management, energy audits, post-licensing fish tissue sampling, funding up to $150,000 for a Power Vista exhibit documenting the culture of the Haudenosaunee and their relationship to the project, scholarships, a pledge for ongoing dialogue after relicensing, and protection from trespass on Tuscarora Nation lands (Relicensing Settlement Agreement Between the Power Authority of the State of New York and the Tuscarora Nation, Niagara Power Project, FERC Project No. 2216, 2005).

Further, the construction of the reservoir inspired contemporary cultural expressions, such as Eric Gansworth's novel *Smoke Dancing,* in which his illustrations speak to the conflict between the Tuscaroras and the New York State Power Authority in representations of the traditional Three Sisters surrounded by gasoline tanks that, in turn, desecrate the wampum belt of the Treaty of Canandaigua (1794). On the frontispiece of his novel, a cigarette is crushed into the back of a Turtle. Tuscarora visual historian, Dr. Jolene Rickard, the granddaughter of activist Chief Clinton

Rickard, visually documented the flooding of the Tuscarora homeland in an installation entitled *Corn Blue Room* (1998), currently located in the Denver Art Museum in Denver, Colorado. Entering the installation, the viewer becomes a part of a visual dialogue between images of corn, the reservoir and transformers. To enter the physical space of *Corn Blue Room* is to experience a place of Tuscarora Nation worldview and identity in dialogue with the appropriation of Tuscarora land by the New York State Power Authority.

Biographies of Notable Figures

Clinton Rickard (Rowadagahrade) (Tuscarora) (1882–1971)

Chief Clinton Rickard was a leader in the 20th-century Indian rights movement. Although he indicates in his autobiography, *Fighting Tuscarora* (1973), that due to health issues he could not be actively involved in demonstrations against the reservoir, his political initiatives were foundational to the Tuscarora Nation's resistance to the incursions of the State Power Authority on the Tuscarora Nation reservation. His son, William Rickard (1918–1964), was also a political activist and a leader of the resistance to the reservoir until his untimely death.

Rickard was born in 1882 on the Tuscarora Nation reservation, the son of George and Lucy Rickard. He served in the United States Army and was stationed in the Philippines from 1902 to 1904 before returning home and raising a family. By 1920, he was a chief of the Beaver Clan on the national council of the Tuscarora Nation, where his name was Rowadagahrade, meaning "Loud Voice." A lifelong activist in the service of Indian rights, he studied the U.S. Code and treaties between the federal government and the Haudenosaunee (Iroquois). In 1926, he was part of a group of Native American activists who founded the Indian Defense League of America (IDLA), setting a precedent for future litigation by using established treaties between the federal government and Indian nations to further land rights and cultural preservation (Johansen and Mann, 257–59).

Rickard challenged the United States and Canada to enforce the provisions of the Jay Treaty (1794), which provided for free passage of Indian nations across the border. He considered this provision as critical to recognition of the sovereign status of indigenous nations in the United States and Canada and came to the defense of Indians who were harassed by border officials, providing legal advocacy and financial assistance through the Indian Defense League of America (IDLA). Although an advocate of Haudenosaunee sovereignty, he is also considered to be a leader in the North American pan-Indian movement for Native American nationalism and considered the 1924 Indian Citizenship Act to be an instrument of social control over Indian nations stating that

> . . . to us, it seemed that the United States government was just trying to get rid of its treaty obligations and make us into taxpaying citizens who could sell their homelands and finally end up in the city slums. (Wallace 2012, 141)

In the 1950s, Rickard fought against the federal policy of tribal termination and considered it a method of extinguishing Indian nations and their sovereignty.

In his autobiography, Rickard states that "the SPA [State Power Authority] got its reservoir, and we were left with scars that never heal" (Graymont 1973, 152). Although the scars refer to the loss of homes and farmland under the reservoir waters, pollution and cultural values, such as relationships to the land, the "scars" in part also refer to the social disruption created by ideological divisions regarding the building of the reservoir (Wallace 2012, 144).

Wallace "Mad Bear" Anderson (Tuscarora) (1927–1985)

Wallace "Mad Bear" Anderson's advocacy of Native American rights and tribal sovereignty began in the 1950s, before the surge of Red Power activism in the 1960s and 1970s. He was born in Buffalo, New York, and raised on the Tuscarora Nation reservation. An advocate of nonviolent demonstrations against government interference and treaty violations, he adopted the name "Mad Bear," given to him by his grandmother in his childhood due to what seemed to her to be his argumentative and confrontational presence. He enlisted in the United States Navy in 1944, serving at Okinawa in WWII and in the Korean War. Upon returning home, he became a leader in many protests against injustice and advocated nonviolent resistance to government interference on reservations and treaty violations.

Returning home after the war, his leadership centered on non-violent protest against Haudenosaunee payment of New York State income tax (1957), resistance to the State Power Authority's appropriation of Tuscarora Nation land for a hydropower reservoir, opposition to government tribal termination policies, Haudenosaunee declarations of sovereignty in Brantford, Ontario (1959), a citizen's arrest for the misconduct of Indian Commissioner Glen L. Emmons in Washington, D.C., and the takeover of Alcatraz Island (1969). In 1967, Anderson established the North American Indian Unity Caravan that traveled to indigenous nations throughout the United States. In the last decades of his life, his advocacy on behalf of indigenous rights moved into an international forum.

Robert Moses (1888–1981)

Robert Moses has been referred to as a "master builder" (Hauptman 1986, 139) who changed the landscape in New York State with his public projects. He was born in

Connecticut in 1888 and grew up in Manhattan, New York. He attended Yale, Oxford, and Columbia Universities.

One of Moses' first projects in public service was at the Municipal Research Bureau in New York, where he worked on restructuring New York City's civil service system. In 1922, he became president of the Long Island State Park Commission, and by 1925 he was chairman of the State Council of Parks. By 1933, Mayor Fiorello La Guardia appointed Moses Director of the Parks Department in New York City, where he undertook major public works, building highways and bridges and renovating the Central Park Zoo. He held several offices, including the secretary of state for New York, commissioner of New York City Department of Parks and, in 1954, he was appointed by Governor Thomas Dewey to be chairman of the New York State Power Authority (Hauptman 1986, 139). He considered the St. Lawrence Seaway Project and the Niagara Project to be his crowning glories in a long and demanding career.

As early as 1946, Moses developed plans to remove the Haudenosaunee (Iroquois) from their lands in New York State for public usage. When he was the Commissioner of the New York State Council of Parks, he hired Colonel William S. Chapin to analyze and develop a report about the impact of a potential dam, the Kinzua dam, in Allegheny State Park. The report revealed a federal plan to purchase the Allegheny Reservation and remove the Senecas to open their reservation for Upper Allegheny flood control and to "develop the land for recreational purposes" (Hauptman 1986, 139–40). Hauptman states that "as early as 1946, Moses had begun to view Iroquois lands as regional sacrifice areas for his vision of America" (Hauptman 1986, 140). He believed that the St. Lawrence Power Project and Seaway and the resulting inexpensive hydroelectric energy would attract substantial business interests to the area.

Given what seemed to be Moses's unbridled power and arrogance, he had many detractors. He was accused of displacing some mostly poor 250,000 urban residents with his massive projects and was considered responsible for Brooklyn's baseball team leaving the city because he refused to build a new stadium. Although he was widely criticized, he left behind a substantial record of accomplishment that included the Lincoln Center for the Performing Arts, Shea Stadium, thirteen bridges, power projects, highways, and numerous parks in New York State. By 1959, Moses no longer worked for the state and had become president of the 1964–65 World's Fair.

DOCUMENT EXCERPTS

The Treaty of Canandaigua (The Pickering Treaty) (1794)

Article II of this treaty is an agreement between George Washington, through his representative, Timothy Pickering, and the Senecas (Six Nations) that the

United States will not interfere in the land rights of the Senecas or any of the Six Nations.

> . . . the United States acknowledges all the land within the aforemen-
> tioned boundaries, to be the property of the Seneca Nation; and the United
> States will never claim the same, nor disturb the Seneca Nation, nor any of
> the Six Nations, or of their Indian friends residing thereon, and united
> with them, in the free use and enjoyment thereof; but it shall remain theirs,
> until they choose to sell the same.

Source: Kappler, Charles. *Indian Affairs: Laws and Treaties*, Volume 2, Treaties. Washington, D.C.: Government Printing Office, 1904.

The Federal Power Act (1920)

*Enacted in 1920, the Federal Power Act created the Federal Power Commission
(FPC), now the Federal Energy Regulatory Commission, that governs the licensing of hydroelectric power projects. In Section 796 (2), it defines reservations.*

> . . . reservations means national forests, tribal lands embraced within
> Indian Reservations, military reservations, and other lands and interests
> in lands owned by the United States, and withdrawn, reserved, or withheld
> from private appropriation and disposal under the public land laws; . . .

Source: 16 U.S. Code Chapter 12.

Federal Power Commission v. Tuscarora Indian Nation (1960)

*In February, 1959, the Federal Power Commission ruled that the Tuscarora Nation
tribal lands were a reservation and that the Tuscarora Nation could not be forced
to sell land to the State Power Authority. Subsequently, the ruling was reheard by
the United States Supreme Court, which, in a 4-to-3 decision, announced on
March 7, 1960, ruled against the Tuscarora Nation, claiming that there was no treaty
obligation to protect their lands, since the lands required for the reservoir, the so-
called Dearborn tract, had been purchased in fee simple, and ruling that Tuscarora Nation land could be seized by eminent domain. Following are excerpts from
Justice Black's dissenting opinion.*

> . . . The Court holds that the Federal Power Act authorizes the taking of
> 22% (1,383 acres) of the single tract which the Tuscarora Indian Nation

has owned and occupied as its homeland for 150 years. Admittedly this taking of so large a part of the lands will interfere with the purpose for which this Indian reservation was created—a permanent home for the Tuscaroras. I not only believe that the Federal Power Act does not authorize this taking, but that the Act positively prohibits it. Moreover, I think the taking also violates the nation's long-established policy of recognizing and preserving Indian reservations for tribal use, and that it constitutes a breach of Indian treaties recognized by Congress since at least 1794.

Whether the Federal Power Act permits this condemnation depends, in part, upon whether the Tuscarora Reservation is a "reservation" within the meaning of the Act. For if it is, 4(e) forbids the taking of any part of the lands except after a finding by the Federal Power Commission that the taking "will not interfere or be inconsistent with the purpose for which such reservation was created or acquired . . ." There is no such finding here. In fact, the Commission found that the inundation of so great a part of the Tuscarora Reservation by the waters of the proposed reservoir "will interfere and will be inconsistent with the purpose for which such reservation was created or acquired." If these Tuscarora homelands are "tribal lands embraced within" an Indian reservation as used in 3(2) they constitute a "reservation" for the purposes of 4(e), and therefore the taking here is unauthorized because the requisite finding could not be made.

I believe the plain meaning of the words used in the Act, taken alone, and their meaning in the light of the historical background against which they must be viewed, require the conclusion that these lands are a "reservation" entitled to the protections of 4(e) of the Act. "Reservation," as used in 4(e), is defined by 3(2) which provides:

> " 'reservations' means national forests, tribal lands embraced within Indian reservations, military reservations, and other lands and interests in lands owned by the United States, and withdrawn, reserved, or withheld from private appropriation and disposal under the public land laws; also lands and interests in lands acquired and held for any public purposes; but shall not include national monuments or national parks . . ."

The phrase "tribal lands embraced within Indian reservations" surely includes these Tuscarora lands. They are tribal lands. They are embraced within the Tuscarora Indian Nation's reservation. The lands have been called a reservation for more than 150 years. They have been so described in treaties, Acts of Congress, court decisions, Indian agency reports, books, articles and maps. In fact, so far as I can ascertain, they have never been called anything else, anywhere or at any time—until today. Even the Court of Appeals and the Federal Power Commission, and the briefs and record in this Court, quite naturally refer to this 10-square-mile tract of land as an Indian reservation. The Court itself seems to accept the fact that the Tuscarora Nation lives on a reservation according to (in its words) the "generally accepted standards and common understanding" of that term. The Court, however, decides that in the Federal Power Act Congress departed from the meaning universally given the phrase "tribal lands embraced within Indian reservations" and defined the phrase, the Court says, "artificially." The Court believes that the words "other lands . . . owned by the United States," which follow, were intended by Congress to limit the phrase to include only those reservations to which the United States has technical legal title. By the Court's "artificial" interpretation, the phrase turns out to mean "tribal lands embraced within Indian Reservations—except when "the lands involved are owned in fee simple by the [Indians]."

Creating such a wholly artificial and limited definition, so new and disruptive, imposes a heavy burden of justification upon the one who asserts it. We are told that many tribes own their reservation lands . . . all such reservation lands are put in jeopardy by the Court's strained interpretation. . . . The fact that the Tuscarora Nation holds technical legal title is fortuitous and an accidental circumstance probably attributable to the Indian land policy prevailing at the early date this reservation was established. Their lands, like all other Indian tribal lands, can be sold, leased or subjected to easements only with the consent of the United States Government. Congress and government agencies have always treated the Tuscarora Reservation the same as all others, and there is no reason even to suspect that Congress wanted to treat it differently when it passed the Federal Power Act.

Source: Federal Power Commission v. Tuscarora Indian Nation (362 U.S. 99, 1960).

Further Reading

Bilharz, Joy A. *The Allegany Senecas and Kinzua Dame: Forced Relocation through Two Generations.* Lincoln and London: University of Nebraska Press, 1998.

Bodley, John H. *Victims of Progress.* Mountain View, CA: Mayfield Publishing Company, 1999.

Branch, Bill. "Indian Families find SPA Generous Winner." *Niagara Falls Gazette* (July 31, 1960).

Chevrier, Lionel. *The Saint Lawrence Seaway.* New York: St. Martin's Press, 1959.

Deloria, Vine. *Behind the Trail of Broken Treaties: An Indian Declaration of Independence.* Austin: University of Texas Press, 1985.

Federal Power Commission v. Tuscarora Indian Nation (362 U.S. 99, 1960).

Graymont, Barbara, Ed. *Fighting Tuscarora: The Autobiography of Chief Clinton Rickard.* Syracuse, NY: Syracuse University Press, 1973.

Grinde, D. and B. Johansen. *Ecocide of Native America.* Santa Fe: Clear Light Publishers, 1995.

Haudenosaunee Environmental Task Force. *The Words That Come Before All Else: Environmental Philosophy of the Haudenosaunee.* Cornwall Island, Canada: Native North American Travelling College, 1999.

Hauptman, Laurence M. *The Iroquois Struggle for Survival: World War II to Red Power.* Syracuse, NY: Syracuse University Press, 1986.

Johansen, Bruce E. and Barbara A. Mann, eds. *Encyclopedia of the Haudenosaunee (Iroquois Confederacy).* Westport, CT: Greenwood Press, 2000.

Keal, Paul. *European Conquest and the Rights of Indigenous Peoples.* Cambridge: Cambridge University Press, 2003.

Landy, David. "Tuscarora Among the Iroquois." In *Handbook of North American Indians: Northeast.* Vol. 15. Edited by Bruce E. Trigger. Washington, D.C.: Smithsonian Institute,1978, 518–524.

Library of Congress. *A Century of Lawmaking for a New Nation: U.S. Congressional Documents and Debates,* 1774–1875. rs6.loc.gov/ammem/amlaw/lawhome.html

McCully, Patrick. *Flooding the Land, Warming the Earth: Greenhouse Gas Emissions from Dams.* International Rivers Network: West Coast Print Center with Solstice Press, June 2002.

Parlato, Frank. "Tuscaroras Fear Contaminated Water Causes Cancer Deaths." *Niagara Falls Reporter,* July 24, 2012.

Trigger, Bruce G., ed. *Handbook of North American Indians: Northeast.* Vol. 15. Washington, D.C.: Smithsonian Institution Press, 1978.

Wallace, Anthony F.C. *The Tuscarora: A History.* Albany: State University of New York Press, 2012.

Williams, Ted. *The Reservation.* Syracuse, NY: Syracuse University Press, 1976.

Wilson, Edmund. *Apologies to the Iroquois.* Syracuse, NY: Syracuse University Press, 1991.

National Indian Youth Council, 1961

Paul McKenzie-Jones

Chronology

1955   Santa Fe Indian Council is formed when college students at the University of New Mexico wish to visit local high schools to inspire Native students to graduate and move into higher education.

1956 University of Chicago anthropology professor Sol Tax creates the Workshops on American Indian Affairs, a six-week summer immersion course intended to provide sympathetic readings of Native cultures and histories to Native students rather than the standard "disappearing savage" rhetoric they received in standard educations forums.

1961 Southwest Regional Indian Youth Council elections see Clyde Warrior galvanize his cohorts with a short but effective "sewage of Europe" speech.

American Indian Chicago Conference is organized by Sol Tax and sees over 500 Native delegates from 75 different Native nations convene to draft the Declaration of Indian Purpose as a challenge to newly elected president John F. Kennedy.

Ten young American Indian activists meet in Gallup, New Mexico, to create the National Indian Youth Council in response to elected and appointed tribal leaders refusing to listen to their calls during the AICC for change in the status quo in Indian affairs.

1964 The fish-ins protest against treaty abrogation in the Pacific Northwest see between 500 to 20,000 Native protestors lead the first mass inter-tribal direct-action protest of the twentieth century.

1966 The National Indian Youth Council/Original Cherokee Community Organization leads a protest against the opening of the Cherokee Traditional Village in Tahlequah, Oklahoma, building upon the legacy of blockading begun at the 1964 fish-ins.

1968 Founder member Clyde Warrior dies of liver failure, aged 28.

Browning Pipestem heads a leadership coup of the NIYC in protest at the direction of the movement under the old guard.

There is a further split in the NIYC as several leading members, including Mel Thom, join forces with Martin Luther King and later Ralph Abernathy as part of the Poor People's Campaign, maintaining a steady presence at Resurrection City even as the protest is broken up.

1970 Gerald Wilkinson becomes new leader of the NIYC and begins to turn the group in a new direction.

1977 NIYC lawyers help fight the *Harjo v. Kleppe* court case, which ends another form of federal paternalism in oversight of tribal politics.

2011 The NIYC celebrates its 50th anniversary as a continuing advocate for tribal rights, cultural sovereignty, healthcare rights, and the protection of sacred sites.

The National Indian Youth Council

In the 1960s, a decade of unprecedented civil unrest and cultural, racial, and political activism, the National Indian Youth Council forged the Red Power Movement as its members led the call to uphold traditional American Indian cultures, languages, and traditions against the American tradition of assimilation. In the face of increasing attempts by the federal government to terminate the federal trust relationship with American Indian nations and finally fully assimilate American Indians into the dominant western culture of the United States, the NIYC campaigned tirelessly for tribal self-determination, treaty rights, cultural preservation, and culturally relevant education for the indigenous peoples of the United States. Through tactics of direct action protest, model schools, and direct dialogue with federal power brokers, the NIYC changed the shape and tone of federal Indian affairs and paved the way for later, more celebrated militant activist organizations to fight for indigenous rights. The NIYC is the second-oldest continuously existing inter-tribal Native organization in the United States, significantly changed the face of American Indian activism in the 1960s, and remains committed to fighting on behalf of indigenous peoples from across the Americas.

On Thursday, August 23, 1961, a group of ten young American Indians convened in a rented office space in Gallup, New Mexico, to discuss their ideas for the future of a "greater Indian America." The meeting, which lasted over three days, resulted in the creation of the National Indian Youth Council. The original ten members, Clyde Warrior (Ponca), Mel Thom (Paiute), Herb Blatchford (Navajo), Shirley Witt (Mohawk), Karen Rickard (Tuscarora), Mary Natani (Winnebago), Joan Noble (Ute), Thomas and Bernadine Eschief (Shoshone Bannock), and Howard McKinley Jr. (Navajo), quickly became the dominant voices of disaffected young, reservation and rurally raised American Indians during the decade that followed. The commitment of these young American Indians to the cultural aspects of their identities was reflected in the choice of location for the meeting, which "coincided" with the week-long Gallup Inter-Tribal Indian Ceremonial. While the origins of the NIYC are often posited as being born of frustration at being shut out and shouted down at the American Indian Chicago Conference earlier in that year, there were many roads that led these young men and women on the path to this pivotal meeting. Born of a confluence of regional college youth council members, Workshops on American Indian Affairs students, and individual tribal activists, the National Indian Youth Council was framed by multiple indigenous voices from all across the United States.

The Southwest Regional Indian Youth Council had originated many years earlier, also in New Mexico. In 1957, the Santa Fe Indian Club expanded its membership to include indigenous students from all across the Southwest. Charles E. Minton,

National Indian Youth Council: From left are Melvin Thom, president of National Indian Youth Council; Allen Jacob, a Chipewyan from Edmonton, Alberta, Canada; and Herb Blatchford, a Navajo from Gallup, New Mexico, and executive director of NIYC. NIYC is active on various issues and is the second-oldest national American Indian organization. (Duane Howell/The Denver Post via Getty Images)

Executive Secretary of the Southwest Association on Indian Affairs, who sponsored the youth councils and their annual conferences, proclaimed three objectives of the SRIYC: "to stimulate Indian youth to acquire . . . skills that would . . . be of service to the tribes and communities; to expand their circle of Indian acquaintance . . . and to acquire an understanding of the varied and complex problems in Indian affairs, so they will work together . . . to improve conditions among Indian people" (Minton, 55). By 1961, the SRIYC had expanded to include Oklahoma and Utah college campuses, which incorporated Mel Thom and Clyde Warrior into the sphere of influence. At almost the same time as the Santa Fe Youth Council was expanding into first the Regional Indian Youth Council and eventually the Southwest Regional Indian Youth Council, University of Chicago anthropologist Sol Tax was creating the Workshops on American Indian Affairs.

The Workshops were conceived of as a practical extension of Tax's concept of "action anthropology" as the ideal intellectual approach toward Native Peoples. Tax

---

Sidebar 1: Red Power

Red Power was first coined by Clyde Warrior and Mel Thom immediately after they heard Stokely Carmichael's call for Black Power in 1966. Over the course of the following decade, Red Power assumed many forms. Originally conceived as a reference to the strength and endurance of indigenous communities, traditions, and cultures despite generations of enforced subjugation at the hands of the federal government, by the end of the 1960s, Red Power had evolved into a more political statement of militant action as the new groups campaigned for tribal self-determination built on the foundations laid by the National Indian Youth Council. By that time, Vine Deloria Jr. and then the American Indian Movement had adopted the phrase as a call to arms in the surge of occupations and direct-action protests that sprang from the occupation of Alcatraz Island in 1969, and was seen by many as best expressed in Deloria's 1969 book *Custer Died for Your Sins*. At the same time, a third expression of Red Power emerged north of the border when Canadian Indian Youth Council founder Harold Cardinal published *The Unjust Society*. In the United States, the pinnacle of the Red Power Movement is seen as being the 73-day siege at Wounded Knee in 1973. In Canada, the same sentiment is reserved for the Oka Crisis at Kanesatake in 1990.

---

was as certain of the Workshops' importance to the history of American Indian education as Minton was of the youth councils'. As Workshops instructor Al Warhrhaftig explained, "action anthropology held that by intervening in a community in such a way that new alternatives can be created without co-opting the power to incorporate only such alternatives as are perceived by its members to be beneficial, anthropologists can observe 'values in action': they can simultaneously study and help" (McKenzie-Jones, 54). Among the young Native students attending the inaugural summer workshops was Herb Blatchford, and in the 1961 summer straddled by the American Indian Chicago Conference and the inaugural NIYC meeting, among the six-week student cohort were Clyde Warrior, Karen Rickard, Bernadine and Thomas Eschief, and Mary White Eagle Natani.

The overlap of the original NIYC cohort containing members who were both youth council and workshops students speaks to the miniscule number of American Indian students attending college in the 1960s. By 1963, "3,141 Indians were attending colleges or universities and 2,290 others were enrolled in post-high school vocational schools" (McKenzie-Jones, 45). The councils and workshops facilitated a unity among what would otherwise have been a disparate number of indigenous students spread thinly across United States college campuses. There were, however, still students attached to neither of these groups, and this is where the American Indian Chicago Conference provides the final piece of the inaugural NIYC jigsaw. Witt attended the conference as a representative of her home community and was introduced to other young caucus members by her childhood friend Karen Rickard. Both Witt and Rickard had been privileged enough to spend their childhood listening to stories from Tuscarora chief Clinton Rickard, famous for his campaigns for the sovereign rights of the Six Nations of the Iroquois Confederacy. As such, Rickard and Witt were both outspoken champions of American Indian rights who gelled seamlessly with the other members of the original NIYC. It was at the AICC, where despite being an integral part of the drafting of the Declaration of Indian Purpose that transpired from the conference, the collective group of young Indians, angry and frustrated at being constantly silenced by the more experienced tribal political leaders, decided to meet later in the year to form their own organization.

The urgency with which these young Native students viewed the relationship between American Indians and the U.S. government was exposed by Beryl Spruce (Laguna) in his inaugural RIYC address, "We Are Born at a Time When the Indian People Need Us," and later at the American Indian Chicago Conference by Shirley Witt. Spruce, controversially at that time, called American Indians themselves to account for being acquiescent in the colonial subservience to white America in which many of them found themselves. He argued, "We're lazy. We're lazy and we're proud that we're little babies sitting in a mud puddle, sitting there and wishing that someone else would come and pull us out. We're saying to ourselves, 'I'm just a poor little Indian. I'm ignorant. If I go to school, I won't make it. I just know I won't make it.' I don't think we're even nearly the proud Indian that used to live long ago. I don't think we even have a right to be proud that we are their descendants . . . They had courage. They had pride and self-discipline. Those are things we seriously lack today. We don't have them anymore. We're cowards" (Shreve, 55).

Witt later recalled that at the conference, "As our youth caucuses felt more and more lifted up by our conviction and commonality of ideas, and as those ideas began to take shape on scraps of paper passed from group to group, we knew that we had something to contribute to the ponderous atavistic deliberations taking place each afternoon in the general assembly" (Shreve, 90). By the end of the conference, however, the constant rejection of their ideas by the assembled tribal political leaders led the youth groups to determine to form their own intertribal organization of indigenous uplift.

Although unrelated, Spruce's speech set a precedent for much of the rhetoric that the later NIYC members, and Clyde Warrior in particular, would mirror. In late 1964, Warrior ran an article in the NIYC's newspaper *ABC, Americans Before*

Columbus, under the headline "Which One Are You? Five Types of American Indian." The types were a reflection of the worst perceptions of Indians by white society, and included "the slob, or hood," who molds himself into the white misconception of Indian-ness "by dropping out of school, becomes a 'wino,' eventually becomes a court case, usually sent off . . . another Indian hits the dust, through no fault of his own" (Warrior 1964, 1). The second was the "joker," who "has defined to himself that to be an Indian is a joke. An Indian does stupid, funny things . . . and he goes through life a bungling clown" (Warrior). The third was the "redskin, white noser or sellout," who "has accepted . . . the definition that anything Indian is dumb, usually filthy, and immoral, and to avoid this is to become a "LITTLE BROWN AMERICAN" by associating and identifying with everything that is white. Thus society has created the fink of finks." (Warrior). The fourth "type" was the "ultra-pseudo Indian" who "is proud that he is Indian but for some reason does not know how one acts. Therefore, he takes his cues from non-Indian sources, books, shows, etc. and proceeds to act 'Indian.' Hence, we have a proud, phony, Indian" (Warrior).

The final type was the "angry nationalist" who "is generally closer to true 'Indianism' than the other types, and they resent the others for being ashamed of their own kind" (Warrior). The "angry nationalist," with whom Warrior himself was usually associated, "tends to dislike the older generations who have been 'Uncle Tomahawks' or 'yes men' to the Bureau of Indian Affairs and whites in general" (Warrior). He claimed that this type viewed the "problems of personality disappearance" with "bitter abstract and ideological thinking" and were labeled "radicals" as they tended to "alienate themselves from the general masses of Indians for speaking as it appears to them, 'TRUTHS' " (Warrior).

While Warrior was becoming the more well-known of the NIYC leaders because of such strident rhetoric, other NIYC members were equally vocal in their critique of the status quo of the iniquity of Indian-white relations. Mel Thom, first president of the NIYC had coined the phrase "A Greater Indian America" in which he positioned American Indians at the forefront of the American consciousness as a juxtaposition of the reality of general American Indian invisibility in American culture. Additionally, one of the first major agreements that the inaugural group made among themselves was the equal voice and importance of all involved, male or female. While this was a reflection of their commitment to common cultural motifs of gender equality in American Indian communities, especially pre-dating European contact, it also set the NIYC apart from many other activist movements of the 1960s, which reflected to more normative patriarchal structures of American society. This commitment to equality was vitally important for the continued support of members such as Witt and Rickard, who were raised in communities where women were significant voices in all decisions of cultural and political significance.

In 1964, the NIYC burst onto the national spotlight of American Indian affairs and pushed American Indian issues into the wider American social consciousness as they helped orchestrate direct-action protests against treaty abrogation in the Pacific Northwest. Long before the more famous occupation of Alcatraz Island by the Indians of All Tribes, the fish-ins of the Pacific Northwest introduced a new militant aspect to intertribal campaigns for self-determination and tribal sovereignty. Soliciting the help of celebrity civil rights advocates Marlon Brando and Dick Clarke, the protests raised awareness of the long history of treaty fishing rights being ignored in the region, and the wider history of treaty abrogation by state and federal agencies nationwide. In the specific case of the Pacific Northwest protests, they eventually culminated in a 1974 federal ruling in favor of the tribes of Washington state (Shreve, 119–38). The Boldt decision awarded 50 percent of the annual allowable catch to treaty tribes in the State. While historian Bradley Shreve locates the fish-ins as the birth of Red Power Movement, the origins of the slogan came later, in 1966, when Clyde Warrior, Mel Thom, Della Warrior, and two other activists rented a car and gate-crashed the annual parade of the National Congress of American Indians. On the car's right side was a banner with the words "Red Power, National Indian Youth Council." On the left, "Custer Died For Your Sins." And in addition to Red Power, the NIYC also introduced phrases such as "Red Apples" and "Uncle Tomahawks" into the language of American Indian affairs to denote those tribal leaders, Native government employees, and other indigenous peoples whom they perceived as being complicit in maintaining the status quo of settler colonial power structures that rendered American Indians as second-class and racially inferior citizens (McKenzie-Jones, 76).

In contrast to these perceived cultural sellouts, the Red Power of the NIYC was framed almost entirely within a cultural framework that reflected their commitment to the "medicine ways" and their traditional upbringings at the feet of their parents and grandparents within the bosom of their communities. This was reflected in the words of both Karen Rickard, when she described listening to her father's stories, such as "how the Tuscarora left the home in the Carolinas" (Shreve, 75), and Clyde Warrior, who recalled listening to his grandparents talk of a time when "the Indians were a great people, when we were rich, when we lived the good life" (McKenzie-Jones, 116). This commitment to the old ways of community life was exemplified by the group's decision to hold all annual meetings on reservation land rather than urban hotels or conference centers.

Following their success in raising awareness over treaty abrogation, the leaders of the NIYC switched their focus to cultural relevancy in education. Their childhood educational experiences, whether in public or boarding schools, had been replete with discussions of Indian savagery, disappearance, and unworthiness, and the activists sought to change this through systematic educational reform, from kindergarten level all the way through college. In addition to simply wishing for a true history of American Indian cultures and languages to be presented in the classroom, there were multiple cultural reasons for their campaign for culturally relevant education. Many were reflected in Warrior's essay on the five types of Indian, and the group were determined to erase one of the most pernicious ways in which Native children were taught to disregard their own cultures, communities, and even parents and elders as worthless. They embarked on an impressive number of educational projects, from sponsoring the United Scholarship Services and Upward Bound educational agencies, to embarking in the late 1960s upon a ten-site model reservation school project, in partnership with the Far West Laboratory for Educational Research and Development. In addition, several leaders, including Clyde Warrior and Browning Pipestem (Oto-Missouria), organized NIYC-sponsored summer workshops in competition with (and eventually replacing) the Boulder, Colorado, workshops of which they were both alumni (McKenzie-Jones, 144–68). These projects, and others that followed, eventually led to the federal government passing the Indian Education Act in 1972.

At the same time, the growing militancy of the NIYC's rhetoric and their impatience toward the removal or restructuring of the federal policies that governed American Indians saw them increasingly at odds with the more established National Congress of American Indians. Having set in motion a series of events that allowed Vine Deloria Jr. to ascend to the executive office of the NCAI at a very young age, NIYC leaders, and Clyde Warrior especially, became disillusioned with his commitment to the organizations preferred path of steady, engaged dialogue with federal government. The relationship descended into often personal acrimony as Warrior, Thom, and others saw Deloria betraying the vitality of youth in his preference to dialogue over protest, while Deloria, in turn, viewed the NIYC leadership as "crass but effective" (McKenzie-Jones).

Events at the end of the 1960s left an indelible mark on the NIYC, as first, founding member Clyde Warrior died of liver failure in 1968, and then a schism appeared among the leadership as Browning Pipestem led a coup at the annual meeting later that same year, due to a schism forming in the organization as factions of the NIYC led the American Indian cohort of the Poor People's Campaign. At the end of the decade, as other American Indian organizations shone in the spotlight, the increased awareness of Native issues saw membership numbers soar, however. While maintaining an initial focus on educational reform, the new leadership, under Cherokee Gerald Wilkinson, also began to initiate legal fights to protect sacred sites and tribal sovereignty, including the significant *Harjo v. Kleppe* case in 1976, as well as creating a new job-placement program for young American Indians that still exists today.

In 2011, the National Indian Youth Council celebrated its 50th anniversary as an intertribal advocate of Native rights, federal treaty obligations, tribal sovereignty,

Sidebar 2: *Harjo v. Kleppe* (1976): A Fight for Tribal Self-Determination

Harjo v. Kleppe was a landmark court case in the fight for tribal self-determination. In a bitterly fought Muscogee Creek leadership election between Allen Harjo and eventual winner Claude Cox, the issue of National Council representation was a key component of both side's election campaigns. Cox wished to write a new tribal constitution that would allow for National Council membership candidates to be chosen from districts rather than traditional towns. Harjo promised to reinstate the National Council under the more traditional format of Creek Town representation as laid out in the nation's 1867 constitution. When Cox won, along with the fact that the new constitution required approval from the Secretary of the Interior, Harjo's supporters urged him to challenge the legal standing of the fact that the office of the President of the United States would only formally recognize the right of the chief to govern and not his National Council. They felt that this failure to recognize the council as a legitimate branch of government was further proof of federal paternalism undermining tribal sovereignty. With the help of NIYC lawyers, Harjo's case against Thomas S. Kleppe, who was deemed representative of the federal government as the Secretary of the Interior, and actually approved Cox's rewritten constitution while the case was pending, ultimately helped end federal paternalism and strengthen tribal sovereignty. The court ruled that the 1906 Five Civilized Tribes Act had, in fact, reinforced the right of the nation to govern itself in the consensual manner it saw fit. In other words, while Cox's redistricted national Council was allowed, he was no longer able to claim complete autonomy over tribal affairs in internal relations or interactions with the federal government.

health care, employment, and culturally relevant education. The longevity of the organization, championed a movement by its first president, Mel Thom, is a testament to the groundbreaking legacy of those young American Indian men and women who were so readily dismissed as callow, inexperienced youths by tribal leaders at the Chicago conference. In those early days, the National Indian Youth Council dramatically changed the way American Indians protested social, cultural, and political inequity and paved the way for the more easily recognized militant protests that followed their lead in the late 1960s and early 1970s. Their dedication to traditional cultural motifs flourishing in the modern world, and the equal standing of Native women within their movement, also set them apart as trendsetters and trailblazers in contemporary American Indian history.

Biographies of Notable Figures

Clyde Warrior (1939–1968)

Clyde Merton Warrior was born into a traditional Ponca family in 1939 and was raised with Ponca as his first language. Raised by his grandparents, who were traditional drum-makers, Warrior was a fluent singer and fluid dancer by his fourth birthday, even leading songs at the drum. This upbringing framed Warrior's worldview and shaped his activism and ideology for Red Power. It was also the defining anchor of his fight for culturally relevant education and his desire to see tribal self-determination reflect the old ways rather than mirror the political system of the United States.

Warrior's route into activism began when he attended Cameron Junior Agricultural College in Lawton, Oklahoma, and joined the Ittanaha Club. From there, Warrior transferred to the University of Oklahoma and won the presidency of the Sequoyah Club. It was during his Sequoyah presidency that Warrior won the presidency of the SRIYC in a landslide with the short but devastating speech, "I am a full-blood Ponca Indian from Oklahoma. This is all I have to offer. The sewage of Europe does not run through these veins." The speech quickly cemented Warrior's position as one of the most bellicose and militant of the young activists who were changing the shape of American Indian protest in the 1960s. Warrior was a reluctant leader, however, and preferred to champion the community rather than himself. One such example was his role in the Cherokee traditionalist protest against the opening of the tribal heritage village and museum in the mid-1960s, and his long-standing commitment to Native education, first as a student researcher and later as a leader of the NIYC. Amongst his many achievements in his short lifetime, Warrior was the creator (alongside Mel Thom) of the Red Power motif and the architect and ideologue of the early and foundational incarnation of the movement. His commitment to the traditional medicine ways of the past infused his every speech and article and clearly framed Red Power as the bedrock of that which American Indians already possessed, in community, tradition, and cultural identity.

Warrior's tragic death from liver failure in 1968 at the age of 28 robbed Indian country of one of its most dynamic speakers and powerful intellects. His words and speeches still resonate with American Indians, young and old, more than 40 years after his death, and he continues to inspire a desire to fight for change in Indian-white affairs.

Mel Thom (1938–1984)

When Thom became the inaugural president of the NIYC, he was also president of the tribe of Many Feathers student group of Brigham Young University. He was a critical choice as figurehead of the NIYC in its early days and was a dynamic and forceful speaker in federal conferences and meetings throughout the 1960s. Raised traditionally on the Walker River Paiute reservation, Thom was a passionate and dedicated advocate for tribal treaty rights and self-determination. At the end of the 1960s, Thom was the lead Indian delegate for the Poor People's Campaign, a member of the Committee of 100, and a major figure in the events surrounding Resurrection City in Washington, D.C. After being ousted of his NIYC leadership by Browning Pipestem in 1968, Thom walked away from national intertribal politics and returned to his home community on the Walker River Reservation in Nevada. Once home, he was elected tribal chairman and served until 1974. In the decade that followed, until his suicide in 1984, Thom established his own construction company and largely avoided involvement in activism or Indian education. When he did attend national conferences, it was with the NCAI rather than the NIYC. His decision to end his own life was based upon deteriorating ill-health related to a car accident that had happened sometime after he returned home and served as tribal chairman.

Shirley Witt (1940–)

Shirley Hill Witt was an instrumental figure in the early years of the NIYC and featured strongly in the creation and growth of the organizations newspaper, including leading the charge to change its name from the original *Aboriginal* to the later *ABC, Americans Before Columbus*. Raised traditionally in the matrilineal framework of Iroquois culture and now a respected clan mother with a prominent position within her community, Witt insisted that the NIYC was almost uniquely gender egalitarian among activist organizations in the 1960s.

After leaving the NIYC to pursue work with the Civil Rights Commission in the late 1960s, Witt earned her PhD in anthropology at the University of New Mexico and went on the be a respected scholar at the university of North Carolina at Chapel Hill and Colorado College through the 1970s. She also served as an American Indian delegate to the United Nations, alongside Kirk Kickingbird, in the Carter administration. There, she campaigned on behalf of indigenous women's rights to equal access to, and equality in, the workplace. In recent years, Witt has returned to the board of the NIYC and continues to advocate for Native rights in the legal, cultural, political, and social spheres of contemporary life.

Karen Rickard (1938–)

Karen Rickard was born on the Tuscarora reservation in New York State as the daughter of the powerful and influential chief Clinton Rickard. While she shared some similarities with Warrior in being raised traditionally on a family farm, her childhood was also spent witnessing her father's tireless campaigning on behalf of the Six Nations of the Iroquois Confederacy. Her political outlook was framed early in life as she listened to her father fight for the rights of Haudenosaunee people on both sides of the U.S.–Canadian border. Besides her work with the NIYC, Rickard, a graduate of State University of New York, Buffalo, taught in Niagara Falls before working with Native freshman students at the University of California, Los Angeles. From UCLA, she moved to Michigan, where she taught high school for twenty-five years until her retirement in 2004.

Herb Blatchford (1928–1996)

Herb Blatchford was considered by many of the early NIYC stalwarts as the glue that kept the organization together in its formative years, stemming from his previous experience in organizing the first Santa Fe Indian Youth Council from which the regional councils sprang. Born in 1928 on the Navajo reservation, and traditionally taught shepherding as a child, although he did attend boarding schools, Blatchford was also the grandnephew of legendary Navajo chief Manuelito. It was he who decided upon Gallup, New Mexico, as the venue for the inaugural meeting, and ensured that office space and sleeping quarters were available for the young activists who attended. Prior to and after his involvement with the NIYC, Blatchford was director of the Gallup Indian community center and worked closely with the local community to reduce alcoholism among relocated Native residents. In the late 1970s, he rejoined the NIYC and helped them fight against coal extraction on the Navajo reservation. After again splitting from the NIYC after disagreements with executive director Gerald Wilkinson, he continued to campaign for environmental causes in Native communities until his death in a house fire in 1996.

DOCUMENT EXCERPT

Declaration of Indian Purpose

In 1961, almost 700 tribal delegates representing 64 tribes attended the American Indian Chicago Conference. The Declaration of Indian Purpose was later presented to incoming President John F. Kennedy as a unified call for self-determination and a challenge from America's indigenous peoples to be included in his New Frontier.

In order to give due recognition to certain basic philosophies by which the Indian people and all other people endeavor to live, We, the Indian People, must be governed by principles in a democratic manner with a right to choose our way of life. Since our Indian culture is threatened by presumption of being absorbed by the American society, we believe we have the responsibility of preserving our precious heritage. . . .

We believe in the inherent right of all people to retain spiritual and cultural values, and that the free exercise of these values is necessary to the normal development of any people. Indians exercised this inherent right to live their own lives for thousands of years before the white man came and took their lands . . .

We believe that the history and development of America show that the Indian has been subjected to duress, undue influence, unwarranted pressures, and policies which have produced uncertainty, frustration, and despair. . . .

The Indians as responsible individual citizens, as responsible tribal representatives, and as responsible tribal councils want to participate, want to contribute to their own personal and tribal improvements and want to cooperate with their Government on how best to solve the many problems in a businesslike, efficient, and economical manner as rapidly as possible.

We believe that where programs have failed in the past, the reasons were lack of Indian understanding, planning, participation, and approval.

A treaty, in the minds of our people, is an eternal word. Events often make it seem expedient to depart from the pledged word, but we are conscious that the first departure creates a logic for the second departure, until there is nothing left of the word.

What we ask of America is not charity, not paternalism, even when benevolent. We ask only that the nature of our situation be recognized and made the basis of policy and action.

Source: American Indian Chicago Conference, June 13–20, 1961, 5–6.

See also: American Indian Movement, 1968

Further Reading

Bruyneel, Stephen. *The Third Space of Sovereignty: The Post-Colonial Politics of U.S.—Indigenous Relations.* St. Paul: University of Minnesota Press, 2007.

Cobb, Daniel, M. *Native Activism in Cold War America: The Struggle for Sovereignt.* Lawrence: University Press of Kansa, 2008.

Cornell, Stephen. *The Return of the Native: American Indian Political Resurgence.* Oxford, UK: Oxford University Press, 1988.

Declaration of Indian Purpose. American Indian Chicago Conference Booklet.

McKenzie-Jones, Paul, R. *Clyde Warrior: Tradition, Community, and Red Power.* Norman: University of Oklahoma Press, 2015.

National Indian Youth Council. *Preamble.*

Shreve, Bradley G. *Red Power Rising: The National Indian Youth Council and the Origins of Native Activism.* Norman: University of Oklahoma Press, 2011.

Steiner, Stan. *The New Indians.* New York: Harper & Row Publishers, 1968.

Warrior, Clyde. "Poverty Community, and Power" *New University Thought,* 4, No. 2, 1965.

"Which One Are You? Five Types of American Indian." *ABC, Americans Before Columbus,* Vol. 1, No. 4, December 1964.

American Indian Movement, 1968

Frances Holmes

Chronology

July 28, 1968	AIM is founded.
1969	AIM establishes the Minneapolis Indian Health Board.
	AIM presents challenges to National Council of Churches conference.
	AIM pressures Minneapolis Mayor Naftalin to establish the first Indian Week to occur anywhere in the country.
	November 20, Alcatraz occupation. Visited and supported by AIM members.
1970	Minnesota Legal Rights Center opens.
	Assists with Lizzy Fasthorse and Muriel Waukazo's takeover of Mount Rushmore.
	Occupies empty building Naval Air Station, Fort Snelling.
	Assists Lac Courte Oreilles Ojibwa of Wisconsin Winter Dam takeover.
	Plymouth Rock takeover. Includes occupation of Mayflower replica and appearance at Thanksgiving pilgrim re-enactment.
1971	AIM members travel to Washington, D.C.; citizen arrest of John Old Crow.
	May prayer vigil at Mount Rushmore.
	July 4th protest at Mount Rushmore.

1972 Heart of Earth Survival School opens, Minneapolis.

Red School House opens, St. Paul.

February 14, death of Raymond Yellow Thunder, Gordon Nebraska.

Trail of Broken Treaties.

1973 Death and trial of Wesley Bad Heart Bull. Custer, South Dakota. Town razed.

71-day Wounded Knee takeover.

We Will Remember Survival School opens, Pine Ridge, SD.

1974 International Indian Treaty Council established in Geneva, Switzerland.

Assists in establishing Gaelic language school, Derry, Northern Ireland.

Clyde Bellecourt addresses World Council of Churches Montreaux, Switzerland.

Wounded Knee trials begin and last through 1976.

1975 AIM sponsors Little Earth of United Tribes Urban Housing Program.

Shootout at Jumping Bull Ranch; FBI agents killed; Leonard Peltier imprisoned with two life sentences.

1976 February 24, prominent AIM member Anna Mae Pictou Aquash is found murdered.

1977 MIGIZI Communications founded—produces indigenous radio news.

United Nations formally recognizes indigenous peoples of the world by granting the International Treaty Council non-governmental organizational (NGO) status.

AIM calls for the enactment of the American Indian Religious Freedom Act.

1978 AIM establishes first prison education for Native adults.

"Longest Walk," Alcatraz to Washington, D.C.

Circle of Life Survival School opens.

1979 AIM establishes American Indian Opportunities Industrialization Center (AIOIC).

1981 Yellow Thunder Camp in the Black Hills is established.

1983 KILI Radio station in Porcupine, South Dakota, is begun.

1984 Federation of Native Controlled Survival Schools is established, consisting of 16 schools.

1988	Elaine Stately/Peacemakers Center opens in Twin Cities.
	Minneapolis patrol is reinitiated due to murdered Native women.
1989	AIM secures boat landing for tribal members' right to spear fish in northern Wisconsin lakes.
1990	First Youth and Elders gathering, Okmulgee, Oklahoma.
1991	AIM Founds National Coalition on Racism in Sports & Media.
1992	National Coalition on Racism protests during the Super Bowl in Minneapolis.
	Demonstrations against the 500th anniversary of Columbus stops parade in Denver, Colorado.
1994	"Walk for Justice" from Alcatraz to Washington, D.C., publicizing Peltier's treatment.
1998	AIM provides security for Ward Valley, California, protest.
1999	AIM occupies Whiteclay, Nebraska.
2008	"Longest Walk 2," Alcatraz to Washington, D.C., with participation of the Maori people.

Introduction

The 1960s and 1970s brought significant social upheaval in the United States. Transitioning from the Vietnam War, citizens were angry, and minoritized populations were frustrated by their social circumstances. Black Panthers, farm workers, and feminists engaged in protests to bring attention and change to their circumstances. Dee Brown had captured the public's sympathies with his book *Bury My Heart at Wounded Knee,* and Vine Deloria Jr. had published an indigenous call to action with *Custer Died for Your Sins: An Indian Manifesto.* While Native Peoples had already experienced lifetimes of resistance as a result of Euro-American genocide, recent decades had brought the Indian Reorganization Act (IRA), with its potential for puppet governments, as well as Termination and Relocation. These circumstances set the stage for new efforts of resistance by Natives through the American Indian Movement (AIM). This chapter provides highlights of the most publicized AIM efforts, achievements, individuals, and underlying meanings of AIM advocacy.

The Origins of AIM

Dennis Banks and George Mitchell, both Ojibwa, initiated the first AIM meeting on July 28, 1968, to discuss the concerns and welfare of Native Peoples. Clyde

American Indian Movement (AIM) co-founders Vernon Bellecourt and Dennis Banks, Ojibwa. AIM was founded in 1968 in Minneapolis, Minnesota, and modeled on the Black Panthers. It initially addressed police harassment and issues that urban Indians faced. (Bettmann/Getty)

Bellecourt, also Ojibwa, who had been working to increase opportunities for "city Indians," also attended. Native Peoples were struggling with racism, discrimination, violence, low wages, and poor housing. AIM was initially composed of urban Natives with an intent to restore dignity and reclaim a sense of "Indian-ness."

Banks, Mitchell, and Bellecourt established a street patrol to protect Natives from the abuse and corruption of local police. The AIM patrol was patterned after an organization established by the Black Panthers. Strangely, "[i]n Minneapolis, only 10 percent of the population was Indian, but 70 percent of the inmates in the city's jails were our [Native] people" (Banks and Erdoes 2004, 63). Minneapolis police regularly stormed Native bars, indiscriminately beating and arresting Natives. AIM canvassed the downtown bar areas and would clear out the bars before police arrived. Within 39 weeks, the arrest rate dropped to near zero (Deloria 1985, 36).

Many urban Natives had lost their sense of spirituality through boarding school, Termination, and Relocation. AIM leaders incorporated the spiritual leadership of Leonard Crow Dog (Lakota) into their decision-making processes. AIM grew to over 5,000 members in more than 79 chapters nationwide (Banks and Erdoes 1995,

Sidebar 1: People Involved with the Early American Indian Movement

Senator James Abourezk	U.S. Senator of South Dakota during Occupation of Wounded Knee. Grew up in South Dakota.
Henry Adams	Native American who provided AIM with its intellectual energy.
Anna Mae Aquash	AIM activist. Found murdered execution-style in South Dakota in 1976.
Dennis Banks	Founder of AIM, significant leader.
Clyde Bellecourt	Founder of AIM, significant leader.
Vernon Bellecourt	AIM member, brother of Clyde.
Pedro Bissonette	Leader of Oglala Sioux Civil Rights Organization (OSCRO), participant in AIM and Trail of Broken Treaties.
Wallace Black Elk	Lakota Spiritual leader.
Marlon Brando	Prominent actor and supporter of AIM. Personal supporter of Dennis Banks and Russell Means.
Lehman Brightman	During Alcatraz occupation, established University of California, Berkeley's Native American Studies department
Wesley Bad Heart Bull	Murdered in 1973. Sentencing hearing for his killer was site of AIM riot in Custer, South Dakota.
Robert Burnette	Tribal Chairman Rosebud Sioux tribe during Wounded Knee Occupation.
Carter Camp	AIM leader from Oklahoma, confidante of Banks and Means.
Frank Clearwater	AIM member, shot and killed during Wounded Knee occupation.
Jack Coler	FBI agent shot and killed at Jumping Bull Ranch in Pine Ridge Reservation.
Leonard Crow Dog	Spiritual leader and member of AIM.
Vine Deloria Jr.	Dakota scholar/writer/lawyer/activist.
Douglas Durham	FBI informant within AIM.
Jimmie Durham	AIM organizer and diplomat for International Indian Treaty Council.
Frank Fools Crow	Oglala spiritual leader—leader of traditional Natives during Wounded Knee.
John Graham	AIM activist convicted of killing AIM activist Anna Mae Aquash.

William Janklow	Lawyer and governor of South Dakota. Previously advocated for Native people, became an antagonist. Stated, "The only real way to deal with these kinds of people is to put a bullet in their heads. Put a bullet in a guy's head, and he won't bother you anymore" (Hendricks 2006, 151).
William Kunstler	Social activist and lawyer. Represented Banks and Means in Wounded Knee trials. Previous clients included Martin Luther King.
Buddy Lamont	AIM member, shot and killed at Wounded Knee occupation.
Arlo Looking Cloud	AIM activist convicted of killing AIM activist Anna Mae Aquash.
Russell Means	Significant AIM leader.
Louis Moves Camp	AIM member who became a federal informant against AIM.
Senator George McGovern	South Dakota U.S. senator during Wounded Knee occupation.
Judge Fred Nichol	Judge in Wounded Knee trials of Means and Banks.
Richard Oakes	Leader of Alcatraz occupation. Murdered in California.
Leonard Peltier	Serving two life sentences for the murder of two federal agents at Jumping Bull Ranch.
Floyd Red Crow Westerman	Native singer and actor. AIM advocate and activist.
Reuben Snake	Advocate and organizer for AIM, American Indian Church roadman.
Ken Tilsen	Primary lawyer for Means and Banks in Wounded Knee trial.
John Trudell	Primary participant of AIM, spokesperson at Alcatraz. Wife and children died from probable house arson. Author and singer.
Ron Williams	Federal agent shot and killed at Jumping Bull ranch at Pine Ridge Reservation
Dick Wilson	Co-opted Pine Ridge chairman. Ran puppet government during Wounded Knee.
Raymond Yellow Thunder	Murdered and found dead five days later in truck sitting in used car lot in the border town of Gordon, Nebraska.

64). Russell Means, Oglala Lakota, had been working to establish an Indian Center in Cleveland, Ohio, but joined forces with AIM after meeting Banks and Bellecourt at a conference in San Francisco (Means and Wolf 2004, 147). Banks and Means became the flashy, charismatic leaders of AIM; neither lacked self-confidence. Both leaders had a gift for thought-provoking sound bites (Nagel 1996, 167).

AIM challenged school curriculum and protested derogatory films, church organizations, welfare workers/offices, and the BIA. Drawing national attention, AIM assisted Lizzy Fast Horse and Muriel Waukazoo in their occupation of Mt. Rushmore in September 1970. Twenty-three protesters, including AIM members' spiritual leader John Fire Lame Deer and activist John Trudell, climbed up the mountain and made camp behind Roosevelt's head (Means and Wolf 1995, 170). Activists remained there for approximately four weeks. The group placed a large flag with the words "Sioux Indian Power" over the monument (Banks and Erdoes, quoting Lizzy Fast Horse, 2004, 110).

November 1970 marked the 350th anniversary of the Plymouth colony and a large celebration and re-enactment had been planned. The Wampanoag people asked AIM for help in staging a protest. AIM led a march through the town, singing and drumming (Johansen 2013, 245). The re-enactors welcomed the over 300 protestors, thinking that they lent an air of authenticity to the celebration. However, Means gave a speech on the pedestal of Wampanoag leader Massasoit's statue. Means called Thanksgiving a national day of mourning. AIMsters (as AIM members call themselves) climbed aboard a replica of the Mayflower in the adjacent harbor and dumped its pilgrim dummies overboard. Means and Bellecourt buried Plymouth Rock with sand and then marched out to a Plymouth plantation, where a feast was taking place. More statements were exchanged; tables and chairs were turned over (Means and Wolf 1995, 175–78).

Raymond Yellow Thunder

In Gordon, Nebraska—a town adjacent to the Pine Ridge Reservation in South Dakota—Raymond Yellow Thunder (Oglala) was found dead and frozen in an unlocked truck at a used car lot. His February 1972 death resulted in an unprecedented backlash from the Native community. Yellow Thunder, a 51-year-old ranch hand, had been out drinking. A group of four whites had stripped and beat him and thrown him into their car trunk. They drove around, eventually throwing him into an American Legion Hall. He wandered out to the street, and the four assailants grabbed him and repeated their actions. Thinking that Yellow Thunder was drunk, the police brought him to jail to sleep it off. The next morning, he staggered out of the building and found his way to a used car lot, where he remained until he was found dead five days later (Smith and Warrior 1996, 112–15).

After a lack of action by the police, Yellow Thunder's family asked AIM to step in. AIM descended on the area and caravanned through town. By the end of the week, there were 1,400 Natives in town—doubling the population of Gordon (Johansen 2013, 303). There were three days of boycotts, demonstrations, and marches. The guilty men were only charged with manslaughter. This effort marked AIM's first collaboration with rural reservations.

Trail of Broken Treaties

In 1972, Robert Burnette suggested a march to Washington, D.C., during the presidential election. The Trail of Broken Treaties originated from several points along the west coast in October. Winding through reservations, the participants met in St. Paul, Minnesota, where a twenty-point position paper was written (Deloria 1997, 46–56). From St. Paul, a four-mile long caravan, comprising a hundred Natives—young and old, urban and rural—arrived in Washington, D.C.

After arriving in Washington, D.C., on November 3, it became clear that Burnette had failed to make lodging arrangements. Frustrated by this and the inability of the federal government to send a representative to hear their grievances, AIM's

---

Sidebar 2: Trail of Broken Treaties Twenty Point Position Paper, October 1972, Minneapolis, MN

The following consists of the 20 points determined through four days of workshops chaired by Reuben Snake with the participants of the Trail of Broken Treaties. Over two days, Hank Adams reformulated the information into 20 points. Vine Deloria Jr. called this "the best summary document of reforms put forth in this century" (Deloria 1997 50).

1. Restoration of constitutional treaty-making authority.
2. Establishment of treaty commission to make new treaties.
3. An address to the American People & joint sessions of congress.
4. Commission to review treaty commitments & violations.
5. Resubmissions of unratified treaties to the senate.
6. All Indians to be governed by treaty relations.
7. Mandatory relief against treaty rights and violations.
8. Judicial recognition of Indian right to interpret treaties.
9. Creation of congressional joint committee on reconstruction of Indian relations.

10. Land reform and restoration of a 110 million-acre Native land base:
    A. Priorities In Restoration of the Native American Line Base
    B. Consolidation of Indians' Land, Water, Natural and Economic Resources
    C. Termination of Losses and Condemnation of Non-Indian Land Title
    D. Repeal of the Menominee, Klamath, and Other Termination Acts.
11. Revision of 25 U.S.C. 163; Restoration of rights to Indians terminated by enrollment and revocation of prohibitions against "dual benefits."
12. Repeal of state laws enacted under public law 280 (1953).
13. Resume federal protective jurisdiction for offenses against Indians:
    A. Establishment of a National Federal Indian Grand Jury
    B. Jurisdiction over Non-Indians Within Indian Reservations
    C. Accelerated Rehabilitation and Release Program for State and Federal Indian Prisoners
14. Abolition of the Bureau of Indian Affairs by 1976.
15. Creation of an "Office of Federal Indian Relations and Community Reconstruction."
16. Priorities and purpose of the proposed new office.
17. Indian commerce and tax immunities.
18. Protection of Indians religious freedom and cultural integrity.
19. National referendums, local options, and forms of Indian organization.
20. Health, housing, employment, economic development, and education.

The full version of the Twenty Points can be found on the AIM website: http://www.aimovement.org/ggc/trailofbrokentreaties.html

intentions shifted to an occupation of the Bureau of Indian Affairs (BIA) building (Nagel 1996, 169). Desks, file cabinets, and chairs were used to block doors, windows, and hallways in the building. As riot police harassed the occupiers, the building became subjected to increased destruction. Negotiations were proposed but never materialized. Administrators promised that the AIMsters would not be prosecuted if they would take money given to them to return home. AIMsters took 20,000 tons of agency files as they left (Johansen 2013, 251).

Custer Courthouse

In Buffalo Gap, South Dakota, in January 1973, a barroom brawl between Wesley Bad Heart Bull (Lakota) and Darld Schmitz occurred. Early in the evening, Schmitz had voiced his intent to kill an Indian. Wesley had gone to the bar for a drink with his mother and wife. The two men exchanged insults, and Schmitz stabbed Bad Heart Bull seven times. Schmitz was arrested and charged with involuntary manslaughter, and released on $5,000 bail (Means and Wolf 1995, 243). He claimed self-defense. The case was then tried at the county seat in Custer, South Dakota.

On February 6, 1973, angry AIM leaders led a caravan of 30 cars, with more than 100 people, through heavy snow to Custer. Riot police greeted them. AIMsters held a rally on the courthouse steps. Only Banks, Means, Peltier, and Dave Hillwere (Choctaw AIMster) were allowed inside to talk with County Attorney Hobart Gates. The AIMsters informed Gates that they wanted Schmitz's charge changed to murder. Gates refused.

Means told the crowd of the decision, which caused an uproar. Wesley's mother was on the steps and attempted to enter the courthouse. Protesters rushed the door, and the riot police began swinging batons and dispensing tear gas. Wesley's mother was grabbed by the police and shoved down the stairs. The riot consumed the town for several days. The courthouse and chamber of commerce building were burned down, and 22 people were arrested. Wesley's killer was acquitted and never served any jail time (Banks and Erdoes 2004, 151–56).

Wounded Knee II—Occupation

Throughout these 1973 events, the Oglala people on Pine Ridge had been suffering. The BIA had set up a land-use situation that originated with the Dawes Act. Land on reservations had been divided into allotments, which were divided further among individual heirs, decreasing their size until useless. The BIA then leased the lands to non-Native ranchers for grazing, divesting the allottees of their land. The Oglala organized the Oglala Sioux Landowners' Association (OSLA) to reform this policy. Oglala Chairman Dick Wilson resisted the organization, and tensions escalated. In response, the Oglala Sioux Civil Rights Organization (OSCRO) was formed with the intent of impeaching Wilson (Mohawk 2010, 465).

Wilson, of mixed blood, had previously proven himself corrupt. He had supposedly received $10,000 from white businessmen promising to support their bootlegging enterprise on a "dry" (no alcohol) reservation. He was also accused of paying and transporting unregistered voters to the poles for his election. Many claimed that Wilson had purchased tribal land for his use at one-quarter the cost, increased his salary by 50 percent, refused to keep a budget, and forged the tribal secretary's signature on a $69,000 check (Hendricks 2006, 47–48).

Wilson cancelled the IRA required council meetings and managed tribal decisions through a handpicked committee. He was concerned that AIM would aid the Oglala people, so he set an ordinance banning AIM and any supporters from the

Pine Ridge reservation. Shortly thereafter, the BIA provided Wilson with $64,000 to establish a policing squad, the "Guardians of the Oglala Nation" (GOONS), which operated at his beck and call. It is speculated that this money influenced Wilson's decision regarding a transfer of uranium-rich land to the U.S. Forest Service (Churchill 2003, 168).

AIMsters filed a complaint with the U.S. Attorney's Office, citing the rules and regulations that Wilson was violating. They received no response. However, as tensions escalated between the AIMsters and Wilson during his impeachment process, the BIA sent 110 federal marshals to protect him. The Pine Ridge tribal headquarters became barricaded, and police were stationed on the rooftops. This Special Operations Group (SOG) of federal marshals walked the streets in bright blue jumpsuits with their side arms, rifles, and machine guns clearly displayed. GOONs were given riot training, judo instruction, batons, and eventually AK-47s. Wilson dominated the impeachment process. Those who opposed him retreated to the community hall in the village of Calico. Calling for AIM to support them, the Calico hall quickly filled with hundreds of Oglalas and AIMsters (Hendricks 2006, 46–57). Spiritual leader Fools Crow asked AIM to make a stand at Wounded Knee, sacred ground.

During the evening of February 28, 1973, 60 to 80 vehicles made their way to Wounded Knee. The contingent consisted of traditional, urban, and spiritual Lakota, as well as representatives from the Iroquois League Nations (Deloria 1985, 75). The intent had been to conduct a news conference, but the action progressed into a 71-day occupation. At Wounded Knee, there was a small store and museum run by non-Natives who had been capitalizing on the scared site. The buildings, and their contents, which included some food and ammunition, were taken over. AIM drew up a list of demands. An FBI special agent met with AIM right away. Means provided him with a copy of their demands, which basically restated the agreements made in the 1868 Laramie treaty—the return of the Black Hills, the re-establishment an independent Oglala Nation, and a task group to investigate the BIA (Means and Wolf 1995, 257–61).

Publicity was drastically skewed. Networks broadcast that AIM had taken white hostages and had executed a commando-type raid with significant firepower. Yet, the Natives were very poorly equipped. AIMsters had brought a few weapons and used hunting knifes from the trading post. So as to appear well armed and to keep the federal marshals at a distance, AIMsters created the illusion of more weapons. AIMsters painted coffee can lids black and attached wires to them. They buried them in full sight of the marshals, leading them to believe that a perimeter of land mines had been set. To simulate a machine gun, AIMsters draped an ammunition belt over a lead pipe and then rapidly fired 10 shotgun rounds (Weyler 1982, 85).

Wilson's GOONS set up roadblocks and surrounded the area. FBI agents, 300 armed field marshals and BIA police SWAT teams arrived, F4 Phantom jets flew overhead and military flares lit up the sky (Johanasen, 2013, 29). Armament included "17 [a]rmored personnel carriers [. . .] 41,000 rounds for grenade launchers and helicopters" (Churchill 2003, 169), and 120 sniper rifles (Hendricks 2006, 132). Additionally, "[m]ilitary officers, supply sergeants, maintenance technicians, chemical officers, and medical teams [were provided on site]" (Churchill, 2003, 169). An estimated half-million rounds were fired. An additional 200 airborne troops in Colorado were put on 24-hour standby. Informants were planted to destabilize and provoke individuals to participate in illegal activity within the AIM organization. Some of these informants tried to suggest violent methods of handling situations, or attempted to corner AIM leadership into purchasing illegal weapons. A few of these informants were discovered, others confessed (Akwesasne Notes 1974, 15).

Smuggling routes were constructed to bring in additional food and ammunition for the AIM occupation. Churchill contends that as many as 13 people who were trying to smuggle in supplies were killed by GOON patrols and secretly buried (Churchill 2003, 170). Negotiations became increasingly strained, and as result, ultimatums were issued. On Friday, March 9, 1973, the government told the AIMsters they needed to leave Wounded Knee, or else the FBI would come in shooting. That afternoon, the Natives from Pine Ridge filled the surrounding roads as they tried to get to their relatives. The National League of Churches stated that it would send representatives to stand between the Natives and the federal marshals. Telegrams and letters of support for the Oglala flooded the White House. Consequently, the federal marshals had to deal with the 300 permanent inhabitants of Wounded Knee as well as the 1,000 Natives descending on the area. Reports indicate that the cars leading into the area were seven miles long (Deloria 1985, 76–77).

Negotiations were re-established. Ceasefires would occur, only to have shooting resume. After AIMsters Buddy Lamont (Oglala) and Frank Clearwater (Apache) were killed, AIM leaders surrendered 71 days into the occupation, with the promise of investigations into Wilson's illegal practices and violations of the 1868 Fort Laramie Treaty—neither happened (Johanasen 2013, 29).

In an overt effort to disable AIM, the FBI made 562 arrests. The entire legal charade resulted in only 15 convictions. AIM leadership was tied up in the courts for years, and all of AIM's monies and fundraising efforts were used for the various litigation fees. While AIM leaders and many of the participants were dealing with their court proceedings, Wilson continued to terrorize the population of Pine Ridge. As Russell Means accounted in his autobiography, over a three-year period after the occupation, at least 69 AIM members on the reservation died violently, and 350 others suffered severe injuries from attack (Means and Wolf 1995, 296, 304).

The Charges, Court Cases, and Decisions Reached from the Wounded Knee Occupation

Although "acts done under a claim or right are not criminal," (Sayer 1997, 37), in 1973 Russell Means consented to arrest once he signed an agreement with the federal government regarding the Wounded Knee occupation. After submitting to the negotiator who was onsite, Means was handcuffed and placed on a helicopter and taken to the Rapid City jail. Once released on bail, he flew to Washington, D.C., to meet with the federal government to discuss the agreements he had made with them. However, Means was told that government representatives would not meet with him because the activists at Wounded Knee had refused to lay down their weapons. Barred from returning to Wounded Knee by the judge who had released him on bail, Means took on speaking engagements at universities and lecture halls to earn money for AIM. After an unfortunate misunderstanding with the press regarding Means's comments associated with the judge who had granted his release, Means was picked up and jailed again in the Minnehaha County, South Dakota, jail, where he stayed for six weeks (Means and Wolf 1995, 284–93).

The federal government stated that if the activists of Wounded Knee would lay down their weapons officials stated that they would meet with the chiefs and leaders of the Lakota. The activists were assured that there would be no arrests, except for outstanding warrants. However, within minutes of the Wounded Knee surrender, the FBI began handcuffing the activists as they left the occupation site (Means and Wolf 1995, 292–93). At the close of the Wounded Knee occupation, several leaders were jailed immediately with significant bail bonds:

Russell Means: $150,000 bond
Pedro Bissonette: $152,000 bond
Stan Holder: $32,000 bond
Leonard Crow Dog: $35,500 bond.

There were over 562 arrests and 185 federal indictments (Johansen 2013, 299). These indictments against Wounded Knee Occupation defendants encompassed eight sections of Titles 18 and 26 of the U.S. Criminal Code. The offenses charged included:

- Impeding or obstructing federal officers during the lawful performance of their duties incident to a civil disorder

- Assaulting a federal officer
- Transporting firearms for the use of disorder
- Using firearms in commission of a felony
- Being in possession of unregistered (illegal) firearms
- Robbery
- Various combinations of burglary and larceny
- Destroying a motor vehicle
- Reckless disregard for the safety of human life
- Conspiring to commit one or more of the charged offenses (Sayer 1997, 44)

"By the fall of 1973, agents had amassed some 316,000 separate investigative file classifications on those who had been inside Wounded Knee" (Churchill, 170, citing Dunbarr Ortiz). However, there were only 15 convictions and none of them were substantial charges (Johansen, 299).

"Banks and Means were specifically charged with three counts of assault on federal officers, one charge each of conspiracy, and one each for larceny. Banks and Means would have each had to serve eighty-five years in prison" (Sayer 1997, 69). The Wounded Knee occupation trial began on January 8, 1974, at 10:00 AM and lasted nine months.

The primary attitude of the defendants in the trial was that it was not merely *United States v. Means and Banks*, but instead a political trial. In fact, AIM attorney William Kunstler had stated, "for the first time in an American jury would have the ability to pass on what has happened to the American Indian" (Sayer 1997, 63). He also remarked: "The major difficulty inherent in representing Native American activists accused of serious federal crimes lies in the apparent willingness of the government to resort to any form of official misconduct to gain convictions" (Kunstler 1985, 611).

The trial was moved from South Dakota to St. Paul, Minnesota, in response to concerns of extreme racism. Several other prominent lawyers came to the aid of AIM leaders, including Ken Tilsen. The defense's needs were so great, and there were of so many volunteers, that the effort became known as the Wounded Knee Legal Defense/Offense committee (WKLDOC). By the end of June 1974, there were 21 lawyers from six states in Rapid City. (Sayer 1997, 49–51).

Throughout the trial, the government provided altered documents, as well as FBI agents and witnesses who lied on the witness stand. Each of these instances was met with Judge Nichol's threat of a dismissal. Kunstler referred to the judge's explanation of his final decision to dismiss the case: "The prosecution in this trial had something other than attaining justice foremost in its mind . . . [i]ncidents of misconduct formed a pattern throughout the course of the trial [leading] me to the belief that this case was not prosecuted in good faith or in the spirit of justice (United States v Banks, 383 F. Supp. 397)" (1985, 611). See below, Document Excerpts, for Judge Nichol's remarks in his dismissal.

AIM's Significant But Less Publicized Activities

AIM initiated many other advocacy-based activities. The leaders established legal support for many urban Natives. AIM was involved in housing issues and established several "Survival Schools" that focused on culturally relevant curriculum. Protests and demonstrations were led against racist and derogatory professional and college sports team mascots. In 1978, the Longest Walk was organized. Participants walked from Alcatraz to Washington, D.C., to educate the American public about the injustices that occur for Native Peoples. AIM has been involved in international indigenous working groups, including the United Nations with its work on indigenous rights. In 1981, an 880-acre area within the Black Hills was occupied with the intent of securing sacred space. It was named after Raymond Yellow Thunder.

Today, AIM chapters are still somewhat active in various locations. Each chapter has a focus unique to the Native Peoples it serves. The Survival Schools established in Minnesota are still in operation. Banks, Bellecourt, and Bill Means (Russell's brother) continue with their dedication to advocacy for Native Peoples in various ways. Trudell died in 2015.

Conclusion

Formed in 1968, AIM was associated with activist events and circumstances advocating for the betterment of Native Peoples and their circumstances. As the movement evolved, it was clear to many people that the fundamental aspect of AIM was land. Reflections from Means and Banks, and other scholars have brought this to light. Specifically, the Fort Laramie Treaty of 1868 stipulated that the Sioux reservation consisted of over two million acres (Deloria 1985, 64). Naturally, land is the foundation, for, by and about Native perspective and existence.

Following the Wounded Knee Occupation, AIM was criticized for its inexperience and opportunism, and for taking advantage of uneducated or unsophisticated rural Natives. But events outlined in this chapter highlight some of AIM's greatest work whereby modern, traditionalist, urban, and rural activists came together to fight their common enemy of colonization. Was it successful? Native

Peoples today are more vocal, more involved, and more present on the minds of Euro-Americans. Elizabeth Cook-Lynn sums up AIM well in her reflection of the life of Russell Means:

> The trend toward greater understanding, some say, would probably not have happened without the influence of the upheaval called the American Indian Movement, and the lifelong dedication to an idea of public dissent by Russell Means and other Indians in the United States. With the absence of dissent and protest the situation on Indian reservations will only get worse.
>
> No one argues that AIM was not ruthless and narcissistic and the leadership exploitive, but those born and raised on South Dakota reservations in the twentieth century, as was Russell Means, know that AIM and its leadership were never irrelevant. AIM represents the obligation of indigenous peoples to keep in touch with what matters to them—the land. (Cook-Lynn 2012, 17)

Biographies of Notable Figures

Dennis Banks (1937–)

Dennis Banks (Ojibwa) was one of several very influential leaders of the American Indian Movement (AIM). Banks was born at his grandparents' home at Federal Dam on the Leech Lake Chippewa Reservation. It was a typical reservation home for that era—no running water, electricity, or plumbing. However, this remote area, which boarders Leech Lake with its 640 miles of shoreline, dotted with streams, forests, and open meadows, was a fragrant and beautiful place for a boyhood. At a feast given in honor of his birth, Banks was given his Ojibwa name of Nowa-Cumig, which means "at the center of the universe" (Banks and Erdoes 2004, 14). Banks's family logged, trapped, fished, sugared, and harvested wild rice.

When Banks was five years old, he and his older brother and sister were forced to attend boarding school in Pipestone, Minnesota. The school was 250 miles from their home. The boarding school era functioned at its height from 1900 to 1930. It was one of the federal government's efforts to deculturate and assimilate Native children. (See Carlisle Indian Industrial School, 1879, this volume.) When Banks and his siblings arrived at the school, they were each scoured with DDT insecticide, and the boys had their heads shaved down to their scalps (Banks and Erdoes 2004, 25). Banks was issued uniform-style clothing and slept in a dorm. He attended Pipestone for nine years, never returning home in the summer. Banks ran away nine times. He was transferred to a junior-high boarding school in Wahpeton,

North Dakota, when he was 11 years old. Two years later, he was transferred to a larger boarding school at Flandreau, South Dakota. From there, he escaped one final time and returned home to Leech Lake (Banks and Erdoes 2004, 31).

In 1954, Banks joined the United States Air Force. He became an aerial photographer of such places as Korea, Manchuria, China, and the Soviet Union. Banks was eventually stationed in Japan. There he became involved with Machiyo Inouye and had a child. Banks, however, was denied permission to marry her. He was then ordered back to the States. Refusing to go, Banks went AWOL twice and was eventually brought back to the United States in chains. He worked, trying to earn enough money to return to Japan but was unable to accumulate enough funds. It was during this period that a significant amount of frustration and anger built up within him (Banks and Erdoes 2004, 57).

Banks then moved to Minneapolis and eventually became a heavy drinker. The St. Paul police would arrest hundreds of Natives weekly at the "Indian Town" bars. Those arrested on drunk-and-disorderly charges would then be used to work on city projects. Banks was pulled into these mass arrests approximately 25 times. In 1966, Banks was arrested for stealing groceries to feed his family of 10. He read about Native history while in jail. From newspapers, he learned about the civil rights movement, Vietnam protests, and the Black Panthers (Banks and Erdoes 2004, 60).

Once Banks was released from prison, he contacted George Mitchell. Together they printed 500 leaflets calling for a meeting on July 28, 1968, to discuss the possibility of starting a movement for the benefit of Native Peoples. Mitchell and Banks went from door to door and called their friends, families, and relatives. On the night of the meeting, sure that no one would show up, the small church basement filled with over 200 people. Clyde Bellecourt, another prominent AIM leader, was in attendance. With Banks as field director and Bellecourt as chairman, AIM was born (Banks and Erdoes 2004, 62).

During the Yellow Thunder Protests (see narrative), Banks met his long-time wife, Darlene Nichols, or Kamook. Together they had three daughters and a son (Banks and Erdoes, 119). After his participation in the Occupation of Wounded Knee (see narrative) and his defense in subsequent trials, Banks was found guilty of assault and riot charges for the Custer courthouse riot (see narrative). On August 5, 1975, he jumped bail for that charge and eluded the authorities by driving between South Dakota and the west coast repeatedly—each time to accomplish different purposes. In the process, Banks stayed with friends, such as the actor Marlon Brando, John Trudell, and Lee Brightman, as well as various other supporters and sympathizers. While staying with Brightman, Banks was apprehended by the FBI (Banks and Erdoes 2004, 314).

Banks was jailed in San Francisco, charged with "unlawful flight to avoid prosecution" and was held for extradition to South Dakota. Upon his release, Banks held a press conference conveying the seriousness of his extradition: the current South Dakota Governor Bill Janklow had publicly proposed putting a bullet through Banks's head. Marlon Brando rallied his friends and supporters, while many of Banks's supporters wrote letters to California Governor Jerry Brown. As a result of these efforts, Governor Brown denied Banks's extradition to South Dakota (Banks and Erdoes 2004, 322).

During his time in California, Banks became the Chancellor of California's Native American DQ University. However, after eight years, Governor Brown chose not to run for office again. The incoming governor, George Deukmejian, made it very clear that if asked he would extradite Banks back to South Dakota. Banks appealed to the Six Nations Confederacy in upstate New York for sanctuary. After a lengthy process of consideration, they granted his request. Banks and his family stayed on the Onondaga reservation for approximately two years (Banks and Erdoes 2004, 337). In 1984, when Bill Janklow was no longer the governor of South Dakota, Banks turned himself over to the sheriff. After a hearing in Custer, South Dakota, Banks was sentenced to three years in prison. He had served one year and two months when he was released on parole (Banks and Erdoes 2004, 346).

After his release, Banks continued to work and provide leadership for Native communities. He has organized sacred runs and protests regarding Native remains and sports mascots, as well as "walks for justice" to bring attention to Leonard Peltier's circumstances.

Russell Means (1939–2012)

Russell Means (Oglala Lakota), a primary leader of AIM, was born November 10, 1939, in Porcupine on the Pine Ridge Reservation. He was the oldest of four boys. His mother was Yankton Sioux, and his father was Oglala Lakota. Her parents lived a very traditional life—growing their food, cattle, and horses while leasing their land to ranchers for grazing. The foundation of Means's Native perspective came from the time and experiences he had with his grandfather as they walked the land together. In this way, Means learned about the plants and animals and stories of Iktomi, the Lakota trickster (Means and Wolf 1995, 12). The Lakota name given to him in his youth was Wanbli Ohitika, or Brave Eagle. Means has often said that he learned his most profound lessons from his grandfather, as he would not provide Means with the end of the story. Instead, Means had to determine the end for himself. From this method of oral teaching, he learned patience and the practice of deep contemplation.

Both of Means's parents attended Indian boarding schools. However, because they moved to Vallejo, California, in 1942, he attended public schools there. His father was a welder and was able to find plentiful work in California. In 1945, after WWII had ended, shipyards laid off thousands of workers, including Means's father. In 1946, Means's mother had twins. As soon as the babies could travel, the family returned to South Dakota, as there was more work available there, however the family eventually returned to Vallejo. Means's adolescent years were rocky. His father was an alcoholic, and his mother was the major influence in his family. Means often fought with his mother and began to struggle academically and socially. Running with a rough crowd, he succumbed to alcohol and drug abuse, skipped school, and committed petty thefts. In an effort to corral his behavior, Means's mother sent him to boarding school in Winnebago, Nebraska (Means and Wolf 1995, 28–57).

Russell Means (Oglala Lakota), American Indian Movement (AIM) leader, speaks to a crowd of followers in South Dakota in 1974. Means was an early leader in 1970s protests. (Bettmann/Getty)

After returning from Winnebago, Means became addicted to drugs and began to deal them. After several rounds of going on and off the drugs, Means stuck primarily to alcohol. Once while driving drunk, Means hit another car and injured the occupants. He was sentenced to jail (Means and Wolf 1995, 66–76). As an adult, Means did accounting, assembly line operations, data processing operations, printing, mail delivery, janitorial, rodeo riding, and dance instruction work. However, Means had also been homeless and arrested for petty theft, drunkenness, assault, and disorderly conduct (Johansen 2013, 187). At various times, Means lived in Los Angeles, on the Rosebud Reservation in South Dakota, and in Cleveland, Ohio. While in L.A., Means married and had two children.

Later, after to moving to San Francisco, Means married again and had a child with his wife, Betty. Soon thereafter, Means and his father participated in the first attempt to take over Alcatraz in 1964. After the takeover, Means left San Francisco and returned to South Dakota. He found a job in Sturgis, South Dakota, as a bookkeeper with a construction company. He would leave his home, wife, and children frequently, although returning many times over during the course of their marriage. After living for a short time in Mission, South Dakota, on the Rosebud Reservation, Means, his wife, Betty, and their two children moved to Cleveland, Ohio. They divorced in 1970. In Cleveland, Means helped to establish an American Indian Center. It was while establishing the center that Means attended a conference in San Francisco, where met Banks and Bellecourt, the leaders and founders of AIM (Means and Wolf 1995).

Weeks after the conference, Banks and Bellecourt called Means and asked him to attend the National Council of Churches conference with them. At the conference, Banks and Bellecourt questioned the council about the money that they had been accumulating on the behalf of Native children while none of it was being spent on Natives. After being shuffled from room to room, Bellecourt grabbed a microphone during a general assembly and demanded to be heard. He questioned the attendees about following their God's commandments, and he publically questioned their morals. Means became exhilarated by the leaders' ability to confront the crowd regarding their wrongdoings, and he realized that he wanted to join AIM.

After the occupation of Wounded Knee, and court proceedings that went on for years (and jail time), Means ran for tribal office, was nominated to run for president on the Libertarian Party's ticket, and also ran for governor of New Mexico. He assisted with the seizure of 880 acres in the Black Hills, naming the land Yellow Thunder Camp. The sacred land of the camp was held for five years. Means supported several international indigenous issues, including the Miskito Indians against the Sandinistas. He wrote *Where White Men Fear to Tread* with Marvin Wolf. Means starred in several films, including *The Last of the Mohicans*, *Pocahontas*, and *Natural Born Killers*. He also created art, wrote music, and sang.

In 2011, Means learned he had esophageal cancer, which had spread and was inoperable. Means declined chemotherapy and turned instead to indigenous therapies. On October 21, 2012, Russell Means walked on to another realm. Means had married five times and divorced four times, and had ten children.

DOCUMENT EXCERPT

Wounded Knee Trials

After a trial lasting nine months, in St. Paul, Minnesota, U.S. District Judge Fred Nichol dismissed charges against Dennis Banks and Russell Means in 1974, for charges against them in the Wounded Knee occupation in South Dakota.

Memorandum Decision

NICHOL, Chief Judge.

This memorandum decision concludes the trial stage of the government's case against two leaders of the 1973 occupation of Wounded Knee, South Dakota, the historic Indian village. The occupation lasted seventy-one days and the trial lasted slightly over eight months. Although the trial was often protracted and tedious, it came to a swift end. After deliberating the case for about nine hours, one of the jurors became ill and could not continue deliberations. The government would not agree to accept the verdict of the remaining eleven jurors. In the meantime the defense team filed a motion for judgment of acquittal, thus giving this court the alternative of granting a mistrial or ruling on the motion. I have decided to dismiss all charges remaining in this trial.

Defendants' motion for judgment of acquittal is based generally on allegations of government misconduct. The alleged misconduct consists of the following: 1) conspiracy to suborn perjury and to cover up said subornation in the case of Louis Moves Camp, a prosecution witness; 2) suppression of an FBI statement exposing the perjury of Alexander David Richards, a prosecution witness; 3) illegal and unconstitutional use of military personnel and material at Wounded Knee and the government's effort to cover up said use; 4) violation of applicable professional, ethical and moral standards; and 5) various other incidents of governmental misconduct. For the reasons given below, this court treats defendants' motion as a motion for dismissal and grants judgment of dismissal.

At the end of the decision, District Judge Fred Nichol had disappointed and harsh criticism against the U.S. government for its prosecution of the case.

Conclusion

This court is mindful of the heavy responsibility that it bears in our criminal justice system. It is unquestionably essential to our society that our laws be enforced swiftly and surely. This court also believes, however, that our society is not bettered by law enforcement that, although it may be swift and sure, is not conducted in a spirit of fairness or good faith. Those who break our laws must be brought to account for their wrongs, but it is imperative that they be brought to this accounting through an orderly procedure conducted in the spirit of justice. This court's first duty, then, is to insure that our laws are fairly enforced, or as Mr. Chief Justice Warren aptly put it: "[our duty] is to see that the waters of justice are not polluted." *Mesarosh v. United States, supra,* 352 U.S. at 14, 77 S. Ct. at 8.

Although it hurts me deeply, I am forced to the conclusion that the prosecution in this trial had something other than attaining justice foremost in its mind. In deciding this motion I have taken into consideration the prosecution's conduct throughout the entire trial. The fact that incidents of misconduct formed a pattern throughout the course of the trial leads me to the belief that this case was not prosecuted in good faith or in the spirit of justice. The waters of justice have been polluted, and dismissal, I believe, is the appropriate cure for the pollution in this case.

Source: United States v. Banks, 383 F. Supp. 389 (D.S.D. 1974).

See also: Occupation of Alcatraz, 1969–1971; Anna Mae Pictou Aquash (1945–1975)

Further Reading

Akwesasne Notes. *Voices from Wounded Knee.* Cornwall Island Reserve, Canada: Akwesasne Notes, 1974.

Banks, Dennis and Richard Erdoes. *Ojibwa Warrior: Dennis Banks and the Rise of the American Indian Movement.* Norman: University of Oklahoma Press, 2004.

Churchill, Ward. *Acts of Violence: The Ward Churchill Reader.* New York: Routledge, 2003.

Cook-Lynn, Elizabeth. "Twentieth-Century American Indian Political Dissent and Russell Means." *Wicazo Sa Review.* Vol. 29, No. 1, 2014.

Deloria, Vine, Jr. "Alcatraz, Activism, and Accommodation." Edited by Troy Johnson, Joane Nagel, and Duane Champagne. *American Indian Activism: Alcatraz to the Longest Walk.* Urbana: University of Illinois Press, 1997.

Deloria, Vine, Jr. *Behind the Trail of Broken Treaties.* Austin: University of Texas Press, 1985.

Hendricks, Steve. *The Unquiet Grave: The FBI and the Struggle for the Soul of Indian Country.* New York: Thunder's Mouth Press, 2006.

Johansen, Bruce. *Encyclopedia of the American Indian Movement.* Santa Barbara, CA: Greenwood, 2013.

Kunstler, William M. "By Hook or by Crook," *Hamline Law Review*, Vol. 8, pp. 611–624, 1985.

Matthiessen, Peter. *In the Spirit of Crazy Horse.* New York: Viking, 1991.

Means, Russell and Marvin J. Wolf. *Where White Men Fear to Tread: The Autobiography of Russell Means.* New York: St. Martin's Press, 1995.

Mohawk, John. "Directions in Peoples Movements." Edited by Susan Lobo, Steve Talbot, and Traci L. Morris. *Native American Voices.* New York: Prentice Hall, 2010, pp. 463–468.

Nagel, Joane. *American Indian Ethnic Renewal: Red Power and the Resurgence of Identity and Culture.* New York: Oxford University Press, 1996.

Sayer, John William. *Ghost Dancing the Law: The Wounded Knee Trials.* Cambridge: Harvard University Press, 1997.

Smith, Paul Chaat and Robert Warrior. *Like a Hurricane: The Indian Movement from Alcatraz to Wounded Knee*. New York: New Press, 1996.

Weyler, Rex. *Blood of the Land: The Government and Corporate War against the American Indian Movement*. New York: Random House, 1982.

Occupation of Alcatraz, 1969–1971

Paul McKenzie-Jones

Chronology of Events

1945   Congress approves the passage of Senator Arthur Watkins House Concurrent Resolution 108, which called for termination of the federal trust relationship between the United States and its indigenous nations.

1956   Congress asks the Bureau of Indian Affairs to implement the Indian Relocation Act, under which a relocation program was aimed at bringing reservation-based American Indians into the cities as a means of improving employment prospects and assimilating into the dominant culture.

1963   The federal government shuts down the high-security prison on Alcatraz Island due to crumbling infrastructure and spiraling maintenance costs.

1964   In what is an admitted publicity stunt, four young Sioux residents of San Francisco "reclaim" Alcatraz Island for American Indians, citing a clause in the 1868 Treaty of Fort Laramie that promised to return any decommissioned federal lands to the Sioux Nations. The occupation lasts four hours.

1968   A traveling band of Native activists, poets, and artisans, calling themselves the White Roots of Peace, begin touring the United States preaching acceptance and culture based upon Iroquois traditions.

1969   The San Francisco Indian center burns down, and the city refuses to allocate funds to rebuild it.

Richard Oakes dives into San Francisco Bay and begins the occupation of Alcatraz Island.

1970   Richard Nixon delivers a "Special Message to Congress" calling for "self-determination without termination."

Richard Oakes's daughter dies after falling down a flight of concrete stairs, forcing him to leave the occupation.

1971 The occupation ends after factionalism, alcohol, and drug issues cause chaos among the last remaining activists on the island.

1975 Congress passes the Indian Self-Determination and Education Assistance Act, which formally recognizes the rights of federally recognized American Indian nations to govern through their own laws and implement their own culturally relevant education policies and programs.

The American Indian Occupation of Alcatraz Island

The 1969 occupation of Alcatraz Island was a landmark moment in contemporary American Indian history. Building upon the militant rhetoric of the National Indian Youth Council, disaffected urban Indians seized the island and catapulted American Indian issues onto the global stage. The occupation signified a major shift in Indian activism as the protestors adopted the mantra of Red Power from a foundation of cultural retention to one of political militancy. Using treaty rhetoric and the language of federal Indian policy as weapons of protest, the Indians transformed the art of activism from protests and blockades to land seizure and reclamation. The event changed the face of Indian/white relations and inspired further movements to organize in the fight for tribal sovereignty and self-determination.

A group of American Indians, members of Indians of All tribes, occupy the former prison at Alcatraz Island in San Francisco Bay, California, on November 25, 1969. The occupation of the island drew public attention to the plight of American Indians and resulted in significant changes in the federal government's policies, including improvements in education and health care. (AP Photo)

On November 20, 1969, several boatloads teeming with American Indian students disembarked on the abandoned federal prison island of Alcatraz. Isolated as it was, alone on a rocky island surrounded by the shark-infested waters of San Francisco Bay, the prison was most famous for being inescapable: in its almost 30-year history as a federal prison until its closure in 1965, there was only one successful escape out of a mere 14 attempts. As such, the thought of a group of people breaking into the island prison just a year after its closure was indeed a strange concept to the general public at that time. In the years before its conversion to a federal prison, Alcatraz served as a military prison, which ironically held American Indian prisoners at various times. The first Indian to be imprisoned on Alcatraz as a military prisoner of the United States was a Paiute who arrived in 1873.

Over the course of the next several years, an estimated ten or eleven Indians of a variety of nations were imprisoned on Alcatraz, including in 1874, Natchez (Paiute), the brother of Sarah Winnemucca, and in 1881, at the height of General George Crook's campaign against the Chiricahua Apache, Kaetana, an influential war chief. Two years after his incarceration, when he was allowed to return to Arizona, Crook sent a letter to General Sheridan noting that "Ka-e-te-na . . . who less than two years ago was the worst Chiricahua of the whole lot, is now perfectly subdued. He is thoroughly reconstructed, has rendered me valuable assistance and will be of great service in helping me to control these Indians in the future. His stay at Alcatraz has worked a complete reformation in his character." The largest number of American Indians prisoners held at the island prison, at least until the occupation, was 19 Hopi Indians incarcerated between January and August 1895 "until they shall evince, in an unmistakable manner, a desire to cease interference with the plans of the government for the civilization and education of its Indian wards, and will make proper promises of good behavior in the future."

The 1969 invasion was not a mere publicity stunt, however, but was rather the result of months of meticulous preparation to begin an unarmed occupation of the island as a means of highlighting treaty abrogation, broken promises of relocation officers, and termination of the federal trust relationship with tribes across the country. Nor was it the first such attempt to take over the island. There had been two previous attempts, both more symbolic gestures than the practical effort of the third attempt. The first occupation lasted four hours and occurred in March 1964. This short-lived occupation was led by Richard McKenzie, a Lakota from the Rosebud reservation, as he and four other Sioux residents of San Francisco laid claim to Alcatraz, citing the 1868 Treaty of Fort Laramie as promising to return all surplus federal land to the Sioux Nations with whom the United States signed the treaty. Within this claim, they also demanded that the island be used as an American Indian university. While the attorney general decided that the claims were without legal foundation, it was only a month later that the island was indeed declared to be surplus federal land.

This rhetoric was recalled and developed six years later during the full 19-month occupation that lasted from November 20, 1969, until June 20 1971. The second, intervening occupation attempt, although intended as the occupation date, ended

Sidebar 1: Termination Policy

In 1953, Senator Arthur V. Watkins of Utah, presented House Concurrent Resolution 103 to Congress. The bill was designed to terminate the federal trust relationship between the government and federally recognized Indian nations. Since the end of World War II, Congress had been focused upon extricating itself from the "Indian business," and Watkins's termination policy offered them just such a route. The policy was enacted by identifying tribes deemed capable of being part of mainstream American society and putting before them a proposal to sign away their rights and expectations to the continued support of the federal government's social and economic treaty obligations. Under the policy, which ran from 1953 until 1968, but was only formally repealed by the 1975 Self-Determination Act, 109 tribes were terminated, with federal jurisdiction and responsibility being handed over to the relevant states. The majority of state governments had no intention of inheriting the federal obligations and acted accordingly (or ignored them). Two of the most famous tribal cases during the Termination era were the Menominee and Klamath tribes. The Menominee, of Wisconsin, had such successful lumber and forestry operations that the BIA was convinced the tribe could function sustainably without federal support. The Klamath, of Oregon, were targeted for similar reasons, having valuable timber resources on their land. Termination was devastating for both tribes, with poverty and homelessness realities for many tribal members. Citizens of both tribes began campaigning to have the process reversed, and recognition restored. While the Menominee were successful in 1973, it took the Klamath until 1986 to win restoration as a federally recognized tribe. During the Termination era, approximately 2.5 million acres of land fell out of federal trust status, and 12,000 American Indians lost their tribal affiliation, thus ceasing to be recognized as Indian by the federal government. (See also Termination Policy, Mid-1940s to Mid-1960s.)

up becoming a dress rehearsal for the student occupiers, calling themselves Indians of All Tribes to represent the multi-tribal coalition of the individuals involved (Smith and Warrior, 11). In both instances, the primary instigators were a young Mohawk student activist named Richard Oakes and a middle-aged civil organizer named Adam Nordwall (Shoshone). Both men were aware of the treaty rhetoric used by the 1964 occupiers but moved in very different circles until they met a Halloween party thrown by journalist Tim Findley just days before the invasion. Each had been devising his own plan for occupation of the island with the intent of

Sidebar 2: Relocation Program

The congressionally mandated Indian Relocation Program ran concurrently with the Termination Policy. Aimed at relieving American Indian poverty by removing Indians from reservations and relocating them into cities, the program resulted in the largest migration of American Indians in U.S. history—larger even than any of the formed removals of the 1830s or post-Civil War era. Modeled after the 1950 Navajo-Hopi Rehabilitation Act, which was deemed a success after four years despite having a ten-year goal to boost economic situations of both people's, the Relocation Program was a response to a 1950 census report that highlighted the massive economic disparity between American Indians and other groups within the United States. According to the census, the average reservation-based American Indian earned $950 per year. This contrasted with the average African American earnings of $2,000 per year, and the average white annual income of $4,000. Nine major U.S. cities were chosen as relocation centers, mainly due to their proximity to the larger number of reservation-based American Indians. As such, Chicago, Denver, Los Angeles, San Francisco, San Jose, St. Louis, Cincinnati, Cleveland, and Dallas saw a huge influx of American Indians in the second half of the twentieth century. While the intention was for the Indians to ultimately assimilate into the larger population, one unintended consequence was the creation of Indian centers, such as the one that burned down in San Francisco, by the newly relocated residents determined to provide a place of community and help for those new relocatees who did not receive the services promised them by the BIA. The oldest continually running urban Indian Center is in Chicago, which first opened its doors in 1953. While many Natives eventually decided that city life was not for them, and returned to the reservations, it is estimated that approximately 750,000 American Indians migrated to cities between 1950 and 1980, mostly as a result of the Relocation Program. To put this into context, in the 1940 census, eight percent of American Indians were city dwellers. In 2000, that figure had risen to 79 percent. (See also Bureau of Indian Affairs American Indian Relocation Program, 1952.)

developing the community center and university that McKenzie and his fellow Sioux had demanded five years earlier, and both were spurred into urgency by the October 10 fire that burned the San Francisco Indian Center to the ground. The center was a focal point for urban Indian residents and a haven of community and friendship for relocated Indians trying to adjust to life in a foreign city. Its sudden loss struck at the heart of San Francisco's Native community as they now had no place to call their own (Smith and Warrior, 13).

While Nordwall, Oakes, and others wondered aloud about the legality of the Fort Laramie claims in relation to Alcatraz (Smith and Warrior, 15), the treaty claim was in many ways a symbolic gesture as no San Francisco land had been exchanged in that 1868 treaty. As such, the Sioux Nations had no real legal claim to the island under the Fort Laramie treaty, Their argument of sovereign indigenous occupancy carried more weight but no 'legal' substance under California law. What they were claiming was ownership on behalf of all Indians rather than specifically for their own people, in response to the myriad of treaty promises that the United States had made, and then broken, during the short, but tumultuous, history of Indian/white relations. The concept of a needing a community "home" in the San Francisco area tied neatly into the concept of reclamation of the land with Alcatraz Island, as everywhere else in the United States, originally being indigenous homelands. The original inhabitants of the coastal region from Point Sur, in central California, to San Francisco in the north, were the Ohlone, a linguistically connected group of almost 50 different indigenous nations. After European contact and colonization, originally by the Spanish, before the United States acquired the land, the populations of Ohlone people had dwindled to fewer than 1,000 people, with the last monolingual fluent speaker dying in 1939. The modern descendants of the various Ohlone nations have consolidated their community into the state-recognized Muwekma Ohlone tribe of the San Francisco Bay area and in the early 21st century began to aggressively pursue culture and language revitalization programs. In 1969, with there being no cohesive Ohlone community present, the urban student coalition Indians of All Tribes attempted to reclaim their land in absentia.

The language of reclamation and treaty abrogation was made clear on November 9, 1969, just eleven days before the full occupation. The moment was exponentially more frenetic an event than either of those that sandwiched it. In the buildup to the proposed landing on Alcatraz, Nordwall briefed local news reporters on their plans, under oath of secrecy, leaking the time and location of the departure from Fisherman's Wharf. At the proposed moment, Nordwall, Oakes, and the rest of the activists turned up to a throng of reporters eager to chronicle the occasion, including a boatload ready to record the actual landing. The only problem was that the prearranged boats to take the Indians across the bay had not turned up. As Nordwall hurriedly tried to track the boats down, and Oakes stalled the reporters with a drawn-out reading of the Alcatraz Proclamation, salvation appeared in the form of a schooner named *Monte Christo*. Nordwall convinced the captain, Richard Craig, to allow them aboard, although he agreed only to take them around the perimeter of the island rather than dock and allow them to disembark (Smith and Warrior, 16).

As the boat neared Alcatraz, Richard Oakes decided that simply circling the island was not enough, stripped off his shirt, and dived in the frigid waters of San Francisco Bay. As he swam to shore, his body attempting to adjust to the exhilaration of his actions as well as the strong current and icy water, the captain turned the ship away from the island, but not quickly enough to prevent three more students jumping ship to catch up with Oakes. Although they were picked up by the Coast Guard and returned to Fisherman's Wharf within the hour, a marker had been laid down. After returning surreptitiously the following night, on a boat called the *New Vera II,* with half a dozen other people, and informing the lone federal employee remaining on the island that they claimed it on behalf of all Indians, Oakes decided that a more emphatic statement needed to be made. Symbolism was no longer enough, and the occupation needed to happen for real (Fortunate Eagle, 82).

Ten days later, in the dark early hours of November 20, several boats carrying a combined total of 78 American Indian students docked on the east side of the island. Among them were Oakes, who was elected as the group's spokesman rather than leader, and LaNada Means, who would later become a prominent figure of the occupation. After the landing became public knowledge, the Coast Guard organized a blockade, and state and federal officials scrambled to draft a response, the island occupiers set about creating as habitable an environment as possible on the abandoned edifice of rock. Amid the euphoria of the successful landing, the proclamation that Oakes had used as a stalling technique a week and a half earlier was released to the public. Amid the rhetoric of land reclamation and treaty inequity, the paucity of American Indian life on reservations across the United States was laid bare in ten poignant observations. These observations, were inserted midway through the proclamation, which was written by Nordwall, who was not on the island, but attending an education conference in Minneapolis. It read,

> "We feel that this so-called Alcatraz Island is more than suitable for an Indian Reservation, as determined by the white man's own standards. By this we mean that this place resembles most Indian reservations in that:
>
> 1. It is isolated from modern facilities, and without adequate means of transportation.
> 2. It has no fresh running water.
> 3. It has inadequate sanitation facilities.
> 4. There are no oil or mineral rights.
> 5. There is no industry and so unemployment is very great.
> 6. There are no health care facilities.
> 7. The soil is rocky and non-productive; and the land does not support game.

8. There are no educational facilities.
9. The population has always exceeded the land base.
10. The population has always been held as prisoners and kept dependent upon others.

Further, it would be fitting and symbolic that ships from all over the world, entering the Golden Gate, would first see Indian land, and thus be reminded of the true history of this nation. This tiny island would be a symbol of the great lands once ruled by free and noble Indians." (American Indian Center, 1969)

While the words themselves were nothing new in Indian affairs, and reflected attacks on the federal administration of Indian peoples and lands by members of the National Indian Youth Council, the National Congress of American Indians, and the Society of American Indians, as well as the government's own early 20th-century Meriam Report, the media attention to the occupation gave the charges an international exposure that none of these previous examples had experienced. The scale of the favorable public reactions to the occupation was exponentially reflected by the number of American Indians who flocked to San Francisco with the intention of beating the Coast Guard blockade and joining their fellow indigenous counterparts on the island.

What they hoped to help create was a vision of turning the desolation described in the proclamation into a thriving focal point of American Indian cultures and values open to any members of all tribes across the nation. Oakes described plans for a enter for Native American Studies, an American Indian Spiritual Center, an Indian Center of Ecology, an Indian Training School, and an American Indian Museum. As a student, and one who had recently been galvanized to fight for what was important by the visit of the White Roots of Peace to the San Francisco Bay area, education was a fundamental necessity to any improvement in American Indian life in America. The reality of life on the island was, however, quickly deteriorating for the occupiers, despite the blockade being lifted. While this enabled supporters to send provisions to the island, it also allowed increasing numbers of supporters to land. The numbers of arrivals, with an estimated total of 5,600 American Indians coming and going from the island during the occupation, meant that the island population almost always exceeded its meager resources.

Within a few short months on the island, the lack of amenities and isolation began to take their toll, with increasing factionalism and violence breaking out among the occupiers. One of the major issues to emerge was growing among the island occupiers toward the attention received by Richard Oakes. As he spent more time away from the island attending dinners and press conferences on the mainland, people began to doubt his commitment to the cause, as well as the influence of those Indians on the mainland who were handling many of the organizational decisions for those on the rock. Matters came to a head in a December 1969 conference when LaNada Means, Richard Oakes, and others sat at a table underneath a banner that read, "Indians on Alcatraz will Rule Alcatraz" (Fortunate Eagle, 160). This public display of unity between the island Indians and Oakes did not last too long, however, and moves were taken behind the scenes to remove him as the de facto leader of Alcatraz. Before these moves could materialize into action, however, a personal tragedy struck Oakes, from which he never recovered.

On January 3, 1970, Yvonne Oakes, the twelve-year-old daughter of Richard and Anne, slipped on the third-floor landing of their apartment building, which had previously housed prison guards and the island's caretaker, and fell straight to the concrete floor below. She lay in a coma for five days in an Oakland, California hospital before finally succumbing to the injuries sustained in the fall. Richard Oakes returned to Alcatraz only long enough to recover his belongings and then left the island permanently. Perhaps surprisingly, given the attempts to subvert his leadership, Oakes's departure left a power vacuum that threatened to devolve into an ungovernable factionalism that would undo all the good work of the occupation. It was here that LaNada Means (Shoshone) and John Trudell (Santee Sioux) stepped into the breach and saved the occupation from imploding. Means had been on the island from the very first day and was a well-respected figure among the people who remained, and was entrusted with trying to push forward with the creation of a permanent Native American university on the island. Trudell, meanwhile, had gained an increasing profile as the voice of Radio Free Alcatraz, an ad hoc broadcast in which he interviewed visitors and residents of the island and expressed the political issues at stake with calm assuredness over the airwaves (Fortunate Eagle, 170).

Life on the island continued to become increasingly tense, however, especially after the authorities cut off all water and power supplies to the island. On June 1, 1970, a fire engulfed sections of the island and burned down the iconic lighthouse. With the water having been cut off on the island, the residents had little left to fight the fire with and simply had to survey the damage the next day. Despite such setbacks, and increasingly belligerent tactics from the state and federal authorities, the occupation continued. Fire, to the San Francisco Indian Center, had been one of the final catalysts to the occupation, after all. It was not going to be allowed to bring it to its knees. Another fire, later in the occupation, seriously burned LaNada Means as she sought to keep the flames from her son, but ultimately it was a second invasion, this time by federal marshals, that brought the occupation to an end. By the time of the June 11, 1971, landing, only 15 Indians remained on the island. Trudell and Means had stayed almost to the end, but they, too, were gone when the marshals landed and removed the final residents.

Throughout the occupation, the federal response to the activists had been a source of frustration. Initially reacting in a somewhat typical manner, by blockading the island and attempting to stop any traffic—either people or supplies, on or off Alcatraz—the government then lifted the blockade and agreed to negotiate with Oakes, Nordwall, and others. Negotiations were more lip service than literal, however, from both sides of the divide. The Indians steadfastly insisted that they would settle for nothing less than the university, cultural center, and museum, while the government was equally trenchant in their demands that the occupation cease, and the Indians leave the island. Neither side was willing to compromise. At most, the federal acquiescence to negotiations was merely a waiting tactic, as government advisors expected the occupation to last a far shorter period of time than it ultimately did. When the federal marshals landed and removed the final 15 residents, Trudell noted that the entire federal strategy had been to lie to them. Many people argue that the occupation of Alcatraz was ultimately a failure, as the demands for free title to the island and the creation of a community center, museum, and university never materialized. This, however, ignores the monumental shifts in public perception, understanding, and law that Alcatraz was responsible for. For several years after the occupation, Indian rights were firmly in the public consciousness, and America's indigenous peoples were no long invisible. The administration of Richard Nixon, already committed to reforming Indian policy and ending termination, went further and pushed for education assistance for American Indians to be written into law. In Indian country, there was a massive shift in outspokenness and cultural advocacy as through the exposure Alcatraz received in comparison to earlier movements, an increasing number of young American Indians found the confidence and inspiration to speak out against the institutional and social injustices they suffered on a daily basis. Historically, the occupation of Alcatraz is a seminal moment, when the culturally focused Red Power of the National Indian Youth Council evolved into a vociferously militant call for political power and recognition through the actions and rhetoric of Indians of All Tribes.

Biographies

Richard Oakes (1942–1972) was born on May 22, 1942, in Mohawk Nation territory at Akwesasne in New York. After a childhood learning the tradition lifeways of the Mohawk people, he started adult life as a high steelworker, a common and contemporary Mohawk tradition for young men seeking work. After visiting San Francisco, however, he decided to pursue higher education and enrolled in San Francisco State University. After a visit by a traveling group of activists preaching traditional Mohawk belief systems, and values of peace, Oakes was galvanized into challenging the university to offer more culturally relevant classes for the Native student population. Oakes himself wrote the curriculum for the Native American studies department that the university eventually agreed to. After the occupation of Alcatraz, Oakes continued to fight for American Indian rights, and aided the Pit River Indians as they attempted to reclaim three million acres of land from Pacific Gas and Electric. Several months after leaving Alcatraz after the death of his daughter, Yvonne, Oakes was left in a coma for several days following a bar fight in which he was hit over the head with a pool cue. A visit to his bedside by Wallace Mad Bear Anderson is credited as the catalyst to his recovery. On September 20, 1972, Oakes was shot to death in an altercation with Michael Morgan, a YMCA camp manager with a reputation for treating Native children in his care badly.

Adam Fortunate Eagle (1929–) was born Adam Nordwall on the Red Lake reservation but spent much of his childhood at Pipestone Indian Training School after his father died. The name Fortunate Eagle was given to him by a Crow elder in 1971. Upon graduating from boarding school, he attended the Haskell Institute of Kansas (now Haskell Indian Nations University). After moving to San Francisco and creating his own successful termite company, *First American Termite Company,* it was he, in his role as chairman of the United Bay Area Council of American Indian Affairs, Inc., who proposed the occupation of Alcatraz. After Alcatraz, Fortunate Eagle taught Native American Studies at California State University Hayward. It was there that, through a colleague, he was invited to attend the International Conference of World Futures in Rome. As he exited the plane, Fortunate Eagle "claimed" Italy through the right of discovery. Also a successful author, Fortunate Eagle has written three books, *Pipestone, My Life in an Indian Barding School, Heart of the Rock,* his account of the Alcatraz occupation, and *Scalping Columbus and other Damn Indian Stories,* a collection of personal stories and anecdotes.

LaNada War Jack (née Means) (1945–) was born and raised on the Shoshone Bannock reservation and sporadically attended BIA boarding schools before becoming the first American Indian student to enroll in the University of California Berkeley. While at Berkeley, Means co-founded an organization called United Native Americans, which became a key player in the years of militant activism that followed Alcatraz. She was also a committed anti-war protestor against the United States' involvement in Vietnam. After the occupation, Means remained committed to American Indian treaty rights and education, receiving her bachelor's degree in Native American law and politics in 1971. In 1999, she gained her doctorate in political science from Idaho State University. She has also served on the Fort Hall Business Council of the Shoshone Bannock tribes as well as spending three years as the tribal executive director, overseeing more than 60 tribal departments and advising council members on organizational and policy initiatives. Since 2008, she has been President of Indigenous Visions network, an educational organization dedicated to increasing awareness of the historical issues of oppression and colonization since European contact.

John Trudell (1946–) was born in Omaha, Nebraska, and raised in a variety of towns in Nebraska and South Dakota. Before Alcatraz, Trudell had dropped out of school at 16 and joined the navy. After serving in Vietnam, he left the navy in 1967 and enrolled in radio and broadcast studies at San Bernardino Community College. After Alcatraz, Trudell was a prominent member of the American Indian Movement and involved in the height of the Native activist protests that culminated in the 1973 armed stand-off with the federal government at the Wounded Knee hamlet at Pine Ridge, South Dakota, including the Trail of Broken Treaties. He was also national chairman of AIM from 1973 to 1979. Trudell lost his wife and children in a tragic fire at the home of his in-laws in 1979. While Trudell firmly believed that the fire was a deliberate arson attack in retaliation for his and his family's activism, the BIA deemed the fire accidental.

After his family's deaths, Trudell turned to music and released the highly acclaimed *Tribal Voices* album in 1983, in which he skillfully wove together a complex thread of spoken word poetry over a layer of traditional northern and southern plains drum songs. As well as being a highly sought after motivational speaker, Trudell was a successful actor and writer. He appeared in several successful films, including *Thunderheart, On Deadly Ground,* and *Smoke Signals,* and also starred in Hallmark's TV movie, *Dreamkeeper.* In 2008, he released *Lines from a Mined Mind: The Words of John Trudell*, a collection of his lyrics, poetry, and essays since he began writing after his wife's death. He is also the subject of a 2005 biographic documentary *Trudell.*

DOCUMENT EXCERPTS

House Concurrent Resolution 108

HCR 108 is the federal bill that is more commonly known as the "Termination Bill," which formally set the federal government on the path of "getting out of the Indian Business."

"Whereas it is the policy of Congress, as rapidly as possible, to make the Indians within the territorial limits of the United States subject to the same laws and entitled to the same privileges and responsibilities as are applicable to other citizens of the United States, to end their status as wards of the United States, and to grant them all of the rights and prerogatives pertaining to American citizenship. . . .

Resolved by the House of Representatives (the Senate concurring),

That it is declared to be the sense of Congress that, at the earliest possible time, all of the Indian tribes . . . located within the States of California, Florida, New York, and Texas . . . should be freed from Federal supervision and control and from all disabilities and limitations specifically applicable to Indians. . . ."

Source: August 1, 1953 | [H. Con. Res. 108] 67 Stat. B122. In Keppler, Charles. *Indian Affairs: Laws and Treaties.* Volume VI, Laws. Washington, D.C.: Government Printing Office.

Indian Relocation Act

The Indian Relocation Act of 1956 was inspired by the success of the Navajo-Hopi rehabilitation bill in removing destitute Navajo and Hopi citizens to nearby urban centers.

"Be it enacted by the Senate and House of Representatives of the United States of America in Congress assembled, That in order to help adult Indians who reside on or near Indian reservations to obtain reasonable and satisfactory employment, the Secretary of the Interior is authorized to undertake a program of vocational training that provides for vocational counseling or guidance, institutional training in any recognized vocation or trade, apprenticeship, and on the job training, for periods that do not exceed twenty-four months, transportation to the place of training, and subsistence during the course of training. The program shall be available primarily to Indians who are not less than eighteen and not more than thirty-five years of age and who reside on or near an Indian reservation, and the program shall be conducted under such rules and regulations as the Secretary may prescribe."

Source: Public Law 959, Chapter 930, [S. 3416] 70 Stat. 986. August 3, 1956.

Alcatraz Proclamation

The Alcatraz Proclamation formally announced the intention of the Indians of All Nations to seize Alcatraz in lieu of broken treaty promises. The document serves as a banner of self-determination even today.

"Proclamation to the Great White Father and All His People

We, the Native Americans, re-claim the land known as Alcatraz Island in the name of all American Indians by right of discovery.

We wish to be fair and honorable in our dealings with the Caucasian inhabitants of this land, and hereby offer the following treaty:

We will purchase said Alcatraz Island for twenty-four dollars ($24) in glass beads and red cloth, a precedent set by the white man's purchase of a similar island about 300 years ago. We know that $24 in trade goods for these 16 acres is more than was paid when Manhattan Island was sold, but we know that land values have risen over the years. Our offer of $1.24 per acre is greater than the 47¢ per acre that the white men are now paying the California Indians for their land. We will give to the inhabitants of this island a portion of that land for their own, to be held in trust by the American Indian Affairs [sic] and by the bureau of Caucasian Affairs to hold in perpetuity—for as long as the sun shall rise and the rivers go down to the sea. We will further guide the inhabitants in the proper way of living. We will offer them our religion, our education, our life-ways, in order to help them achieve our level of civilization and thus raise them and all their white brothers up from their savage and unhappy state. We offer this treaty in good faith and wish to be fair and honorable in our dealings with all white men."

Source: http://www.historyisaweapon.com/defcon1/alcatrazproclamationandletter.html

Alcatraz Letter

This letter was sent out as a call to arms to raise awareness and support of the Alcatraz occupation.

December 16, 1969

Dear Brothers and Sisters:

This is a call for a delegation from each Indian nation, tribe, or band from throughout the United States, Canada, and Mexico to meet together on Alcatraz Island in San Francisco Bay, on December 23, 1969, for a meeting to be tentatively called the Confederation of American Indian Nations (CAIN).

On November 20, 1969, 78 Indian people, under the name "Indians of All Tribes," moved on to Alcatraz Island, a former Federal Prison. We began cleaning up the Island and are still in the process of organizing, setting up classes and trying to instill the old Indian ways into our young.

We moved onto Alcatraz Island because we feel that Indian people need a Cultural Center of their own. For several decades, Indian people have not had enough control of training their young people. And without a cultural center of their own, we are afraid that the old Indian ways may be lost. We believe that the only way to keep them alive is for Indian people to do it themselves.

While it was a small group which moved onto the island, we want all Indian people to join with us. More Indian people from throughout the country are coming to the island every day. We are issuing this call in an attempt to unify all our Indian Brothers behind a common cause.

We realize that there are more problems in Indian communities besides having our culture taken away. We have water problems, land problems, "social" problems, job opportunity problems, and many others.

And as Vice President Agnew said at the annual convention of the National Congress of American Indians in October of this year, now is the time for Indian leadership.

We realize too that we are not getting anywhere fast by working alone as individual tribes. If we can gather together as brothers and come to a common agreement, we feel that we can be much more effective, doing things for ourselves, instead of having someone else doing it, telling us what is good for us.

So we must start somewhere. We feel that if we are going to succeed, we must hold on to the old ways. *This is the first and most important reason we went to Alcatraz Island.* [Italics in the letter.]

Source: http://www.historyisaweapon.com/defcon1/alcatrazproclamationandletter.html

Nixon's Special Message

Nixon's special message was his declaration to seek ways in which American Indian governments could function more autonomously, and is seen as the beginning of the self-determination era, even though the Self-Determination Act was not passed until 1975.

To the Congress of the United States:

The first Americans—the Indians—are the most deprived and most isolated minority group in our nation. On virtually very scale of measurement -employment, income, education, health—the condition of the Indian people ranks at the bottom.

This condition is the heritage of centuries of injustice. From the time of their first contact with European settlers, the American Indians have been oppressed and brutalized, deprived of their ancestral lands and denied the opportunity to control their own destiny. Even the Federal programs which are intended to meet their needs have frequently proved to be ineffective and demeaning.

This, then, must be the goal of any new national policy toward the Indian people to strengthen the Indian's sense of autonomy without threatening this sense of community. We must assure the Indian that he can assume control of his own life without being separated involuntary from the tribal group. And we must make it clear that Indians can become independent of Federal control without being cut off from

Federal concern and Federal support. My specific recommendations to the Congress are designed to carry out this policy . . .

Source: Public Papers of the Presidents of the United States: Richard Nixon, 1970. Washington, D.C.: Government Printing Office, 1971, 564–76.

See also: National Indian Youth Council, 1961; American Indian Movement, 1968

Further Reading

Alcatraz History. Accessed July 17, 2015. www.alcatrazhistory.com

American Indian Center Seizure of Alcatraz Island. 1969. Digital History ID 721. Digital History. Accessed February 28, 2016. http://www.digitalhistory.uh.edu/disp_textbook.cfm?smtid=3&psid=721

Fortunate Eagle, Adam. *Heart of the Rock: The Indian Invasion of Alcatraz,* Norma: University of Oklahoma Press, 2002.

History Is a Weapon. "Alcatraz Letter and Proclamation." Accessed July 12, 2015. http://www.historyisaweapon.com/defcon1/alcatrazproclamationandletter.html Accessed July 12, 2015

Johnson, Troy. *The American Indian Occupation of Alcatraz Island: Red Power and Self-Determination.* Lincoln: University of Nebraska Press, 2008.

Josephy, Alvin and Troy Johnson. *Red Power: The American Indians' Fight for Freedom.* Lincoln: University of Nebraska Press, 1999.

Nagel, Joane. *American Indian Ethnic Renewal: Red Power and the Resurgence of Identity and Culture.* Oxford, UK: Oxford University Press, 1997.

Smith, Paul Chaat and Robert Warrior. *Like a Hurricane: The Indian Movement from Alcatraz to Wounded Knee.* New York: The New Press, 1996.

U.S. National Park Service. Alcatraz Island. "We Hold the Rock." 2016. Accessed July 17, 2015. http://www.nps.gov/alca/learn/historyculture/we-hold-the-rock.htm

Winton, Ben. "The Occupation of Alcatraz: Don't Give Us Apologies. Give Us What We Really Want." Feb. 28, 2012. Accessed July 31, 2015. http://www.thenativepress.com/life/alcatraz.php

7

Self-Determination and Sovereignty, 1970–Present

Ojibwe Treaty Rights, 1974

Patty Loew

Chronology of Events

1837 The Lake Superior tribe of Chippewa (Ojibwe) signs a cession treaty giving up over 13 million acres in what would become northern Wisconsin and east central Minnesota. Treaty signers reserve the rights to hunt, fish, and gather in the ceded territory.

1842 The Ojibwes cede just over 19 million acres in present-day Wisconsin and Michigan's Upper Peninsula, again reserving harvesting rights in the ceded territory.

1854 The Ojibwes cede an additional 6 million acres in present-day northeastern Minnesota and establish permanent reservations in Wisconsin, Minnesota, and Michigan. The treaty contains no language related to harvesting rights.

1901 Chief Blackbird is arrested and convicted of violating Wisconsin conservation laws on the reservation. The Wisconsin Supreme Court reverses the decision, ruling that the state has no jurisdiction within the reservation boundaries.

1974 Two brothers from the Lac Courte Oreilles Ojibwe (LCO) band are cited for violating Wisconsin conservation laws related to spearfishing off the reservation. LCO sues the state of Wisconsin.

1978 Federal Judge James Doyle rules against the Ojibwe. LCO and other Ojibwe bands who signed the 1837 and 1842 treaties appeal.

1983 The U.S. Court of Appeals for the Seventh Circuit reverses Judge Doyle's decision in what becomes known as the *Voigt* decision. The state of Wisconsin appeals. The U.S. Supreme Court refuses to hear the case. Governor Anthony Earl issues Executive Order 31, which orders all state agencies to abide by the ruling and work "in a spirit of cooperation."

1984 The Ojibwe bands form Great Lakes Indian Fish and Wildlife Commission (GLIFWC), which manages harvesting activities in the ceded territory. Federal court proceedings continue in three phases to determine the scope, regulation, and damages to which the Ojibwes are entitled.

1985 Under GLIFWC supervision, tribal members move off reservation to spearfish in ceded territory lakes. They are met by small groups of anti-treaty protestors.

1986 Treaty rights become a major issue in the gubernatorial campaign. Anti-treaty groups, including Protect Americans' Rights and Resources (PARR) and Stop Treaty Abuse-Wisconsin (STA-Wisconsin), form. Gubernatorial candidate Tommy Thompson meets with PARR, and STA-Wisconsin, promises to fight treaty rights, and wins election.

1987 Judge Doyle imposes regulations to protect the fishery, but rules that the Ojibwes are entitled to harvest on private lands *if* "public lands were insufficient to support a modest living." The state Wisconsin appeals and is sanctioned by appellate judges for filing a "frivolous appeal." After Judge Doyle dies, Judge Barbara Crabb takes over the case. Anti-treaty protests swell.

1988 Anti-treaty groups organize massive protests on northern Wisconsin boat landings during spring spearfishing. STA-Wisconsin sells "Treaty Beer" as a fundraiser. Treaty-support groups successfully boycott the manufacturer. Witness for Non-Violence for Treaty and Rural Rights (Witness) organizes caravans of treaty supporters from Milwaukee and Madison. Witness documents civil rights abuses.

1989 Protests grow so massive and violent that Governor Thompson calls out the National Guard to keep peace on the boat landings during the spring spearing season. The state offers $60 million to "lease" treaty rights from the smallest and largest band of Ojibwe spearfishers, but tribal members reject both proposals. Stories about spearfishing violence dominate national print and broadcast media. The U.S. Commission on Civil Rights launches an investigation. The state's request for an injunction to stop the Ojibwes from spearing is denied.

1990 Judge Crabb rules that the Ojibwes cannot collect damages under *Voigt*. Boat landing violence and national news media coverage reach an apex, threatening both the Ojibwes and Wisconsin's tourism industry. The U.S. Senate Select Committee on Indian Affairs begins an investigation.

1991 The ACLU, acting on behalf of the Ojibwes, successfully seeks an injunction against STA-Wisconsin, whose members are ordered to stay away from the boat landings. STA-Wisconsin founder Dean Crist is fined $182,000. The U.S. Senate Committee releases its *Casting Light Upon the Waters* report, which concludes that spearing has not damaged Wisconsin's fishery. Judge Crabb issues her summary decision. Neither the state nor the Ojibwes appeal.

1992 The Mille Lacs Band sues the state of Minnesota, arguing that Minnesota suppressed its rights secured in the 1837 treaty. *Minnesota v. Mille Lacs* involves the same issues and the same Ojibwe bands as in the Wisconsin case.

1993 The Minnesota legislature rejects an agreement worked out among Mille Lacs, the governor, and the Minnesota DNR. Mille Lacs resumes its lawsuit.

1994 Federal Judge Diane Murphy rules in favor of Mille Lacs. The state of Minnesota appeals.

1998 The U.S. Supreme Court agrees to hear *Minnesota v. Mille Lacs*. The Ojibwe organize the Waabanong Run from Lac du Flambeau to Washington, D.C., to bring attention to Indian treaty rights.

1999 The U.S. Supreme Court rules 5–4 in favor of Mille Lacs.

The Struggle for Treaty Rights for Chippewa People

Chippewa Treaty Rights refers to a 25-year struggle (1974–1999) over off-reservation hunting, fishing, and gathering rights established by the Lake Superior tribe of Chippewa in three nineteenth-century land-cession treaties negotiated with the U.S. government. Two major court rulings, *Lac Courte Oreilles Band of Lake Superior Chippewa Indians, et al., v. Lester P. Voigt, et al.* (also known as the "*Voigt* decision") and *Minnesota v. Milles Lacs Band of Chippewa Indians* (also known as the "*Mille Lacs* decision"), bookended a period of furious lawsuits and violent confrontations, primarily over spearfishing and gill netting by Chippewa bands in Michigan, Wisconsin, and Minnesota. Ultimately, in the *Mille Lacs* decision, the U.S. Supreme Court definitively ruled in favor of the Chippewas (or Ojibwes, as they call themselves), a decision that many legal scholars interpret as a reinforcement of tribal sovereignty and acknowledgment of Indian treaty rights. The Chippewa treaty rights struggle has had far-reaching implications. Since the court ruling, treaty rights have been used successfully by the Ojibwes and their allies to block perceived environmental threats, including sulfide and iron mining proposals, in the ceded territories where off-reservation hunting, fishing, and gathering rights are legally presumed to exist.

In March 1974, when two Chippewa brothers informed the local sheriff that they intended to spearfish off-reservation in accordance with three nineteenth-century treaties, they intended to get arrested. What Fred and Mike Tribble of the Lac Courte Oreilles Band of Lake Superior Chippewa could not have imagined, however, was that their act of civil disobedience would become the genesis of one of the most important Indian treaty rights lawsuits of modern times. The case transformed the political landscapes of three Midwestern states and continues to affect the way communities across the country relate to Indian nations on environmental issues.

Between 1778 and 1871, the United States negotiated hundreds of treaties with Indian nations. Article Six of the U.S. Constitution explicitly declared treaties to be "the supreme law of the land." Like other Indian nations coerced into land-cession treaties, the Chippewas, also known as the Ojibwes or Anishinaabes, agreed in three nineteenth-century treaties to give up roughly the northern third of present-day Wisconsin, a portion of northeastern Minnesota, and a small slice of Michigan's Upper Peninsula. The territory ceded contained an estimated 39 million acres, for which the Ojibwes received a total cash payment of $602,500 or 64 cents per acre. The government paid its obligation in annuities spread out over a period of 20 to 25 years.

During the treaty negotiations, the Ojibwes expressed concern over access to fish, wild rice, and maple trees and other resources that had sustained them for generations. In the first two of three treaties, negotiated in 1837, 1842, and 1854, the Ojibwes explicitly insisted upon the continued rights to hunt, fish, and gather in the territories ceded to the U.S. government (Satz 1991, 131–85). It was this language that formed the basis of the 25-year court battle touched off by the Tribble brothers' spearfishing incident.

In 1848, when Wisconsin became a state, officials assumed their jurisdiction, and authority extended to everyone, including members of sovereign Indian nations, within the boundaries of the state. Conservation wardens arrested tribal members who ventured off-reservation to hunt, fish, and gather in accordance with their treaties, and confiscated their weapons. Even those who exercised their rights *on* the reservation sometimes faced prosecution. In 1901, a Bad River tribal member was found guilty of setting a gill net on the reservation. By the time a district court ruled that the state had no authority to impose its fish and game laws on the reservation, the accused had already served his sentence—30 days at hard labor.

Allotment, the systematic privatization of tribal lands begun in earnest after the 1887 General Allotment Act, and the transformation of the landscape due to western expansion, restricted tribal access to traditional hunting, fishing, and gathering places. Throughout the nineteenth and twentieth centuries, attempts to hunt deer or spear fish off-reservation drove those activities underground. "A lot of times I'd lay out in the grass hiding," Red Cliff elder Ike Gokee related, "afraid to move because there was a car close by, and we didn't know whether it was the game warden" (Gokee, 1994).

The Ojibwes were not alone in their struggle. During the 1950s and 1960s, similar battles occurred in Washington State. Tribal members held well-publicized "fish-ins," in which they attempted to net fish in support of their treaty rights and in violation of state law. Commercial fishing, industrial pollution, and hydroelectric dams, among other factors, had seriously depleted the Native salmon runs. The decline of the resource only heightened tensions between Native and non-Native fishers and led to violent confrontations. The fish-ins culminated in a federal lawsuit against the state of Washington. The resulting 1974 *Boldt* decision, which established a 50–50 allocation of fish for Native and non-Native harvests, would later be invoked by the federal judge presiding over the Wisconsin case.

In contrast to the events in Washington, the first nine years of the Chippewa treaty rights case were quiet. Even the Wisconsin Department of Natural Resources had forgotten about *Voigt*, according to George Meyer, who succeeded Department of Natural Resources Secretary Lester Voigt, for whom the suit is named. When the appellate court issued its ruling, "It was like a train hitting a wall," according to Meyer (Meyer, 2010). Public reaction was swift and confrontational. Anti-treaty rights groups, including Protect American Rights and Resources (PARR) and Stop Treaty Abuse-Wisconsin (STA), organized protest rallies and developed legal strategies to thwart the Native harvest. The eleven member bands of Lake Superior Ojibwe, in turn, established the Great Lakes Indian Fish and Wildlife Commission (GLIFWC) to provide natural resource management, regulate the harvests, and provide public information about treaty rights and sovereignty. GLIFWC represented its 11 member bands in court battles and in negotiations with the state.

In 1985, when Ojibwe tribal members first moved off the reservation to spear walleye, they were met by angry crowds of white hunters and fishers, resort owners, and others connected to the tourism trade. Spearers attempting to launch their boats walked a gauntlet of rock-throwing, jeering mobs. On the water, spearers were even more vulnerable. Spearing occurs at night in shallow waters during spawning season (usually the last two weeks of April or the first two weeks of May), so tribal boats moved perilously close to private homes and docks. While one occupant sits and steers, the other, wearing a battery-operated helmet light, stands and spears—making the spearer a bright target against a dark sky. As spearing boats neared the shoreline, they faced gunshots, protest boats attempting to ram or swamp them, and projectiles fired from high-powered sling slots. "My people are suffering," Lac du Flambeau Tribal Chair Mike Allen declared in 1989. "We are under incredible physical and verbal attack" (Whaley 1994, 106).

The escalating violence over treaty rights led the state in 1989 to offer $50 million to the largest spearing band, Lac du Flambeau, and $10 million to the smallest band, Mole Lake, to "lease" their treaty rights. The notion of paying the Ojibwes not to harvest walleye infuriated anti-treaty groups like PARR and STA-Wisconsin. Ironically, on that point the general membership of both tribes agreed, voting overwhelmingly against the lease. The proposal touched off a political struggle between the Lac du Flambeau Tribal Council, which endorsed the lease, and Wa-Swa-Gon Treaty Association, an opposing faction led by Tom Maulson and Nick Hockings, who lobbied to defeat it. Lac du Flambeau members would later turn their leadership out of office and elect Maulson as president.

The lease also drew the wrath of the other Ojibwe bands, who accused the state of mounting a "divide and conquer" campaign against them. Terms of the lease required the Lac du Flambeau to identify their traditional spearing lakes, which would preclude other bands from spearing in them. The other bands argued they were *all* signatories to the treaties and held the rights *in common*. Traditionalists likened the "buyout" to the state paying Catholics not to go to church on Sunday or bribing Jews not to commemorate Passover. As Hockings explained, "If you sever these webs that connect us to the earth—whether it's the deer or whether it's fish or whether it's the timber or the gathering rights—if you sever these, you start losing the identity of who you are" (Hockings 1990).

Wisconsin Governor Tommy Thompson responded to the failed lease attempt by seeking an injunction, not against the protestors, but against the spearers. In refusing his request, an angry Judge Crabb likened the request to efforts during the 1960s to suppress black voters and civil rights. "If this court holds that violent and lawless protests can determine the rights of the residents of this state," she asked, "what message will that send?" (*Lac du Flambeau v. Stop Treaty Abuse-Wisconsin*, 991 F.2d 1249 (7th Cir. 1993)). Americans who tuned into national network news programs that same week were subjected to disturbing images from Wisconsin. CNN broadcast a story featuring an interview with a protester holding the effigy of an Indian head on a spear. A local ABC affiliate interviewed a protestor holding a sign that read, "Hay [sic] Tommy T., our north timber is for timber wolves, not timber niggers."

The obvious racial undertones of the dispute prompted the U.S. Commission on Civil Rights to investigate. Its 1989 report concluded that "physical threats and racial harassment of Chippewa Indians in northern Wisconsin have been commonplace" (U.S. Commission on Civil Rights 1989, 3). Some of the harassment had been documented by members of treaty support organizations, including Witness for Non-Violence for Treaty and Rural Rights in Northern Wisconsin (Witness). Borrowing techniques used in the black voting drives of 1964's Freedom Summer, Witness trained hundreds of observers, including students and clergy primarily from Milwaukee and Madison, in non-violent strategies. They formed protective circles around the spearers and their families on the landings and used cameras and audio recorders to document civil rights violations. Judge Crabb cited that evidence in her 1991 decision to grant injunctive relief to the Ojibwes in a petition filed by the ACLU on their behalf.

Between 1974 and 1999, there were 54 major legal decisions related to Chippewa treaty rights—11 in Michigan, 19 in Wisconsin, and 18 in Minnesota. An additional six rulings involved STA-Wisconsin, the anti-treaty group, whose leader, Dean Crist, was ordered to pay a $182,000 fine. In granting a preliminary injunction against STA-Wisconsin, Judge Crabb ordered the group to stay away from the boat landings and refrain from interfering with tribal spearfishing. U.S. Court of Appeals for the Seventh Circuit upheld the injunction, declaring, "the stench of racism is unmistakable" (*Lac du Flambeau Band v. Stop Treaty Abuse-Wisconsin* 1990).

The 1991 injunction was one of two major factors that contributed to the collapse of the anti-treaty movement. The other was the release that same year of a federal report, *Casting Light upon the Waters: A Joint Fishery Assessment of the Wisconsin Ceded Territory*, spearheaded by Senator Daniel Innouye (D–HI), who headed the U.S. Senate Select Committee on Indian Affairs. The report concluded that spearfishing was not threatening the walleye fishery and implored all stakeholders to move forward together in a new era of cooperation. That same spring Judge Crabb issued her summary decision on the treaty rights issue and gave each side three months to appeal. Both the state and the Ojibwes had won concessions during the 19 appearances in federal court, and neither side was willing to risk losing those advantages. No appeals were filed.

A year later, in 1992, the issue resurfaced in Minnesota. The Mille Lacs Band sued, alleging that Minnesota had violated the same 1837 treaty in suppressing hunting, fishing, and gathering rights in that state. Fearing a repeat of boat landing violence, the Mille Lacs Band, the governor, and the Minnesota Department of Natural Resources worked out a compromise. The band agreed to drop its lawsuit and to limit its walleye harvest on Lake Mille Lacs to 24,000 pounds. In return the Mille Lacs Band would have received $8.6 million and 7,500 acres of land from the state, along with exclusive fishing rights to just under five percent of the lake (Squires 2015). After the Minnesota legislature rejected the agreement, Mille Lacs resumed its lawsuit. In 1994, federal Judge Diane Murphy ruled in favor of the Ojibwes, a decision the state of Minnesota immediately appealed.

The Minnesota Hunting and Angling Club, led by former Minnesota Vikings Coach Bud Grant, held an anti-treaty rights rally at the state capitol. A short time

Sidebar 1: The Educational Mandate of Act 31

Perhaps the most enduring legacy of the Chippewa Treaty Rights controversy was passage of Act 31, an educational mandate inserted into the 1989–91 biennial budget by the Wisconsin legislature. The legislation requires the study of Wisconsin American Indian history, culture, and tribal sovereignty. Hailed by some as a long-term strategy to educate Wisconsin residents about the eleven federally recognized Indian nations in Wisconsin, it was criticized for failing to provide funds to implement the initiative. Specifically the Act created five statutory sections:

Act 31

s. 115.28(17)(d) *Treaty Rights Curriculum*

In conjunction with the American Indian Language and Culture Education Board, develop a curriculum for grades 4 to 12 on the Chippewa Indian's treaty-based, off-reservation rights to hunt, fish, and gather.

s. 118.01(c)7–8 *Human Relations*

Each school board shall provide an instructional program designed to give pupils:

7. An appreciation and understanding of different value systems and cultures.

8. At all grade levels, an understanding of human relations, particularly with regard to American Indians, Black Americans, and Hispanics.

s. 118.19(8) *Teacher Certification*

Beginning July 1, 1991, the state superintendent may not grant to any person a license to teach unless the person has received instruction in the study of minority group relations, including the history, culture, and tribal sovereignty of the federally recognized tribes and bands located in the state.

s. 121.02(1)(h) *Instructional Materials*

Each school board shall:

Provide adequate instructional materials, texts, and library services which reflect the cultural diversity and pluralistic nature of American society.

s. 121.02(1)(L)4 *K-12 Social Studies Instruction*

Each school board shall:

Beginning September 1, 1991, as part of the social studies curriculum, include instruction in the history, culture, and tribal sovereignty of the federally recognized American Indian tribes and bands located in the state of Wisconsin at least twice in the elementary grades and at least once in the high school grades.

Source: http://dpi.wi.gov/amind/state-statues

later, the protest group Proper Economic Resource Management (PERM) formed and raised money for six landowners who joined a lawsuit filed against Mille Lacs by the state and nine counties. Over the next five years, various facets of off-reservation hunting, fishing, and gathering rights found their way into federal district and appeals courts. Although Minnesotans braced for violence, the dispute never reached the level of contentiousness that marked the Wisconsin experience. However, in 1998, when the U.S. Supreme Court agreed to hear the case, the decision shocked the Ojibwes. The justices take up a limited number of cases each year, and both the Seventh and the Eighth Circuits had ruled favorably for the tribe. The Ojibwe reasoned that if the high court intended to uphold the tenets of their off-reservation rights, it would have let the lower court rulings stand. By agreeing to hear the case, the court left the door open for some or all of the *Voigt* decision to be overturned.

In fall 1998, GLIFWC organized the Waabanong Run in order to draw attention to treaty rights. Runners, representing not only the Ojibwes but also other Native and non-Native supporters, carried the eagle staff from the Lac du Flambeau reservation to the nation's capital. The three-week relay culminated in drumming and speeches on the steps of the U.S. Supreme Court building just as the justices prepared to hear oral arguments.

In March 1999, in a 5–4 decision, the high court ruled in favor of the Ojibwes, a decision that effectively ended 25 years of litigation. Ironically, it was Sandra Day O'Connor, an ardent states' rights justice, who delivered the ruling, stating: ". . . the tribe's treaty rights to hunt, fish, and gather on state land can coexist with state natural resource management" (O'Connor in *Minnesota v. Mille Lacs* 1999).

Since 1999, the Mille Lacs decision has been invoked in dozens of Indian law cases, ranging from those involving tribes such as the Skokomish in the Pacific Northwest and the Navajo in the Southwest to Plains nations, including the Oglalas, Santees, and Yankton Sioux, to the Mattaponis in Virginia. It is significant not only because of the clear affirmation of Indian treaty rights, but also because the high court reinforced important judicial canons—that treaties must be interpreted as the Native signers would have understood them at the time of the negotiations and that ambiguity in the treaties must be resolved in favor of the Indian nations.

The Chippewa treaty rights issue has also played a major role in environmental struggles involving non-Indian enterprise in the ceded territories. During the late twentieth and twenty-first centuries, treaty rights were invoked in tribal efforts to block two major mine proposals. In 1994, Exxon resurrected a plan to create a large copper and zinc mine near Crandon, Wisconsin. Over the next ten years, the Sokaogon Chippewa Community (also known as the Mole Lake Ojibwe), whose reservation lay adjacent to the mine site, argued that the mine threatened its wild rice *on* the reservation and hunting, fishing, and gathering rights *off* the reservation. Environmental groups, hunting and fishing organizations, many local residents, and several other tribes lent their support to Mole Lake. Exxon and its successors eventually pulled out of the project, and in 2003 Mole Lake and the Forest County Potawatomis purchased the mine site and promised that mining would never take place there.

In 2011, the Bad River Band of Lake Superior Chippewa invoked treaty rights when the Gogebic Taconite Company announced plans to site a massive open-pit taconite mine at the headwaters of the Bad River watershed, a project that tribal members feared would destroy their rice beds. Again, the Ojibwes and their supporters used their treaty rights to rally support for their position. Three years later, the company announced it would withdraw from the project.

The Chippewa treaty rights struggle is important within the context of other high-profile national "Red Power" activities, among them the takeover at Alcatraz Island (1968), the American Indian Movement (AIM) occupation of the Bureau of Indian Affairs building in Washington D.C. (1972), and the AIM takeover at Wounded Knee, South Dakota (1973). The legal implications of the court decisions surrounding the Ojibwes and their treaties not only solidify the rights specific to the Lake Superior tribe of Chippewa, but also lend weight to those established in hundreds of other treaties negotiated over a span of 250 years.

Biographies

Walter Bresette (Red Cliff Ojibwe) was a spokesperson for the Ojibwes' treaty rights and a founder of Witness for Non-Violence for Treaty and Rural Rights. Witness trained observers and organized caravans of treaty supporters who traveled to northern Wisconsin boat landings and formed protective circles around the spearers and their families. Bresette later co-founded the Wisconsin Green Party.

Dean Crist was the founder of Stop Treaty Abuse-Wisconsin, one of the most confrontational groups opposed to Indian treaty rights. Crist organized scores of protests on northern Wisconsin boat landings in the late 1980s and early 1990s. The demonstrations, which sometimes featured mass arrests, became so unruly the National Guard was called out. In 1991, the American Civil Liberties Union successfully sought an injunction to keep STA-Wisconsin members from the boat landings. A federal judge fined Crist $182,000.

Tom Maulson was co-founder of Was-Swa-Gon Treaty Association, the group of Ojibwe spearfishers actively engaged in the exercise of treaty-based fishing, hunting, and gathering rights during the boat landing protests. When the tribal leadership of Lac du Flambeau voted to approve a $50 million proposal by the state in which the Ojibwes would agree not to spear walleye, Maulson strongly opposed it.

Not only did Lac du Flambeau members reject the lease, they replaced their leadership and elected Maulson president.

George Meyer was lead negotiator for the state of Wisconsin and in 1993 became Secretary of the Wisconsin Department of Natural Resources, a post he held for eight years. Although early on he was cast in an adversarial role, Meyer eventually became a staunch defender of Indian treaty rights.

Tommy Thompson became governor of Wisconsin in 1987, running on a platform that included strong opposition to the *Voigt* decision and a promise to end Ojibwe spearfishing in the ceded territory. During his 14 years in office, he directed the state's attorney general to contest and appeal more than a dozen federal court directives. In 2001, he left office to become U.S. Secretary of Health and Human Services under President George W. Bush.

DOCUMENT EXCERPT

Discrimination against Chippewa Indians in Northern Wisconsin: A Summary Report

In 1989, during the height of protest and violence on northern Wisconsin boat landings, the Wisconsin Advisory Committee to the U.S. Commission on Civil Rights released a report on Chippewa Treaty Rights. The document included historical and legal background on the dispute, described the scope of discrimination directed at the Ojibwe, and offered recommendations toward a peaceful resolution of the controversy. Here is an excerpt from the report, which formed the committee's conclusions:

Summary

This report summarizes views and opinions provided at a forum conducted by the Wisconsin Advisory Committee in Wausau on April 27, 1989. It reports the perspectives of a number of knowledgeable persons interested in, but with opposing views and opinions on, issues related to Indian treaty rights, which the Advisory Committee may decide merit further investigation and analysis.

The information received primarily focused on the historical and legal framework of Indian treaty rights; efforts by State and local authorities to protect and enforce treaty rights; efforts made to educate and inform the public regarding Indian treaty rights and culture; the extent to which forms of discrimination may occur due to resentment of Chippewa treaty rights; efforts that are underway by State and local government to address discrimination that may occur; and recommendations for alleviating any discrimination or injustice against Indian people. Perspectives on these issues were provided by State government officials, tribal groups, community-based organizations and advocacy groups, and representatives from the media and business. The Committee hopes the information received will encourage ongoing and constructive dialogue on the issues and provide an ameliorating effect on existing problems regarding this matter.

The Advisory Committee found that tensions between Indians and non-Indians have been present for many years in northern Wisconsin. Since the *Voigt* decision in 1983, affirming the rights of Chippewa Indians to fish, hunt, and gather timber and other resources, tensions have transformed into increased racial hostility and fears of violence. This increased hostility has been particularly provoked by spearfishing. During the spring of 1989 tensions soared after the ruling by U.S. district court Judge Barbara Crabb allowing tribal fishermen to take 100 percent of the safe harvest and reducing of bag limits for non-Indian fishermen.

The Wisconsin attorney general and a history professor provided an overview of the historical and legal framework of Indian treaty rights. Both acknowledged that whatever views one has on the reinterpretation of the treaty, the court rulings on this issue are law and must be obeyed.

State officials admitted that the protests at the boat landings had been tainted with racism but contended that this had involved only a small group of people. Enforcement agencies were notified of these anti-Indian activities to ensure that civil rights violation did not occur.

Local law enforcement officials were praised for their professional and prompt response to protests at the boat landings. Since the forum, the Federal Bureau of Investigation is looking into possible civil rights violations by protestors who allegedly threw rocks and shouted racial slurs.

According to reports by the tribal leadership and other pro-treaty rights groups, "Save a Walleye, Spear an Indian" and "Save a Deer, Shoot an Indian" are examples of slogans directed at Indians and placed on promotional items such as hats, handguns, bumper stickers, and beer.

A spokesman for an antitreaty rights group claimed that his organization does not encourage or sanction racial hostility against Indians. He indicated that any racial hostility exhibited is due to fear that increased fishing and hunting rights by Indians threatens tourism, business, and personal and recreational real estate of the area.

There were numerous complaints regarding the lack of public knowledge about Indian treaty rights. The state and local education agencies were accused of failing to provide courses on Indian and treaty rights. Also, the local print and broadcast media in northern Wisconsin were accused of failing to cover stories related to treaty rights accurately and objectively.

The State and antitreaty rights groups specifically complained of the Federal Government's failure to provide assistance in resolving the problems surrounding treaty rights. Since the forum, the Governor and members of the Wisconsin delegation have met with the U.S. Interior Secretary to request assistance.

Overall, the information received indicated that little has changed since the Committee's last review of Indian treaty rights in 1984, except for an increase in racial polarization. However, a wide variety of suggestions were made by presenters that they believe should be considered in resolving treaty rights issues and the discrimination that has occurred as a result of their implementation. These suggestions are outlined below:

State Government

1. Continued condemnation of racist acts associated with treaty rights.
2. Promotion of education and ongoing discussion of Indian treaty rights and culture in schools.
3. A negotiated settlement of treaty rights that is fair to the Chippewas while accommodating the needs of tourism and business.
4. Greater Federal Government involvement and assistance in the resolution of problems associated with treaty rights.

Tribal Representatives

1. Observation of boat landing protests by the U.S. Justice Department, Community Relations Division.
2. Greater Federal scrutiny of the law enforcement efforts in the exercise of treaty rights.
3. Statewide educational efforts to increase public awareness and knowledge of Indian treaty rights.

Community-Based Organizations and Advocacy Groups

1. Eliminate Federal Indian policy.
2. Abrogate Indian off-reservation treaty rights.

Pro-treaty Groups

1. Review and reconsideration of the recommendation made by the Wisconsin Ad Hoc Commission on Racism in a report dated November 1984.

2. Require mandatory curriculum on Indian treaty rights and culture in public schools.
3. Formation of a coalition involving local and State government, tribal government, churches, and other community groups to address Indian issues.

News Media

1. The news media of northern Wisconsin need to increase their efforts to report accurately and objectively Indian treaty rights issues.
2. Increase efforts to recruit Native Americans into broadcast and print media fields.

Source: Wisconsin Advisory Committee to the U.S. Commission on Civil Rights, *Discrimination Against Chippewa Indians in Northern Wisconsin: A Summary Report* (Madison, WI: Wisconsin Advisory Committee to the U.S. Commission on Civil Rights, 1989).

Casting Light upon the Waters

In 1991, the U.S. Senate Select Committee on Indian Affairs released its report on the Chippewa treaty rights controversy. Casting Light upon the Waters *examined the historical and contemporary socio-political factors that contributed to the dispute and concluded that the fishery had not been harmed by spearing. It called for a new era of cooperation for the betterment of Wisconsin's natural resources. Here is an excerpt from the report.*

Conclusion Regarding the State of the Resource. People concerned about the fishery resource of northern Wisconsin can be confident that it is being carefully studied and is protected. Chippewa spearing has not harmed the resource. Fish populations in the ceded territory are healthy. Three major factors currently impact northern Wisconsin fisheries: 1) reaffirmation of the Chippewa tribes as harvesters; 2) heavy angling pressure; and 3) continually changing environmental factors. As a result, popular fish species, such as walleye and muskellunge, are subjected to considerable stresses.

Available information suggests a number of conclusions concerning the effects of these stresses on the northern Wisconsin fishery. At this time; fish populations are not being over-exploited in most cases. For example, the average harvest of walleye does not exceed the agreed-upon maximum of 35 percent of the available adult stocks. In the lakes sampled, tribal spearing harvest of walleye has never exceeded this level. However, overall exploitation in some waters is of particular concern because lakes under 500 acres are more vulnerable to overfishing and environmental pressures than larger lakes. Further studies in such lakes are needed to monitor the effects of harvest levels and management actions. Moreover, current fish populations in most cases meet or exceed agreed- upon population goals. In 70 percent of walleye lakes studied, the populations are at or above the established goals. The number of female age classes exceed the agreed-upon goals in all lakes examined during 1986–90. This indicates stable reproductive capacity in those lakes. However, in 30 percent of the lakes, walleye numbers are below desired levels. This indicates that such lakes must receive further study to determine why the numbers are low and to ensure that the lakes are not being over-harvested.

Current information does not allow biologists to draw any conclusions about long-term trend s in individual fish populations. While current information indicates relatively healthy fisheries, long-term population trends currently cannot be detected. Fish managers recognize that there is a need to establish a reliable mechanism for assessing changes in fisheries and aquatic ecosystems. . . .

The tribal, state, and federal managers have embarked upon one of the largest studies of fishing ever conducted. They are using state-of- the-art methods and have collected a large pool of valuable information. They have established joint population goals and are standardizing assessment methods.

Preparation of the report yielded one very clear conclusion: The fishery of the ceded territory faces increasing pressures from all factors. The managers must continue to monitor populations and harvest levels, and evaluate assessment methods and management strategies. The pressures on the fishery require a continuation and further expansion of the joint monitoring and assessment efforts. The managers have demonstrated that they have the expertise to manage the Northern Wisconsin fishery for the benefit of all users. They are committed to management efforts that will assure that Northern Wisconsin's fishery resource remains one of the best protected and best managed in the country.

Source: US Department of the Interior, *Casting Light upon the Waters: A Joint Fishery Assessment of the Wisconsin Ceded Territory* (Minneapolis: Bureau of Indian Affairs, 1991).

Further Reading

Lac du Flambeau v. Stop Treaty Abuse-Wisconsin, 991 F.2d 1249 (7th Cir. 1993)

Loew, Patty and James Thannum. "After the Storm: Ojibwe Treaty Rights 25 Years after the Voigt Decision." *American Indian Quarterly,* Vol. 35, No. 2 (spring 2011).

McClurken, James. *Fish in the Lakes, Wild Rice, and Game in Abundance: Testimony on behalf of Mille Lacs Ojibwe Hunting and Fishing Rights.* East Lansing: Michigan State University Press, 2000.

Nesper, Larry. *The Walleye War.* Lincoln: University of Nebraska Press, 2002.

Satz, Ron. *Chippewa Treaty Rights.* Madison: Wisconsin Academy of Sciences, Arts and Letters, 1991.

U.S. Department of the Interior. *Casting Light upon the Waters: A Joint Fishery Assessment of the Wisconsin Ceded Territory*. Minneapolis: Bureau of Indian Affairs, 1991.

Whaley, Rick and Walter Bresette. *Walleye Warriors*. Philadelphia: New Society Publishers 1994.

Wilkinson, Charles. "To Feel the Summer in the Spring: The Treaty Fishing Rights of the Wisconsin Chippewa." Oliver Rundell Lecture. Madison: University of Wisconsin Law School, Continuing Education and Outreach, 1990.

Wisconsin Advisory Committee to the United States Commission on Civil Rights, *Discrimination against Chippewa Indians in Northern Wisconsin Summary Report*. Madison: Advisory Committee to the United States Commission on Civil Rights, 1989.

Oliphant v. Suquamish, 1978

Amy Casselman

Chronology

1786 The Treaty of Hopewell is signed with the Choctaw Nation. The treaty states that the Choctaws have criminal jurisdiction over non-Indians who settle on their land.

1788 The Constitution of the United States of America is ratified. Article I recognizes American Indian political sovereignty, and Article VI grants Congress the power to make treaties with Indian nations.

1831 The United States Supreme Court issues a ruling in *Cherokee Nation v. Georgia*. It rules that American Indian nations are not fully sovereign entities but instead "domestic dependent nations" whose relationship to the federal government resembles that of a "ward to his guardian."

1832 The United States Supreme Court issues a ruling in *Worcester v. Georgia*. It rules that states do not have criminal jurisdiction in Indian country.

1855 The Treaty of Point Elliott is signed between the Suquamish Indian tribe (among others) and the United States. The treaty establishes the Suquamish Indian tribe's Port Madison Indian Reservation.

1871 The Indian Appropriations Act becomes law and ends the process of treaty making with Indian tribes.

1885 The Major Crimes Act becomes law and extends federal jurisdiction over all "major crimes" in Indian country, including crimes committed by an Indian against an Indian. The law does not preclude dual jurisdiction with tribal governments.

1887 The General Allotment Act (also known as the Dawes Act) becomes law. It starts the process of land division and privatization in Indian country and causes massive land loss for Native People. It dramatically affects the Suquamish tribe as a large number of non-Indians settle on the Port Madison Indian Reservation.

1903 The United States Supreme Court issues a ruling in *Lone Wolf v. Hitchcock.* It rules that Congress has plenary power to abrogate (break) treaties with American Indian nations.

1953 Public Law 280 becomes law. It forces six states to assume criminal jurisdiction over some or all of the Indian country within its borders. State governments assume criminal jurisdiction over Indian country for the first time. Subsequently, some states voluntarily adopt the law; others retrocede or alter its application.

1968 The Indian Civil Rights Act becomes law, extending most of the U.S. Bill of Rights to Indians in Indian country. It limits tribal sentencing authority to no more than a $500 fine and six months in jail for a single offense. This is later amended to a $15,000 fine and three years in jail under the Tribal Law and Order Act of 2010.

1973 The Suquamish establish a Law and Order Code that covers a variety of criminal offenses and extends criminal jurisdiction over both Indians and non-Indians.

1973 Mark Oliphant is allegedly involved in a drunken brawl and is arrested by Suquamish Tribal Police on the Port Madison Indian Reservation. He is incarcerated for five days in lieu of $200 bail.

1976 In *Oliphant v. Schlie,* Mark Oliphant appeals for a writ of habeas corpus to the Ninth Circuit Court of appeals. He argues that as a non-Indian, the Suquamish lack criminal jurisdiction over him. The Ninth Circuit denies his request.

1978 Mark Oliphant appeals the Ninth Circuit's decision to the United States Supreme Court in *Oliphant v. Suquamish.* The Court sides with Oliphant, reversing the Ninth Circuit Court's decision, and ruling that all Indian tribes lack criminal jurisdiction over non-Indians unless specifically authorized by Congress.

1990 The United States Supreme Court issues a ruling in *Duro v. Reina.* It holds that tribal criminal jurisdiction is limited to members of the prosecuting tribe. In response, Congress passes the "Duro Fix," extending tribal criminal jurisdiction over all Indians, regardless of membership.

2010 The Tribal Law and Order Act of 2010 becomes law. It addresses epidemic levels of Indian country crime and jurisdictional challenges by increasing coordination among tribal, state, and federal agencies. It specifically upholds the ruling in *Oliphant v. Suquamish.*

2013 The Violence Against Women Reauthorization Act of 2013 becomes law. Among other things, the law addresses epidemic levels of violence against Native women in Indian country by granting participating tribes special domestic-violence criminal jurisdiction over non-Indians.

Tribal Criminal Jurisdiction: *Oliphant v. Suquamish*

Mark Oliphant v. The Suquamish Indian Tribe (Oliphant v. Suquamish) is a 1978 United States Supreme Court case concerning tribal criminal jurisdiction. The plaintiff, Mark David Oliphant, argued that as a non-Indian his arrest by Suquamish tribal police on the Port Madison Indian Reservation in Washington State was unlawful because the tribal government lacked criminal jurisdiction. In contrast, the Suquamish Indian tribe asserted that as a federally recognized tribe, they possessed the inherent sovereignty to prosecute crimes committed on their land, regardless of the racial identity of the perpetrator. In a six-to-two decision, the United States Supreme Court ruled in favor of Oliphant, holding that tribal governments do not have criminal jurisdiction over non-Indians unless specifically authorized by Congress. The ruling in *Oliphant* is a significant event in the history of American Indian political sovereignty and has had far-reaching consequences for American Indian people and governments.

The 1978 *Oliphant* decision stems from an alleged altercation that transpired during the annual Chief Seattle Days celebration on the Port Madison Indian Reservation of the Suquamish Indian tribe. At approximately 4:30 a.m. on August 19, 1973, Mark Oliphant was allegedly involved in a drunken brawl with attendees who were camped on Suquamish land. This alleged altercation led to Oliphant's arrest by Suquamish tribal police, who charged him with assaulting a police officer and resisting arrest. Pursuant to a contract with the nearby City of Bremerton, Oliphant was incarcerated in an off-reservation jail in lieu of $200 bail, and after five days he was released on his own recognizance.

Oliphant challenged Suquamish tribal jurisdiction, arguing that tribal governments do not have the authority to prosecute crimes committed by non-Indian perpetrators. He appealed his case to the United States District Court for the Western District of Washington and was denied a writ of habeas corpus. He then appealed his case to the Ninth Circuit Court of appeals in *Mark David Oliphant v. Edward Schlie (Oliphant v. Schlie),* which also denied his request.

In *Oliphant v. Schlie,* the court issued a near unanimous ruling upholding Suquamish tribal jurisdiction over crimes committed on tribal land. To arrive at this conclusion, the court reviewed treaties and congressional acts and evaluated Oliphant's argument on the basis of congressional trends, constitutionality, and practical considerations. It determined that no treaty or congressional act had extinguished the Suquamish's inherent sovereign right to exercise criminal jurisdiction on their land. Further analysis revealed that strengthening tribal criminal justice systems was consistent with congressional trends toward supporting tribal communities and bolstering law and order in Indian country (the legal term for Indian reservations and other land within the boundaries of Indian communities). As a practical consideration, the court also noted that tribal criminal jurisdiction over non-Indians in Indian country was necessary for public safety, since federal institutions (the alternative to tribal police) were not designed for local law enforcement.

Oliphant then appealed his case to the United States Supreme Court in *Mark Oliphant v. The Suquamish Indian Tribe.* The issue before the court remained the extent to which an Indian tribe may exercise criminal jurisdiction over non-Indians for crimes committed on Indian land. There were a number of possible outcomes. The Court could take a broad approach and issue a ruling applicable to all federally recognized tribes unilaterally confirming or denying the right of criminal jurisdiction. Alternatively, the Court could issue a narrower ruling specific to jurisdiction in this particular case without applying it to all Indian tribes. Finally, it could have accepted the Suquamish tribe's argument for a "subject matter jurisdiction test" that could ascertain which cases warranted tribal jurisdiction.

Ultimately, the Supreme Court opted for a unilateral holding overturning the lower courts' rulings and prohibiting all Indian tribes from exercising criminal jurisdiction over non-Indians unless specifically authorized by Congress. Justice William Rehnquist authored the majority opinion (with Justices Stewart, White, Blackmun, Powell and Stevens concurring). To arrive at this conclusion, the Supreme Court rejected the Ninth Circuit Court's analysis of treaties, congressional acts, congressional trends, and other factors.

The U.S. Supreme Court's reasoning rested on a radically different notion of tribal sovereignty vis-à-vis the lower courts. The Ninth Circuit Court adhered to the longstanding legal principle that tribes maintain all of their rights as sovereign nations except those that have been specifically ceded via treaty or explicitly extinguished by Congress. And since the Suquamish had never relinquished criminal jurisdiction by treaty or by statute, and since maintaining law and order is *sine qua non* (essential and inherent) to political sovereignty, the Ninth Circuit Court rejected Oliphant's claim. In contrast, the U.S. Supreme Court interpreted tribal sovereignty to exist to the extent of what was *granted to* tribes by Congress and via treaty. Since the Court could not supply a treaty or Congressional action that specifically *conferred* criminal jurisdiction upon the Suquamish, they assumed that it did not exist.

The Supreme Court's radically different interpretation of tribal sovereignty was based in part on the assumption that tribes had no formal system of law and order until recently. As such, the Court reasoned that criminal jurisdiction could not have been assumed to be part of the tribe's inherent sovereignty during the treaty-making process because at the time, a modern notion of criminal jurisdiction did not exist for Native People. The Court's holding also rested on the argument that exercising criminal jurisdiction over non-Indians was inconsistent with their status as "domestic dependent nations" (political entities that are not fully sovereign due to their dependence on the United States).

The Supreme Court bolstered its argument by using primary documents to develop a doctrine of implicit divestment. Its rationale held that tribal rights could be implicitly terminated—even without explicit Congressional action—if those rights were deemed inconsistent with their status. As the majority opinion noted, "While Congress never expressly forbade Indian tribes to impose criminal penalties on non-Indians, we now make express our implicit conclusion of nearly a century ago that Congress consistently believed this to be the necessary result of its repeated legislative actions" (*Oliphant v. Suquamish Indian Tribe*, 435 U.S. 191, 204).

Curiously, some of the primary documentation to support the doctrine of implicit divestment came from congressional testimony over policy that was debated but never became law, and from treaties that themselves specified tribal criminal jurisdiction over non-Indians. For example, the Court cited the 1786 Treaty with the Choctaws that states, "If any citizen of the United States . . . shall attempt to settle on any of the lands hereby allotted to the Indians to live and hunt on, such person shall forfeit the protection of the United States of America, and the Indians may punish him or not as they please." While this language appears to confirm criminal jurisdiction for tribal governments, the Court used it to argue the opposite. Instead, the Court proffered that since these provisions became less prevalent over time, their gradual absence supported the doctrine of implicit divestment. Finally, while the Court's analysis centered on developing an *implicit* understanding of Congressional intent during an *historic* era, it appeared to ignore the argument presented in both the Suquamish tribe's brief and the opinion of the Ninth Circuit Court, that *contemporary* congressional policy was *explicitly* investing in tribal self-sufficiency and sovereignty.

Justice Thurgood Marshall authored the dissenting opinion with Chief Justice Warren Burger concurring. (Justice Brennan did not participate.) The dissent rested on the same argument as the lower court in *Oliphant v. Schlie*, that in the absence of explicitly ceding criminal jurisdiction over non-Indians, Indian tribes are assumed to maintain it.

Oliphant in Context

Local criminal jurisdictional authority is a fundamental right in most American communities. Recognizing that justice is best meted out at the local level, most American cities are governed by municipal regulations that are policed by city law enforcement in accordance with state and federal law. With some exceptions, such was the case for tribal governments prior to *Oliphant* where most crimes perpetrated in Indian country fell under tribal criminal jurisdiction regardless of the racial identity or tribal membership of the perpetrator. Before *Oliphant*, non-Indians who committed crimes could expect to be arrested, tried, and convicted in tribal court under the doctrine of implied consent (the notion that one forfeits the jurisdiction of one entity and assumes the jurisdiction of another when crossing a border into a new state or country). After *Oliphant*, tribes retained the ability to prosecute crimes committed by Indians in Indian country but were prohibited from exerting jurisdiction over non-Indian perpetrators.

After *Oliphant*, state and federal entities were tasked with adjudicating all non-Indian perpetrated crime on tribal land. Unfortunately, state and federal governments generally failed to fulfill their new roles in Indian country law enforcement. As a result, crime in Indian country has steadily increased, and in some cases reached epidemic levels. This is especially true for offenses such as drug production and trafficking, assault, and other violent crimes. Of particular concern is the level of sexual assault and domestic violence perpetrated against Indian women by non-Indian men. The interracial aspect of this crime is a statistical anomaly in the

---

Sidebar 1: Jurisdictional Authority for Crimes Committed in Indian Country* after *Oliphant v. Suquamish*

	Indian Perpetrator	**Non-Indian Perpetrator**
Indian Victim	Tribe+Concurrent State or Federal[†]	Exclusive State or Federal[†‡]
Non-Indian Victim	Tribe+Concurrent State or Federal[†]	Exclusive State or Federal[†]

* Indian Country is defined as "all land within the limits of any Indian reservation under the jurisdiction of the United States government." See 18 U.S.C. § 1151.

[†] State jurisdiction is determined by Public Law 280 status.

[‡] Unless the assault qualifies for Title IX exemptions for special domestic violence jurisdiction under the Violence Against Women Reauthorization Act of 2013.

Note—In rare cases it is possible for the U.S. Military to also assert criminal jurisdiction. For example, see *Lavetta Elk v. United States.* No. 05-186L 2009.

United States and is partially explained by the climate of race-based impunity created under *Oliphant*.

Historically, American Indian nations exercised effective local jurisdiction over the people and activities on their land. Even after contact with Europeans, the inherent sovereignty of American Indian nations remained intact and acknowledged by alien governments. Article 1 of the Constitution of the United States recognizes American Indian political sovereignty, and the more than 400 treaties signed between Native nations and the United States reaffirm the sovereign status of American Indian nations. However, changing views of Native People in the context of 19th-century westward expansion led to steady encroachment into American Indian political sovereignty and criminal jurisdiction, ultimately paving the way for the *Oliphant* decision.

One of the earliest and most significant inroads to American Indian sovereignty was the 1831 U.S. Supreme Court case *Cherokee Nation v. Georgia.* Though Native nations were once viewed as *pre* and *extra*-Constitutional (existing both before the birth of the United States as a country, and independent from the sovereignty it draws from the Constitution), the ruling in this case instead deemed Native nations "domestic dependent nations." As a result, the sovereignty of American Indian nations is now significantly limited in that they may no longer function as fully sovereign entities, but rather as distinct communities with limited political sovereignty under the supremacy of United States federal law. The *Cherokee Nation* case was foundational to the *Oliphant* decision, with the majority's argument resting in large part on the status of American Indian nations as "domestic dependent nations."

After *Cherokee Nation,* additional law and policy significantly limited tribal criminal jurisdictional authority in Indian country. The Major Crimes Act of 1885, 1953's Public Law 280, and the Indian Civil Rights Act of 1968 limited the types of crimes that could be adjudicated in tribal court, transferred criminal jurisdiction over certain crimes to state governments, and limited tribal sentencing authority. The ruling in *Oliphant* builds on previous laws to further restrict tribal criminal jurisdiction by specifying race as a jurisdictional determinant.

As the result of *Oliphant,* Indian country is unique in that it is virtually the only place in the world in which a perpetrator can commit a crime in a community yet have no legal accountability to the local government. Coupled with other earlier laws limiting tribal jurisdiction, *Oliphant* creates an exceptional legal framework in which the location, type of crime, and the racial identity of perpetrator(s) and victim(s) must be determined in order to adjudicate crime. Under this schema, crimes committed by non-Indians against Indians are especially difficult to prosecute. Consequently, not only has Indian country crime increased in general, but crime perpetrated by *non*-Indians against Indians has also increased in particular.

Sidebar 2: Who Is An "Indian"? Congress's "Duro Fix"

The ruling in *Oliphant v. Suquamish* held that Indian tribes lack criminal jurisdiction over non-Indians and instead limited their ability to adjudicate crime over "Indian" people only. However, the ruling did not specify who would be considered "Indian" for the purpose of criminal jurisdiction, leading to additional complications for law enforcement. This issue was at the heart of the 1990 U.S. Supreme Court case *Duro v. Reina,* in which Albert Duro allegedly killed a 14-year-old boy in the Salt River Pima Maricopa Indian Community. The Court ruled that though Duro was a member of the Torres-Martinez Desert Cahuilla Indians, he was not a member of the prosecuting tribe and was therefore immune to their jurisdiction. This ruling further limited tribal sovereignty in that it restricted tribal jurisdiction to crime committed by tribal members only. In response, Congress passed what is now known as the "Duro Fix," which restored tribal criminal jurisdiction over all "Indians" regardless of membership with the adjudicating tribe. Despite the "Duro Fix," ambiguity remains because federal, state, and tribal definitions of "Indian" vary significantly throughout the country. Thus, a definition of who an "Indian" is for the purposes of criminal jurisdiction under *Oliphant* remains unclear.

Notably, the Oliphant case itself is a clear example of the public safety challenges stemming from the Supreme Court's ruling. Mark Oliphant was living on Indian land, attending an event hosted by an Indian community, and was arrested for allegedly assaulting an Indian member of that community. Yet, in *Oliphant v. Suquamish,* the Supreme Court ruled that as a non-Indian, Oliphant should have no criminal accountability to that Indian community. Prior to the alleged assault, the Suquamish tribe requested police support from the Bureau of Indian Affairs (the federal agency responsible for managing tribal land). This request was denied, leaving the Suquamish tribal police as the only law enforcement agency on duty during Oliphant's alleged assault. And though the Supreme Court ruled that Oliphant's case falls under federal jurisdiction, the federal government did not prosecute him. Here, the federal government failed in both policing and prosecution, thus allowing crime perpetrated by a non-Indian against an Indian to be met with impunity.

Tribal governments, state and federal legislators, and Native activists have pursued a variety of methods to address crime in Indian country in the wake of *Oliphant,* including strengthening tribal civil codes, advocating for better state and federal policing, promoting increased sovereignty drawn from treaty rights, and lobbying Congress for legislative changes. Significant progress was made along those lines in 2010 when President Obama signed the Tribal Law and Order Act (TLOA) into law. The TLOA is a federal law that addresses Indian country crime by increasing communication between law enforcement agencies, compiling federal declination and Indian country crime statistics, facilitating cross-deputization agreements, and increasing funding for tribal justice institutions. The law specifically upholds the *Oliphant* ruling, stating, "Nothing in this Act confers on an Indian tribe criminal jurisdiction over non-Indians" (25 U.S.C. 2801 § 206), and instead frames addressing jurisdictional challenges post-*Oliphant* through increased coordination among tribes, states, and the federal government.

To many, The TLOA represented significant progress in addressing crime in Indian country. However, many tribal advocates argued that it still did not do enough to address crime committed by non-Indian perpetrators, especially as it relates to epidemic levels of violence against Indian women. In response, Congress passed Title IX of the Violence Against Women Reauthorization Act of 2013 (VAWA 2013). Title IX: Safety for Indian Women extends special tribal criminal jurisdiction over non-Indian perpetrators of dating violence, domestic violence, and violations of protection orders. Title IX applies to non-Indian perpetrators of said crimes who live or work on Indian land or are a "spouse, intimate partner, or dating partner" of an Indian on tribal land (Public Law 113–4 § 904).

Though limited in scope, Title IX has received serious criticism by some members of Congress and others who view it as a threat to non-Indian civil liberties. In contrast, Title IX has garnered praise from tribal governments and Indian people as a significant restoration and recognition of the sovereignty they have always possessed. Since its passage, several tribal governments have exercised special domestic violence jurisdiction under Title IX and have used it to arrest and prosecute non-Indian perpetrators.

Though Title IX's significance is usually read in terms of its challenge to *Oliphant*, it is important to note that nothing in VAWA 2013 extends criminal jurisdiction over crimes like those allegedly perpetrated by Mark Oliphant. Even though he lived on the Port Madison Indian Reservation, his alleged assault of a tribal police officer was not domestic in nature and therefore would not fall under Title IX. Additionally, Title IX—rather than streamline Indian country jurisdiction—adds more layers to an already complex jurisdictional scheme that remains mostly intact. Per Title IX, in addition to the location of the crime, the type of crime, and the racial identities of the persons involved, law enforcement must also now factor the nature of the crime (domestic/non domestic) and the relationships between the perpetrator, the victim, and the tribal community in order to determine jurisdiction. However, despite this persistent complexity, it is clear that VAWA 2013 is a significant shift in federal Indian policy. Not only is it a legislative check on the anti-tribal sovereignty trend characteristic of the Rehnquist court, but it also significantly shifts the trajectory of federal Indian law toward meaningful investments in American Indian sovereignty.

Today, the ruling in *Oliphant v. Suquamish* remains one of the most significant events that have shaped American Indian history. Historically, it fundamentally altered the way that tribal sovereignty was viewed by the federal government, resulting in challenges to public safety in Indian country that persist to this day. In the face of these challenges, it also spurred advocacy from tribal governments, Indian people, and their allies to continue to invest in tribal sovereignty and ensure law and order in tribal communities. The result of that advocacy—notably the TLOA and VAWA 2013—has dramatically reshaped the trajectory of American Indian tribal sovereignty towards self-determination for Indian nations.

Biography

Sarah Deer (1972–)

Sarah Deer is a citizen of the Muscogee (Creek) Nation and is one of the most influential figures in the modern anti-violence movement for Native women, especially as it relates to law and policy. Deer is a lawyer, author, activist, and law professor at William Mitchell College of Law in St. Paul, Minnesota. In 2014, she was awarded the prestigious MacArthur Fellowship for her work in tribal justice and anti-violence advocacy. Her work has resulted in some of the most significant changes in federal Indian policy in recent history. Today, she continues to advocate for tribal governments and American Indian women.

Since receiving her law degree from the University of Kansas, Deer has published extensively in both tribal law and federal Indian policy. Her work traces the impact of American colonization on traditional indigenous justice systems, and challenges the way that federal Indian policy has divested American Indian governments of political sovereignty. Deer incorporates gender into her analysis, comparing the experience of Native women under traditional tribal justice systems to their experience within the modern American justice system. In doing so, her work highlights the way that American law and federal Indian policy have shaped the epidemic levels of violence against Native women in Indian country. As such, she advocates for a survivor-centered model of justice within a context of reinvigorating tribal sovereignty, expanding tribal criminal jurisdiction, and reforming federal Indian law.

The outcome of *Oliphant v. Suquamish* figures prominently in Sarah Deer's work. Deer situates the case as one of many that divested tribal nations of their inherent sovereignty and produced a jurisdictional structure that creates a public safety crisis in Indian country. Her analysis of *Oliphant* illustrates the way that an already complex jurisdictional structure has been racialized, creating a climate of race-based impunity for non-Indian criminals. This, she notes, is particularly gendered in that *Oliphant* disproportionately affects Native women targeted by non-Native men.

Sarah Deer was instrumental in data collection and analysis for Amnesty International's groundbreaking 2007 report *Maze of Injustice: The Failure to Protect Indigenous Women from Sexual Violence in the USA*. As a co-author of the project, Deer collected data from all over the nation to reveal the complex nature of jurisdiction in Indian country and the way that it impacts Native women. Through statistical data, interviews, and legal analysis, Deer and her colleagues revolutionized the discourse on violence against Native women by framing it as an international human rights issue. In doing so, Deer was instrumental in garnering national and international attention to an issue relatively unknown outside of the Native community.

After *Maze of Injustice*, Deer continued to advocate for anti-violence strategies in Indian country. She testified before Congress and authored additional publications demonstrating the need to revitalize tribal justice systems in order to combat epidemic levels of violence against Native women. Her work on *Maze of Injustice* and subsequent activism directly led to significant changes in federal Indian policy through the Tribal Law and Order Act of 2010 (TLOA) and the Violence Against Women Reauthorization Act of 2013 (VAWA 2013).

The TLOA invests in American Indian sovereignty to increase tribal sentencing authority, improve services for American Indian women, develop federal accountability to American Indian governments and citizens, coordinate policing between multiple agencies, and bolster funding to tribal governments to help maintain law and order. As a result, tribal governments have more resources to adjudicate crime in their communities and hold the federal government accountable to its responsibility to protect Native women.

The passage of the TLOA was hailed as a major victory for Native women and Indian country communities. However, it failed to fully address the jurisdictional complications identified in *Maze of Injustice* and did nothing to address the outcome of *Oliphant v. Suquamish*. As such, Deer continued to lobby Congress and was instrumental in the passage of VAWA 2013.

VAWA 2013 builds on The TLOA by expanding tribal jurisdiction over non-Indian perpetrators for some of the most common crimes committed against Native women. In doing so, it challenges the Supreme Court's ruling in *Oliphant* and addresses public safety in Indian country by re-investing in tribal sovereignty.

The impact of Sarah Deer's work is broad and far-reaching. Deer has radically redirected federal Indian policy and advocated for Native women in the context of re-Indigenizing tribal law. In her moving essay "What She Says, It Be Law," Deer discusses her own tribe's traditional law as it relates to jurisdiction and violence against Native women. Deer points out that, unlike the modern justice system, the Muscogee (Creek) Nation traditionally shaped law around the experience of the survivor and her vision of justice. As such, she pushes the boundaries of what "justice" means for Native women and tribal governments in order to shape a more vibrant future for Native People as a whole. (*See also* Deer's biography in Tribal Law and Order Act, 2010.)

DOCUMENT EXCERPTS
The Suquamish Indian tribe's Legal Brief

The following is an excerpt from the Suquamish Indian tribe's legal brief submitted to the Ninth Circuit Court of Appeals. The brief outlines details of the alleged incident involving Mark Oliphant as well as the Suquamish tribe's argument for criminal jurisdiction over non-Indians.

Appellant was arrested at approximately 4:30 A.M. The only law enforcement officers available to deal with the situation were tribal deputies. Without the exercise of jurisdiction by the tribe and its courts, there could have been no law enforcement whatsoever on the Reservation during this major gathering which clearly created a potentially dangerous situation with regard to law enforcement. Public safety is an underpinning of a political entity. If tribal members cannot protect themselves from offenders, there will be powerful motivation for such tribal members to leave the Reservation, thereby counteracting the express Congressional policy of improving the quality of Reservation life [. . .]

Federal law is not designed to cover the range of conduct normally regulated by local governments. Minor offenses committed by non-Indians within Indian reservations frequently go unpunished and thus unregulated. Federal prosecutors are reluctant to institute federal proceedings against non- Indians for minor offenses in courts in which the dockets are already overcrowded, where litigation will involve burdensome travel to witnesses and investigative personnel, and where the case will most probably result in a small fine or perhaps a suspended sentence. Prosecutors in counties adjoining Indian reservations are reluctant to prosecute non-Indians for minor offenses where limitations on state process within Indian country may make witnesses difficult to obtain, where the jurisdictional division between federal, state and tribal governments over the offense is not clear, and where the peace and dignity of the government affected is not his own but that of the Indian tribe [. . .]

Traffic offenses, trespasses, violations of tribal hunting and fishing regulations, disorderly conduct, and even petty larcenies and simple assaults committed by non-Indians go unpunished. The dignity of the tribal government suffers in the eyes of Indian and non-Indian alike, and a tendency toward lawless behavior necessarily follows.

Source: Suquamish Tribal Brief, pp. 27–28, as quoted in *Oliphant v Schlie,* 544 F.2d 1007 (Ninth Circuit 1976): 9, 10.

The Ninth Circuit Court's Ruling in *Oliphant v. Schlie* (1976)

Below are excerpts from Ninth Circuit Court's ruling in Oliphant v. Schlie. *The decision relies on the assumption that tribes maintain all of their rights as sovereign nations unless those rights have been specifically ceded via treaty or explicitly extinguished by Congress.*

Oliphant argues that the Suquamish have no jurisdiction over non-Indians because Congress never conferred such jurisdiction on them. This misstates the problem. The proper approach to the question of tribal criminal jurisdiction is to ask "first, what the original sovereign powers of the tribes were, and, then, how far and in what respects these powers have been limited" [. . .]"It must always be remembered that the various Indian tribes were once independent and sovereign nations . . ." [. . .] who, though conquered and dependent, retain those powers of autonomous states that are neither inconsistent with their status nor expressly terminated by Congress [. . .]

The question is not whether Congress has conferred jurisdiction upon the tribe. The tribe, before it was conquered, had jurisdiction, as any independent nation does. The question therefore is, did Congress (or a treaty) take that jurisdiction away? The dissent points to no action by the Congress, and no treaty language, depriving the tribe of jurisdiction [. . .]

Surely the power to preserve order on the reservation, when necessary by punishing those who violate tribal law, is a sine qua non of the sovereignty that the Suquamish originally possessed.

Source: Oliphant v. Schlie, 544 F.2d 1007 (Ninth Circuit 1976): 1, 3.

Circuit Judge Kennedy's Dissenting Opinion in *Oliphant v. Schlie* (1976)

Below are excerpts from Ninth Circuit Court Judge Anthony Kennedy's dissenting opinion in Oliphant v. Schlie. *Kennedy's dissent challenged the notion of inherent criminal jurisdiction proffered in the majority decision. He would later become an associate Justice of the Supreme Court of the United States under President Ronald Reagan.*

The concept of sovereignty applicable to Indian tribes need not include the power to prosecute nonmembers. This power, unlike the ability to maintain law and order on the reservation and to exclude undesirable nonmembers, is not essential to the tribe's identity or its self-governing status. [. . .] Therefore I do not find the doctrine of tribal sovereignty analytically helpful in this context and instead find it necessary to look directly at the applicable legislation to determine whether Congress intended the tribal courts to have the power to exercise jurisdiction over nonmembers [. . .]

I am persuaded that Indian tribal courts were not intended to have jurisdiction over non- Indians. Although Congress has never explicitly so provided, it has repeatedly acted in accord with this premise. Unlike the majority, I would not require an express congressional withdrawal of jurisdiction. A presumption in favor of any inherent, general jurisdiction for tribal courts is wholly inconsistent with the juridical relations between the federal government and the Indian tribes that has existed for the past 100 years. Viewing tribal courts in their historical and cultural context, in light of the fact that virtually no white man appears to have been tried by an Indian tribunal in the past century, congressional silence on this point can hardly be viewed as assent.

Source: Oliphant v. Schlie, *544 F.2d 1007 (Ninth Circuit 1976): 12, 19.*

Justice Rehnquist's Majority Opinion in *Oliphant v. Suquamish* (1978)

Below are excerpts from the majority opinion in Oliphant v. Suquamish, *authored by Justice William Rehnquist. Rehnquist was joined by Justices Stewart, White, Blackmun, Powell, and Stevens.*

While Congress never expressly forbade Indian tribes to impose criminal penalties on non-Indians, we now make express our implicit conclusion of nearly a century ago that Congress consistently believed this to be the necessary result of its repeated legislative actions [. . .]

By themselves, these treaty provisions would probably not be sufficient to remove criminal jurisdiction over non-Indians if the tribe otherwise retained such jurisdiction. But an examination of our earlier precedents satisfies us that, even ignoring treaty provisions and congressional policy, Indians do not have criminal jurisdiction over non-Indians absent affirmative delegation of such power by Congress. Indian tribes do retain elements of "quasi-sovereign" authority after ceding their lands to the United States and announcing their dependence on the Federal Government [. . .] But the tribes' retained powers are not such that they are limited only by specific restrictions in treaties or congressional enactments [. . .]

By submitting to the overriding sovereignty of the United States, Indian tribes therefore necessarily give up their power to try non-Indian citizens of the United States except in a manner acceptable to Congress. This principle would have been obvious a century ago when most Indian tribes were characterized by a "want of fixed laws [and] of competent tribunals of justice." H.R. Rep. No. 474, 23d Cong., 1st Sess., 18 (1834). It should be no less obvious today, even though present-day Indian tribal courts embody dramatic advances over their historical antecedents. [. . .]

We recognize that some Indian tribal court systems have become increasingly sophisticated, and resemble in many respects their state counterparts. We also acknowledge that, with the passage of the Indian Civil Rights Act of 1968, which extends certain basic procedural rights to anyone tried in Indian tribal court, many of the dangers that might have accompanied the exercise by tribal courts of criminal jurisdiction over non-Indians only a few decades ago have disappeared. Finally, we are not unaware of the prevalence of non-Indian crime on today's reservations which the tribes forcefully argue requires the ability to try non-Indians [. . .] But these are considerations for Congress to weigh in deciding whether Indian tribes should finally be authorized to try non-Indians. They have little relevance to the principles which lead us to conclude that Indian tribes do not have inherent jurisdiction to try and to punish non-Indians. The judgments below are therefore *Reversed*.

Source: Oliphant v Suquamish Indian Tribe, 435 U.S. 191 (1978): 205, 209, 211–13.

Justice Marshall's Dissenting Opinion in *Oliphant v. Suquamish* (1978)

The following is Justice Thurgood Marshall's dissenting opinion in Oliphant v. Suquamish. *Marshall's reasoning is congruent with the rationale of the Ninth Circuit Court of Appeals. Chief Justice Burger joined Marshall in dissent. Justice Brennan did not participate.*

I agree with the court below that the "power to preserve order on the reservation . . . is a *sine qua non* of the sovereignty that the Suquamish originally possessed" [. . .] In the absence of affirmative withdrawal by treaty or statute, I am of the view that Indian tribes enjoy, as a necessary aspect of their retained sovereignty, the right to try and punish all persons who commit offenses against tribal law within the reservation. Accordingly, I dissent.

Source: Oliphant v. Suquamish Indian Tribe, 435 U.S. 191 (1978): 213.

See also: Tribal Law and Order Act, 2010; Violence Against Women Act, Title IX: Safety for Indian Women, 2013

Further Reading

Amnesty International. *Maze of Injustice: The Failure to Protect Indigenous Women From Sexual Violence in the USA*. New York: Amnesty International Publications, 2007.

Barker, Joanne, ed. *Sovereignty Matters: Locations of Contestation and Possibility in Indigenous Struggles for Self-Determination*. Lincoln, NE: University of Nebraska Press, 2005.

Cherokee Nation v. Georgia, 30 U.S. 1 (1831).

Deer, Sarah. "What She Say, It Be Law." *Mending the Sacred Hoop Newsletter.* 4.2 (2000): 1.

Deer, Sarah. "Sovereignty of the Soul: Exploring the Intersection of Rape Law Reform and Federal Indian Law." *Suffolk University Law Review* 38 (2005): 459.

Deer, Sarah and Carrie E. Garrow. *Tribal Criminal Law and Procedure*. New York: Altamira Press, 2007.

Goldberg, Carole, Kevin K. Washburn, and Philip P. Frickey, eds. *Indian Law Stories*. St. Paul: Foundation Press, 2011.

Indian Country Defined. 18 U.S.C. § 1151.

Johnson, Steven. "Jurisdiction: Criminal Jurisdiction and Enforcement Problems on Indian Reservations in the Wake of Oliphant." *American Indian Law Review* 7.2 (1979): 291–317.

Lavetta Elk v. United States. No. 05-186L (U.S. Court of Federal Claims, 2009).

Oliphant v. Schlie, 544 F.2d 1007 (Ninth Circuit 1976).

Oliphant v. Suquamish Indian Tribe, 435 U.S. 191 (1978).

Pevar, Stephen L. *The Rights of Indians and tribes*. Oxford, UK: Oxford University Press, 2012.

Tribal Law and Order Act of 2010 P.L. 111–211, 25 U.S.C. 2801.

Violence Against Women Reauthorization Act of 2013 P.L. 113–14.

Worcester v. Georgia, 31 U.S. 515 (1832).

Indian Child Welfare Act of 1978

Azusa Ono

Chronology

1609   The Virginia Company authorizes the capture of Indian children for the purpose of conversion, assimilation, and use of their labor.

1819   The Civilization Fund Act passes. It is the first federal law affecting Indian children. It provides funds to private agencies and churches to establish programs to "civilize the Indian."

1879   The Carlisle Indian School, the first off-reservation boarding school, is founded in Pennsylvania by General Richard Henry Pratt.

1884   The "placing-out" system is established. The program sent a great number of Indian children to farms in the East and Midwest so that they could learn the "values of work and the benefits of civilization."

1953   Congress adopts House Concurrent Resolution 108, which declares that "it is the policy of Congress, as rapidly as possible, to make the Indians within the territorial limits of the United States subject to the same laws . . . , to end their status as wards of the United States and to grant them all the rights and prerogatives pertaining to American citizenship."

            Congress passes P.L.83–280 (commonly known as PL280). The act transfers most civil and criminal jurisdiction from the federal government and local tribe to the state where the reservation is located.

1958–67   The Bureau of Indian Affairs (BIA) and the Child Welfare League of America (CWLA) undertake the Indian Adoption Project (IAP). During its nine-year existence, IAP coordinated adoption of 395 Native American children and made referrals for over 5,000 families interested in adopting Indian children.

1968   IAP is folded into the broader Adoption Resource Exchange of North America (ARENA).

            This non-governmental organization defined the Indian youth as "hard-to-place children" and rigorously sought adoptees.

1969   The Association of American Indian Affairs (AAIA) publishes a study on Indian adoption. It reveals an extremely high rate of adoption and foster care of Indian children, as well as conflicting motives for their removal from homes and tribal communities.

1974   Congress initiates its first hearing on Indian child welfare.

AAIA publishes another study on Indian adoption and begins publishing *Indian Family Defense*, a newsletter focused on Indian child-welfare problems.

1976   Senator James Abourezk (D–SD), chairman of Senate Subcommittee on Indian Affairs, introduces the Indian Child Welfare Act (ICWA).

1978   President Jimmy Carter approves ICWA. The act 1) establishes the primary jurisdiction of tribal courts in child welfare proceedings for Native American children, 2) establishes priorities for the placement of Native children, and 3) provides funding to improve child welfare and family development and preservation programs on reservations.

1982   First usage of the "existing Indian family exception." The Kansas State judicial system implemented it for the first time in the *Adoption of Baby Boy L.* case, and it has since evolved. The "existing Indian family exception" is a court-decreed doctrine that bars application of ICWA when neither the child nor the child's parents have not maintained a significant social, cultural, or political relationship with his tribe.

1989   The U.S. Supreme Court decides the case of *Mississippi Band of Choctaw Indians v. Holyfield* (490 U.S. 30, 1989). The Court holds that tribal courts have jurisdiction over children when both biological parents live on a reservation, even though they were born off of the reservation.

1992   The Northwest Indian Child Welfare Association renames itself as the National Indian Child Welfare Association (NCWA).

1994   Congress passes the Social Security Act Amendments of 1994 (P.L.03–432), which require states to develop specific measures for compliance with ICWA within their Child and Family Service Plan.

2001   Shay Bilchik (Executive Director of the Child Welfare League of America) formally apologizes for IAP at a meeting of the National Indian Child Welfare Association and puts the Child Welfare League of America on record in support of the Indian Child Welfare Act. He states, "No matter how well intentioned and how squarely in the mainstream this was at the time, it was wrong; it was hurtful; and it reflected a kind of bias that surfaces feelings of shame."

2003   ICWA amendments are proposed to reject the "existing Indian family exception," but Congress never passes them.

2008   The Fostering Connections to Success and Increasing Adoptions Act (P.L.110–351) becomes a law. The act provides tribal access to Title IV-E funds of the Social Security Act either directly from the federal government or through an intergovernmental agreement with states.

2013   The Supreme Court rules in the case of *Adoptive Couple v. Baby Girl* in favor of non-Indian adoptive family over a Cherokee biological father. The court claims that provisions that prohibit the termination of a biological father's parental rights never applied to him as he never knew or had custody over the child.

Introduction

The Indian Child Welfare Act of 1978 (ICWA, P.L.95–608) is a law that seeks to ensure the survival of tribal cultures and traditions through tribal jurisdiction. The law arose in response to the destructive practices of the public and private welfare systems that removed Native American children from their families and tribal communities. Senator James Abourezk of South Dakota first introduced the bill on August 27, 1976, and President Jimmy Carter signed it in 1978. The act:

1. Established the primary jurisdiction of tribal courts in child welfare proceedings for on-reservation children and enrolled off-reservation children.
2. Established priorities for the placement of Native children (the child's extended family, followed by members of the child's tribe and other Native families, before any other adopter). By creating this hierarchy, the law sought to honor the extended family arrangements and sustain tribal cultures.
3. Provided funding to improve child welfare and family development and preservation programs on reservations.

Congress also appropriated $5.5 million for tribes to operate family-development centers in an effort to strengthen family life and prevent separation of Indian children from their families.

Removal of Indian Children Prior to ICWA

Adoption of Native American children by non-Native families is a part of a long-lasting assimilationist policy that the federal government had embraced since the foundation of the nation. Before the removal of Indian children through adoption and foster care, the federal government and interested non-Indian organizations and religious groups had removed, often forcibly, Indian children to make them attend boarding schools. By the end of 19th century, boarding schools became the only option for a lot of Indian families to provide adequate housing, clothing, food, and education, a pattern that persisted throughout the 20th century. Given limited choices, more parents became willing to send children to off-reservation boarding schools, hoping they would provide a better life for their children.

The first off-reservation boarding school, the Carlisle Indian School in Pennsylvania, opened its doors in 1879. Its founder, Richard Henry Pratt, believed that the boarding schools would successfully "Kill the Indian and save the man." Pratt's philosophy persisted when the wholesale Indian adoption program started in 1958.

1958–67 Indian Adoption Project (IAP)

Between 1958 and 1967, the Child Welfare League of America (CWLA) contracted with the BIA to promote the adoption of Indian children with non-Indian foster families. This is a unique example of U.S. public policy whereby the federal government transferred children of one race to families of another race.

The IAP director Arnold Lyslo had spent a lot of time working on public relations to win support for his adoption project from the general public. He characterized the adoption of Indian children as a benevolent act that would help unwed Indian mothers who had to ask for assistance from their extended families. To convince social workers in the field that adoption of Indian children was successful, Lyslo published articles in *Child Welfare*, a journal whose primary audience was in the field of social work. Lyslo characterized Native children as "forgotten" youth who were "unloved and uncared for on the reservation" ("Adoptive Placement," 4).

The IAP had three major objectives. First, it sought to prove that Indian children were adoptable. Second, it wanted to expand from a pilot program, which would place 50 to 100 children, to a large-scale permanent, national plan. Finally, it conducted research based on the earlier placement process, the outcome of which was Robert Fanshel's *Far from the Reservation: The Transracial Adoption of American Indian Children* (1972).

To be eligible for IAP, Indian children, family, and the court system needed to meet the specific criteria. Children had to have at least one-quarter of Indian blood and be physically and mentally capable of benefitting from adoption. Second, the birth parent(s) must have decided to relinquish the child after casework and counseling because it was best for the child. Third, if the child was forcibly removed from home for abandonment or neglect, the jurisdiction of state courts, not tribal courts, had to be clear enough to ensure that the child was legally free for adoption (Lyslo, "Background," 40).

During its first year of operation, IAP operated on 13 reservations in five states (Arizona, Montana, Nevada, North Carolina, and South Dakota). Of these five states, South Dakota and Arizona had the most active IAP operation. During its nine-year existence, IAP coordinated the adoption of 395 Native American children. Children mostly from reservations in the Western and Midwestern states were adopted by non-Indian families in the Eastern and Midwestern states. In 1967, for instance, out of 119 Indian children adopted through IAP, 41 came from Arizona, and 24 from South Dakota. Meanwhile, the largest number of non-Indian adopting families resided in Massachusetts (16) followed by Indiana (14), Illinois (13), New York (13), and New Jersey (11) (Department of Interior News Release, March 24, 1968).

IAP developed as a part of the "termination" policy, which aimed for withdrawal of the federal government's trust relationship with Indian tribes. Supporters of termination policy argued that adoption of Indian children by non-Indian families was more cost-effective than placing the children in government-funded boarding schools.

The termination policy advanced with the adoption of House Concurrent Resolution 108, followed in 1953 by the passage of PL280. The resolution declared that transfer of the Indian child welfare cases to state systems would save the BIA money. Supporters of termination and IAP also contended that adoption by non-Native private families also meant that Indian children would no longer require federal or state support once adopted by a middle-class non-Native family. For Native Americans, on the other hand, the adoption of their children was another example of government policies of individual "termination" and assimilation.

PL280 aimed the transfer of most of civil and criminal jurisdiction as well as social services from the federal government and local tribe to the state where the reservation was located. By making Indian people eligible for state-administered services, including public assistance and child welfare service, the act sought elimination of the federal government's responsibility over tribes. States that accepted the PL-280 policies first included California, Minnesota (except for the Red Lake Chippewa Reservation), Nebraska, Oregon (except for the Warm Springs Reservation), Wisconsin, and Alaska (upon statehood). Later Arizona, Florida, Idaho, Iowa, Montana, Nevada, Utah, North Dakota, South Dakota, and Washington became PL 280 states.

In 2001, Shay Bilchik, the executive director of the CWLA, formally apologized for the excesses of the IAP at a meeting of the National Indian Child Welfare Association. He put the CWLA on record in support of the Indian Child Welfare Act. Said Bilchik, "No matter how well intentioned and how squarely in the mainstream this was at the time, it was wrong; it was hurtful; and it reflected a kind of bias that surfaces feelings of shame" (NICWA website).

The Adoption Resource Exchange of North America (ARENA)

The Adoption Resource Exchange of North America (ARENA) took shape in mid-1967 and began full operation by early 1968 under the direction of Clara Swan. It started as a three-year demonstration project in CWLA funded by the HEW, the American Contract Bridge Association, and the BIA. By 1977, almost 800 Native children had been placed through these programs.

ARENA sought to develop the First National adoption resource exchange to effectively find homes for "hard-to-place children." Indian children were considered such children who were characterized as of minority race, children with physical or mental disabilities, older children, or part of larger sibling groups. Distribution of Indian youth among the ARENA-identified families proved to be extremely high. For instance, in 1971, 95 children out of 249 ARENA-placed adoptees were Native.

In the early 1970s, CWLA emphasized identification of homes for Native children within their culture. In reality, the vast majority of Native youth were adopted by non-Native (mostly Caucasian) families. Behind this trend existed the "shortage" of so-called "blue-ribbon" (blond, blue-eyed, and visibly "white") babies. The 1970s witnessed the introduction of birth control, increased wage work opportunities for women, and the 1973 legalization of abortion. Women of all ethnic groups enjoyed more reproductive rights, including the means to avoid pregnancy and to choose options other than placing their babies for adoption. This perceived "shortage" led to the popularity of Native American children for adoption as well as an increased interest in overseas adoption.

Statistics on Removal of Indian Children

The American Association of Indian Affairs report published of 1969 declared the Indian adoption situation as a crisis. It revealed that an extremely high rate of removal (25–35 percent) of all Native children were removed from their homes and placed into foster care, adoption homes, or institutions. In Minnesota, one in every four Indian children under the age of one year had been adopted between 1971 and 1972 (Byler, 1).

In addition to the adoption, foster care, and institutionalization, many Indian children lived in BIA-operated facilities. In 1971, 34,538 Indian children stayed in the Bureau's residential facilities rather than at home (Byler, 1). Among the Navajos, approximately 20,000 children or 90 percent of the BIA school population in grades K–12 lived at boarding schools (Byler, 2).

A majority of those children living in foster care did so with non-Indian families. A 1969 survey of 16 states found that 85 percent of all children in foster care did not reside with Indian families (Byler, 2). They and their parents also faced discriminatory standards for foster care, based on American middle-class values. Due to the widely shared ideology that appreciated middle-class nuclear family orientation over the extended family orientation of Indian families, it was almost impossible for Indian families to be qualified as foster families (Byler, 4).

Campaign for ICWA

The Devils Lake Sioux of Fort Totten, North Dakota, were among the first groups to voice resistance to ongoing removal of Indian children from their tribal communities, subsequent to their placement with non-Indian foster care and/or adoption (Jacobs, 98). In 1968, the concerned women of the Fort Totten reservation asked for the AAIA's assistance and sent delegates to Washington, D.C., to lobby Congress. The AAIA's study on the Devils Lake Sioux declared that out of 1,100 young people under the age of 21, 275 (25 percent of the total) had been separated from their families (Jacobs, 101).

During the 1978 Congressional hearings, a number of Indian activists, advocates, tribal government officials, social workers, and parents testified in support of the Indian Child Welfare Act. Many pointed out that child welfare workers neither understood nor supported Native cultures and their childrearing traditions. This failure to respect Native American culture had emphasized child removal instead of integrated services to support and sustain Indian communities.

Witnesses also testified that welfare agencies rarely made an effort to make an early intervention, provide alternatives to out-of-home placement, or offer support for family and children to prevent the removal process. Federal or state agency personnel who had little or no knowledge of Indian culture or child-rearing practices, or who had poor training in dealing with Indian child welfare, nonetheless made decisions about removal. Indian youth often would be taken away without any court order or due process (Mindell and Gurwitt, 63). Non-Indian social workers would visit family's homes and convince the Indian mothers to relinquish their children, claiming that they would be better served with non-Indian adoptees. As Senator Abourezk stated in 1977, "public and private welfare agencies seem to have operated on the premise that most Indian children would really better off growing up non-Indian" (ICWA Hearing, 1977, 1). When faced with the loss of their children, Indian parents and families had little choice but to accept the judgment of government personnel, even if it was far from ideal as they rarely understood their parental rights or means of redress. Those parents who opposed this policy in court often failed to locate an advocate to represent their interests (Mindell and Gurwitt, 63).

Proponents of the ICWA also claimed that adoption of Indian children by non-Indian families separated them from tribal heritage. Instead, they demanded a transition from a system based on acculturation to mainstream values to one that emphasized Indian self-determination.

Psychiatrists also became concerned about the impact of institutionalization and adoption of Indian children by non-Indian families. The American Academy of Child Psychiatry (AACP) established a Committee on the American Indian Child in 1973 and collaborated with AAIA in their effort to pass the welfare act. During the hearings, psychiatrists testified that foster care and adoption by non-Indian families placed undue burdens impact on Indian children, especially in their adolescent years. A representative of the Academy claimed in a hearing on January 25, 1975: "There is much clinical evidence to suggest that there Native American children placed in off-reservation non-Indian homes are at risk in their later development. Often enough they are cared for by devoted and well-intended foster or adoptive parents. Nonetheless, particularly in adolescence, they are subject to ethnic confusion and a pervasive sense of abandonment with its attendant multiple ramifications" (ICWA Hearing 1977, 114). Indian children's out-of-home experiences for extended periods of time seriously impaired their ability as parents, and transferred the problem to future generations.

Opponents of the welfare act came from the federal government agencies. The Departments of Interior, Health, Education and Welfare (HEW), and Justice, and the Office of Management and Budget (OMB) expressed disapproval of the bill. The BIA and the HEW saw no need for the ICWA, preferring an amendment to the Social Security Act to accomplish the goal. Private groups actively involved in the removal and placement of Indian children with non-Indian families, such as the CWLA, also spoke in opposition. The Church of Jesus Christ of Latter Day Saints believed that the ICWA would interfere with its Student Placement Program in which over 2,500 Indian youth (almost 5,000 at its peak in 1972) were taken into Mormon homes. These groups argued that the welfare act represented "reverse" racial discrimination by requiring that Indian children be placed only with Indian families.

The campaign for passage in the 1970s of the ICWA became part of a larger quest for Indian self-determination and sovereignty. The Red Power movement had employed more confrontational and militant tactics, as seen with the occupation of Alcatraz Island in San Francisco Bay in 1969, and the takeover in 1973 of Wounded Knee, South Dakota. The campaign for the welfare act was less visible to the general public. Grassroots activism included passage of tribal resolutions, revision of legal codes, and development of social service programs (Jacobs, 119). Such initiatives drew less media coverage than the more radical events staged by the American Indian Movement (AIM) and the National Indian Youth Council (NIYC).

Misunderstanding and Inappropriate Interpretation of Indian Parents' Behavior

Among those Indian children placed for adoption, very few children were removed due to physical abuse. According to a study conducted in North Dakota and in the Northwest, in 99 percent of all cases, the adoption process resulted from charges of neglect, social deprivation, and emotional damage of children living with their parents (Byler, 2). Indian parents, observing the removal of their children, could engage in poor parental behavior and avoidance of emotional attachments to their youth.

Child welfare officials also could be insensitive to traditional Indian child rearing practices where the extended family offered significant child care. Non-Indian social workers and authorities often perceived the willingness of an Indian mother or father to allow a child to live with a relative as a sign of abandonment. Relatives, such as aunts, uncles, and grandparents, often were the primary source for child abuse prevention in Indian communities.

Compounding this situation was a traditional Native belief that children are gifts from the Creator, instead of parents' property. Members of extended families often showed extraordinary patience and tolerance toward the young, emphasizing children's self-discipline. Therefore, children were usually brought up without restraint or severe physical punishment. This alternative to close parental supervision and physical punishment by Indian parents was viewed as indications of parental neglect (ICWA Hearing 1974, 103).

Challenges after the ICWA

Advocates of the Indian Child Welfare Act won their battle with the passage in 1978 of the legislation. Yet, challenges arose to hinder application of the law. Funding for tribal foster care and adoption services has been always a problem, as Title II of the ICWA provides only a small grant program for tribes. The largest share of funding is administered by the Department of Health and Human Services (HHS) under the provisions of the Social Security Act. Title IV-B of that law allows tribes to have access to funds to support their child welfare services. This also became the only monitoring tool available to the federal government for examination of state ICWA compliance.

Another major issue in the application of the welfare act is the development of "existing Indian family exception" (also known as "Indian family exception doctrine" or "the Indian family doctrine") The "existing Indian family exception" doctrine arose from a judge's opinion that bars application of the ICWA when neither the child nor the child's parents have not retained a significant social, cultural, or political relationship with his tribe (Atwood, 204).

In 2013, the "Baby Veronica" case (*Adoptive Couple v. Baby Girl*) made national headlines as a custody battle was fought between the adoptive parents of an Indian child and her biological father. As seen here, protests supporting the biological father occurred outside of the courthouse. The Indian Child Welfare Act of 1978 was cited by both parties in the legal proceedings, with the courts ultimately ruling that the adoptive parents would gain custody. (AP Photo/Sue Ogrocki)

This exception was first used in 1982, when the Kansas Supreme Court decided in the case of *Adoption of Baby Boy L.* (231 Kan. 199). When an unwed non-Indian mother tried to voluntarily place her son for adoption with a non-Indian adoptive family, the Indian father and his tribe objected it. The court supported the adoption, arguing that the ICWA would not apply in this case, as no family had existed before adoption (Atwood, 205). Since the first implementation of this exemption, a number of courts have used it to protect non-Indian adoptive family's interests including the 2013 U.S. Supreme Court case of *Adoptive Couple v. Baby Girl.*

Biography of Notable Figure

Evelyn Lance Blanchard (1938–) is a Laguna Pueblo and Pascua Yaqui social worker and Indian activist. She was an important proponent of the welfare act and had been called the "Mother of ICWA" (Johnson, 149). She received a B.A.

**Sidebar 1: Supreme Court Decision Related to ICWA,
1989 *Mississippi Band of Choctaw Indians v. Holyfield*
(490 U.S. 30, 1989)**

Jennie Bell, a member of the Mississippi Band of Choctaw Indians, was a 24-year-old single mother of two when she became pregnant with twins by a Choctaw man who was married to another woman, and who had two children of his own. Upon deciding to place her twins for adoption, Jennie Bell left the reservation to give birth. She immediately put her twins up for adoption with a non-Indian couple: Orrey Curtiss Holyfield, a Methodist minister, and his wife, Vivian Joan. They had been looking for a child to adopt, but had encountered difficulties in locating one, partially because of their advanced age (Orrey, 60 years old, and Vivian, 44 years old) and Orrey's poor health.

The issue in this case was whether the tribal jurisdiction extends to an Indian child whose mother gave birth off-reservation. The U.S. Supreme Court held that as both biological parents lived on a reservation, tribal courts had jurisdiction over the children even though they had been born off-reservation. The tribal court, also considering the psychological attachment of children to the adoptive parents, ruled that the twins could stay with the Holyfields. The decision reinforced tribal jurisdiction over child custody cases of tribal members.

---

in sociology from the University of New Mexico in 1962 and a master's degree in social work from the University of Denver in 1969. In 2010, she submitted to the UNM American Studies Department her dissertation entitled "To Prevent the Breakup of the Indian Family: The Development of Indian Child Welfare Act of 1978." Her passion for the fight against the unfair removal of Indian child from their family and community comes from her own family's generational history of child removal and institutionalization. Her father was taken from his home in Laguna, New Mexico, to attend Carlisle Indian School in Pennsylvania. Blanchard herself was removed from her parents in her teenage years (Johnson, 155; Jacobs, 111–12).

When the hearings on the ICWA began in 1974, Blanchard served as an assistant area social worker in the BIA Albuquerque Area Office. At the 1974 hearing, she submitted a statement making it clear that she was not representing the BIA, even though she was an agency employee. Blanchard saw an urgent need for hiring more Indian social workers who understood the tribal culture. She stated, "The only solution is in providing competent social workers who are given the funds to work

Sidebar 2: ICWA Supreme Court Decision Related to ICWA, 2013 *Adoptive Couple v. Baby Girl* (the Baby Veronica case)

Baby Veronica was born to Christy Maldonado, a non-Native mother, and Dusten Brown, a member of Cherokee Nation and an Iraq war veteran. While Maldonado was still pregnant, her relationship with Brown ended, and she decided to put her child up for adoption. The non-Indian adoptive couple, Matt and Melanie Capobianco, supported Maldonado during her pregnancy and attended the delivery. Four months after Veronica's birth, the adoptive couple served Brown with a notice of pending adoption. He signed papers stating that he was "not contesting the adoption," only to contact a lawyer one day later to seek custody of his infant daughter.

In September 2011, the South Carolina Family Court and South Carolina Supreme Court awarded custody of Veronica to Brown, the biological father. The courts held that the adoptive family had failed to prove that the biological father's custody would cause harm to the child, and that they sought to provide preventive measures to avoid the adoption of the child by a non-Native family. After this decision, the Capobiancos released Veronica to her biological father, who lived in Oklahoma.

The Capobiancos and their supporters appealed the case to the U.S. Supreme Court, arguing that the ICWA ignored the best interests of children. In June 2013, the Court overturned the state courts' decisions in a 5–4 ruling. The court held that provisions that barred the termination of the biological father's parental right never applied to him as he had never known or had custody over the child before her adoption.

Following the Supreme Court decision, in September 2013, Dusten Brown unwillingly gave up his daughter to the Capobiancos after fighting the order for few months. The Cherokee Nation also dropped the case. The case drew national media attention, especially after *Dr. Phil,* a daytime television talk show, had highlighted the adoption issue on October 18, 2012, eight months before the Supreme Court decision.

within the community. We must be allowed to develop programs and facilities on the reservation which will enable the child who has to be removed from the home, the source of his distress, to develop not according to the norms and mores of the outside but according to his or her own needs and the prevailing conditions and precepts of his or her tribe. Emphasis must be placed on keeping children with their own or substitute families" (ICWA Hearing 1974, 216).

Blanchard would take a leave from the BIA in New Mexico and move in the mid-1970s to the Pacific Northwest to provide assistance to the tribes in Washington state who sought to change the state's administrative codes related to Indian child welfare (Jacobs, 109, 131). She has held a number of leading positions in the area of social work, including the program director of the National Center for American Indian and Alaskan Native Mental Health Research and Development (Whitecloud Center) in Portland, Oregon. Blanchard also has been secretary of the Association of American Indian and Alaska Native Social Workers.

Before the passage of the welfare act, Indian activists, the Association of American Indian Affairs, and their supporters worked with individual states to change the state codes to adopt the new policy of Indian self-determination for child welfare. Blanchard contributed to the transformation of the Washington State's codes related to Indian child welfare. In 1976, Washington State included new regulations that gave tribes greater involvement in the placement of their youth (Jacobs, 131).

The CWLA and ARENA understood the best interest of Indian child as to find a permanent home rather than staying within the tribal community, and emphasized permanency and saving Indian children over the preservation and strengthening of Indian families. (Jacobs, 151–52) In an article entitled "Question of Best Interest," Blanchard objected to such a position and claimed, "How the courts define 'best interest' negates the right of an Indian person to look for strength and assistance from his tribal identity by denying it as a resource, keeps the Indian parent, child and tribe in a dependent position in this era of self-determination and individual rights, and effectively kills more Indian people through the smothering arms of the helping process" (Blanchard, 60).

The passage of the ICWA occurred because of tireless work and the efforts of Indian activists and social workers like Blanchard, who have dealt with the issue of Indian child welfare on a constant basis. They knew only too well about the problems confronting Indian children, families, and tribes. The welfare act strengthened the ideal of Indian self-determination, as Blanchard claimed that "Indian tribes and communities can manage their own affairs" (Blanchard, 1977, 42).

DOCUMENT EXCERPTS

Before the passage of ICWA, numerous Indian witnesses testified before Congress in support of the act. One of the main arguments that advocates of ICWA made was that the removal of Indian children from their home and tribal community undermined the group rights and sovereignty of Indian tribes and nations as well as threatening the survival of tribal traditions and cultures. Here Calvin Issac, tribal chief of the Mississippi Band of Choctaw Indians and representative of the National Tribal Chairmen's Association, testifies as to the importance of Indian children in preservation of Indian cultures and traditions, calling them "the only real means for the transmission of the tribal heritage."

Testimony by Calvin Issac, Tribal Chief of the Mississippi Band of Choctaw Indians and a Member of the National Tribal Chairmen's Association, before the House of Representatives Subcommittee on Indian Affairs and Public Lands, S.1214, The Indian Child Welfare Act, February 9, 1978.

I testified before the Senate Select Committee on Indian Affairs last year on the importance to the Indian tribal future of federal support for tribally controlled educational programs and institutions. I do not wish to amend anything I said then, but I do want to say that the issue we address today is even more basic than education in many ways. If Indian communities continue to lose their children to the general society through adoptive and foster care placements at the alarming rates of the recent past, if Indian families continue to be disrespected and their parental capacities challenged by non-Indian social agencies as vigorously as they have in the past, then education, the tribe, Indian culture have little meaning or future. This is why NTCA supports S. 1214, the Indian Child Welfare Act.

Our concern is the threat to traditional Indian culture which lies in the incredibly insensitive and oftentimes hostile removal of Indian children from their homes and their placement in non-Indian settings under color of state and federal authority. Individual child and parental rights are ignored, and tribal governments, which are legitimately interested in the welfare of their people, have little or no part in this shocking outflow of children.

The problem exists both among reservation Indians and Indians living off the reservation in urban communities: an inordinately high percentage of our Indian children are separated from their natural parents and placed in foster homes, adoptive homes, or various kinds of institutions, including boarding schools. The rate of separation is much higher among Indians than in non-Indian communities. In 1976 Task Force Four of the Policy Review Commission reported Indian adoption and foster care placement statistics for 19 states. Of some 333,650 Indians in those states under the age of 21, 11,157, or at least one in every 30, were in adoptive homes. Another 6,700 were in foster care situations. Comparison of Indian adoption and foster placement rates with those of the non-Indian population for the same state invariably showed the Indian rate was higher, usually at least two to four times as high and sometimes 20 times higher. Where the statistics were available they showed that most of the adoptions and placements, sometimes 95 percent of them, were with non-Indian families.

One of the most serious failings of the present system is that Indian children are removed from the custody of their natural -parents by nontribal government authorities who have no basis for intelligently evaluating the cultural and social premises underlying Indian home life and childrearing. Many of the individuals who decide the fate of our children are at best Ignorant of our cultural values, and at worst contemptful (sic) of the Indian way and convinced that removal, usually to a non-Indian -household or institution, can only benefit an Indian child. Removal is generally accomplished without notice to or consultation with responsible tribal authorities.

Often the situation which ultimately leads to the separation of the child from his family is either not harmful to the child, except from the ethnocentric viewpoint of one unfamiliar with the Indian community, or is one which could be remedied without breaking up the family. Unfortunately, removal from parental custody is seen as a simple solution. Typically the parents do not understand the nature of the proceeding, and counsel represents neither parents nor child.

Not only is removal of an Indian child from parental custody not a simple solution, under present policies it is no solution at all. The effect of these practices can be devastating—both for the child and his family, and in a broader sense, for the tribe. The child, taken from his Native surroundings and placed in a foreign environment is in a very poor position to develop a healthy sense of identity either as an individual or as a member of a cultural, group. The resultant loss of self-esteem only leads to a greater Incidence of some of the most visible problems afflicting Indian communities: drug abuse, alcoholism, crime, and suicide. The experience often results, too, in a destruction of any feeling of self -worth of the parents, who are deemed unfit even to raise their own children. There is a feeling among professionals who have dealt with the problem that this sort of psychological damage may contribute to the Incidence of alcohol abuse.

Culturally, the chances of Indian survival are significantly reduced if our children, the only real means for the transmission of the tribal heritage, are to be raised in non-Indian homes and denied exposure to the ways of their People. Furthermore, these practices 'seriously undercut the tribes' ability to continue as self-governing communities. Probably in no area is it more important that tribal sovereignty be respected than in an area as socially and culturally determinative as family relationships.

The ultimate responsibility for child welfare rests with the parents and we would not support legislation, which Interfered with that basic relationship. What we are talking about here is the situation where government, primarily the state government has moved to intervene in family relationships. S. 1214 will put govern mental responsibility for the welfare of our children where it belongs and where it can most effectively be exercised, that is, with the Indian tribes. NTCA believes that the emphasis of any federal child welfare program should be on the development of tribal alternatives to' present practices of severing family and cultural relationships. The jurisdictional problems addressed by this bill are difficult and we think it wise to encourage the development of good working relationships in this area between the tribes and nontribal governments whether through legislation, regulation, or tribal action. We would not want to create a situation in which the anguish of children and parents are prolonged by jurisdictional fights. This is an area in which the child's welfare must be primary.

Source: Hearings on Indian Child Welfare before the Senate Subcommittee on Indian Affairs. 95th Cong., 1st Session (1977).

Further Reading

Atwood, Barbara Ann. *Children, Tribes, and States: Adoption and Custody Conflicts over American Indian Children.* Durham, NC: Carolina Academic Press, 2010.

Blanchard, Evelyn. "The Question of Best Interest," in Steven Unger, ed. *The Destruction of American Indian Families.* New York: Association on American Indian Affairs, 1977, 57–60.

Byler, William. "The Destruction of American Indian Families." In *The Destruction of American Indian Families.* Edited by Steven Unger. New York: Association on American Indian Affairs, 1977, 1–11.

Fanshel, David. *Far from the Reservation: The Transracial Adoption of American Indian Children.* Metuchen, NJ: The Scarecrow Press, Inc., 1972.

Harness, Susan Devan. *Mixing Cultural Identities through Transracial Adoption: Outcomes of the Indian Adoption Project (1958-1967).* Lewiston, NY: Edwin Mellen Press, 2008.

Jacobs, Margaret D. *A Generation Removed: The Fostering and Adoption of Indigenous Children in the Postwar World.* Lincoln: University of Nebraska Press, 2014.

Johnson, Troy R., ed. *The Indian Child Welfare Act the Next Ten Years: Indian Homes for Indian Children. Conference Proceedings, August 22–24, 1990.* Los Angeles: American Indian Studies Center, University of California at Los Angeles, 1991.

Lyslo, Arnold L. "Background Information on Indian Adoption Project: 1958 through 1967." In David Fanshel, *Far from the Reservation: The Transracial Adoption of American Indian Children.* Metuchen, NJ: The Scarecrow Press, Inc., 1972, 33–49.

National Indian Child Welfare Association website. May 4, 2015. http://www.nicwa.org/

Simon, Rita J. and Sarah Hernandez. *Native American Transracial Adoptees Tell Their Stories.* New York: Lexington Books, 2008.

Unger, Steven, ed. *The Destruction of American Indian Families.* New York: Association on American Indian Affairs, 1977.

U.S. Department of Interior News Release, "Indian Children Adopted during 1967 at Almost Double the 1966 Rate," March 24, 1968. Accessed May 4, 2015. http://www.bia.gov/cs /groups/public/documents/text/idc017233.pdf

U.S. House of Representatives, *Hearings on Indian Child Welfare Act of 1978 before the Subcommittee on Indian Affairs and Public Lands on the Committee on Interior and Insular Affairs*, 95th Cong., 2nd Sess., Washington, D.C.: U.S. GPO, 1981.

U.S. Senate, *Hearings on Indian Child Welfare Act of 1977 before the Select Committee on Indian Affairs*, 95th Cong., 1st Sess., Washington, D.C.: U.S. GPO, 1977.

American Indian Religious Freedom Act, 1978

Angelique EagleWoman (Wambdi A. WasteWin)

Chronology

Time immemorial	Native Americans in the Western Hemisphere practice religious and ceremonial cultural lifeways guided by seasonal calendars and administered to sacred geographical sites to keep the world in balance.
1600s–1700s	Europeans establish colonies in North America with many fleeing from religious persecution in England. Newly created churches categorized Native Americans as non-Christian and therefore "pagans" and "savages."
1787	U.S. Constitution is adopted with the following First Amendment language on religious freedom: "Congress shall make no law respecting an establishment of religion, or prohibiting the free exercise thereof."
1823	U.S. Supreme Court announced in the *Johnson v. McIntosh* decision the "doctrine of discovery" as the legal basis for asserting title to all American Indian lands in North America.
1879	Carlisle Indian School is established as the model to "civilize" American Indian children and convert them to Christianity based upon a military regimen.
1880s	Compulsory attendance is imposed on American Indian children in government and/or religious boarding and day schools with rigid requirements of English-only standards for the children, U.S. patriotism instruction, and conversion to Christianity as "civilization" training.

1882	U.S. Indian Commissioner Hiram Price delivers his annual address supporting the proselytization of American Indians into Christian denominations.
1884	The U.S. Bureau of Indian Affairs creates the Indian Religious Crimes Code with enforcement in the U.S. Courts of Indian Offices to punish American Indians practicing traditional cultural and ceremonial lifeways.
1890	December 26. To prohibit the ceremonial Ghost Dance, the largest number of U.S military forces since the U.S. Civil War are mobilized to the Dakota Territory. The U.S. military commits the Wounded Knee Massacre, killing more than 300 unarmed men, women, and children.
1924	The Indian Citizenship Act is enacted by the U.S. Congress, creating dual citizenship for American Indians as tribal citizens and U.S. citizens.
1970s	American Indian governments, organizations, and people voice public protests regarding the ongoing U.S. religious persecution of those practicing traditional cultural and religious lifeways.
1978	August 11. American Indian Religious Freedom Act (AIRFA) is enacted by the U.S. Congress with no enforcement mechanism provided.
1994	AIRFA is amended to recognize the usage of peyote as part of traditional American Indian religious ceremonies and directed that no criminal penalties be assessed or, public-benefit deprivation occur, for an American Indian using peyote in a bona fide religious practice.
1996	U.S. President Bill Clinton issues Executive Order No. 13007 directing federal agencies to provide access and accommodation for American Indians to sacred sites on federal public lands.

Introduction

The American Indian Religious Freedom Act of 1978, 42 U.S.C. § 1996, was enacted in response to the petitions of tribal governments, organizations, and individuals to change the policies of the United States in seeking to convert Native Americans to Christianity and to suppress the traditional cultural and ceremonial lifeways of Native Americans. Native Americans sought a federal law that would provide legal protection for the practice of traditional cultural and ceremonial

A Northern Arapaho tribal member who killed a bald eagle in 2005 for use in a religious ceremony makes his way into the 10th Circuit Court of Appeals at the Federal Courthouse in Denver, 2007. A federal government decision to allow the Wyoming tribe to kill two bald eagles for a religious ceremony was a victory for American Indian religious freedoms. In the following year, the American Indian Religious Freedom Act of 1978 would offer federal protection for traditional and ceremonial practices. (AP Photo/ Bill Ross)

lifeways, for access and ceremonial practices at sacred sites on federal public lands, and the protection of ceremonial items.

In response, a bill was sponsored with three main purposes identified during the congressional hearings: 1) allowing Native Americans access to sacred sites located on federal public lands, 2) protecting the use of peyote as a sacrament by the Native American Church free of federal or state prosecution for possession of an illegal substance, and 3) allowing Native Americans the continued use of eagle feathers and other ceremonial items without the threat of federal prosecution under eagle-protection laws. On behalf of the U.S. Department of Justice, Assistant U.S. Attorney General-Legislative Affairs Patricia M. Wald submitted a letter of support for the bill with the understanding that no change to any existing federal or state laws would be required.

The bill as enacted was described in the Congressional Record by Representative Morris K. Udall as having "no teeth in it." The text of the first section of the act provided access to sacred sites and the ability to possess sacred items. The second section directed a review of federal agency policies and procedures for alignment with the policy statement in the first section.

In 1994, AIRFA was amended to accomplish the protection of sacramental peyote use by Native Americans free of criminal prosecution in the federal or state judicial systems. The amendment also protected Native Americans engaged in the bona fide ceremonial use of peyote from public-benefits deprivations based upon that usage.

The U.S. Governmental Policy of Eliminating Native American Religious Practice

With the formation of the United States, Euro-Americans viewed non-Christians as inferior and lacking the same religious freedom protections as Christians. The Christian faiths rely on a written text and practitioners may travel to any location. For Native Americans, cultural and religious practices are interwoven with the natural world. In the Native American worldview, the earth is a living being and referred to as "Mother Earth," which denotes a cultural and spiritual relationship. Further, all Native American religious practices adhere to the viewpoint of the inter-relationship of the natural world and human society. In contrast, the written text for Christianity places human beings in superior ranking to the natural world, which allows for exploitation.

With these fundamental differences, the history in the United States has been one of religious persecution for Native Americans. The efforts of proselytizing American Indians to Christianity began with the first Europeans to travel to the western hemisphere and continue to the present day. Under U.S. Indian policy in the 1800s, U.S. officials advocated for the "civilization" of American Indians, and particularly of children. The U.S. Indian policy era of assimilation and allotment during the late 1800s was intended to drastically reorient American Indians from traditional cultural and religious lifeways to emulate Euro-American Christian farmers. Three major efforts formed the U.S. Indian policy of this era: 1) outlawing American Indian religious and cultural practices; 2) enforcing compulsory U.S. education on American Indian children with a focus on conversion to Christianity; and 3) dividing the reserved homelands of tribal nations into small parcels of land to convert Indians into Christian farmers through the 1887 General Allotment Act.

Indian Religious Crimes Code

In 1882, U.S. Indian Commissioner Hiram Price delivered his annual report on the work of the U.S. Bureau of Indian Affairs (BIA), in which he advocated for Christian missionaries to provide education to American Indians as furthering the civilization mission of the U.S. government. "I am decidedly of the opinion that a liberal encouragement by the government to all religious denominations to extend their educational missionary operations among the Indians would be of immense benefit . . . In no other manner and by no other means, in my judgment, can our Indian population be so speedily and permanently reclaimed from the barbarism, idolatry and savage life, as by the educational and missionary operations of the Christian people of our country" (Prucha, 156). In his November 1, 1883, annual report, U.S. Secretary of the Interior Henry Teller similarly asserted that tribal medicine men were imposters and should be compelled to stop their practices (Prucha, 159).

In furtherance of these sentiments, Commissioner Price developed the Indian Religious Crimes Code to be implemented in the U.S. Courts of Indian Offenses on Indian reservations. The BIA regulations were issued in 1884 establishing the courts (Haas, 6), The fourth rule of the code provided:

> 4th. The "sun-dance," the "scalp-dance," the "war-dance," and all other so-called feasts assimilating thereto, shall be considered "Indian offenses," and any Indian found guilty of being a participant in anyone or more of these "offenses" shall, for the first offense committed, be punished by withholding from the person or persons so found guilty by the court his or their rations for a period not exceeding ten days; and if found guilty of any subsequent offense under this rule, shall by punished by withholding his or their rations for a period not less than fifteen days, nor more than thirty days, or by incarceration in the agency prison for a period not exceeding thirty days.

To directly punish medicine men practicing traditional cultural and religious lifeways, the sixth rule of the code provided:

> 6th. The usual practices of so-called "medicine-men" shall be considered "Indian offenses" cognizable by the Court of Indian Offenses, and whenever it shall be proven to the satisfaction of the court that the influence or practice of a so-called "medicine-man" operates as a hinderance [sic] to the civilization of a tribe, or that said "medicine-man" resorts to any artifice or device to keep the Indians under his influence, or shall adopt any means to prevent the attendance of children at the agency schools, or shall use any of the arts of a conjurer to prevent the Indians from abandoning their heathenish rites and customs, he shall be adjudged guilty of an Indian offense, and upon conviction . . . shall be confined in the agency prison for a term not less than ten days, or until such time as he shall produce evidence satisfactory to the court, and approved by the agent, that he will forever abandon all practices styled Indian offenses under this rule.

This set of rules was later revised in 1892 by Commissioner of Indian Affairs Thomas J. Morgan to set the term of imprisonment between ten and thirty days, and subsequent offenses to be charged for a maximum term of six months (Prucha, 186).

Many American Indians continued in opposition to these policies. On the Standing Rock Reservation, the Lakota medicine man and leader Chief Sitting Bull (Tatanka Iyotake) had allowed the practice of the Ghost Dance near his home. The local Indian agent sent out agency police to bring in Sitting Bull, and in doing so, the leader was killed. Following his death, Lakota Chief Big Foot sought safety at the Pine Ridge agency and proceeded to fly a white flag of surrender and peace when the group was intercepted by U.S. cavalry. The cavalry escorted them to a campsite set up by the military near the village of Wounded Knee.

The next morning, on December 26, 1890, the U.S. cavalry opened fire on the unarmed men, women, and children at the campsite. Survivors have related the horrific events that became known as the Wounded Knee Massacre of 1890 (Cohen's Handbook, 965). Thus, a message was sent to American Indians that the United States intended to use military force to suppress the Ghost Dance and other religious practices.

Allotment and Loss of Tribal Sacred and Cultural Sites

A third thrust of U.S. Indian policy to assimilate American Indians was division of tribal lands into separate parcels to diminish the tribal landholdings. Specific federal legislation had been passed for particular tribal nations. The U.S. Congress approved the 1887 General Allotment Act (commonly referred to as the "Dawes Act" after its primary sponsor Senator Henry Dawes). Through the law, the U.S. President determined a reservation subject to allotment, and U.S. Indian agencies implemented the land-division process. Through this process, the Indian agent created a tribal roll of members eligible to receive an allotment within reservation boundaries. Allotments were held by the U.S. government as trustee on behalf of the landowner for an initial 25-year period, later extended indefinitely. After allotments were determined, the U.S. government considered the remaining lands as "surplus" and set its purchase price to gain the lands as federal public lands.

Between 1887 and the repeal of the law in 1934, approximately two-thirds of all Indian lands—close to 27 million acres—were lost. A second loss of land occurred through the surplus determination resulting in another 60 million acres leaving tribal ownership (Royster, 12–13). U.S. President Theodore Roosevelt championed the allotment policy and was also known for acquisition of federal public lands designated as conservation acres. With many sacred and cultural sites on the lands claimed by the U.S. government, Native Americans lost access to their most sacred spiritual places to conduct traditional religious practices. Additionally, those tribal nations removed by the U.S. military from their homelands during this period lost access to their ancestral cemeteries and sacred spiritual places, as well as their abilities to conduct their ceremonial seasonal practices.

Congressional Hearings, Reports, and the Enactment of the American Indian Religious Freedom Act

With the vocal protests of the Civil Rights Movement of the 1960s and 1970s, American Indian leaders, organizations, and individuals became more public in their assertions for religious freedom. With the Indian self-determination gaining momentum in the mid to late 1970s, petitions, lobbying efforts, and public protests resulted in a bill to support American Indian religious freedom, co-sponsored by Senator James Abourezk of South Dakota and Representative Morris Udall of Arizona.

On February 24 and 27, 1978, the U.S. Senate Select Committee on Indian Affairs held hearings on American Indian religious freedom issues in furtherance of the bill. Several major concerns were expressed from tribal representatives from across the country. Witnesses at the hearings came from as far as the Yakama tribe in Washington to the Onondaga Nation of New York to deliver their statements to the committee. Common themes presented included the misunderstandings of non-Indian federal agency officials about access to sacred sites, the criminalization by all forms of law enforcement when Native Americans possessed ancient ceremonial items, and the desecration of Native American spiritual places. Several witnesses testified to the long history of U.S. governmental suppression of American Indian religious practices.

Deep gratitude was also expressed for the consideration of the new law. As Frank Tenario of the All Indian Pueblo Council explained, "We strongly support the efforts to get a consistent government-wide policy and procedures regarding the protection and preservation of Indian religious practices" (American Indian Religious Freedom Hearing on February 24 and 27, 1978, 15).

The testimony of Kurt Blue Dog and Walter Echo-Hawk underscored the disproportionately large numbers of American Indians in state and federal prisons who had been denied basic religious freedom rights. They offered examples of Indian males denied the ability to wear their hair long as an expression of spirituality, denial of the right to build a sweat lodge at prisoner facilities, and denial of the use of sacred pipes in ceremonies within prisons. This was juxtaposed with the federal and state prison systems' provision of chapels, religious text meetings, and other religious freedoms to incarcerated non-Indians (American Indian Religious Freedom Hearing on February 24 and 27, 1978, 151–61).

When the bill was debated in the U.S. House of Representatives, several congressmen questioned the need for the law, the process of implementation, and the lack of a list of sacred sites held by the federal government. In response, Congress-man Udall addressed the concerns that the law would provide access on federal pub-lic lands, not private lands; that there should not be a list of sacred sites kept by the federal government; and that the law would have "no teeth in it" (Congressional Record-House (July 18, 1978), p. 21445).

The American Indian Religious Freedom Act was formally enacted on August 11, 1978, through a joint resolution of the Senate and House of Representatives and codified at 42 U.S.C. § 1996. In the introduction of the resolution, the U.S. Congress found that "the lack of a clear, comprehensive, and consistent Federal policy has often resulted in the abridgment of religious freedom for traditional Amer-ican Indians." The first section of the law provided: "On and after August 11, 1978, it shall be the policy of the United States to protect and preserve for American Indians their inherent right of freedom to believe, express, and exercise the tradi-tional religions of the American Indian, Eskimo, Aleut, and Native Hawaiians, including but not limited to access to sites, use and possession of sacred objects, and the freedom to worship through ceremonials and traditional rites." The second section instructed the U.S. President to require all federal agencies to review and evaluate their policies and procedures in consultation with Native traditional reli-gious leaders to determine whether changes were necessary to carry out the purposes of the law.

The federal agency review resulted in a report to the U.S. Congress within the one-year deadline given. The 98-page report, P.L. 95–341, was delivered August 1979 from the Federal Agencies Task Force chaired by Secretary of the Interior, Cecil Andrus. The report dealt with many common misconceptions about Native American religious practices and provided comprehensive recommendations.

The conclusion section recognized the major step forward in understanding between the indigenous peoples and the mainstream ideas on religions.

Many issues raised by the passage of the American Indian Religious Free-dom Act reflect the prejudices and rigidity of past eras and not the matured understanding which characterizes contemporary America. Behind many objections may lurk the suspicion which the unfamiliar invokes in the mind before it comes to a more perfect understanding. It is clear from the direction of growth in understanding that has characterized American soci-ety in this century and from the adoption of a specific statement on Ameri-can Indian religious freedom by the Congress, that a policy of removing barriers to Indian religious freedom is perceived as the next step in the growth of American religious freedom and political maturity. (AIRFA Report, August 1979, 97)

Sidebar 1: Two Federal Cases Highlighting the Lack of Protection for Sacred Sites

1. *Lyng v. Northwest Indian Cemetery Association,* 485 U.S. 439 (1988)

The Six Rivers National Forest, near the Hoopa Valley Indian Reservation in northern California, has significance to numerous Native American Nations in the area. In 1982, the U.S. Forest Service (U.S.F.S.) proposed a timber road through the Chimney Rock area, a place of sacred ceremonial significance. A lawsuit was filed by a coalition of organizations, tribes, and individuals in federal court seeking an injunction to stop construction. The original decision by the federal district court and the Ninth Circuit Court of Appeals to uphold this junction was appealed to the U.S. Supreme Court by the U.S.F.S.

In an opinion authored by Justice Sandra Day O'Connor, the Court reversed the injunction and denied the claims by American Indians. Because the U.S.F.S. allowed access to the sacred site, the Court found no constitutional violation of the First Amendment's Free Exercise Clause. Rather, the decision focused on the land-ownership aspects of the case as determinative to permit the U.S.F.S. to build the timber-hauling road.

2. *Navajo Nation v. U.S. Forest Service,* 535 F.3d 1058 (9th Cir. 2008 en banc) (*Snowbowl* Case)

Three sacred peaks, the largest referred to as Humphrey's Peak in the Coconino National Forest, compose the San Francisco Peaks under the land management of the U.S.F.S. Numerous tribal nations have nurtured the peaks as sacred since time immemorial, including the Havasupai, Hopi, Hualapai, Navajo, White Mountain Apache, and Yavapai-Apache Nations. The U.S.F.S. approved the building of a ski run on Humphrey's Peak in the 1930s. known as the "Snowbowl." When an expansion was planned, tribal groups filed suit in federal court in the 1980s. Federal courts held that the expansion did not burden the religious practices of American Indians, because they had not been denied access to the Peaks.

In February 2005, the U.S. Forest Service approved the private contractor of the Snowbowl's proposal to generate snow from recycled wastewater to spray on the ski slopes due to lack of snowfall in northern Arizona. To stop the use of the recycled wastewater, tribal groups filed for an injunction in federal court. The injunction was denied. On appeal to the Ninth Circuit after a favorable ruling by a three-judge panel, a full en banc panel reheard the case and denied that the Forest Service approval burdened religious freedom under the 1993 Religious Freedom and Restoration Act.

The American Indian Religious Freedom Act signaled a change from federal suppression to federal support. However, many of the issues raised by tribal representatives were not fully addressed, and the lack of an enforcement mechanism in the law led many to criticize the AIRFA as not accomplishing its stated purpose.

American Indian Religious Freedom Act Amendment in 1994: The Sacramental Use of Peyote

Not addressed in the 1978 American Indian Religious Freedom Act was specifically the use of peyote as a sacrament by the practitioners of the Native American Church. Under federal and state laws, possession and ingestion of peyote has been considered a criminal act subject to prosecution. Although the use of peyote was for religious and sacramental purposes, federal and state authorities viewed Native American use as strictly criminal activity. In 1990, the U.S. Supreme Court upheld the denial of unemployment benefits and the state classification of sacramental use of peyote as a felony and therefore found no violation of the U.S. Constitution's First Amendment Free Exercise Clause in *Employment Division, Department of Human Resources of Oregon v. Smith*, 494 U.S. 872.

In the aftermath of the U.S. Supreme Court decision, tribal organizations, leaders, and individuals again sought federal protection of the use of peyote as part of American Indian religious practice. A thorough and compelling report from the House Representatives Committee on Natural Resources provided background information on the usage of peyote by Native Americans.

Anthropologists date the sacramental use of the peyote cactus among indigenous peoples back 10,000 years. Native American religious use of peyote was discovered by Spanish explorers in the 1600s and has continued to the present. Such use exists today, largely through the Native American Church (NAC), among more than 50 Indian tribes in the United States. The NAC is the present-day embodiment of one of the oldest religious traditions in the western hemisphere. (Report on AIRFA Amendments of 1994, August 1994, 3)

Sidebar 2: Further Federal Action to Protect Sacred Items and Sites

Native American efforts continued for the protection of sacred items, cemeteries, and the return of human remains. These efforts culminated in the enactment of the 1990 Native American Graves Protection and Repatriation Act (NAGPRA), codified at 25 U.S.C. § 3001 et seq. Under the law, a review committee was established to report regularly to the U.S. Congress on the implementation of the NAGPRA.

Without an enforcement mechanism in the American Indian Religious Freedom Act, tribal leaders found it difficult to interact with federal agencies in accessing and protecting sacred sites on federal public lands. This was addressed through executive action. In 1996, U.S. President William Clinton signed Executive Order No. 13007, directing all federal agencies to accommodate access to sacred sites on federal lands for Native Americans, to prevent adverse impact to such sacred sites, and to protect the confidentiality of the sites as appropriate. The second section required federal agencies to provide a report detailing changes to existing policies to comply with the order, including a process for consultation with tribal leaders (61 Fed. Reg. 26771). This order facilitated consultation on sacred sites on public lands but did not require that tribal recommendations be followed after the consultation.

The report also provided a summary of the recent U.S. Supreme Court decision and the resulting inconsistent legal status for religious practitioners subject to varying state laws.

In response, the U.S. Congress enacted 42 U.S.C. § 1996a titled: "Traditional Indian religious use of peyote" and 42 U.S.C. § 1996(b)(1), which directly dealt with the religious possession and use of peyote. Under the latter section: "(1) Notwithstanding any other provision of law, the use, possession, or transportation of peyote by an Indian for bona fide traditional ceremonial purposes in connection with the practice of a traditional Indian religion is lawful, and shall not be prohibited by the United States or any State. No Indian shall be penalized or discriminated against on the basis of such use, possession or transportation, including, but not limited to, denial of otherwise applicable benefits under public assistance programs." With this federal enactment, the ruling in the *Smith* decision was effectively nullified.

Biography

Suzan Shown Harjo (Cheyenne and Hodulgee Muscogee) was born in 1945 in El Reno, Oklahoma, and is recognized as one of the preeminent advocates for American Indian religious and cultural rights. Descended from the Cheyenne Chief Bull Bear, Suzan was determined to give voice to American Indians in their fight for cultural and religious survival. In the 1960s, she married Frank Harjo and co-produced the first Native American news radio program aired in New York City. Then in 1974, she moved with her son and husband to Washington, D.C., where she served as legislative liaison for two law firms specializing in American Indian law.

In 1978, U.S. President Jimmy Carter appointed her as special assistant for Indian Legislation in his administration. Her efforts contributed to the passage of the American Indian Religious Freedom Act of 1978 and other significant legislation positively impacting tribal communities. During an interview in 2010, Harjo reported: "I am very proud of having been a Carter political appointee and having been the primary author of his 1979 Report to Congress on American Indian Religious Freedom. Even though we didn't get everything we wanted, the act as a policy statement and as a process for follow-on legislation was and is invaluable" (Interview by Jennifer Weston, Cultural Survival Organization, Winter 2010).

In memory of her husband, she founded The Morning Star Institute, a Native rights advocacy organization, in 1984. Today, she serves as president of the Institute. From 1984 to 1989, she also served as the executive director of the National American Indian Congress (NCAI). Throughout her decades of activism, she has stood firmly as a voice for protection of sacred sites and items. She has continued her advocacy, stating, "Our churches are being attacked and our people can't go to them to pray. It's a fight against white men with gold in their eyes" (Indian Country Today, *9 Sacred Sites Quotes to Remember*, 6/17/15). Since the early 1990s, she has been a force behind the litigation to cancel the trademark of the NFL's Washington D.C. team based on its offensive Indian mascot.

Her advocacy also influenced the enactment of the 1989 National Museum of the American Indian Act, the 1990 Native American Native American Graves Protection and Repatriation Act, and the signing of Executive Order No. 13007 on Protection of Sacred Sites. In November 2014, Suzan was awarded the U.S. Presidential Medal of Honor.

DOCUMENT EXCERPT

On the 25th anniversary of the AIRFA, the Senate Select Committee on Indian Affairs held a hearing to determine whether further federal action was necessary for implementation of the law. The hearing was held on July 14, 2004, and included concerns on the failure of federal agencies to follow the directive to allow access to sacred areas on public lands, to prevent the destruction of those sites, and to protect the privacy of their locations.

Testimony of Suzan Shown Harjo, President, The Morning Star Institute

It has been 25 years that we have been waiting for a cause of action to protect sacred places; 26 years ago, the Forest Service was successful in lobbying Congress to strip the American Indian Religious Freedom Act of a cause of action and to make statements on the House floor that would guarantee that there would be no cause of action in this bill.

The Supreme Court, because of that action and that successful lobby effort by the Forest Service, basically said in 1988 that, not only did the Religious Freedom Act not offer a cause of action, but the freedom of religion clauses of the First Amendment did not offer any protection for us.

We have no way of getting into court on this matter. We have no way of staying in court to protect our sacred places. The Federal agencies know that. That is why they are pretty cavalier about ignoring what we have to say about access and protection of our sacred places on what they view as their land.

The authority for the Forest Service and other Federal agencies to allow us access to medicine places, for example, is in fact that those lands are our lands. They were confiscated by the Federal Government. They were taken by these Federal agencies and I believe held illegally. But even if you allow that they are taken and held under the color of law, it does not make it right, and we still have prior and paramount rights to those gathering areas.

There should be no question that Federal agencies can permit closure of certain areas for ceremonial purposes, permit taking of what was referred to in one testimony as "forest products." Those are our medicine plants. Those are our sacred objects. Those are our sacred items. Those things are guaranteed to us by the natural laws, the original laws, by the laws that put us in these places.

Source: Religious Freedom Act. Hearing before the Committee on Indian Affairs, Senate, 108–630. July 14, 2004. Washington, D.C.: Government Printing Office, 2004, 11–12.

See also: Native American Graves Protection and Repatriation Act, 1990

Further Reading

Executive Order No. 13007, 61 Fed. Reg. 26771 (May 24, 1996).

Haas, Theodore H. *The Indian & The Law-1.* United States Indian Service, Lawrence: Haskell Institute, 1949.

Newton, Nell Jessup, ed. *Cohen's Handbook of Federal Indian Law*. LexisNexis, 2012. [Cohen's Handbook in text]

Prucha, Francis Paul, ed. *Documents of United States Indian Policy*. Lincoln and London: University of Nebraska Press, 2000.

Royster, Judith V. "The Legacy of Allotment." *Arizona State Law Journal*, 1995, 27: 1–78.

Smith, Andrea. "Soul Wound: The Legacy of Native American Schools." *Amnesty International Magazine*. 2007. Accessed June 23, 2015. http://www.amnestyusa.org/node /87342.

United States Federal Agencies Task Force, *American Indian Religious Freedom Report P.L. 95–341*, Washington, D.C.: U.S. GPO, 1979.

U.S. House of Representatives Committee on Natural Resources, *Report on American Indian Religious Freedom Act Amendments of 1994*, 103rd Cong., 2nd Sess., Washington, D.C.: U.S. GPO, August 5, 1994.

U.S. Senate Select Committee on Indian Affairs, *Hearings on American Indian Religious Freedom*, 95th Cong., 2nd Sess., Washington, D.C.: U.S. GPO, Feb. 24 and 27, 1978.

Santa Clara Pueblo v. Martinez, 1978

Torivio A. Foddor

Chronology of Events

ca. 1378 Santa Clara Pueblo established. While the Tewa people have lived in northern New Mexico since time immemorial, the U.S. Supreme Court has acknowledged that Santa Clara Pueblo has existed for over six hundred years. Experts, however, believe that the Pueblo was actually founded in the early 1500s.

1541 Explorer Francisco Vásquez de Coronado visits Santa Clara Pueblo on his expedition through what would become the southwestern United States.

1680 Pueblo revolt against the Spanish. Tewa religious leader Popé of Ohkay Owingeh led a rebellion of 2,000 pueblo warriors, driving the Spanish out of New Mexico.

1692 The Spanish reconquer New Mexico under the leadership of Diego de Vargas. Despite the reconquest, the pueblos are given substantial land grants by the Spanish Crown and are able to retain much of their culture and language throughout the ensuing centuries.

1908 Thurgood Marshall is born in Baltimore, MD.

1939   Santa Clara Pueblo pass membership ordinance limiting tribal membership to children born of marriages between members of the pueblo; children born of marriages to male members and nonmembers; and expressly *excluding* children born of marriages to female members and non-members of the tribe.

1941   Julia and Myles Martinez marry. Julia is a member of the Santa Clara Pueblo. Myles Martinez is a member of the Navajo Nation.

1946   Audrey Martinez is born. Julia Martinez attempts to enroll Audrey in the Santa Clara Pueblo. Her application for membership is denied.

1967   Thurgood Marshall is appointed to United States Supreme Court, becoming the first African American to sit on the highest federal court in the United States.

1968   Congress passes the Indian Civil Rights Act (ICRA). The legislation has two primary objectives: 1) to ensure that tribal members are afforded individual civil rights, and 2) to encourage tribal self-government.

1975   Julia Martinez and her daughter, Audrey Martinez, file suit in the U.S. district court for the State of New Mexico challenging Santa Clara Pueblo's denial of membership "to children born of marriages between female members of Santa Clara Pueblo and non-members." Martinez argues that the ICRA provides an implied opportunity to bring her case to federal court.

             The court agrees that it has jurisdiction to hear the case under the ICRA, but upholds the tribal membership ordinance for Santa Clara Pueblo.

1976   Martinez appeals the court's opinion to the U.S. Court of Appeals for the Tenth Circuit.

             Once again, the court agrees that the ICRA provides jurisdiction for the court to hear the case, but holds that Santa Clara Pueblo's membership ordinance violates the equal protection guarantee of the ICRA.

1978   Santa Clara Pueblo appeals the 10th Circuit Court of Appeals ruling to the United States Supreme Court.

             In an opinion by Justice Thurgood Marshall, rather than determining the permissibility of the tribe's ordinance, the Court concludes that the ICRA only provides habeas corpus relief for individuals who believe that their detention by a tribe is unlawful. As a result, it finds no jurisdictional basis for the Court to hear Martinez's claims.

In circumstances where tribal members wish to challenge the legality of their detainment, they may appeal their case to the federal courts of the United States. For all other claims against tribes that fall under the ICRA, the only legal forums available to them are those found within tribal court systems.

Santa Clara Pueblo v. Martinez: Conflicting Values in the Struggle for Tribal Self-Determination

Santa Clara Pueblo is located along the dusty banks of the Rio Grande River in Northern New Mexico. A stone's throw away from the Los Alamos National Laboratory, the gravel roads of the pueblo twist and bend amid the arid foothills of the Jemez Mountains. The nearby town of Española, New Mexico, has served the area as a railroad outpost since the late 1880s, providing the region with access to goods and services from the Rio Grand Western Railroad line. To visit the area is to embrace a community that has navigated the delicate balance of diversity and culture for nearly six centuries.

Given the remoteness of the Pueblo, it may seem surprising that such a small place, boasting a population of nearly 4,000 residents, could have such a significant impact on American Indian history. And yet, the saga that became the U.S. Supreme Court case *Santa Clara v. Martinez*, 436 U.S. 49 (1978) emanated from exactly this quiet corner of Indian country. Eventually, a disagreement about membership among tribe members in the Pueblo resulted in a legal case traveling all the way to the U.S. Supreme Court, and the opinion by the Court set a major precedent for tribal governments, entrusting tribal court systems to adjudicate claims brought against them under the Indian Civil Rights Act, and enabling them to maintain control over their internal affairs without the threat of outside interference.

In discussing any historic event related to the Pueblos of Northern New Mexico, it is important to note that their history did not begin with the arrival of the Spanish. The Tewa-speaking peoples of this region have made their home along the banks of the Rio Grande since time immemorial, developing distinct cultures that have overlapped and intersected with one another for as long as the waters have passed over the rocks that set the foundations of time. This vibrant past is alive and well in the dances, ceremonies, and religious traditions of New Mexico's Pueblos.

And yet, the first recorded contact with the Pueblo of Santa Clara begins with the 1541 expedition of Spanish explorer Francisco Vásquez de Coronado, who visited Santa Clara Pueblo on his expedition through what would become the southwestern United States. The result of this initial encounter would eventually lead to the establishment of Spanish missions among the Pueblo communities of the Rio Grande Valley, and within the Santa Clara Pueblo community in 1628. Other Pueblos in the region would strike a similar balance with the new arrivals, opening their communities to Spanish missionaries, settlers, and traders, often by force.

As waves of Spanish settlers began to arrive, the Pueblos became increasingly frustrated by the imposition of the Catholic religion on their people, and the suppression of their traditional religions—sometimes through the execution of traditional elders and leaders. This tension came to a head in the Pueblo Revolt of 1680. Led by Tewa religious leader Popé of Ohkay Owingeh (formerly San Juan Pueblo), the Pueblos of the Rio Grande Valley were able to forge a military coalition of some 2,000 pueblo warriors extending as far west as the Zuni and Hopi tribes, located along the border of present-day eastern Arizona and western New Mexico. The rebellion was able to successfully drive the Spanish from their provincial capital in Santa Fe, forcing them to retreat to El Paso del Norte, now the modern-day city of Ciudad Juárez in Mexico.

Ultimately, the Spanish would reconquer New Mexico in 1692, under the leadership of Diego Vargas. As the Spanish progressed northward, one by one the Pueblos fell to the better-armed Spanish forces. Despite the eventual colonization of the region, the Pueblo success in the 1680 revolt led to the Spanish crown granting certain concessions to the Pueblo, including land grants to their villages. As a result, many of the Pueblos, including Santa Clara, were able to preserve much of their culture and traditional religions, and live in relative peace, despite the arrival of settlers in the region.

The history noted above is crucial to understanding the context of Pueblo governance as it relates to the *Santa Clara v. Martinez* case. As a function of their relative isolation from the influences of mainstream society, and the preservation of their centuries-old systems of governance, the people of Santa Clara Pueblo were able to exist and carry on with life, largely unimpeded by western influences. While many Pueblo residents embraced Catholicism and the Catholic missions within their communities, they were able to do so on their own terms. Many Pueblos, including Santa Clara, combined elements of traditional, Pueblo religions and practices with the teachings of the Catholic Church. This enabled them to arrive at a unique religious balance that helped preserve their communities. Similarly, the Pueblos' governments functioned in a manner that allowed them to retain traditional values and societies while also carrying out modern functions of government.

As a part of its efforts to carry out modern governmental functions according to the traditional customs of the Pueblo, in 1939, the Santa Clara Pueblo sought to use the western legal process of creating laws to preserve its traditional values regarding tribal membership (*Martinez* 1976, 1040). In the 1930s, a number of marriages took place between Pueblo members and non-members. Traditionally, marriages had been arranged or had taken place between male and female members of the tribe. This eliminated most controversies over tribal membership, since both individuals were already members of the tribe. Even in instances where tribal members had married outside of the tribe, Santa Clara Pueblo had determined tribal membership on a case-by-case basis. Under this system, in a number of instances, the Pueblo had actually permitted children born to marriages of female tribal members and non-members to become members of the tribe (*Martinez* 1976, 1040).

However, Pueblo elders became increasingly concerned about the increase in mixed marriages between female tribal members and non-members, and its effects on the resources of the tribe, including tribal lands, water, and other resources (*Martinez* 1976, 1040). As a result, the Pueblo Council passed a tribal ordinance that restricted membership in the Pueblo according to the following regulations:

- Children born of marriages between tribal members were permitted to become members of the tribe.
- Children born of marriages between male tribal members and non-tribal members were permitted to become members of the tribe.
- Children born of marriages between female tribal members and non-tribal members were NOT permitted to become members of the tribe.
- "Naturalization" as members of the tribe was not to be permitted under any circumstances (*Martinez* 1975, 6).

The result of the 1939 ordinance led to the categorical exclusion from tribal membership of any children born to female tribal members who married outside of the tribe. This change in policy directly affected numerous individuals who called Santa Clara Pueblo home, including the children of Julia Martinez (*Santa Clara* 1978, 52). While Julia Martinez was a "full-blooded member of the Santa Clara Pueblo," she married a man from the Navajo Nation in 1941. As a result, under the tribe's 1939 membership ordinance, Julia Martinez's children were excluded from membership in the Santa Clara Pueblo, despite the fact that Julia resided on the reservation and was a member of the Pueblo herself. For Martinez's children, this meant that they could not become members of the Pueblo, vote in tribal elections, hold office, or inherit their mother's home or interests in tribal lands (*Santa Clara* 1978, 52–53). On the other hand, culturally, her children were very much able to participate in the life of the Santa Clara community. They were allowed to speak the Tewa language, take part in the practice of the tribe's religion, and participate in the traditions and customs of the Pueblo (*Martinez* 1976, 1041).

Despite her efforts to persuade the tribe to change its membership rules, Martinez was ultimately unsuccessful. In the intervening years, however, Congress passed the Indian Civil Rights Act of 1968 (ICRA), which carried with it "two distinct and competing purposes." The first was to "strengthen the position of individual tribal members" in their dealings with the tribe. The second was to promote the federal "policy of furthering Indian self-government" (*Santa Clara* 1978, 62). One of ICRA's provisions regarding individual rights sought to ensure that tribes did not "deny to any person within its jurisdiction the equal protection of its laws or deprive any person of liberty or property without due process of law" (25 U.S.C. § 1302 (A)(8)). The language of the provision seemed to apply to the Martinez case, and Julia and her adult daughter, Audrey, filed suit in the U.S. District Court for the State of New Mexico in 1975. The two argued that the Santa Clara membership ordinance violated the equal protection provisions of the ICRA (*Martinez* 1975, 6).

In order for a federal court to hear a case regarding the laws that govern the rights of American Indians and Indian tribes, it must first possess the jurisdiction, or the power to make legal decisions over the matter at hand. This is because tribal courts in their capacities as quasi-sovereign governments have "exclusive jurisdiction over wholly internal tribal subject matter such as membership disputes" (Canby Jr. 2015, 226). So, in order for the court to consider Julia and Audrey Martinez's claims, the federal district court first had to determine whether or not it had the appropriate jurisdiction to hear the case.

Sidebar 1: Jurisdiction Definition

The question of jurisdiction ultimately factored quite heavily into the Supreme Court's final opinion in *Santa Clara v. Martinez*. According to the Legal Information Institute at Cornell University, jurisdiction is defined as the power of a court to adjudicate cases and issue orders (Legal Information Institute 2015). In Indian country, tribes exercise broad civil jurisdiction over their internal affairs. As a result, the Court was obliged to consider whether Congress had expressly granted it the authority to consider the claims brought by Julia and Audrey Martinez. While the lower courts found an implicit grant of jurisdiction to hear the claims, the Supreme Court concluded that absent an express allocation of authority, it did not have jurisdiction to consider the claims.

The matter would have been much easier for the court to determine, except that the ICRA was completely silent on the matter of jurisdiction. In the actual text of the ICRA, there was simply no language to guide the court as to whether or not it had the jurisdiction to hear the case. As a result, Santa Clara Pueblo argued that the court lacked jurisdiction to consider the Martinezes' claims (*Martinez* 1975, 7). Despite absence of guiding language, and the arguments of the tribe to the contrary, the district court nonetheless concluded that it possessed jurisdiction to hear the Martinezes' case. The court noted that the claims of equal protection violations being raised against the tribe were far from "frivolous" and required the court to make a judgment on the actual claims being alleged by Julia and Audrey Martinez (*Martinez* 1975, 9).

Regarding the claims brought by Julia and Audrey, the court reached a much different conclusion. The court noted:

> Even assuming plaintiffs [Julia and Audrey Martinez] are correct, the equal protection guarantee of the Indian Civil Rights Act should not be construed in a manner which would require or authorize this court to determine which traditional values will promote cultural survival . . . such a determination should be made by the people of Santa Clara; not only because they can best decide what values are important, but also because they must live with the decision every day (*Martinez* 1975, 18).

Ultimately, the result of the district court's interpretation of the ICRA was to uphold the Santa Clara membership ordinance by promoting the sovereignty of the tribe. The court concluded that a tribe must be able to make and enforce its decisions about membership as a part of its cultural identity, and that an external authority should not interfere with such determinations (Martinez 1975, 18–19).

Given the outcome in the federal district court, Julia and Audrey Martinez appealed their case to the U.S. Court of Appeals for the Tenth Circuit, hoping for a different result. Following the same line of reasoning as the district court, the court of appeals concluded that the ICRA was intended "to provide protection against tribal authority" on behalf of individual Indians. Moreover, Congress must have intended to allow courts to hear such claims—"otherwise, it [the ICRA] would constitute a mere unenforceable declaration of principles" (*Martinez* 1976, 1042). Having dispatched with the question of jurisdiction, the court then considered whether the Santa Clara Pueblo membership ordinance violated the equal protection provision of the ICRA.

In determining the outcome of the case, the court observed that it must weigh the importance of tribal sovereignty against the individual right to fair treatment under the law in order to determine whether the membership ordinance could be upheld (Martinez 1976, 1045). Under this analysis, the court considered whether a tribe could extend certain rights to men while denying the same rights to women, and still be lawful under the ICRA. On this point, the court simply concluded that under the facts of the case, and the particular circumstances of the Martinez family, that the tribal membership ordinance did not justify treating male and female tribal members differently. The court also noted that the tribe failed to demonstrate how such different treatment of men and women promoted cultural survival (Martinez 1976, 1047).

The result of the second case was, of course, very different from the conclusion reached by the district court. In the first opinion, the lower court expressly held that the tribes should make such determinations of tribal values. In the court of appeals, the Tenth Circuit concluded that the individual Indian interest in tribal membership and equal justice exceeded the ability of the tribe to define its membership (*Martinez* 1976, 1047–1048).

Given the outcome of the second case, it is little surprise that the Santa Clara Pueblo would appeal the Tenth Circuit opinion to the United States Supreme Court. On appeal, the tribe argued that the ICRA did not waive its "sovereign immunity from suit" (*Santa Clara* 1978, 58). As a concept, tribal sovereign immunity is the legal doctrine that tribal governments cannot be sued without their consent. The same is true for state governments and the federal government. There are, of course, many exceptions to this doctrine, but it remains a viable legal principle that the courts must consider. In examining the tribe's argument, the Court observed that legal precedents indicate that in order to waive a tribe's sovereign immunity from suit, it must be "unequivocally expressed." The provisions of the ICRA, however, do not mention an express waiver of immunity. As a result, the Court concluded that lawsuits against tribes (such as the one brought by Julia and Audrey Martinez)

Sidebar 2: Tribal Sovereign Immunity

Sovereign immunity is the legal doctrine by which a government may not be sued without its consent. Under the laws of the United States, Indian tribes are considered to be domestic dependent nations, possessing a degree of sovereignty and self-government over their own affairs. Given this relationship with the government of the United States, tribal sovereign immunity has been recognized by the U.S. Supreme Court as an official element of Indian tribal governance.

under the ICRA are "barred by [tribal] sovereign immunity from suit" (*Santa Clara* 1978, 59).

Given the fact that there was no explicit waiver of immunity, the Court proceeded to analyze whether an "implicit" waiver of immunity is contained within the ICRA. This was the same question addressed by the district court in 1975. On this point, the Court observed that the only relief provided to those filing claims against the tribe was limited to habeas corpus relief. Habeas corpus relief, in this case, is the opportunity for individuals who have been arrested by a tribe to challenge their detention in federal court. Such a remedy would not apply to Julia and Audrey Martinez, because they were not challenging an arrest (indeed, they had not at all been arrested by the tribe), but were seeking to bring a lawsuit against the tribe for violations of the ICRA's equal protection provision. As a result, the Court concluded that there was simply no jurisdiction for it to consider the claims brought by the Martinez family (*Santa Clara* 1978, 71–72).

The analysis of the Supreme Court was ultimately very different from the opinions of the district and appeals courts. Both lower courts had concluded that the ICRA provided jurisdiction for them to consider the claims brought by the Martinez family. The Supreme Court, led by Justice Thurgood Marshall, concluded that there was no jurisdictional basis for it to consider the claims of the Martinez family, because the tribe had invoked its sovereign immunity from suit, and because the ICRA did not provide jurisdiction for the Court to consider the claims. As a result, the Santa Clara tribal membership ordinance was upheld, and the Court never considered the equal protection arguments raised by Julia and Audrey Martinez.

While the legal history of the case is a bit convoluted, the outcome was widely considered to be a major victory for proponents of tribal self-government—perhaps at the expense of the individual liberty guarantees ensured to tribal members under the ICRA. In his dissent, Justice White criticized the majority opinion on exactly this point, declaring that he could not believe that Congress intended to leave the "enforcement of [ICRA] rights to be left up to the very tribal authorities alleged to have violated them" (*Santa Clara* 1978, 82). Nevertheless, the opinion set an astounding precedent for tribal governments, entrusting their court systems to adjudicate claims brought against them under the ICRA, and enabling them to maintain control over their internal affairs without the threat of outside interference.

In 2012, the members of the Santa Clara Pueblo voted in favor of membership change. The implementation of the tribal vote, and its implications for the children of female tribal members and non-tribal members remains a point of ongoing debate for the tribe.

Biographies

Popé (also Popay, and Po he yemu)

The backdrop of American Indian history is littered with tales of peoples massacred, battles lost, and ultimately of lands lost—all to the invading tides of colonialism. And yet, the story of Popé and the Pueblo Revolt of 1680 is a crucial story for the positions that Native People took for self-government and for resisting conquest, signaling a moment outside of space and being where the Indians actually won, and managed to successfully drive the invading European powers from their lands.

The early life of the man behind the Pueblo Revolt of 1680 is largely lost to the annals of time. Even the meaning of his name, Popé, is a matter of some controversy, with scholars, linguists, and Pueblo members translating it as "Squash Mountain," "Red Moon," and even "Ripe Cultigens," respectively (Roberts 2004, 159). However, there is little debate about the significance of Popé to Pueblo peoples, and his role in orchestrating the most successful American Indian rebellion in history.

Popé could, perhaps, best be described as a religious leader. A leader of the summer moiety at San Juan Pueblo (now know by its Tewa name, Ohkay Owingeh), Popé's reputation at the height of his power spanned dozens of communities nearly 400 miles apart. He was a known "dissident" who rejected all things Spanish prior to the revolt of 1680 (Roberts 2004, 160). When Spanish Governor Juan Francisco Treviño arrived in the New Mexico province in 1675, he immediately launched a campaign to round up Pueblo spiritual leaders and deal with the problem of Indian sedition once and for all. His efforts saw the capture of some 47 medicine men from various Pueblos, all of whom he accused of practicing witchcraft (Gutiérrez 1991, 131). Three of the spiritual leaders were hanged, and the others publically flogged, for refusing to abandon their traditional religions. Among these leaders was the San Juan medicine man Popé (Calloway 2012, 92).

After learning of the religious leaders capture, Tewa warriors from a bevy of Pueblo communities marched on Santa Fe, demanding Popé's release. Gov. Treviño, perhaps wary of sparking further insurrection among the Pueblos, opted to grant their demands (Roberts 2004, 159–60). Following his release, Popé would flee to Taos Pueblo, the northernmost Pueblo in New Mexico, and one of the most traditional and isolated. It would be from there, nestled in the heart of the Sangre De Cristo mountain range, that Popé would begin to plot nothing less than a revolution to throw off the Spanish yoke once and for all.

Having escaped the clutches of Spanish might, Popé's reputation among the Pueblos grew. According to the *Declaration of Indian Juan* (1681), Pueblos throughout New Mexico were inclined to participate in the rebellion that would follow because of Popé's ability to communicate with the "devil," and on account of his willingness to use brutal tactics to ensure compliance—including the murder of a son-in-law whom he perceived to be a threat to the rebellion (Calloway 2012, 120–21). Popé's message to the Pueblo masses was that the Christians and their god had to be destroyed in order for the ancient gods to show favor to the people once again. Given that the Spanish had stolen Pueblo crops, confiscated Pueblo lands, and suppressed Pueblo culture, Popé's message was one of "liberation" (Gutiérrez 1991, 132).

With his coalition solidified, Popé began to plan his attack on the Spanish. While there were multiple opportunities, the Pueblo coalition opted to hit the Spanish during a crucial moment, attacking when their supplies were low and before reinforcements could arrive. If the plan were successful, the Spanish would be isolated from their capital city, Santa Fe, and the surrounding communities would be vulnerable to further attacks by Pueblo warriors (Calloway 2012, 92).

After conferring with his deputies, Popé set the date of the attack for August 11, 1680, the first night of the new moon. On August 9, 1680, August Popé dispatched runners to all of the Pueblo coalition, carrying cords with two knots tied into them—one knot for each day until the Pueblos would strike. The plan seemed pretty well on point until religious leaders opposed to the rebellion were able to learn the date of the attack, and leak word to Spanish Governor Otermín (Gutiérrez 1991, 132).

In response, leaders from Tesuque Pueblo urged Popé to move the attack to the next day. As Pueblo runners carried the new date of the rebellion to the rest of the coalition, the others prepared for war. Despite the Governor Otermín learning of the attack, the change in date was successfully communicated to the rest of the coalition. On August 10, 1680, the Pueblo Revolt began. Its execution was well planned. The warriors began by stealing or killing the Spanish modes of transportation, primarily their horses and mules. Without horses, the Spanish would be unable to communicate with Santa Fe and other outposts in New Mexico (Gutiérrez 1991, 133). The second objective of the Pueblo coalition was to isolate Santa Fe. To accomplish this, Pueblo warriors blocked all roads leading into Santa Fe and destroyed the surrounding villages one by one.

With Santa Fe effectively cut off from the rest of New Mexico, all that remained was to take the capital city. Popé's men accomplished this by first cutting off access to food and water, before laying siege to the city. After nine days, realizing that his people could not last long under such conditions, Governor Otermín launched a counterattack aimed at temporarily repelling the Pueblo coalition, and buying enough time for the remaining colonists in Santa Fe to make their escape. The plan worked. While the Pueblo warriors regrouped from the Spanish counteroffensive, the remaining colonists made a hasty retreat south, passing the charred remains of their settlements and countrymen along the way (Gutiérrez 1991, 133–35). With the last of the Spanish on their way out of New Mexico, the Pueblo Revolt passed from military excursion into a cause for celebration. For once, the Pueblos had won.

The effects of the rebellion would be relatively short-lived, earning freedom for the Pueblos for some 12 years following the attack. But for Popé, the Pueblo Revolt would see him earn an almost mythical status in the Pueblo consciousness, transforming him from a simple medicine man to a national hero. In 2005, the State of New Mexico honored Popé's legacy by unveiling his statute in the rotunda of the United States Capitol.

DOCUMENT EXCERPTS

The following document is an excerpt from the 1939 Santa Clara Pueblo member-ship ordinance that ultimately sparked the Supreme Court decision in Santa Clara v. Martinez.

Santa Clara Pueblo Membership Ordinance—1939

Be it ordained by the Council of the Pueblo of Santa Clara, New Mexico, in regu-lar meeting duly assembled, that hereafter the following rules shall govern the admission to membership to the Santa Clara Pueblo:

1. All children born of marriages between members of the Santa Clara Pueblo shall be members of the Santa Clara Pueblo.
2. All children born of marriages between male members of the Santa Clara Pueblo and non-members shall be members of the Santa Clara Pueblo.
3. Children born of marriages between female members of the Santa Clara Pueblo and non-members shall not be members of the Santa Clara Pueblo.
4. Persons shall not be naturalized as members of the Santa Clara Pueblo under any circumstances.

Source: Santa Clara Pueblo v. Martinez, 436 U.S. 49 (1978)

The Indian Civil Rights Act of 1968 (ICRA) provided the legal basis for Julia and Audrey Martinez to challenge Santa Clara Pueblo's membership requirements. The two argued that the Pueblo's membership requirements were in violation of ICRA's provisions guaranteeing equal protection to tribal membership.

The Indian Civil Rights Act of 1968 (Emphasis added)

In general—No Indian tribe in exercising powers of self-government shall—

(1) make or enforce any law prohibiting the free exercise of religion, or abridging the freedom of speech, or of the press, or the right of the people peaceably to assemble and to petition for a redress of grievances;

(2) violate the right of the people to be secure in their persons, houses, papers, and effects against unreasonable search and seizures, nor issue warrants, but upon probable cause, supported by oath or affirmation, and particularly describing the place to be searched and the person or thing to be seized;

(3) subject any person for the same offense to be twice put in jeopardy;

(4) compel any person in any criminal case to be a witness against himself;

(5) take any private property for public use without just compensation;

(6) deny to any person in a criminal proceeding the right to a speedy and public trial, to be informed of the nature and cause of the accusation, to be confronted with the witnesses against him, to have compulsory process for obtaining witnesses in his favor, and at his own expense to have the assistance of counsel for his defense (except as provided in subsection (b));

(7)

    (A) require excessive bail, impose excessive fines, or inflict cruel and unusual punishments;

    (B) except as provided in subparagraph (C), impose for conviction of any 1 offense any penalty or punishment greater than imprisonment for a term of 1 year or a fine of $5,000, or both;

    (C) subject to subsection (b), impose for conviction of any 1 offense any penalty or punishment greater than imprisonment for a term of 3 years or a fine of $15,000, or both; or

    (D) impose on a person in a criminal proceeding a total penalty or punishment greater than imprisonment for a term of 9 years;

(8) deny to any person within its jurisdiction the equal protection of its laws or deprive any person of liberty or property without due process of law;

(9) pass any bill of attainder or ex post facto law; or

(10) deny to any person accused of an offense punishable by imprisonment the right, upon request, to a trial by jury of not less than six persons.

Source: 25 U.S.C. §§ 1301—1304.

The following document is an excerpt from the actual U.S. Supreme Court case Santa Clara v. Martinez. *After differing opinions from two federal courts, the effect of the Supreme Court's decision would preserve Santa Clara Pueblo's tribal membership ordinance.*

Santa Clara Pueblo v. Martinez (1978)

Mr. Justice MARSHALL delivered the opinion of the Court.

This case requires us to decide whether a federal court may pass on the validity of an Indian tribe's ordinance denying membership to the children of certain female tribal members.

Petitioner Santa Clara Pueblo is an Indian tribe that has been in existence for over 600 years. Respondents, a female member of the tribe and her daughter, brought suit in federal court against the tribe and its Governor, petitioner Lucario Padilla, seeking declaratory and injunctive relief against enforcement of a tribal ordinance denying membership in the tribe to children of female members who marry outside the tribe, while extending membership to children of male members who marry outside the tribe. Respondents claimed that this rule discriminates on the basis of both sex and ancestry in violation of Title I of the Indian Civil Rights Act of 1968 (ICRA), 25 U.S.C. §§ 1301–1303, which provides in relevant part that "[n]o Indian tribe in exercising powers of self-government shall . . . deny to any person within its jurisdiction the equal protection of its laws." § 1302(8).1

Title I of the ICRA does not expressly authorize the bringing of civil actions for declaratory or injunctive relief to enforce its substantive provisions. The threshold issue in this case is thus whether the Act may be interpreted to impliedly authorize such actions, against a tribe or its officers in the federal courts. For the reasons set forth below, we hold that the Act cannot be so read.

I

Respondent Julia Martinez is a full-blooded member of the Santa Clara Pueblo, and resides on the Santa Clara Reservation in Northern New Mexico. In 1941 she married a Navajo Indian with whom she has since had several children, including respondent Audrey Martinez. Two years before this marriage, the Pueblo passed the membership ordinance here at issue, which bars admission of the Martinez children to the tribe because their father is not a Santa Claran.

Although the children were raised on the reservation and continue to reside there now that they are adults, as a result of their exclusion from membership they may not vote in tribal elections or hold secular office in the tribe; moreover, they have no right to remain on the reservation in the event of their mother's death, or to inherit their mother's home or her possessory interests in the communal lands.

Following a full trial, the District Court found for [the tribe] on the merits. While acknowledging the relatively recent origin of the disputed rule, the District Court nevertheless found it to reflect traditional values of patriarchy still significant in tribal life. The court recognized the vital importance of respondents' interests, but also determined that membership rules were "no more or less than a mechanism of social . . . self-definition," and as such were basic to the tribe's survival as a cultural and economic entity.

On respondents' appeal, the Court of Appeals for the Tenth Circuit upheld the District Court's determination that 28 U.S.C. § 1343(4) provides a jurisdictional basis for actions under Title I of the ICRA. * * * The Court of Appeals disagreed, however, with the District Court's ruling on the merits. While recognizing that standards of analysis developed under the Fourteenth Amendment's Equal Protection Clause were not necessarily controlling in the interpretation of this statute, the Court of Appeals apparently concluded that because the classification was one based upon sex it was presumptively invidious and could be sustained only if justified by a compelling tribal interest. * * * The court held that the tribe's interest in the ordinance was not substantial enough to justify its discriminatory effect.

We granted certiorari, and we now reverse. * * *

III

* * * It is settled that a waiver of sovereign immunity " 'cannot be implied but must be unequivocally expressed.' " * * * Nothing on the face of Title I of the ICRA purports to subject tribes to the jurisdiction of the federal courts in civil actions for injunctive or declaratory relief. Moreover, since the respondent in a habeas corpus action is the individual custodian of the prisoner, see, e. g., 28 U.S.C. § 2243, the provisions of § 1303 can hardly be read as a general waiver of the tribe's sovereign immunity. In the absence here of any unequivocal expression of contrary legislative intent, we conclude that suits against the tribe under the ICRA are barred by its sovereign immunity from suit.

IV

As an officer of the Pueblo, petitioner Lucario Padilla is not protected by the tribe's immunity from suit. * * * We must therefore determine whether the cause of action for declaratory and injunctive relief asserted here by respondents, though not expressly authorized by the statute, is nonetheless implicit in its terms.

In addressing this inquiry, we must bear in mind that providing a federal forum for issues arising under § 1302 constitutes an interference with tribal autonomy and self-government beyond that created by the change in substantive law itself. * * * Although Congress clearly has power to authorize civil actions against tribal officers, and has done so with respect to habeas corpus relief in § 1303, a proper respect both for tribal sovereignty itself and for the plenary authority of Congress in this area cautions that we tread lightly in the absence of clear indications of legislative intent. * * * Not only are we unpersuaded that a judicially sanctioned intrusion into tribal sovereignty is required to fulfill the purposes of the ICRA, but to the contrary, the structure of the statutory scheme and the legislative history of Title I suggest that Congress' failure to provide remedies other than habeas corpus was a deliberate one. * * *

A

Two distinct and competing purposes are manifest in the provisions of the ICRA: In addition to its objective of strengthening the position of individual tribal members vis-à-vis the tribe, Congress also intended to promote the well-established federal "policy of furthering Indian self-government." * * * This commitment to the goal of tribal self-determination is demonstrated by the provisions of Title I itself. Section 1302, rather than providing in wholesale fashion for the extension of constitutional requirements to tribal governments, as had been initially proposed, selectively incorporated and in some instances modified the safeguards of the Bill of Rights to fit the unique political, cultural, and economic needs of tribal governments. Thus, for example, the statute does not prohibit the establishment of religion, nor does it require jury trials in civil cases, or appointment of counsel for indigents in criminal cases.

The other Titles of the ICRA also manifest a congressional purpose to protect tribal sovereignty from undue interference. * * * *

Where Congress seeks to promote dual objectives in a single statute, courts must be more than usually hesitant to infer from its silence a cause of action that, while serving one legislative purpose, will disserve the other. Creation of a federal cause of action for the enforcement of rights created in Title I, however useful it might be in securing compliance with § 1302, plainly would be at odds with the congressional goal of protecting tribal self-government. Not only would it undermine the authority of tribal forums, but it would also impose serious financial burdens on already "financially disadvantaged" tribes.

Moreover, contrary to the reasoning of the court below, implication of a federal remedy in addition to habeas corpus is not plainly required to give effect to

Congress' objective of extending constitutional norms to tribal self-government. Tribal forums are available to vindicate rights created by the ICRA, and § 1302 has the substantial and intended effect of changing the law to which these forums are obliged to apply. Tribal courts have repeatedly been recognized as appropriate forums for the exclusive adjudication of disputes affecting important personal and property interests of both Indians and non-Indians. Non-judicial tribal institutions have also been recognized as competent law-applying bodies. Under these circumstances, we are reluctant to disturb the balance between the dual statutory objectives which Congress apparently struck in providing only for habeas corpus relief.

B

Our reluctance is strongly reinforced by the specific legislative history underlying 25 U.S.C. § 1303. This history, extending over more than three years, indicates that Congress' provision for habeas corpus relief, and nothing more, reflected a considered accommodation of the competing goals of "preventing injustices perpetrated by tribal governments, on the one hand, and, on the other, avoiding undue or precipitous interference in the affairs of the Indian people."

In settling on habeas corpus as the exclusive means for federal-court review of tribal criminal proceedings, Congress opted for a less intrusive review mechanism than had been initially proposed. * * *

By not exposing tribal officials to the full array of federal remedies available to redress actions of federal and state officials, Congress may also have considered that resolution of statutory issues under § 1302, and particularly those issues likely to arise in a civil context, will frequently depend on questions of tribal tradition and custom which tribal forums may be in a better position to evaluate than federal courts. * * * As is suggested by the District Court's opinion in this case, efforts by the federal judiciary to apply the statutory prohibitions of § 1302 in a civil context may substantially interfere with a tribe's ability to maintain itself as a culturally and politically distinct entity.

As we have repeatedly emphasized, Congress' authority over Indian matters is extraordinarily broad, and the role of courts in adjusting relations between and among tribes and their members correspondingly restrained. Congress retains authority expressly to authorize civil actions for injunctive or other relief to redress violations of § 1302, in the event that the tribes themselves prove deficient in applying and enforcing its substantive provisions. But unless and until Congress makes clear its intention to permit the additional intrusion on tribal sovereignty that adjudication of such actions in a federal forum would represent, we are constrained to find that § 1302 does not impliedly authorize actions for declaratory or injunctive relief against either the tribe or its officers.

The judgment of the Court of Appeals, is, accordingly,

Reversed.

Source: Santa Clara Pueblo v. Martinez, 426 U.S. 49 (1978).

Further Reading

Calloway, Colin G. *First Peoples: A Documentary Survey of American Indian History,* 4th ed. Boston: Bedford/St. Martin's, 2012.

Canby, Jr., William C. *American Indian Law in a Nutshell,* 6th ed. St. Paul: West, 2015.

Getches, David H., et al. *Cases and Materials on Federal Indian Law,* 5th ed. St. Paul: Thompson-West, 2005.

Gutiérrez, Ramón A. *When Jesus Came, the Corn Mothers Went Away: Marriage, Sexuality, and Power in New Mexico, 1500–1846.* Stanford, CA: Stanford University Press, 1991.

Legal Information Institute, Cornell University. https://www.law.cornell.edu/wex/jurisdiction

Martinez v. Santa Clara Pueblo, 402 F.Supp. 5 (1975).

Martinez v. Santa Clara Pueblo, 540 F.2d 1039 (1976).

Roberts, David. *The Pueblo Revolt: The Secret Rebellion that Drove the Spaniards Out of the Southwest.* New York: Simon & Schuster, 2004.

Santa Clara Pueblo v. Martinez, 436 U.S. 49 (1978).

Anna Mae Pictou Aquash, 1945–1975

Claudia J. Ford

Chronology

1945	March 27. Annie Mae Pictou is born in the Shubenacadie band (now called the Indian Brook First Nation) reserve in Nova Scotia, Canada.
1962	After a childhood of poverty and dropping out of school despite being a good student, Anna Mae moves from the Mi'kmaq reservation to Maine, for factory work.
1964–1971	Aqaush moves among Boston, Maine, and New Brunswick and gives birth to two daughters, Denise Maloney (1964) and Deborah Maloney (1965). During this period, Aquash begins a lifelong interest in improving the formal education and tribal cultural education of Indian youth.

1968	The American Indian Movement (AIM) is formed to protest police brutality against American Indians and to improve prison justice for Native Americans. As it grows, it expands to broad goals for protesting racism and improving lives of Indians.
1970–1973	Aquash becomes a member of AIM and takes part in various AIM protests: the anti-Thanksgiving National Day of Mourning at Plymouth, Massachusetts, in November 1970; the Trail of Broken Treaties, and the occupation of the Bureau of Indian Affairs (BIA) in Washington, D.C., in the Summer of 1972; and the 71-day occupation of Wounded Knee, South Dakota, in February through April of 1973.
1973	Aquash meets Nogeeshik Aquash, an Ojibwa political activist, and they marry in a traditional Lakota ceremony during the AIM occupation of Wounded Knee, although the marriage eventually breaks up.
1974–1975	Aquash works for AIM and participates in many activist actions alongside Native Peoples in Canada and the United States. She is arrested multiple times and faces charges related to weapon possession and subversive activities. Aquash has established herself in the inner circles of the AIM leadership.
1975	Because of sustained federal government efforts to break up AIM, some in AIM believe that Aquash is an informant.
1975	November. While in Denver, she is kidnapped from a safe house and brought to South Dakota, where she is interrogated. In late November or early December, she is shot and believed to have been executed by AIM members.
1976	February 24. Anna Mae Aquash's body is discovered at the bottom of a cliff in the Pine Ridge Lakota reservation, with a bullet in the back of her head.
2004	Arlo Looking Cloud and John Graham, members of AIM, are convicted of the Aquash murder in 2004, though many close to the case believe that others in AIM were involved.

The Death of an American Indian Activist, Anna Mae Aquash

Anna Mae Aquash, born Annie Mae Pictou was a Mi'kmaq woman who worked through the 1960s and early 1970s as an activist for American Indian political, gender, and educational justice. Her life was dedicated to efforts to recognize Native land and cultural rights, and she was a committed member of the American Indian

Movement (AIM). Aquash was born on March 27, 1945, in Shubenacadie, Nova Scotia, Canada. She grew up on the Mi'kmaq reservation with her mother, Mary Ellen Pictou, her stepfather, Noel Sapier, and her brother and two sisters, Francis, Mary, and Rebecca. Throughout her childhood and adolescence, Aquash experienced the hardships of poverty that were common to reservation life. She and her siblings struggled with poor housing, no electricity or plumbing, and insufficient food. Under these harsh conditions, Aquash developed tuberculosis at age eight. Despite being a very strong student, she dropped out of elementary school, demotivated by the blatant racism she faced as an Indian child in the Canadian educational system, and also so that she could help her family by taking low-wage agricultural work in nearby potato fields and berry patches. Despite the challenges of poverty, her upbringing was culturally rich, and Aquash grew up under the strong influence of Mi'kmaq traditions.

At age 17, Aquash moved from the reservation to Maine, where she did factory work. She then moved to Boston with the man who became her first husband, Jake Maloney, also a Mi'kmaq tribal member. In the seven years between 1964 and 1971,

---

Sidebar 1: Mi'kmaq History and Culture

Located primarily in Nova Scotia and New Brunswick, the Mi'kmaq peoples are the original inhabitants of the Atlantic Provinces, or Maritimes, of Canada. Mi'kmaq tribal members can also be found throughout Newfoundland, Québec, Maine, and Massachusetts, and the Mi'kmaq are members of the Wabanaki Confederacy along with the Maliseet, Passamaquoddy, Penobscot, and Abenaki peoples. The Mi'kmaq have occupied their traditional lands for more than 10,000 years. There is evidence that the Mi'kmaq were in contact with European fisherman, explorers, and traders from at least the 1500s. Mi'kmaq cultural traditions are based around respect for their land and environment, and the relationships between and among humans and the natural world that allowed their communities to flourish in harmony with the rhythms of the forests, seas, and seasons. The land base allowed the Mi'kmaq to hunt, fish, and gather plants and plant medicines to meet their needs. Families lived in communities of wigwams, organized by a Grand Council and led by a chief. In the past, chiefs were selected by prestige; today, both men and women can stand for tribal chief, an elected position. The Mi'kmaq are famous for their porcupine quill artisans as well as beadwork, basket making, and wampum beading. Sweat lodges and storytelling are important parts of Mi'kmaq ceremonial life, and Glooskap is a major figure in Mi'kmaq mythology.

while moving among Boston, Maine, and New Brunswick, Aquash gave birth to two daughters, Denise and Deborah. During this time, Aquash began a lifelong interest in how both formal education and tribal cultural education could empower Indian youth. Aquash was committed to assisting Indian youth with overcoming the frustrations of urban poverty and racism, and she sought to promote the importance of tribal traditions like those she had grown up with. Aquash increased her understanding of Native rights and history through the influence of Mi'kmaq Chief Peter Barlow of Indian Island, New Brunswick, Canada. Aquash became active in providing social and educational services for a number of Native communities. In Boston, while Aquash worked as a seamstress, and as a childcare worker in the African American community of Roxbury, she also helped to found the Boston Indian Council. Aquash continued to advocate for Indian youth, education, and social services and worked in a school for Native teens in Bar Harbor, Maine.

Native activism was reborn in the 1970s with the Lakota protest of the desecration of Native sacred land at Mount Rushmore and simultaneous with the political and social change and upheaval reflected by the anti-war, African American civil rights, and Chicano farm worker social justice movements. The American Indian Movement, better known as AIM, was born out of a movement to improve Native prison justice and to protest police brutality actions of the 1970s. Aquash actively participated in some of AIM's most important national political events including the anti-Thanksgiving National Day of Mourning at Plymouth, Massachusetts in November 1971, the Trail of Broken Treaties and the occupation of the Bureau of Indian Affairs (BIA) in Washington, D.C., in the Summer of 1972, the 71-day occupation of Wounded Knee, South Dakota in February through April of 1973, and the one-month occupation by the Menominee Warrior Society of the Alexian Brothers' Novitiate in Gresham, Wisconsin in 1975. Aquash became a member of AIM and participated in these actions and others, sometimes accompanied by her young children or alongside Nogeeshik Aquash, an Ojibwa political activist, whom Aquash married in a traditional Lakota ceremony during the AIM occupation of Wounded Knee.

The smuggling from the BIA in 1972 of documents that detailed systematic racism against Native communities and that were incriminating to the federal government, as well as the killing of two Federal Bureau of Investigation (FBI) agents on the Pine Ridge Reservation in 1975, brought AIM into sustained conflict with the federal government. Members of AIM saw a campaign of persistent harassment of members and purposeful destabilization of the movement. The undermining of AIM was escalated in part through infiltration of the organization by government operatives and informers, and the planting of disruptive rumors of internal spying within AIM membership. During these years, Aquash was influential in AIM's organizing and fundraising for the legal defense of their membership, and she

Sidebar 2: Urban Indian Youth Education

Life on Indian reservations was always a challenge as reserves were established to make it difficult for Native People to own working land, find employment, or maintain their cultural traditions. Levels of poverty were shockingly high, and basic services, especially housing, health, education, and recreation, were substandard or nonexistent. It became increasingly common for some Native People to migrate from the reservation to major cities for the majority of the year, and to return only periodically to their home reservations. Over the decades, there have been successive waves of outmigration from reservations. Under the Indian Relocation Act of 1956, the Eisenhower administration initiated a removal effort to persuade American Indians to leave reservations for urban areas, where they were promised housing and employment opportunities that did not often materialize. In the 1960s, Indian youth, especially, were attracted to urban areas because of the opportunities for work, education, and decent housing. While some of these opportunities existed, Native youth were also met with the urban realities of alcohol, drugs, crime, and American society's racist discrimination towards Native Peoples. One response to the marginalization of urban Indian youth in the 1970s was the establishment of culturally oriented schooling. Aquash was at the forefront of this movement as she had been raised within the linguistic and cultural traditions of Mi'kmaq tribal life, and understood firsthand how these traditions might be used to educate and empower Native youth. She was involved with some of the earliest efforts to promote Native education and culture through the Boston Indian Council that continues as the North American Indian Center of Boston; the Teaching and Research in Bicultural Education (TRIBE) school established from 1970 to1972 by the Wabanaki in Bar Harbor, Maine; and, the Red School House survival schools that were set up in Minneapolis/St. Paul by AIM under Title IV of the 1972 Indian Education Act, as alternatives to the public, BIA, boarding, and religious schools normally available to Native youth. See also Davis, Julie L. *Survival School: The American Indian Movement and Community Education in the Twin Cities*. Minneapolis: University of Minnesota Press, 2013.

continued her dedication to the education of Native youth, and the promotion of Native pride, land rights, culture, and language. As a prominent member of AIM, Aquash was vulnerable to government persecution and she fell victim to the government's destabilization tactics. Some people believe that Aquash was falsely accused of being an informant, and that certain members of AIM, the BIA, and agents from the FBI had worked together in arranging to have her murdered.

In the months preceding her death in the fall of 1975, Aquash was arrested twice and traveled among Minnesota, South Dakota, California, Washington, Canada, and Colorado as a fugitive. While in Denver in November 1975, she was kidnapped from a safe house and taken to South Dakota, where she was interrogated and executed by AIM members. She was 30 years old. Aquash's body was discovered in a ravine near a ranch in a remote part of the Pine Ridge reservation in February 1976. Her death was originally attributed to exposure, and she was hastily buried. However, in a subsequent postmortem requested by her family, it was determined that she had been executed by a single bullet to the back of her head and likely killed in late November or early December of 1975. The exact circumstances around the murder of Aquash remain shrouded in uncertainty, despite

Rebecca Julian, left, Anna Mae Pictou Aquash's eldest sister, and Aquash's eldest daughter, Denise Maloney, hold a portrait of Aquash (Mi'kmaq), June 20, 2003, at Shubenacadie, Nova Scotia. AIM activist Aquash was killed in late 1975 on the Pine Ridge Indian Reservation. In 2004 and 2010 two AIM members were convicted for her murder. (AP Photo/Carson Walker)

the fact that two AIM members—Arlo Looking Cloud and John Graham—were convicted of the Aquash murder in 2004, and the case was considered closed in 2010. There remains uncertainty about the facts of the murder, and for her family members the ultimate responsibility for Aquash's murder remains unresolved. In June 2004, the body of Anna Mae Pictou Aquash was brought home to her family and community in Nova Scotia, and she was provided with a traditional Mi'kmaq ceremonial burial on the Indian Brook First Nation land, befitting her standing as a Native woman warrior and activist.

DOCUMENT EXCERPTS

Arlo Looking Cloud's Murder Conviction Is Upheld in Appeals Court

In 2005, Arlo Looking Cloud appealed his conviction for Anna Mae Aquash's murder (also convicted was John Graham) in the United States Court of Appeals, Eighth Circuit. The first paragraph describes Looking Cloud's reasons for appealing the conviction, but the court upheld the conviction in an opinion written by Judge John R. Gibson.,

Fritz Arlo Looking Cloud appeals his conviction for the first degree murder of Anna Mae Aquash following a jury trial. His grounds for appeal are: (1) admission of irrelevant, prejudicial evidence; (2) admission of hearsay and an improper limiting instruction; (3) ineffective assistance of counsel; and (4) insufficient evidence to support his conviction. The district court 1 sentenced him to life in prison. We affirm. . . .

Looking Cloud's final argument is that the evidence at trial was not sufficient to support his conviction and the district court erred in rejecting his motion for judgment of acquittal. The jury convicted Looking Cloud of first degree murder or of aiding and abetting that murder under 18 U.S.C. §§ 1111 and 1153. The elements Looking Cloud disputes are (1) that he killed or aided and abetted in the killing of Aquash; (2) that he did so with malice aforethought; and (3) that the killing was premeditated.

We review the sufficiency of the evidence de novo and will reverse a conviction only if, after viewing the evidence in the light most favorable to the jury's verdict and giving the government the benefit of all reasonable inferences that may be drawn from the evidence, no construction of the evidence will support the jury's verdict. See *United States v. Simon*, 376 F.3d 806, 808 (8th Cir. 2004). Either direct or circumstantial evidence may provide a basis for conviction; adducing direct evidence at trial is not a requirement. Id.

The evidence adduced at trial was as follows. The testimony established that nearly twenty members of the American Indian Movement suspected Aquash was an informant or had at least heard the rumor. Darlene Nichols, who joined the Movement in 1972 and had been an active member, testified that several members, one of whom had already threatened Aquash's life because he suspected she was an informant, took Aquash away for weeks to "watch her."   Nichols said that Aquash was constantly watched, was not allowed to go anywhere alone, and was not permitted to go home despite her requests to do so. Mathalene White Bear, another former member who provided shelter to Aquash in 1975, testified that Aquash believed her life was in danger as early as September of that year.

In November 1975, Aquash left Pierre and went to Denver, where she stayed in the home of a Movement member. Other Movement members frequently gathered at this house. Several members held a meeting at the house in November 1975 because they had received a phone call saying that Aquash was an informant and needed to be taken to Rapid City, South Dakota. The group decided Looking Cloud, Clark, and Graham would take Aquash to Rapid City. Janis testified that those three carried Aquash to the car against her will, crying; her wrists were bound and she was tied to a board and unable to walk on her own. They put her in the back end of a hatch-back Pinto and drove to Rapid City. After meeting with more American Indian Movement members at the Wounded Knee Legal Defense/Offense Committee house in Rapid City, they drove Aquash to Rosebud. Yellow Wood said that Looking Cloud stayed with Aquash in the car while Graham and Clark went into a house. There, Aquash begged to be let go and told Looking Cloud that the others were inside deciding her fate and were probably going to make him pull the trigger. John Trudell, chairman of the American Indian Movement from 1973–1979, testified that Looking Cloud, Graham, and Clark were not decision-makers for the American Indian Movement, and that the group did not make but rather received orders to kill Aquash before they left the house in Rosebud. The jury could reasonably infer from Looking Cloud's participation in carrying Aquash out to the car, tied to a board, that he knew they were going to kill her. In further support of that inference was evidence that Aquash also knew in advance that she was going to be killed. Aquash mailed a ring back to White Bear before she died; it was a signal the two friends had previously arranged so White Bear would know something had happened to Aquash.

Trudell testified that Looking Cloud told him that when Graham and Clark returned to the car for the last time, Aquash cried and begged them not to kill her. They drove to an area near Wanblee and parked the car. Yellow Wood testified that Looking Cloud told him that Aquash continued to cry, pray, and beg for her life as they forced her out of the car and marched her up the hill to a cliff. Two Elk testified that Looking Cloud told him he handed a gun to Graham and nodded at him.

Aquash knelt to the ground, possibly to pray, and Graham held the gun to the back of her head and pulled the trigger. Afterwards, the three buried the gun under a bridge nearby.

From the testimony, the jury could reasonably infer that from the time the car left the house in Rosebud, Looking Cloud understood that the plan was to kill Aquash. Although Looking Cloud told others that Graham pulled the trigger, and the government introduced no evidence to the contrary, the jury could at least reasonably believe that Looking Cloud helped force Aquash out of the car and up the hill and that he assisted in the murder by handing the gun to Graham to shoot and kill Aquash. This constitutes sufficient evidence to support the jury's finding that Looking Cloud killed or aided and abetted in the killing of Aquash, with malice aforethought, and that the killing was premeditated.

We affirm the district court's judgment of conviction.

Source: United States of America, Plaintiff-Appellee, v. Fritz Arlo LOOKING CLOUD, Defendant-Appellant. No. 04-2173. Decided August 19, 2005.

See also: American Indian Movement, 1968

Further Reading

Annie Mae Pictou Aquash. *American National Biography Online.* Accessed February 27, 2016. http://www.anb.org/articles/15/15-01365.html

Brand, Johanna. *The Life and Death of Anna Mae Aquash.* Toronto: James Lorimer, 1978.

Konigsburg, Eric. "Who Killed Anna Mae?" *New York Times Magazine,* April 25, 2014. Accessed November 1, 2015. http://www.nytimes.com/2014/04/27/magazine/who-killed -anna-mae.html?_r=0

Mihesuah, Devon A., Denise Maloney-Pictou and Deborah Maloney-Pictou. "Interview with Denise Maloney-Pictou and Deborah Maloney-Pictou." *American Indian Quarterly* 24, No. 2 (Spring 2000): 264–278.

Mihesuah, Devon A. "Anna Mae Pictou-Aquash: An American Indian Activist." In *Sifters: Native American Women's Lives,* edited by Theda Perdue, 204–222. New York: Oxford University Press, 2001.

Poliandri, Simone. *First Nations, Identity, and Reserve Life: The Mi'kmaq of Nova Scotia.* Lincoln: University of Nebraska Press, 2011.

The Spirit of Annie Mae. Documentary. DVD. Directed by Catherine Anne Martin. Montréal: National Film Board of Canada, 2002.

Weir, David and Lowell Bergman. "The Killing of Anna Mae Aquash." *Rolling Stone* (April 7, 1977): 51–55.

Witt, Shirley Hill. "The Brave-Hearted Women: The Struggle at Wounded Knee." *Civil Rights Digest* 8 (Summer 1976): 38–45.

United Nations Working Group on Indigenous Populations, 1982

Nikki Dragone

Chronology of Events

1960   U.N. Declaration on the Granting of Independence to Colonized Countries and Peoples.

1966   U.N. adopts the International Covenant on Civil and Political Rights and the International Covenant on Economic, Social and Cultural Rights.

1971   The Economic and Social Council authorizes the Sub-Commission to initiate a study on "Problem of Discrimination against Indigenous Populations." Study is undertaken by Special Rapporteur Jose R. Martinez Cobo.

1974   World Council of Indigenous Peoples is established and obtains NGO consultative status.

1975   International Indian Treaty Council is established and obtains NGO consultative status.

1977   NGO-sponsored Conference on Discrimination against Indigenous Peoples in the Americas.

1980   Fourth Russell Tribunal on the Rights of the Indians of the Americas.

1981   International NGO Conference on Indigenous Peoples and the Land. Recommendations based on this conference include establishing a more permanent forum at the U.N. for indigenous peoples.

1981   Based on his ongoing study, Special Rapporteur Cobo recommends the establishment of a more permanent forum at the U.N. for indigenous peoples.

1982   The Working Group on Indigenous Populations is established and holds its first meeting in Geneva, Switzerland.

1985   United Nations Voluntary Fund for Indigenous Populations is established.

1985   The Working Group on Indigenous Populations begins drafting a universal declaration on the rights of indigenous peoples.

1985	Special Rapporteur Cobo finishes his five-volume study.
1989	ILO adopts Convention No. 169 on Indigenous and Tribal Peoples.
1993	The Working Group finalizes and submits the draft Declaration on the Rights of Indigenous Peoples to the Sub-Commission.
1994	The Sub-Commission approves the draft Declaration and submits it to the Commission on Human Rights.
1995	The Commission on Human Rights establishes an inter-sessional Working Group to review the draft Declaration.
2000	The United Nations Permanent Forum on Indigenous Issues is established.
2001	The Special Rapporteur of Human Rights and Indigenous Issues is established.
2006	The Human Rights Council approves the draft Declaration and submits it to the U.N. General Assembly for its approval. Based on a petition filed by Namibia on behalf of the African nation-states, the General Assembly tables the vote on the draft Declaration until the 61st session.
2007	The Working Group on Indigenous Populations holds its final meeting. It is replaced by the newly established Expert Mechanism on the Rights of Indigenous Peoples.
September 13, 2007	The U.N. General Assembly adopts the Declaration on the Rights of Indigenous Peoples.

Introduction

On September 13, 2007, the United Nations General Assembly adopted the Declaration on the Rights of Indigenous Peoples. The original draft Declaration, which recognizes the rights enjoyment of individual and collective human rights of indigenous peoples in both their daily and communal lives, was born out of 11 years of negotiations among indigenous representatives, state government representatives, and human rights experts serving as members of the United Nations Working Group on Indigenous Populations. Established in 1982, the Working Group on Indigenous Populations (also known as the Working Group or WGIP), was the first formalized body within the United Nations that provided a forum for indigenous peoples to speak for themselves, to tell their own stories about the often violent abuse of their human rights, and to tell these stories in a way that enabled them to redefine the terms of their own survival as peoples. To understand why the WGIP

Japanese members of Ainu Association of Hokkaido listen to speeches during the opening session of the UN Working Group on Indigenous Populations in Geneva, Switzerland, 2004. Over 1,000 representatives of indigenous peoples and communities from around the world joined government delegates, non-governmental organizations, and United Nations agencies in Geneva for the largest international meeting on indigenous peoples' rights. (AP Photo/ Keystone/Laurent Gillieron)

is an important benchmark in American Indian history, this chapter will explore innovations in the composition of the Working Group that set it apart from other human rights bodies in the U.N. system; the WGIP's mandate to review developments concerning the protection and promotion of indigenous rights and to draft an international standard; and its continued legacy.

Between 1960 and 1981, a series of events transpired that led to the establishment of the Working Group on Indigenous Populations. The first of these events was the codification of the peoples' right to self-determination in Article 1 of two U.N. human rights treaties ratified in 1966: the International Covenant (treaty) on Civil and Political Rights and the International Covenant on Economic, Social and Cultural Rights. By implementing the right of self-determination, colonized peoples in Africa and other parts of the world became independent self-governing nations. Self-determination became a major rallying point around which indigenous peoples unified in their own struggle for the protection of their collective human rights as distinct peoples. Throughout the 1960s and 1970s, indigenous peoples and organizations became more active at U.N. human rights bodies and conferences. Consequently, in 1971, the U.N.'s Economic and Social Council (ECOSOC) authorized the "Study of the Problem of Discrimination against Indigenous Populations" (the Cobo Study). This study called for the establishment of a U.N. forum on indigenous issues, as did the indigenous delegates who attended both the 1977, NGO Conference on Discrimination against Indigenous Peoples in the Americas and the 1981 NGO Conference on Indigenous Peoples and the Land. Thus, in 1981, the U.N. authorized the establishment of the Working Group of Indigenous Populations.

1982–1985: Innovations in the WGIP's Structure and Composition

Established as a subsidiary body of the Sub-Commission on the Prevention on Discrimination and Protection of Minorities (hereinafter called the Sub-Commission), the WGIP held its first session at the U.N.'s Geneva, Switzerland, headquarters from August 9 through August 13, 1982. With the exception of 1986, when the U.N.'s financial crises temporarily suspended the work of the Sub-Commission and all its subsidiary bodies, the WGIP met annually until 2006. Their yearly meetings, ranging from five to ten days in duration, were held just prior to the Sub-Commission's meetings (Pritchard 1998, 41).

The question remains, what exactly was the Working Group on Indigenous Populations? First of all, it was a subsidiary body of the Sub-Commission on the Prevention of Discrimination and Protection of Minorities. As such, it functioned at the lowest level of the U.N.'s hierarchy of human rights bodies. This means any recommendations, reports, and standards authored by the WGIP required approval by the Sub-Commission, the Commission on Human Rights (CHR), and ECOSOC before being passed on to the U.N. General Assembly (Pritchard 1998, 42). Second, as with other Working Groups organized under the Sub-Commission, the WGIP was composed of only five members, one from each of the following regions: Africa, Asia, Eastern Europe, Western Europe and Others (WEO), and Latin America. The "others" of the WEO region include Australia, Canada, New Zealand, and the United States (Sanders 1994). While the WGIP's members were drawn from the Sub-Commission, they were considered to be independent experts because they served in their capacity as international law experts independent of any political status they might have as representatives of their nations. They were appointed to two-year terms; however, incumbent members had an "unspoken right" to retain their seats (Sanders 1994).

The annual sessions of the Sub-Commission's various Working Groups were formal, highly structured events. Without access to independent sources of information to complete their mandates, most working groups rely on reports and studies submitted by government representatives, specialized agencies, inter-governmental organizations, and NGOs. Additional information could be submitted through oral statements and written interventions of the observers, like NGOs and state representatives, whose status permitted them to attend and participate in annual sessions (Maiguascha 1990, 31–32). However, due to the formalized structure of these meetings, observer participants were required to maintain proper decorum. Consequently, the member elected as the chairperson strictly mediated meetings. It was his or her responsibility to ensure that speakers adhered to specific time limits and to rule out of order those oral statements, written interventions, or dialogue that might be considered irrelevant or cumulative (Williams 1900, 677).

At the time of the WGIP's first session in 1982, only three of the 14 indigenous organizations in attendance had obtained NGO consultative status: WCIP, IITC, and the Indian Law Resource Center. Their attendance resulted in what is arguably the most important innovation introduced to the U.N. system by the WGIP. Indeed, after consulting with the indigenous representatives present, the WGIP's first chairman, Asbjørn Eide, determined that in order to complete the two tasks ECOSOC entrusted to the WGIP the WGIP, "the best possible experts" were needed. Over the protestations of some state representatives, Eide concluded that the "best possible experts" were indigenous representatives. Indigenous representatives were not only allowed to attend and to speak to the WGIP, but they also were empowered to submit interventions, working papers, reports, and proposals (Eide 2007, 45–46). Thus, completely breaking with U.N. tradition, the WGIP was opened up to all possible participants.

Though the numbers of attendees do not indicate it, the fact that the WGIP held its annual sessions in Geneva made it difficult for indigenous diplomats and leaders from less financially solvent communities or third-world nations to attend these meetings. The truth is even the delegates from Canada and the United States had difficulty obtaining the funds necessary to cover the annually incurred costs of travel or food and lodging in Geneva. Many indigenous leaders were able to attend only because of what one indigenous representative described as the "random acts of kindness" of non-indigenous persons and organizations (Henderson 2008, 42). Recognizing that Chairman Eide was right in opening the WGIP up to full participation by indigenous peoples, in 1985, the U.N. General Assembly established the "Voluntary Fund for Indigenous Peoples" to cover travel costs for the more financially disadvantaged indigenous representatives. Within its first four years, the Voluntary Fund ensured the participation of 39 indigenous representatives from over twenty countries (Maiguascha 1994, 32). By the date of the WGIP's final meeting in 2006, nearly 100 travel grants were awarded to disadvantaged male and female indigenous representatives attending U.N. meetings (Eide 2008, 46).

Due to these two innovations, the WGIP became the most active and heavily attended Working Group in U.N. history. In 1982, a total of 30 observer participants attended the WGIP's first session. By 1993, nearly two-thirds of the representatives attending the WGIP were from Latin America, the Soviet Union, South East Asia, and the Pacific. By 1999, some 971 people attended the WGIP. The following year, representatives from 45 states and 248 indigenous and non-indigenous groups attended, a total of 1,027 people. Even after it was determined that a permanent U.N. body was to be established to replace the WGIP, over 580 people attended the Working Group's final meeting in 2006 ("Working Group on Indigenous Populations").

1982–1993: Working Group's Mandate to Review Indigenous Rights Developments

During its first few years, the WGIP worked solely on the first of two mandated tasks: reviewing the developments regarding the human rights of indigenous peoples. It is important to note that this part of their mandate did not authorize the WGIP to examine concrete complaints and allegations of indigenous peoples and organizations against nation-states or vice versa. Nor did it authorize the WGIP to issue recommendations for state action or to issue court-like decisions based on allegations. With this in mind, the WGIP was authorized solely to collect the information necessary to fulfill the second part of their mandate: drafting a set of international standards on indigenous rights.

The information gathered by the WGIP came from a variety of sources, including studies on specific issues completed by the members of the WGIP themselves. One example of this is the study Miguel Alfonso Martinez completed in 1999 on "Treaties, Agreements and Constructive Arrangements between States and Indigenous Peoples." Additionally, the WGIP received reports from governments, intergovernmental bodies, NGOs, and other U.N. bodies. Finally, they received information through the oral statements and written interventions submitted by observer participants to their annual meetings.

The oral interventions and review of written statements and reports resulted in quite a bit of dialogue among observer participants. As their shared grievances often painted terrifying portraits of nation-state violations of indigenous rights, it is no surprise that friction and animosity sometimes erupted when indigenous participants' oral submissions narrated the horrors they endured, and continued to endure, because of state and military policies imposed upon them. These horrors included: genocide, ethnocide, extrajudicial killings, forced removals, expropriation of lands and resources without consent or compensation, and other forms of cultural and religious discrimination (Eide 2007, 41; Henderson 2008, 33). Likewise, when states denounced indigenous peoples as terrorists, denied the veracity of the allegations being lodged against them, or forcefully deflected the allegations by reminding the WGIP that it was not "a chamber of complaints" and, consequently, could not "act upon specific allegations concerning the violations of human rights," it is no surprise that indigenous delegates often responded with anger (Thornberry 2002, 371). And yet, the WGIP developed into a forum where states could not easily dismiss indigenous concerns as simply the complaints of minority populations disgruntled over government policies. In fact, the innovation that permitted all indigenous persons in attendance to participate fully in the WGIP's dialogue and debate, transformed it into a forum where indigenous peoples told their stories, and states had to listen.

It goes without saying that there were, and still are, some states who will not hear what indigenous peoples have to say. However, according to Potawatomi lawyer R. Tim Coulter—who attended nearly every WGIP meeting since 1982 in his capacity as the director of the Indian Law Resource Center (an NGO with consultative status)—the stories indigenous delegates shared with the WGIP "brought astonishing changes in the behavior of states" (Rostkowski 2012). For example, state practices and policies became more friendly to indigenous peoples in that outright massacres and politically motivated removals of indigenous peoples in Latin America slowed down. Canada and other settler states revised their policies and practices to be more supportive of the continued survival of indigenous communities as culturally distinct.

Enabling direct participation of indigenous peoples at the WGIP also necessitated a change in the focus on indigenous rights at the international level. Since the Working Group is a subsidiary body of the Sub-Commission, it initially saw indigenous peoples as a type of minority population, which led to the WGIP's initial focus on investigating the discriminatory practices that prevented indigenous peoples from integrating into the economic, social, and cultural life of the state. However, as the WGIP acted more and more as a forum from which to illustrate the ways state policies and practices curtailed indigenous rights, and states began to take indigenous peoples' claims more seriously, the WGIP's focus shifted from protecting indigenous peoples' rights as minorities to protecting their collective rights to life and self-determination as culturally distinct peoples. This shift is important because it sets the backdrop for the completion of the second part of the WGIP's mandate (Eide 2007).

In fulfilling its mandate to review developments related to indigenous peoples' rights by enabling the direct participation of all indigenous attendees, the WGIP facilitated the development of an international indigenous diplomacy network. Indigenous delegates from all over the world traveled to the WGIP's annual sessions. In many cases, communication necessitated the help of linguistic interpreters. It seemed that the very nature of their vast cultural, spiritual, and historic diversity, precluded consensus and/or unity among indigenous participants. However, as they listened to each other's stories and participated with each other collectively through the formal and informal indigenous caucuses they created in the Working Group, indigenous participants began to recognize they not only had a shared history of colonial oppression, but also shared many traditional values, including the respect for diversity. For all their diversity, it soon became clear that they were unified in their recognition that all of their other human rights flowed from their collective right, as peoples, to self-determination (Henderson 2008, 48–50).

1985–1993: WGIP's Mandate to Draft International Standards on Indigenous Rights

In 1985, the WGIP shifted its focus to the second part of its mandate, the drafting of the document that would ultimately become the UN Declaration on the Rights of Indigenous Peoples. As a starting point, the WGIP produced a list of 14 principles to be included in the future draft. While this draft maintained the WGIP's early focus on the right to equality and freedom from discrimination, it also highlighted the shift in focus toward collective human rights, such as the rights to exist, to be protected from genocide, to maintain ethnic character and identity, and to be protected against state actions that would forcibly assimilate or integrate indigenous peoples into the dominant society (Thornberry 2002, 371; Williams 1990, 682–83). Notably absent from these 14 principles is the right of self-determination. However, Annex I, appended to the report, outlines the WGIP's "plan of action," which includes a promise to consider the collective rights of self-determination, sovereignty and autonomy in future WGIP sessions (Thornberry 2002, 371–72). Also appended to the report in Annex III and IV are the World Council of Indigenous People's Declaration of Principles and NGOs draft Declaration of Principles (authored by a group of indigenous NGOs), both of which clearly state that at the heart of indigenous peoples' struggle is the collective right of self-determination (Williams 1990, 693).

Two years later, when Chairperson Erica-Irene Daes received her mandate to draft a Universal Declaration of Indigenous Rights, the WGIP elected to adopt the 14 principles into the preliminary wording of the draft. In 1988, Daes drafted a working paper on the proposed Universal Declaration. As with the principles upon which this working paper was based, the right of self-determination still was conspicuously absent. Before the end of the 1988 session, this draft was tabled to allow for the submission of comments by state and indigenous representatives (Sanders 1989, 427).

The first mention of self-determination showed up in the 1989 preamble of the first revised draft, which states that "nothing in this declaration may be used as a justification for denying any people [. . .] their right to self-determination" (qtd. by Thornberry 2002, 372–73). The following year, the WGIP broke down into three drafting groups. As is evidenced by paragraph one of their draft, Group Two offered the strongest support for including the indigenous right of self-determination in the draft Declaration: "Indigenous peoples have the right of self-determination, by virtue of which they may freely determine their political status, freely pursue their own economic, social and cultural development, and determine their own institutions" (qtd. by Thornberry 2002, 373).

By the time the WGIP members approved and submitted their final draft to the Sub-Commission for its approval in 1993, the peoples' right of self-determination had been interpreted as applying to the specific situation of indigenous peoples. Despite bitter opposition by some of the state representatives who feared that recognizing indigenous peoples as peoples possessed of the full rights of self-determination may adversely impact the sovereignty of states over their lands and resources, the WGIP agreed to incorporate the right of self-determination into the body of the draft Declaration. Article 3 of the WGIP's draft Declaration read as follows: "Indigenous peoples have the right to self-determination. By virtue of that right they freely determine their political status and freely pursue their economic, social and cultural development" (qtd. by Thornberry 2002, 373, 455).

After 11 years of sometimes bitter negotiations among the WGIP's members, the states, indigenous representatives, NGOs, and other interested parties, the completion of the draft Declaration was a remarkable achievement. In reflecting on the Declaration after its adoption by the U.N. General Assembly on September 13, 2007, Madame Daes remarked, "No other United Nations instrument has ever been elaborated with so much direct participation of its intended beneficiaries" (Daes 2008, 36). Her predecessor, Asbørn Eide, lauded the Declaration as reflecting both "the needs and aspirations of indigenous peoples" and the "concerns of the state" (Eide 2007, 41–42).

1994–2006: The Legacy of the Working Group on Indigenous Populations

Ultimately, the legacy of the WGIP is the Declaration on the Rights of Indigenous Peoples. However, it does not stand alone. In August of 1982, when the WGIP met for the first time, it was the only international human rights forum open to indigenous peoples. By the time the WGIP concluded its final meeting in 2006, there were two other human rights forums dedicated to indigenous peoples: the U.N. Permanent Forum on Indigenous Issues (UNPFII, established 2002) and the Special Rapporteur on the Rights of Indigenous Peoples (established 2001). In 2007, after the U.N.

Sidebar 1: U.N. Declaration on the Rights of Indigenous Peoples: 1985–2007

The international instrument today known as the UN Declaration on the Rights of Indigenous Peoples (UNDRIP) grew out of the second mandate of the UN Working Group on Indigenous Populations (WGIP). Established in 1982, the WGIP was charged with reviewing developments concerning the protection of indigenous rights and drafting an international standard on indigenous rights. After eight years of working with indigenous representatives, NGOs, and state representatives, in 1993 the WGIP finalized the draft Declaration and submitted it to the U.N. Sub-Commission on the Prevention and Elimination of Discrimination. The Sub-Commission approved the draft Declaration the following year and submitted it to the U.N. Commission of Human Rights (CHR) for their approval. The CHR established an open-ended Inter-sessional Working Group and charged it with resolving nation-states' concerns and ensuring the adoption of the draft Declaration. For 12 years, the inter-sessional Working Group met annually to discuss the draft Declaration. Limited participation by indigenous representatives and NGOs was allowed. Finally, in June of 2006, the Commission of Human Rights adopted the draft of the Declaration submitted to them by the Inter-sessional Working Group. It was submitted to the U.N. General Assembly. On September 13, 2007, the U.N. General Assembly adopted the U.N. Declaration on the Rights of Indigenous Peoples.

General Assembly adopted the Declaration, a third forum was established, specifically to replace the WGIP. This forum, known as the Expert Mechanism on the Rights of Indigenous Peoples (EMRIP), is mandated to provide the Human Rights Council with "thematic expertise" on indigenous peoples' rights. Like the WGIP, both EMRIP and the UNFPII are open to the participation of all indigenous peoples and organizations. Unlike the WGIP, the experts chosen to serve as members of EMRIP and the UNPFII, and in the position of the Special Rapporteur can be of indigenous origin.

What does all of this mean? It means that the innovations made to the Working Group on Indigenous Populations have had long-lasting effects on the way that the U.N. Human Rights system is organized and the way people gain access to it. It means that the legacy of the WGIP is that indigenous peoples will continue to represent themselves directly, to speak on their own behalf, and to continue to redefine the terms of their own survival by their storytelling at these and other U.N. fora.

Sidebar 2: Content of the UNDRIP

The preamble and 46 articles comprising the U.N. Declaration on the Rights of Indigenous Peoples (UNDRIP) outline not only the collective and individual rights of indigenous peoples, but also the actions the U.N.'s nation-state members must take to ensure that indigenous rights are protected. The rights recognized in this international instrument may be grouped together in the following broad categories: (1) foundational rights; (2) life and security; (3) language, cultural and spiritual identity; (4) land, territories, and resources; (5) political and economic rights; (6) education, information and employment. A brief description of some of the rights recognized in this document follows:

Foundational Rights: This section recognizes and protects indigenous peoples' rights to freely determine their political status and to freely pursue their economic, social, and cultural development; it also protects their rights to free, prior, and informed consent to any decision affecting their lives, lands, and resources.

Life and Security: These rights protect the basic needs of indigenous persons and peoples and help them to feel safe where they are and to be free from genocide, ethnocide, forced assimilation or integration into a nation-state, and/or attempts by state and economic interests to destroy indigenous cultures; the collective rights to live together as a community, a language group, or a nation in accordance with cultural traditions; and to be free of forced removals or relocations without their free, prior, and informed consent.

Language, Cultural, and Spiritual Identity: These rights include freely practicing and expressing one's culture and language; maintaining, protecting, and developing cultural property; practicing spiritual and religious traditions, in privacy; and revitalizing, using, developing, and passing on indigenous ways of knowing and being.

Political and Economic Rights: These rights protect indigenous peoples' free participation in the following: the political, social, and economic life of the state; in all decisions affecting them; and in the political, social, and economic life of their own community.

Lands, Territories, and Resources: Indigenous peoples have the right to use and develop their traditionally owned and occupied lands and territories; compensation for lands and resources taken without their free, prior, and informed consent; and a safe, clean environment. They have the right to maintain, control, and protect their cultural heritage, traditional knowledge, science, and technologies.

Biography

Robert Tim Coulter (1945–)

Robert Tim Coulter played an extremely vital role with the United Nations Working Group on Indigenous Populations (UN WGIP) in the drafting and adoption of the United Nations Declaration on the Rights of Indigenous Peoples (UNDRIP). Additionally, Coulter and the law office/non-governmental organization (NGO) he helped found in 1977 continue to be key players in ensuring the UNDRIP is enforced in both the domestic law of nation-states like the United States and Canada, and in international human rights law. Tim Coulter, a citizen of the Citizen Potawatomi Indian nation, was born in 1945 in Rapid City, South Dakota, to Joseph and Vivian Coulter. He was raised in Norman, Oklahoma. In 1966, Coulter completed his bachelor's degree at Williams College in Williamstown, Massachusetts. Believing a law degree would enable him to contribute to the political and social activism of the day, Coulter completed his Juris Doctor and was graduated cum laude from Columbia Law School. For the past 46 years, Coulter has used his law degree and considerable experience fighting for the recognition and protection of indigenous peoples' rights throughout the western hemisphere. He and his wife, Samantha Sanchez, currently reside in Helena, Montana.

While in law school, Coulter engaged with the civil rights movement and fought for the equal and voting rights and social equality of African Americans. In addition, he worked as a military draft counselor. After his graduation, Coulter directed a Maryland-based inmate grievance committee before taking a position as a staff attorney with the Native American Legal Defense and Education Fund. In 1975, Coulter began representing the Onondaga Nation and the Haudenosaunee (the Iroquois Confederacy). The six member nations of the Haudenosaunee Confederacy—Mohawk, Oneida, Onondaga, Cayuga, Seneca, and Tuscarora—insisted that they were true nations and that appealing to the United Nations (UN) might be the best way to assert their legal rights as a confederacy of nations. According to Coulter's legal research, they were right. In 1976, when he was asked to help prepare for what would become the 1977 non-governmental organization (NGO)-sponsored conference on Discrimination Against the Indigenous Populations in the Americas, Coulter saw the conference not only as an opportunity to make an international case on behalf of American Indians, but also to improve international law by obtaining recognition of indigenous peoples' human rights. In preparation for this conference, Coulter worked with Haudenosaunee leaders to draft what became the Declaration of Principles submitted at the 1977 NGO Conference as the delegates' main proposal. This same Declaration of Principles ultimately served as one of the foundational documents of the UN Declaration on the Rights of Indigenous Peoples.

In 1977, Coulter collaborated with John Mohawk (Seneca), Jose Barreiro (Taino), and Dr. Richard Chase and Dr. Shelton Davis of the Anthropology Resource Center to establish the Indigenous Peoples Network (IPN). This network was quickly extended to other Indian/indigenous writers, professionals, and academics. Using a combination of print and radio communications, computer networking, and data storage, IPN was able to focus considerable attention on violations of indigenous peoples' human, land, and environmental rights, often effecting immediate relief.

The establishment of the IPN was followed by one of Coulter's most important contributions to indigenous peoples in the United States and throughout the Western hemisphere. Coulter and fellow attorney Steve Tullberg founded the Indian Law Resource Center (ILRC) in 1978. Originally based in Washington, D.C., the ILRC is a non-profit organization providing legal advocacy for American Indian nations and the indigenous peoples of the Western Hemisphere in protecting their human, land, natural resource, and environmental rights, as well as sovereignty and self-governance. Representing Latin and South American Indians, the ILRC has won favorable rulings before the Organization of American States' Inter-American Court of Human Rights and Inter-American Commission on Human Rights. In particular, with the help of the ILRC, the Awas Tingni of Nicaragua and the Maya of Belize have had their land rights recognized. As an NGO with consultative status with the UN, the ILRC played a pivotal role in the drafting of the UNDRIP by the Working Group on Indigenous Populations. Collaborating with other NGOs, in 1985 it submitted the Declaration of Principles, a document that harked back to the Declaration submitted to the 1977 NGO Conference and became a foundational document of the UNDRIP.

Within the United States, the ILRC has helped American Indian peoples win many victories, as well. For example, it was instrumental in helping Alaska Native groups to negotiate an agreement for the cleanup of toxins in the Yukon River watershed. It successfully represented the Cheyenne River Sioux in their struggle to have their religious rights at Devil's Tower protected. Through ILRC advocacy, the Oglala Sioux successfully settle their claims against the federal government for mismanagement of trust funds. Working out of the Helena, Montana, office, Tim Coulter serves as both a member of ILRC's board of directors and as its executive director.

Coulter's work with the Native American Legal Defense and Education Fund and the Haudenosaunee, with the group of American Indian leaders and International Law Experts, and with the delegates attending the 1977 NGO Conference not only led to the establishment of the IPN and the ILRC, but also opened the doors for him to make significant contributions in many other arenas. From 1977 to 1978, Coulter served as the acting executive director of the Institute for the Development of Indian Law. He worked on the U.S. Commission on Civil Rights. From 1982 to 1984, he served as the chairperson of the American Bar Association Committee on the Problems of the American Indian, Section of Individual Rights and Responsibilities. In 1985, he became Harvard Law School's Ralph E. Shikes Visiting Fellow. From 1998 to 2003, he served on the Board of Directors of River Network. He continues to be a member of the American Society of International Law. In 2004, Coulter was elected as a Justice to Citizen Potawatomi Nation's Supreme Court, allowing him the opportunity to come full circle by giving back to his own nation and its growth and development.

DOCUMENT EXCERPTS WITH INTRO
Declaration of Principles (1985)

The Declaration of Principles was drafted by the following non-government organizations, and submitted to the UN Working Group on Indigenous Populations: Indian Law Resource Center, Four Directions Council, National Aboriginal and Islander Legal Service, National Indian Youth Council, Inuit Circumpolar Conference, and International Indian Treaty Council. This document is important because the ideas contained in it bridge the Declaration of Principles submitted by indigenous delegates in 1977 to the NGO Conference on the Discrimination Against Indigenous Populations of the Americas and the UN Declaration on the Rights of Indigenous Peoples, which was adopted by the UN General Assembly on September 13, 2007.

1. Indigenous nations and peoples have, in common with all humanity, the right to life, and to freedom from oppression, discrimination, and aggression.
2. All indigenous nations and peoples have the right to self-determination, by virtue of which they have the right to whatever degree of autonomy or self-government they choose. This includes the right to freely determine their political status, freely pursue their own economic, social, religious and cultural development, and determine their own membership and/or citizenship, without external interference.
3. No State shall asset any jurisdiction over an indigenous nation or people, or its territory, except in accordance with the freely expressed wishes of the nation or people concerned.
4. Indigenous nations and peoples are entitled to the permanent control and enjoyment of their aboriginal ancestral-historical territories. This includes surface and subsurface rights, inland and coastal waters, renewable and nonrenewable resources, and the economies based on these resources.
5. Rights to share and use land, subject to the underlying and inalienable title of the indigenous nation or people, may be granted by their free and informed consent, as evidenced in a valid treaty or agreement.

6. Discovery, conquest, settlement on a theory of TERRA NULLIUS and unilateral legislation are never legitimate bases for States to claim or retain the territories of indigenous nations or peoples.

7. In cases where lands taken in violation of these principles have already been settled, the indigenous nation or people concerned is entitled to immediate restitution, including compensation for the loss of use, without extinction of original title. Indigenous peoples' desire to regain possession and control of sacred sites must always be respected.

8. No State shall participate financially or militarily in the involuntary displacement of indigenous populations, or in the subsequent economic exploitation or military use of their territory.

9. The laws and customs of indigenous nations and peoples must be recognized by States' legislative, administrative and judicial institutions and, in case of conflicts with State laws, shall take precedence.

10. No State shall deny an indigenous nation, community, or people residing within its borders the right to participate in the life of the State in whatever manner and to whatever degree they may choose. This includes the right to participate in other forms of collective action and expression.

11. Indigenous nations and peoples continue to own and control their material culture, including archeological, historical and sacred sites, artifacts, designs, knowledge, and works of art. They have the right to regain items of major cultural significance and, in all cases, to the return of the human remains of their ancestors for burial in accordance with their traditions.

12. Indigenous nations and peoples have the right to be educated and conduct business with States in their own languages, and to establish their own educational institutions.

13. No technical, scientific or social investigations, including archeological excavations, shall take place in relation to indigenous nations or peoples, or their lands, without their prior authorization, and their continuing ownership and control.

14. The religious practices of indigenous nations and peoples shall be fully respected and protected by the laws of States and by international law. Indigenous nations and peoples shall always enjoy unrestricted access to, and enjoyment of sacred sites in accordance with their own laws and customs, including the right of privacy.

15. Indigenous nations and peoples are subjects of international law.

16. Treaties and other agreements freely made with indigenous nations or peoples shall be recognized and applied in the same manner and according to the same international laws and principles as treaties and agreements entered into with other States.

17. Disputes regarding the jurisdiction, territories and institutions of an indigenous nation or people are a proper concern of international law, and must be resolved by mutual agreement or valid treaty.
18. Indigenous nations and peoples may engage in self-defense against State actions in conflict with their right to self-determination.
19. Indigenous nations and peoples have the right freely to travel, and to maintain economic, social, cultural and religious relations with each other across State borders.
20. In addition to these rights, indigenous nations and peoples are entitled to the enjoyment of all the human rights and fundamental freedoms enumerated in the international Bill of Rights and other United Nations instruments. In no circumstances shall they be subjected to adverse discrimination.

Source: United Nations. Declaration on the Rights of Indigenous People. September 13, 2007. UN Doc. E/CN.4/Sub.2/AC.4/1985/WP.4/Add.4. Available online at http://www.un .org/esa/socdev/unpfii/documents/DRIPS_en.pdf. Used by permission of the United Nations.

Further Reading

Daes, Erica-Irene. *Indigenous Peoples: Keepers of our Past, Custodians of our Future.* Copenhagen: IWGIA | International Working Group for Indigenous Affairs. 2008.

Eide, Asbjørn. "Rights of Indigenous Peoples—Achievements in International Law During the Last Quarter of the Century." *Galdu Čá la: Journal of Indigenous Rights.* 2007 (4): 41–82.

Henderson, James (Sa'ke'j) Youngblood. *Indigenous Diplomacy and the Rights of Peoples.* Saskatoon: Pulrich Publishing Ltd., 2008.

Maiguascha, Bice. *The Role of Ideas in a Changing World: The International Indigenous Movement 1975-1990.* North York: CERLAC/York University. 1994. Accessed January 18, 2008. http://www.yorku.ca/cerlac/documents/Maiguaschca.pdf

Pritchard, Sarah. *Indigenous Peoples, the United Nations and Human Rights.* London: Zed Books, 1998.

Rostkowski, Joelle. "Robert Tim Coulter, Lawyer, Founder and Director of the Indian Law Resource Center." *Conversations with Remarkable Native Americans.* Albany: State University of New York Press, 2012.

Sanders, Douglas. "Developing a Modern International Law on the Rights of Indigenous Peoples." 1994. Accessed April 24, 2015. http://www.anthrobase.com/Browse/home /hst cache/Developing.doc.htm

Sanders, Douglas. "The U.N. Working Group on Indigenous Populations. *Human Rights Quarterly.* 1989 (11.3): 406–33. *JSTOR.*

Selden, Ron. "Determined Law Resource Center Continues to Fight for Justice." *Indian Country Today Media Network.com*, June 19, 2003. Accessed June 23, 2015. http:// indiancountrytodaymedianetwork.com/2003/06/19/determined-law-resource-center -continues-fight-justice-88914

Thornberry, Patrick. *Indigenous Peoples and Human Rights*. England: Manchester University Press, 2013.

Williams, Robert A., Jr. "Encounters on the Frontiers of International Human Rights Law: Redefining the Terms of Indigenous Peoples' Survival in the World." *Duke Law Journal*. 1990: 39.4: 660–704. *JSTOR*.

"Working Group on Indigenous Populations." *United Nations Human Rights | Office of the High Commissioner for Human Rights*. Accessed April 30, 2015. http://www.ohchr .org/ EN/Issues/IPeoples/Pages/WGIP.aspx

The Election of Chief Wilma Mankiller, 1983

Daniel Winunwe Rivers

Chronology of Events

1945   Wilma Mankiller born in Tahlequah, Oklahoma.

1956   The Mankiller family relocates to San Francisco under a postwar federal Indian relocation plan designed to facilitate tribal termination.

1963   Wilma Mankiller marries Hugo Olaya, with whom she will have two daughters, Felicia and Gina.

1969   Alcatraz Island in the San Francisco Bay is occupied by a group of Native American activists, the Indians of All Tribes, calling for increased tribal sovereignty and a recognition of the long pattern of breaking treaties on the part of the federal government.

1977   Wilma Mankiller and her two daughters move to Oklahoma, and Mankiller begins working on economic development for the Cherokee Nation.

1981   The Bell Community Revitalization Project begins.

1983   Wilma Mankiller is elected Deputy Chief of the Cherokee Nation.

1985   Ross Swimmer resigns, and Wilma Mankiller becomes Principal Chief of the Cherokee Nation.

1987   Wilma Mankiller is elected Principal Chief.

1991   Wilma Mankiller is re-elected for a third term and receives 82.5 percent of the vote.

2010   April 6. Wilma Mankiller dies at home at the age of 64, in Adair County, Oklahoma.

The Election of the First Woman Chief of the Cherokee Nation, Wilma Mankiller

In 1983, Wilma Mankiller was elected deputy chief of the Cherokee Nation. She was the first woman to hold this position. When the man who had chosen her as his running mate, Principal Chief Ross Swimmer, took a federal position in 1985, Mankiller became the first female Principal Chief of the Cherokee. She ran for the office herself in 1987 and won. In all, Wilma Mankiller served three terms as Principal Chief, from 1985 to 1995. Her election and subsequent political work is an important element of the emergence of feminist Native American political perspectives in the later half of the twentieth century. She also represents the increasing power of tribal self-government and the impact of the Red Power movements of the late 1960s and 1970s on a generation of Native American politicians and activists.

Chief Wilma Mankiller (1945–2010) served as principal chief of the Cherokee Nation of Oklahoma from 1985 to 1995. Mankiller grew up in rural poverty in Stillwell, Oklahoma, and her family moved to the Bay Area of California when she was 11. Mankiller was inspired by the occupation of Alcatraz Island in 1969 and returned to Oklahoma in 1977 to work for her tribe. (AP Photo)

Wilma Mankiller was born in November 1945. Her mother, of Dutch-Irish descent, and her Cherokee father married in 1937, and Mankiller was the sixth of their eleven children. She spent her early years on the allotment land of her grandfather, John Mankiller; he received the 160-acre plot in eastern Oklahoma after federal laws mandated the sale of communally held tribal property. The Mankiller family had then settled on these lands in the first decade of the twentieth century. In 1957, Wilma Mankiller's life was turned upside down when she moved with her family to the San Francisco Bay Area as part of a government-approved urban relocation program. This diasporic migration politicized Mankiller, as it did a generation of Native Americans within the United States. After being deeply affected by the emergence of radical Native American rights activism in the Bay Area in the late 1960s, especially the takeover of Alcatraz Island by the tribes of All Nations in 1969, Mankiller would become one of the most important indigenous feminist leaders of the twentieth century.

The political and intellectual work and influence of Wilma Mankiller was grounded in her Cherokee tradition and the history of the forced march that cost a quarter of tribal members their lives—a brutal military occupation and ethnic cleansing known as the "Trail of Tears." This forced migration pushed the Cherokees off their southeastern Appalachian land to that of Mankiller's childhood, eastern Oklahoma. The Cherokees and other removed tribes would again face government and military intervention in the late 19th century as a result of the Dawes and Curtis Acts. By the first decade of the twentieth century, federal mandates had broken their land into privately held allotments, and in 1907 Oklahoma became a state.

Mankiller grew up in the eastern portion of the state of Oklahoma, in a community she described as deeply shaped by the Cherokee values and ethics of "reciprocity and a sense of interdependence" (Mankiller, "Introduction" 2008, xv). For Mankiller and others, these values connect indigenous cultures and distinguish them from the market capitalism of settler colonial nations.

Before the widespread adoption of European values and the forced marches to the west, the Cherokee people had been a matrilineal, matrilocally organized society. Women were in charge of agriculture and manufacturing, were the primary property owners, and held significant political authority in Cherokee councils. The worlds of men and women were sharply divided in a form of gender complementarity but were not unequal. This sense of partnership in difference coincided with a Cherokee belief in the importance of measured balance. Within this framework, strong Cherokee women were celebrated. Mankiller herself and Cherokee historians like Theda Perdue have identified the importance of the role of women and of the idea of the Beloved Woman in Cherokee culture (Perdue 1998, 18–59; Mankiller and Wallis 1993, 19; Janda 2007, 102–03).

Cherokee women clearly had complex and critical political, military, spiritual, and social power prior to the early 19th century—a power that was grounded significantly in their central role in the cultivation and celebration of corn, including the Green Corn Dance ceremony (Perdue 1998, 25). However, as Cherokee society was increasingly affected by interaction with Anglo-European society, women's position within the tribe suffered. By the early years of the 19th century, American Christian missionaries had made significant inroads into Cherokee society. A small minority of the Cherokee elite had even embraced the planter culture of the Southeast, including rigidly patriarchal gender roles, slave owning, and plantation agriculture. Within this milieu, Cherokee women faced the rapid decline of their social and political influence (Perdue 1998, 115–58). Indeed, by the time Wilma Mankiller first took the role of Principal Chief of the Cherokee, becoming the first female chief of the tribe, she faced overt sexism and resistance to the idea of a female leader of the Cherokee Nation (Mankiller and Wallis 1993, 240–41).

The nineteenth-century laws of the Cherokee Republic, formed in 1809, diminished women's previous power within the tribe. Influenced by the governmental structure of the United States, the Cherokee elite eliminated the traditional roles of women in tribal affairs. The new laws replaced the traditional clan system and matrilineal traditions with a set of regulations that declared that property would pass from parents to their children, weakening women's control over family and property. The emergence of a national government meant that local town councils, where women had contributed significantly to political discussion, lost power. By 1826, the Cherokee General Council explicitly excluded women from a constitutional convention. The resulting constitution then denied suffrage to women, marking their final loss of political power (Perdue 1998, 135–58).

Support for these legal changes largely came from the elite class among the Cherokees, who had gradually adopted Anglo-American plantation agriculture, slave owning, and patriarchal gender roles. Many of the Cherokees also thought adoption of Anglo-American governmental, economic, and religious practices would convince the United States government to allow them to remain in their homeland in modern-day Georgia and Tennessee. This, however, was not the case, and pressure to force the Cherokees off their land grew in direct defiance of earlier treaties. By the mid-1830s, both the United States government and the state of Georgia were pressuring the Cherokees to give up their land and relocate to the west.

In this period, a split deepened within the Cherokee Nation. On one side were the vast majority of the Cherokees and the tribe's leader, John Ross, for whom removal from the Cherokee homeland was unthinkable. On the other side was a faction that believed removal was inevitable and that the Cherokees should agree to it to prevent destruction and cultural dissolution at the hands of Georgia settlers. This pro-removal faction was led by a Cherokee plantation owner, Major Ridge,

Sidebar 1: President Andrew Jackson's Attacks against the Cherokees

In 1828, Andrew Jackson was elected president of the United States. Jackson had grown up in a poor, white community in backwoods North Carolina and virulently hated Native Americans. He saw them as enemies to white settlement in the American Southeast and regularly went on raids to kill Cherokee warriors while working as a rural Tennessee attorney. (Remini 2001, 7–49). His election to the presidency meant that the removal of the Cherokees from their land to facilitate white settlement of the region became a national priority. Calls for Cherokee removal were also strengthened significantly by the discovery of gold in the Cherokee Nation by miners from Georgia. In 1830, with Jackson's encouragement, the United States Congress passed the Indian Removal Act, which gave the president the power to remove and relocate any tribe east of the Mississippi to land set aside for that purpose in the West.

The Cherokee fought this alienation from their homelands diligently, under the leadership of their Principal Chief, a mixed-blood Cherokee man named John Ross, who opposed removal, spoke English fluently, and believed the Cherokee's fate lay in using the American legal system to fight for their rights under treaty. For the case of Cherokee sovereignty and treaty law, the Supreme Court, under Chief Justice John Marshall, ruled in favor of tribal sovereignty, declaring that under treaty the Cherokees were a distinct and separate nation that held the right of autonomy over their own territory. This argument was in direct contradiction to the rights of removal and relocation given to the president by the Indian Removal Act (Perdue and Green 2007, 59–89).

President Andrew Jackson's response to the decision in *Worcester v. Georgia* was one of complete dismissal. He ignored the decision by the Supreme Court and refused to enforce it, providing encouragement to Georgian settlers who were regularly encroaching on Cherokee lands. Violent attacks by Georgians began to occur regularly, including the 1835 occupation by the Georgia militia of the Cherokee Council House and destruction of the printing press used to print the tribal newspaper, *The Cherokee Phoenix* (Perdue and Green 2007, 71–74; Miles 2005, 154; Mankiller and Wallis 1993, 92).

his son, John Ridge, and his nephew, Elias Boudinot, the editor of the *Cherokee Phoenix*. In the face of massive waves of Georgia settlers emboldened by state legislation permitting white winners of a land lottery to take the land and property of the Cherokees, and President Andrew Jackson's elimination of any legal recourse, distrust and conflict grew between John Ross and the Ridge faction. On December 29, 1835, in this chaotic environment, and convinced that they had to leave for the west, the Ridge faction signed the Treaty of New Echota—surrendering all Cherokee lands and agreeing to be removed to the west—without the approval of the Cherokee people, the vast majority of whom did not wish to leave their land (Perdue and Green 2007, 91–115).

The treaty of New Echota set 1838 as the date for Cherokee removal. The 1830 Indian Removal Act had not specified the form that removal would take, but earlier removals of other tribes from the Southeast, including the Choctaw and Chickasaw, had been military operations, controlled by the United States Army, and had resulted in numerous deaths. In 1838, United States soldiers began rounding up Cherokees, taking them from their homes and impounding their property. The Cherokee were imprisoned in forts and camps where food and clean water were scarce, disease rampant and untreated, and shelter inadequate. Many died in these camps before the march even began. In a series of removals involving thousands of Cherokees each, the tribe was forcibly marched on foot by various routes from the Southeast to the land that is present-day Oklahoma. Despite the promises of the Indian Removal Act that the government would provide adequate funding for the removal process, money for supplies was not forthcoming, food was rotten, adequate supplies and clothing were scarce, and disease spread quickly. In the end, an estimated one-quarter of the Cherokee people perished on what came to be known as the Trail of Tears. (Perdue and Green 2007, 116–140; Mankiller and Wallis 1993, 93–95).

In Indian Territory, the Cherokees faced hardships and discord that sprang from the chaotic and violent nature of forced removal; Major Ridge, John Ridge, and Elias Boudinot were assassinated for their betrayal of the Cherokee people. Their deaths exacerbated factionalism and left scars that disrupted Cherokee society in the new territory. By the mid-1840s, however, this chaotic period was largely resolved, and the Cherokees turned in earnest to creating a new community in Indian Territory. One important focus of the tribe was the development of schools—the Cherokee established both a male and a female seminary as well as numerous primary schools. (Denson 2004, 15–51). Publication of the tribal newspaper resumed in Indian Territory under the name *The Cherokee Advocate* (Debo, 1940). The elite class of the Cherokees continued practicing slave-labor plantation agriculture, while at the same time, anti-slavery beliefs grew in the tribe. Divisions over slavery and fears of federal intervention were part of what drove different Cherokee groups to side with either the Union or the Confederacy in the Civil War. (Denson 2004, 53–88).

By the late nineteenth century, the Cherokee faced the threat of federal takeover of their lands again. Although the Treaty of New Echota had promised a "permanent home" where the Cherokees would be able to "establish and enjoy a government of their choice and perpetuate such a state of society as may be most consonant with their views, habits and condition," westward expansion had contributed to the growth of a sizable non-tribal population that wanted land; the white population of Indian Territory and neighboring states began calling for the breakup and sale of the lands promised to the removed tribes. Under the Dawes and Curtis Acts, Congress demanded that the tribes in Indian Territory, regardless of previous treaties, break up their communally owned land and live on individually owned allotments. The tribes who had been forced to leave their homelands on the brutal marches of the 1830s were betrayed and would soon lose their new tribal homes as settlers flooded in and Oklahoma became a state in 1907.

Under the process of "allotment," each member of a tribe received a base allotment of 160 acres of land. However, the federally mandated program led to massive theft of tribal lands, as newcomers cheated Native Americans out of their allotted land, and the railroads claimed huge tracts for commercial enterprises. The land where Wilma Mankiller would spend the first ten years of her life was the allotment given to her grandfather as the Cherokee lands were broken up and white settlers poured in to Indian Territory. Unlike many others, however, John Mankiller retained this land and passed it on to later generations, who lived on it throughout the twentieth century (Debo 1940, 23; Mankiller and Wallis 1993, 4–5).

This, then, was the historical legacy of the community in which Wilma Mankiller was raised. The history of the tremendous loss that the Cherokees had suffered, the importance of community and the land, and a belief in Cherokee resilience were all central parts of her political development. In combination with these deep historical understandings was an awareness of the ways that vulnerability and change were central elements of modern Native life. Mankiller understood intimately how the turbulence of American postwar society had affected the Cherokee and other tribes. In 1956, Mankiller and her family moved to San Francisco, like other Native Americans who were relocated to urban centers in the 1950s (Mankiller and Wallis 1993, 70–71).

The Movement of Native Peoples after World War II

The movement of Native Peoples from their land to urban metropoles was first accelerated by the Second World War. As wartime industry expanded, Native Americans joined others migrating to the cities for jobs. During the war, 40,000 Indians had moved in search of work. Schools set up by the Bureau of Indian Affairs offered courses in war-related skills, such as welding and mechanics. Native men and women worked in the aircraft industry, as clerks and teachers, and in construction.

Although some firms, like Lockheed, maintained racist hiring practices and refused to hire Native Americans, most industrial employers did so willingly, although sometimes at unfair and unequal wages when compared to their white counterparts. These Native workers entered the unfamiliar cities and laid the foundation for communities that would expand in the postwar era. (Bernstein 1999, 64–88). There were also fewer voluntary migrations during the war. In her autobiography, Wilma Mankiller describes the forced removal of 45 Cherokee families from allotted land by the U.S. Army for the enlargement of a military base in 1942. (Mankiller and Wallis 1993, 62–63).

In the decade following the war, the informal migration of many Native Americans from Indian land to the city for employment was followed by a much more systematic and brutal government-sponsored program of relocation designed to facilitate tribal termination. Echoing earlier attempts to force tribal peoples to assimilate and to give up their indigenous cultures, the federal Bureau of Indian Affairs instituted a program designed to move Native Americans from tribal spaces to the cities and to facilitate their becoming laborers in modern American society. This program was overseen by Dillon Myer, a strong proponent of Indian tribal termination and the erasure of traditional tribal lifeways who had been the architect of the forced internment of Japanese Americans during the war and saw Native cultures as "primitive" (Mankiller and Wallis 1993, 63–69; Fixico 2000, 9–10).

The federal relocation program began in 1950 and grew throughout the decade. Although technically voluntary, many aspects of the program's implementation were decidedly coercive. First, Myer supported the reduction of loans offered on reservations and the facilitation of loans for Native Americans who were willing to remove to the cities, a factor that pushed many to leave Native land. In addition, BIA officials, who wielded considerable economic and political power on reservations, often strongly encouraged Native youth and families to relocate. Often, Native People who relocated off reservations to cities felt alienated by the lack of communal ties and support, the coldness they experienced in modern capitalism, and the unfamiliar customs in urban areas. Many of the jobs that the federal government had optimistically predicted would be available disappeared as the beginnings of decline hit the industrial cities of the Northeast, and Native families often found themselves pushed by poverty and postwar housing shortages into poor neighborhoods. Wilma Mankiller and her family found themselves living in Hunter's Point, an impoverished neighborhood in South San Francisco (Edmunds 2006, 400–401; (Mankiller and Wallis 1993, 66–74; Fixico 2000, 8–25).

Although the federal attack on tribal communities and cultures, as well as the difficulties that many Native families faced in the migration and relocation process, made life in the postwar Native American diaspora difficult, this large-scale migration also led to the development of new community ties and pan-Indian relationships that would facilitate the rise of Native American activism in the 1950s and 1960s. As Native American migrants to the cities sought to build community there, they founded American Indian centers in their new locations. American Indian centers were founded in Phoenix (1947), Chicago (1953), and Seattle (1960), as well as many other cities across the United States. These centers were vital spaces for inter-tribal dialogue, personal survival, community formation, and activism (Fixico 2000, 123–40; Lagrand 2002, 162–67).

Wilma Mankiller remembered the San Francisco American Indian Center as a deeply important place for her family after they relocated to the Bay Area in 1956. The staff at the center, Mankiller wrote, "helped us to adjust to urban living." She recalled that the Center was "the heart of a vibrant tribal community" and the gathering place for community activists (Lobo 2002, xv; Fixico 2002, 137). Weekly dinners provided a space for gathering with other Indians and discussing different political perspectives, as well as education programs for urban Native youth. Another important center for Native community in the San Francisco Bay Area was the Intertribal Friendship House (IFH), founded in 1955. The IFH served as a place for community gatherings, youth groups, and communal meals. Pow-wows, also important for the forging of community ties, were organized at the San Francisco Center and the IFH. As a new era of Native American activism that included the Red Power movement emerged, centers such as the one in San Francisco served as critical sites of organizing (Lobo 2002, 28–31, 77, 92; Fixico 2000, 135; Lagrand 2002, 204–08).

In 1963, Mankiller married Hugo Olaya, an Ecuadorian immigrant studying business at San Francisco State University and in quick succession had two children. This was a powerful and dynamic time of activism and social change in the Bay Area. Mankiller admired the social programs and defiant stance of the Black Panther Party as it came out of Oakland in 1966, and deeply identified with the struggles of the United Farm Worker's Union—bringing with her an understanding of labor activism that tied back to her father's work as a longshoreman. And in Mankiller's neighborhood of Hunter's Point, violence between people on the street and police officers intensified, reflecting a history of frustration and racism. Amid these currents of social change, and while she raised her children, Mankiller's political views developed (Mankiller and Wallis 1993, 143–55).

A critical part of Wilma Mankiller's political development was her involvement in the Red Power movement of the late 1960s in the San Francisco Bay Area. In the late 1960s, encouraged by her Klamath friend and mentor, Gustine Moppin, Wilma Mankiller began taking classes at Skyline Junior College and went on to continue her studies at San Francisco State University. (Mankiller and Wallis 1993,

158). This put her at the center of Native American activism in the Bay Area. In 1968, Lanada Boyer (Shoshone-Bannock) and Lehman Brightman (Sioux-Creek) founded a group called United Native Americans (UNA). UNA published a newsletter called *Warpath* and was a part of the 1968 Third World Liberation Front strike at SF State and the 1969 Third World Liberation Front Strike at UC Berkeley, which resulted in the formation of ethnic studies departments at State and UC (Boyer 1997, 89–90). From the Native Studies programs at SF State and Berkeley emerged a group of radicalized Native students, among them Richard Oakes, a Mohawk man from Akwesane, New York, and LaNada Boyer, who had gone to the Bay Area from Idaho (Johnson 1996, 82–84).

In 1969, after the Indian Center where Mankiller spent her teen years burned down, discussions among youth groups of a possible occupation of Alcatraz Island took on new urgency. On November 20, 1969, 89 American Indians landed on Alcatraz Island and claimed it, calling themselves the Indians of All Tribes. They occupied the island for a year and a half, bringing national attention to the injustices facing Native communities and serving as inspiration for a generation of Native American activists. Mankiller's siblings and nieces and nephews were among the occupiers of the island while she managed support from the shore. The occupation had a deep political influence on Mankiller. (DeLuca 1983; Mankiller and Wallis 1993, 192–99).

In this milieu, involved in political work and going back to school, Mankiller began to question her marriage and become seriously involved in community development work. She started working with the Pit River tribe in a land struggle against PG&E, the state power utility, which gave her important legal training in tribal rights, community activism, and economic development (Janda 2007, 85–86). These experiences would not only help Mankiller in her rise to the office of Principal Chief, but would also guide her priorities throughout her political career.

Mankiller, like many women of the era who left previous marriages, suffered an economic downturn as she retrained herself and lost financial support from her husband. In 1977, Mankiller and her two daughters moved back to Oklahoma. Mankiller took a job as economic stimulus coordinator for the Cherokee Nation, and soon she was finding her voice in local Cherokee tribal politics. In 1979, Mankiller was involved in a tragic accident. A car moved into her lane to pass and hit her in a head-on collision. The other driver, who was killed, was her close friend Sherry Morris. In the course of her long recovery, Mankiller also became aware of her own myasthenia gravis and underwent surgery for this condition (Mankiller and Wallis 1993, 215–229; Janda 2007, 88, 114). Out of all of these struggles, Wilma Mankiller emerged strong and determined.

In her position as economic stimulus coordinator from 1977 to 1983, Mankiller helped found and direct an economic development initiative called the Bell

Community Revitalization Project. Bell was a community in Adair County, Oklahoma that was 95 percent Cherokee, and Mankiller successfully used grants to enable the people living there to change their fundamental circumstances. Following recovery from her car accident and subsequent surgery, Mankiller put renewed determination into the Bell project with powerful results. What had begun as the poorest per capita community in Oklahoma became a nationally known success story. The chief of the Cherokees, Ross Swimmer, chose Wilma Mankiller to run as Deputy Chief on his ticket in 1983. Swimmer's decision was surprising—he himself was a conservative Republican, and Wilma Mankiller was a liberal Democrat. Part of what led to Swimmer's nonpartisan choice was Mankiller's trustworthiness and proven record on the Bell community project. Swimmer faced criticism from conservative allies while Mankiller herself faced opposition because she was a woman, a part of a younger generation radicalized by the Red Power movement, and a partial outsider as someone who had not grown up entirely in Oklahoma (Mankiller and Wallis 1993, 232–242; Janda 2007, 89–94).

Wilma Mankiller won the election for Deputy Chief in 1983 and became Principal Chief in 1985 when Ross Swimmer left the position to work in Washington, D.C. Mankiller's rise to the most powerful political office in the Cherokee Nation of Oklahoma made her an internationally known figure. She became a symbol of resurgent Native pride, the strength of indigenous women, and Native American feminism. In her work as Principal Chief, she continued to emphasize grassroots community development and economic empowerment. She focused on health care, education, and programs for Cherokee youth. Working from her staunch belief in the struggle for Native sovereignty, a focus that testified to her roots in the Red Power movement, Mankiller fought for new agreements from the federal government giving the Cherokee independence in overseeing tribal programs and governance (Janda 2007, 97–119).

As the first female Principal Chief of the Cherokee Nation, Wilma Mankiller was one of the most visible figures in Native American politics in the latter half of the twentieth century. Her rise to political office was part of the emergence to power of a generation marked by a new demand for Native sovereignty. Her childhood instilled in her a deep empathy for impoverished Cherokee communities and led her to see community development as a fundamental necessity for tribal prosperity. Her work and her proud identification as a Native American feminist increased the visibility of Native American women and communities in general. Mankiller was the recipient of numerous prestigious awards, including the Presidential Medal of Freedom and the American Association of University Women's Achievement Award, and was inducted into the National Women's Hall of Fame in 1993. She died of pancreatic cancer at her home in Adair County, Oklahoma, on April 6, 2010.

Biographies of Notable Figures

John Ross (1790–1866)

John Ross was born on October 3, 1790. He was raised in a Cherokee world that was already reeling from tremendous change and intrusion from Anglo settlers. After the American Revolution, as white settlers poured into Cherokee lands in Georgia and what in 1796 would become the state of Tennessee, they wreaked havoc on the tribe. The Cherokees, who had sided with the British during the Revolutionary War out of fear of the colonists, lost a tremendous amount of land and suffered greatly during this period. But by 1800, the Cherokees still had about 50,000 square miles of territory and in the early years of the nineteenth century made a remarkable comeback. It was in this world that the young John Ross was brought up (Hicks 2011, 28–32).

John Ross's mother, Mollie, was a Cherokee woman and a member of the Bird Clan. His father, Daniel, was a Scotsman who had come into the Tennessee Valley as a young man to try his luck as a trader. He had met and fallen in love with Mollie McDonald while working as a clerk in a trading post in Cherokee territory. As Mollie's husband, Daniel Ross became a member of the Bird Clan and an important figure in Cherokee society. In his youth and early adulthood, John Ross lived in a world of mixed European and Cherokee ancestry, where traditional tribal customs were rapidly mixing with the customs and practices of Anglo-American society. From his family, John Ross would learn to value both the sovereignty and culture of the Cherokee tribe as well as the government and culture of the United States. He grew up in a home that was organized in the traditional ways and celebrated festivals that had always been sacred to the tribe, while also learning English and the politics of the new nation working at his grandfather's trading post (Mankiller and Wallis 1993, 85; Hicks 2011, 31–32, 43–45).

After being educated at the Kingston Academy in Tennessee, Ross returned to his home in Cherokee country to work in business. He was successful and gradually became better known in the tribe. In 1813, Ross married a Cherokee woman named Elizabeth Brown Henley, also known as Quatie. As settlers continued to move into Indian country, tensions and factionalism mounted. The same year that John Ross and Quatie were married, a rebellion known as the Redstick Rebellion began among the Creek tribe. John Ross and many other Cherokee sided with the American government in a war with the rebellious Creeks, believing that doing so would show their willingness to assist the new nation and help preserve Cherokee sovereignty; however, when Jackson indiscriminately took a huge amount of land from both rebel and loyal Creeks, as well as the Cherokee, at the end of the war, John Ross learned that many American leaders were determined to take Native land and could not be trusted. In the face of this, Ross saw the critical importance of continued Cherokee independence (Hicks 2011, 48, 50–51, 56–69; Mankiller and Wallis 1993, 85–86).

In 1816, John Ross accompanied a delegation of Cherokee statesmen to Washington, D.C. His literacy in English was of great value to the Cherokee. In this mission, John Ross stood out for his diplomatic skills, knowledge of previous treaties that the Cherokee had signed with the United States government, and his bilingualism. He pushed the United States representatives to give the tribe back land that Jackson had taken at the end of the Creek War in exchange for cession of land in South Carolina. This agreement was seen as a major victory by the Cherokees, who were less concerned with the land in South Carolina than the territory that Jackson had taken. Although Jackson quickly and very questionably got the land back, Ross's capable negotiations in Washington gained him the trust of the Cherokee people and a reputation as a statesman (Hicks 2011, 83–89).

In 1817, as part of their effort to consolidate their control of their territory in the face of white aggression, the Cherokee formed a National Committee. This new governmental body of thirteen members constituted a new, powerful executive branch of the Cherokee tribe that oversaw political affairs to prevent any one Cherokee chief from signing away more land to the United States government. John Ross was elected a member of the National Committee. In the face of increased pressure to leave their lands, John Ross, now an appointed Indian commissioner, became more determined to help his people retain their homelands and traditional culture. Increasingly, Ross became the voice of resistance to Andrew Jackson's ploys and threats to force removal. In 1828, in the middle of intensified struggle with the United States over the issue of removal, John Ross was sworn in as Principal Chief of the Cherokees (McLoughlin 1986, 157–58; Hicks 2011, 95, 163).

As Principal Chief, Ross attempted to lead his people through the violence of the Georgia settlers who sought to take their land and the insistence of President Jackson that they be removed to the west. Ross kept the interests of his people at the forefront and believed that the way forward lay in using the laws of the United States and appealing to the rights of the Cherokee under treaties signed with the United States government. Although he ultimately failed to stop the forced removal of his tribe from their eastern homelands, John Ross is remembered as a great hero of the Cherokee people.

Dr. LaNada Boyer (1947–)

LaNada Boyer (Bannock-Shoshone) was born in 1947 and grew up on the Bannock-Shoshone Fort Hall Reservation in Idaho. The Shoshone and the Bannock tribes had been forced onto the Fort Hall Reservation by the American military in 1867. Boyer grew up poor, one of 12 children, and would tell a *Ramparts* magazine writer in 1970 that "we were always hungry." (Collier 1970, 28). She was raised to understand the struggles and betrayals her people had suffered at the hands of the United States and to value political work. Her father was tribal chairman when she was young, and worked to resist government encroachment onto Shoshone and Bannock land. The racism that Native Americans faced was everywhere—visible in the signs in the windows of the stores in the small towns that surrounded the Fort Hall reservation that read, "No Indians or Dogs Allowed" and the presence of separate Indian stalls in public bathrooms. This virulent racism gave Boyer an early understanding of the difficulties facing Native Peoples (Collier 1970, 28–30; Boyer 1997, 88).

As a girl, Boyer attended St. Mary's School for Girls in Springfield, South Dakota. Much of the coursework was designed to prepare Boyer and other Native youth for domestic work and menial labor. Boyer was eventually expelled for being "too outspoken." She was again expelled from public school on the Fort Hall reservation at the age of 15 for speaking up about racism toward Indians in the curriculum. She was sent to Chilocco Indian School in Oklahoma, where she made the honor roll but was expelled again. Boyer was sent to another BIA boarding school, Stewart Institute, in Carson City, Nevada, where she was expelled after only one day. During this series of expulsions, Boyer was labeled "difficult" and threatened with incarceration. At the age of seventeen, Boyer passed the G.E.D. exam and began classes at Idaho State College (Collier 1970, 28–30; Johnson 1997, 104–105).

In 1965, LaNada Boyer joined other Native Peoples taking part in the federal relocation programs and left the Fort Hall reservation on a Greyhound bus for San Francisco. Her decision to go was based on the fact that there were few jobs available for Indians on the Fort Hall reservation except for menial labor. Boyer felt that if she were to take part in the BIA relocation program, she might find a better situation. She would later come to see these programs as a sham set up by the government to dispossess Native Americans. On arriving in San Francisco, Boyer waited in vain for the BIA to help her get the job she had been promised. Instead, once she herself found employment as a barmaid, the BIA immediately ended her $140 monthly stipend. Like many others who relocated, Boyer was alienated and poor and ended up getting pregnant at the age of 17 (Collier 1970, 30; Johnson 1997, 105).

It was at that point that Boyer, determined to continue her education, was accepted into the Economic Opportunity Program for minority students at the University of California at Berkeley as the first Native student in the program. Although she did well in her classes, Boyer felt that she had been accepted out of "tokenism" and experienced pressure to be more "white"—echoes of the antagonism she had experienced in public schools when she was labeled "difficult." She also recalled wanting to learn about Native American history and being unable to find these classes at Berkeley (Boyer 1997, 89; Collier 1970, 30; Johnson 1997, 105–06).

Boyer began getting more involved in Bay Area Native activism. In 1968, she co-founded United American Indians with Lee Brightman (Sioux-Creek). The organization published a newspaper called *Warpath* that was strongly critical of BIA policies. In 1969, Boyer began working on the Third World Liberation Front Strike at UC Berkeley and San Francisco State, which would lead to the establishment of the first ethnic studies programs in the United States (Boyer 1997, 89–90).

In 1969, after the San Francisco American Indian Center burned down, resentment at the poor treatment of Native Americans by the federal government increased. At the same time, discussion had emerged over what to do with Alcatraz Island, the site of a former federal penitentiary in San Francisco Bay. The prison had been closed in 1963, and the next year a group of five Sioux men had attempted to reclaim the island for indigenous Americans. A Texas developer had proposed a controversial plan to turn the land into a commercial site that had been endorsed by the San Francisco City Council. Instead, a group of California college students, including LaNada Boyer, formed a group they called the Indians of All Tribes and planned to occupy the island. On November 20, 1969, they landed and declared the island to be an occupied territory, reclaimed for the Native Peoples of the United States (DeLuca 1982, 7–14).

Lanada Boyer emerged as one of the leaders of the occupation of Alcatraz, along with Richard Oakes (Mohawk). Not only was she one of the core organizers of the action, but she remained at the center of the occupation throughout the year and a half that it lasted. She served on the council organized by the occupation to oversee the occupation and managed relations with media and government representatives. At the one-year anniversary of the occupation, Boyer was one of five original members of the Indians of All Tribes who remained. With John Trudell, she developed a plan to create a university free for Native Americans called Thunderbird University on the island and on the eve of the government removal of the occupiers from the island was organizing students at UC Berkeley and San Francisco State in support of the occupation. In 1997, Boyer wrote that "The island is a reminder of our ongoing relationship with the federal government. It is an infamous prison that carries the burden of the wicked deeds of others, the bondage and captivity of our people, the painful stories of misery and suffering. The federal government has never recognized our claim and has failed to enforce many treaties and federal laws protecting our rights and many others." (Boyer 1997, 100, 96–99; Johnson 1997, 206).

In 1999, Boyer completed her PhD in Political Science at Idaho State University. Her dissertation, a detailed comparison of western European and Native worldviews, argued for the "incorporation of Native American perception into mainstream political discourse" as a way of combatting disconnections between the natural world and human society embedded in Western political and philosophical thought (Chavers 2007, 499; Boyer 1999, 1–44).

See also: Indian Removal Act and the Trail of Tears, 1830; Cherokee Cases, 1831–1832

Further Reading

Bernstein, Alison. *American Indians and World War II: Toward a New Era in Indian Affairs* Norman, Oklahoma: University of Oklahoma Press, 1999.

Boyer, LaNada. "Reflections of Alcatraz." In *American Indian Activism: Alcatraz to the Longest Walk*. Edited by Troy Johnson, Joane Nagel, and Duane Champagne. Chicago: University of Illinois Press, 1997.

Boyer, LaNada. "Epistemology of a Muted Group: Native American Perceptions of the Natural World with Implications for the Political Policy Process." PhD Dissertation. Idaho State University, 1999.

Chavers, Dean. *Modern American Indian Leaders: Their Lives and Their Work, Volume Two.* New York: The Edwin Mellen Press, 2007.

Collier, Peter. "Better Red Than Dead," *Ramparts*. (February 1970): 27–38.

Debo, Angie. *And Still The Waters Run: The Betrayal of the Five Civilized Tribes*. Princeton, NJ: Princeton University Press, 1940.

DeLuca, Richard. " 'We Hold the Rock!: The Indian Attempt to Reclaim Alcatraz Island." *California History*, Vol. 62, No. 1 (Spring 1983): 2–22.

Denson, Andrew. *Demanding the Cherokee Nation: Indian Autonomy and American Culture*, 1830–1900. Lincoln, Nebraska: University of Nebraska Press, 2004.

Edmunds, David, Frederick E. Hoxie, and Neal Salisbury. *The People: A History of Native America*. Belmont, CA: Wadsworth Cengage Publishing, 2006.

Fixico, Donald. *The Urban Indian Experience in America*. Albuquerque: University of New Mexico, 2000.

Genetin-Pilawa, C. Joseph. *Crooked Paths to Allotment: The Fight Over Federal Indian Policy after the Civil War*. Chapel Hill: The University of North Carolina Press, 2012.

Goldstein, Margaret. *You Are Now on Indian Land: The American Indian Occupation of Alcatraz Island*. Minneapolis: Twenty-First Century Books, 2011.

Hicks, Brian. *Toward the Setting Sun: John Ross, the Cherokees, and the Trail of Tears*. New York: Atlantic Monthly Press, 2011.

Hoikkala, Paivi H. "Mothers and Community Builders: Salt Rivers Pima and Maricopa Women in Community Action." In *Negotiators of Change: Historical Perspectives on Native American Women*. Edited by Nancy Shoemaker. New York: Routledge, 1995.

Janda, Sarah Eppler. *Beloved Women: The Political Lives of LaDonna Harris and Wilma Mankiller*. Dekalb: Northern Illinois University Press, 2007.

Johnson, Troy R. *The Occupation of Alcatraz Island: Indian Self-Determination and the Rise of Indian Activism*. Chicago: University of Illinois Press, 1996.

Krouse, Susan Applegate. "What Came Out of the Takeovers: Women's Activism and the Indian Community School of Milwaukee." *American Indian Quarterly*, Vol. 27, No. 3 and 4 (Summer/Autumn 2003): 533–547.

Lagrand, James. *Indian Metropolis: Native Americans in Chicago, 1945–75*. Chicago: University of Illinois Press, 2002.

Langston, Donna Hightower. "American Indian Women's Activism in the 1960s and 1970s." *Hypatia*, Vol. 18, No. 2 (Spring 2003): 114–132.

Lobo, Susan and Kurt Peters, eds. *American Indians and the Urban Experience*. Lanham, MD: Alta Mira Press, 2001.

Lobo, Susan, ed. *Urban Voices: The Bay Area Indian Community*. Tucson: University of Arizona Press, 2002.

Mankiller, Wilma and Michael Wallis. *Mankiller: A Chief and Her People*. New York: St. Martin's Press, 1993.

Mankiller, Wilma. *Every Day is a Good Day: Reflections by Contemporary Indigenous Women*. Golden, CO: Fulcrum Publishing, 2004.

Mankiller, Wilma. "Introduction." In Albert Hurtado, *Reflections on American Indian History*. Norman: The University of Oklahoma Press, 2008.

McLoughlin, William G. *Cherokee Renascence in the New Republic*. Princeton, NJ: Princeton University Press, 1986.

Miles, Tiya. *Ties That Bind: The Story of an Afro-Cherokee Family in Slavery and Freedom*. Berkeley: University of California Press, 2005.

Nagel, Joane. *American Indian Ethnic Renewal: Red Power and the Resurgence of Identity and Culture*. Oxford, UK: Oxford University Press, 1996.

Puisto, Jaakko. " 'We Didn't Care for It,' the Salish and Kootenai Battle against Termination Policy, 1946–1954." *Montana: The Magazine of Western History*, Vol. 52, No. 4 (Winter 2002): 48–63.

Perdue, Theda. *Cherokee Women: Gender and Culture Change 1700–1835*. Lincoln: The University of Nebraska Press, 1998.

Perdue, Theda and Michael Green. *The Cherokee Nation and the Trail of Tears*. New York: Viking Penguin Publishers, 2007.

Remini, Robert. *Andrew Jackson and His Indian Wars*. New York: Viking, 2001.

Rosenthal, Nicolas G. *Reimagining Indian Country: Native American Migration and Identity in Twentieth-Century Los Angeles*. Chapel Hill: University of North Carolina Press, 2012.

Shreve, Bradley G. " 'From Time Immemorial': The Fish-in Movement and the Rise of Intertribal Activism." *Pacific Historical Review*, Vol. 78, No. 3 (August 2009): 403–34.

Shreve, Bradley. *Red Power Rising: The National Indian Youth Council and the Origins of Native Activism*. Norman: University of Oklahoma Press, 2011.

Smoak, Gregory E. *Ghost Dances: Prophetic Religion and American Indian Ethnogenesis in the Nineteenth Century*. Berkeley: University of California Press, 2006.

The American Indian College Fund, 1989

Azusa Ono

Chronology

1965 Office of Economic Opportunity funds a feasibility study for the creation of a junior or community college on the Navajo Reservation. The study recommends the establishment of a tribally controlled community college.

1968 Navajo Community College is established as the first tribal college in the United States. Classes start in January 1969 at the BIA-operated Many Farms High School in Arizona with 309 students (196 full-time).

1969 The Report of the Senate Special Subcommittee on Indian Education entitled *Indian Education: A National Tragedy, a National Challenge* (also known as the Kennedy Report) is issued. It reveals Indian students' extremely high dropout rate (twice the national average) and recommends Indian control over education.

1971 Congress passes the Navajo Community College Act (P.L.92–189) to provide federal support for the college, and appropriates $5.5 million for construction of campus and operational costs.

1972 Navajo Community College and five other tribal colleges start the American Indian Higher Education Consortium (AIHEC). Gerald One Feather of Oglala Sioux Community College became its first president.

The Office of Indian Education is established within the U.S. Department of Education.

Congress passes the Indian Education Act (P.L.92–318), which provides funds for special programs for Indian children attending public schools both on- and off-reservation. The law requires increased participation of Indian parents in the decision-making process to ensure Indian self-determination in education.

1973 AIHEC establishes headquarters in Denver, Colorado, with initial funding from the Ford, Carnegie, and Donner Foundations.

1975 President Richard Nixon signs the Indian Self-Determination and Education Act (PL93-638) to further tribal control of education, social services, and health care.

1976 Navajo Community College attains accreditation by the North Central Association Commission on Institutions of Higher Education and became the first tribally controlled institution to be accredited as a two-year college

1978 President Jimmy Carter signs the Tribally Controlled Community College Assistance Act (P.L. 95–471) to assist tribal colleges on or near reservations, in the form of per-student operational funds (initially $4,000 per full-time student). Senator James Abourezk (D–SD) originally sponsors the bill.

Congress passes the Education Amendments Act (P.L.95–561), which increases financial aid for Native American college students and funding for Native American studies and programs.

1983 Oglala Lakota College and Sinte Gleska College, both in South Dakota, become the first two accredited tribal colleges to offer bachelor's degree programs.

1989 The American Indian College Fund (the College Fund) is established within the AIHEC to raise private-sector money for Tribal Colleges and Universities (TCUs), and scholarships for their students. The College Fund sets its annual budget at $3 million and raises $1 million in the first year of its operation.

Sinte Gleska College becomes the first tribal college to offer a master's degree program.

1990 President George H. W. Bush signs the Native American Languages Act (P.L. 101–477). This law recognizes the federal government's obligation "to preserve, protect, and promote the rights and freedom of Native Americans to use, practice, and develop Native American languages." It officially reverses the historical policy of suppressing Native American languages.

1991 The Indian Nations at Risk Task Force, established by Secretary of Education Lauro Cavazos in 1990, issues its final report. It identifies the failure of schools to educate a large number of Native American children and adults as one of four reasons why Indian nations are at risk.

1992 The White House Conference on Indian Education (authorized by P.L. 100–297) is held. The delegates adopt 111 resolutions, 31 of them related to higher education. They include federal support for the recruitment and retention of Native American faculty and students.

1994 Congress extends the Morrill Land-Grant Act through the passage of the Equity in Educational Land-Grant Status Act (P.L. 103–382) to offer land grant status to 34 TCUs. It entitles those institutions to receive funds and benefits for the improvement of agriculture and sciences programs and facilities.

1996 President Bill Clinton issues Executive Order 13021, "Tribal Colleges and Universities," that directs all federal departments and agencies as well as the private sector to increase their support to TCUs.

2002 The College Fund's headquarters relocate from New York City to Denver.

2007 Congress passes the College Cost Reduction and Access Act (P.L. 110–84), which includes an additional $60 million for TCUs.

2008 AIHEC secures an increased budget authorization ($8,000 per full-time student) for TCUs.

2009 President Barack Obama donates partial proceeds from his Nobel Peace Prize to the College Fund for TCU student scholarships.

2011 President Obama signs Executive Order 13592, "Improving American Indian and Alaska Native Educational Opportunities and Strengthening Tribal Colleges and Universities." The order creates the White House Initiative on American Indian and Alaska Native Education.

2014 Twenty-fifth anniversary of the College Fund and the *Tribal College Journal: Journal of American Indian Higher Education*.

2015 The College Fund holds 25th Anniversary Gala in Los Angeles and Chicago.

The Development of the American Indian College Fund

The American Indian College Fund (the College Fund) was established in 1989 within the American Indian Higher Education Consortium (AIHEC), which had been founded in 1972. The primary role of the College Fund was to seek contributions from the private sector. The fund would offer support to the tribal colleges and universities (TCUs), and scholarships to their students. In 2002, the original headquarters in New York City relocated to Denver, Colorado.

The College Fund came into being as a result of the tribal college movement of the 1960s. A number of Indian tribes and nations sought to provide higher education opportunities for their members on reservations so that they could attend college without leaving their tribal community.

Changes in federal Indian policy also pushed the tribal college movement further, as it shifted from termination to self-determination. Thus, tribes won general support for self-control of their affairs. One such example was the development of Indian Community Action Programs within the Office of Economic Opportunity (OEO). Tribes acquired more autonomy in administering their own programs on reservations (Carney, 106).

As with the American population as a whole, the 1960s saw Native Americans begin to enroll in college in larger numbers. In 1969, 3,500 students took advantage of the BIA's financial assistance to college students; four years later, 13,500 had received BIA funding. By comparison, in 1968, 739 public community colleges were in existence, a number that increased by 1978 to 1,047 (Stein, 6). The need for local community colleges on and near isolated reservations arose with similar demands from Indian tribes.

In 1968, Navajo Community College (today's Diné College) was founded by the Navajo Nation as the first tribal college in the United States. Dr. Robert Roessel, former director of the Rough Rock Demonstration School in Arizona and the Center for Indian Education at Arizona State University, became the first president of Navajo Community College.

The Navajo Nation initially had established a higher education scholarship fund in 1957 to send qualified youth to off-reservation colleges. They soon learned that more than 50 percent of scholarship awardees had returned home by the end of their freshman year. This disappointing outcome led to a 1959 conversation among the tribal education committee about the creation of the tribe's own higher education institution (Stein, 11).

The effort to establish a tribal college was truly a community effort. Yazzie Begay, a member of the Navajo Community College's first board of regents, donated family lands at Tsaile, Arizona, to build the campus. The isolated location, however, was far from the concentration of Navajo people. The college then opened branch campuses in places like Chinle, Shiprock, and Tuba City (Reyhner and Eder, 296–97). The college enrolled Navajos of different ages. One-third of the students were in academic courses, while two-thirds took vocational training courses (Prucha, 1147).

With the success of Navajo Community College, the federal government extended its support for TCUs with the passage of the Tribally Controlled Community College Assistance Act (P.L. 95–471) to assist tribal colleges on or near reservations. The law provided grants for the operation and improvement of TCUs, most of which had operated in deteriorated buildings, and sometimes even in trailers.

Within five years of passage of the Tribally Controlled Community College Assistance Act, TCUs began to earn accreditation. In 1983, Oglala Lakota College and Sinte Gleska College became the first two accredited tribal colleges to offer four-year bachelor's degree programs. In 1989, Sinte Gleska College became the first tribal college to offer master's degrees programs.

The number of TCUs has grown since the creation of AIHEC when, there were only six TCUs. Today, 37 colleges are in operation in the United States. The number of students attending TCUs has also grown. In 1997, approximately 25,000 Native American students attended one of the TCUs. Today, these colleges serve approximately 30,000 full- and part-time students. According to fall 2010 enrollment data, 8.7 percent of Native American college students attended one of the 32 accredited tribal colleges. American Indian students constituted 78 percent of the combined total enrollment of these institutions (*Review of Federal Agencies' Support to Tribal Colleges and Universities*, 2010).

The American Indian Higher Education Consortium (AIHEC)

In 1973, Navajo Community College and five of the first tribal colleges started the American Indian Higher Education Consortium (AIHEC). This would be an informal organization of member colleges to assist TCUs and would serve as a lobbyist group representing TCUs. Gerald One Feather of Oglala Lakota Community College became the first president of AIHEC, followed by Lionel Bordeaux, president of Sinte Gleska College. AIHEC's first five-year plan included working on curriculum, research and data, accreditation, institutional development, and human services. With the funds provided by the Rockefeller Foundation, AIHEC awarded its first leadership grant to the American Association of Colleges and Junior Colleges. The grant funded interns at Sinte Gleska and Navajo Community Colleges (Gipp, 12).

Today, AIHEC represents 37 TCUs in the United States and one in Canada. AIHEC's mission is to provide "leadership and influences public policy on American Indian higher education issues through advocacy, research, and program initiatives; promotes and strengthens indigenous languages, cultures, communities, and tribal nations; and through its unique position, serves member institutions and emerging TCUs" (AIHEC website).

The American Indian College Fund (The College Fund)

The American Indian College Fund (the College Fund) began in 1989 within the AIHEC to raise funds from the private sector. In its first year of its operations, the College Fund raised $1 million. It also established its own endorsement fund supported by a challenge grant from the MacArthur Foundation and a donation from the Hearst Foundation (Houser, 98). Some of the major funders included the Eli Lily Corp. ($31 million for facility development) and the W. K. Kellogg Foundation Higher Education Initiative ($27 million) (Gipp, 13). In 2013, the College Fund distributed more than 6,000 scholarships, not only for TCU students, but also to those who enrolled in the BIA-operated institutions and in mainstream colleges and universities. Since 1989, the College Fund has distributed nearly 100,000 scholarships totaling approximately $78 million. (U.S. Senate Hearing, Statement of

American Indian College Fund (AICF) Flame of Hope 2005 Gala. AICF was founded in 1989 to raise funds from private contributors to support scholarships and resources for tribal colleges. The headquarters were originally located in New York City and relocated to Denver, Colorado, in 2002. (Jemal Countess/WireImage/Getty Images)

Cheryl Crazy Bull, 2014, 28). The demand for financial assistance has always been greater than the supply of scholarships, due to high poverty rates among Native American students, their lower average age compared the United States' total, and the growing number of American Indian students seeking college degrees.

The official mission of the College Fund is to transform "Indian higher education by funding and creating awareness of the unique, community-based accredited tribal colleges and universities, offering students access to knowledge, skills, and cultural values, which enhance their communities and the country as a whole." The current goal of the College Fund is to "educate 60% of Native American people served by TCUs by 2025" (The College Fund website). Today, the College Fund supports 34 fully accredited tribal colleges and universities on or near reservations in 13 states. These colleges and universities serve 30,000 full-time students.

The Tribally Controlled College Assistance Act of 1978

Another limited, but essential, federal funding source for TCUs became available with passage of the Tribally Controlled College Assistance Act of 1978. The act provided $4,000 per full-time equivalent (FTE). The key justifications for the law were (1) geographic isolation of reservations, (2) lack of access among tribal members to mainstream higher education, (3) cultural difference between Indian and non-Indian society, (4) better chances of educational success in local and community setting, (5) local control over higher education to tribal members, and (6) lack of local tax or state funding available to the TCUs (Gipp, 11).

Later, Congress agreed to increase the fund to $6,000 per full-time equivalent (FTE). Under the Reagan administration and throughout the 1980s, the actual appropriation would shrink. According to the Carnegie Foundation's research, in 1980, $5 million in federal fund was distributed under the Tribally Controlled Community College Act, offering approximately $3,000 per FTE. In 1989, the appropriation had grown to $8.6 million, but the tribes received only $1,900 per FTE (The Carnegie Foundation, 36–37). Federal funding never matched the rapid growth of TCUs, and the funds available for each FTE plummeted. In 2008, AIHEC successfully secured $8,000/FTE to meet inflation (AIHEC website).

Encouraged by this support from the federal government, more tribes sought to establish their own TCUs in their communities. This, however, led to more demands from tribal colleges for more funds and technical support. The tribes could exercise Indian self-determination in education in place more easily in elementary and secondary schools as these had predated the self-determination policy. The BIA simply transferred its control, facilities, employees, and funding to the tribes. On the other hand, post-secondary institutions were previously nonexistent, so the tribes had to build them from the ground up.

Funding for TCUs

Despite its positive development and progress, tribal colleges remain the least-funded higher education institutions in the nation. As most TCUs are located on reservations, local property taxes are not available to support them, and states have no obligation to fund them. Thus, major funding for TCUs comes primarily from the federal government, including the Tribally Controlled Community College Assistance Act of 1978, which is administered by the BIA, and Title III of the Higher Education Act. In this situation, the College Fund's ability to raise funds from the private sector is essential to the survival of tribal institutions.

To keep higher education inexpensive, TCUs have maintained lower rates of tuition for their students. The average annual cost of attendance at a TCU in 2013–14

Sidebar 1: Five Most Important Laws for the Creation and Support of Tribally Controlled Colleges and Education of Native Americans

1. The Navajo Community College Act of 1971 (P.L. 92–189).
   The act appropriated $5.5 million for construction, maintenance, and operation of Navajo Community College. The funds were made available for the college to provide educational opportunity for Navajos and other applicants that would suit their unique needs and interests. The original bill was sponsored by Representative Wayne Aspinall (D–CO), chairman of the House Committee on Interior and Insular Affairs. These permanent funds were extremely important for the newly founded Navajo Community College, as other funds were one-time grants.

2. The Indian Self-Determination and Education Act of 1975 (P.L. 93–638).
   The act provided "to encourage the development of human resources of the Indian people; to establish a program of assistance to upgrade Indian education; to support the right of Indian citizens to control their own educational activities." It acknowledged that the federal government's control over the programs related to services for Native Americans had limited rather than enhanced the progress of Indian people and their communities. The Indian Education section of the law offered financial support for the public schools enrolling Native American children to meet the special needs of their students.

3. The Tribally Controlled College Assistance Act of 1978 (P.L. 95–471).
   The act established direct federal assistance to Native American higher education institutions operated on or near reservations. The act provided for "the operation and improvement of tribally controlled community colleges to insure continued and expanded educational opportunities for Indian students." It appropriated $25 million for fiscal year 1979 and $30 million for fiscal year 1980. The fund would be available for TCUs on a per-student basis ($4,000 for each full-time equivalent student attending the college).

4. The Native American Languages Act of 1990 (P.L. 101–477).
   The act recognized federal government's policy "to preserve, protect, and promote the rights and freedom of Native Americans to use,

practice, and develop Native American languages." The act supported that higher education institution would offer the same academic credit comparable to a foreign language course and that elementary, secondary, and higher education institutions would include Native American languages in their curriculum. It also encouraged the use of Native American languages by Indian tribes and other Native governing bodies to conduct their business. The passage of this act was significant as it officially reversed the historical policy of suppressing Native American languages.

5. The Equity in Educational Land-Grant Status Act of 1994 (P.L. 103–382).

The legislation provided Land Grant status for qualified tribal colleges and universities to offer equity funding, access to research and extension programs, and other federal grants and loans. Those TCUs were considered to play the same role of that land grant institution that emphasized education and research in agriculture and mechanic arts. It entitled those TCUs to funds and benefits for the improvement of agriculture and sciences programs and facilities. The act was amended in 2014 and today provides funds to thirty-five TCUs. Prioritized areas are same as national critical needs areas including sustainable energy, global food security and hunger, nutrition and preventing childhood obesity, and sustainable rural economies.

was $14,168 (including room, board, books, and tuition) (The College Fund website). It is considerably lower when compared to the cost of a four-year public university, which stood at $18,749 per year (excluding books) in 2013–14 (The College Fund website). Like many community colleges nationwide, TCUs also have been open-admission institutions from which no applicant will be rejected. This policy puts pressures on already tight budgets, even as the growth of the student body (18,881 in 2012) is positive news for TCUs.

Profiles of TCU Students

A lack of stable funding has led to the closure of TCUs, even as financial difficulty has posed serious challenges for Native American students. The 2010 census reported that 28.4 percent of American Indians lived below the poverty level, nearly double the rate of 15.3 percent of all Americans (2010 Census). According to the College Fund's study, only five percent of Indian scholarship applicants can afford to attend college without financial assistance. The average income of first-time entering students at TCUs is $15,262, while the average cost of education at TCUs is $13,800 (The College Fund website). For a number of TCU students, the financial, technical, and academic support from the College Fund is critical for their success.

A majority of students at TCUs are nontraditional, with more than half over age 25. About 35 percent are single parents, 63 percent are female, and 60 percent attend college on a full-time basis (AIHEC, 2012). Many such students are adults, work full-time, and have family and community obligations while attending college. Many of them are in the first generation of college students in their family, have poor academic preparation, and hold negative impressions of formal education (Stein, 2009, 26).

These characteristics of TCU students, many of which are shared by underrepresented groups in higher education, require more financial assistance, academic and non-academic advising, and special educational and training programs.

Faculty at Tribal Colleges

The distribution and characteristics of faculty at TCUs provide another area that needs improvement. According to the American Indian Higher Education Consortium's 2009-2010 survey conducted in 2009 and 2010, 57 percent of faculty were non-Indian while 79 percent of TCU students were American Indian or Alaska Native. This distribution of American Indian/Alaska Native faculty is significantly higher than that of non-TCUs, yet there remained a considerable gap between them and the student body (AIHEC AIMS Fact Book, 2009-2010). Non-Native faculty members tended to have higher levels of college education, compared to their Native American peers. In 2003, approximately 68 percent of non-Indian faculty had a master's or doctoral degree, while 55 percent of their Indian counterparts did so (Voorhees, 4).

This gap was created partially due to the failed educational policy toward Indian people, and the number of available Native American educators has been limited. For the TCU faculty members who seek graduate degrees, the College Fund has offered scholarships for not only the students at tribal colleges, but also faculty members who since 2002 have sought a terminal degree. In 2014, the College Fund provided over 46 fellowships to TCU faculty to complete a master's or terminal degree (The College Fund, 2013–14 Annual Report, 9).

Missions of Tribal Colleges

One of the most important missions of TCUs is to preserve and promote tribal cultures, languages, and histories. Native studies and language programs are at the center of the TCUs curriculum. Yet, the tribal colleges, like their peers in the mainstream society, also need to prepare students for the 21st-century job market. Balancing the two missions, to educate students in two different, and often opposing, knowledge bases—one of western civilization and another of tribal cultures—poses a difficult task (Carney, 110).

As TCUs commit themselves to serve their local communities and provide services that fit the needs of a specific community, they have diverse missions, curricula, educational emphases, philosophies, and services. Outside the classroom, TCUs play a significant role for the betterment of their tribes by offering important social and economic programs (The Carnegie Foundation, 4). Such programs include health care (health centers, education and prevention of diabetes and HIV) and educational institutions and opportunities (libraries, computing centers, language classes, life-long learning programs, and daycare) (The College Fund website).

Between 1976 and 2010, Native American enrollment in undergraduate degree-granting institutions more than doubled (from 76,100 to 179,278). Yet, they struggle to enroll college students, and their retention late in 2010 was as low as 15 percent (The College Fund, "Fostering Success," 2). Compared to the Native American students at mainstream colleges and universities, the TCU students have a better chance of success when remaining in the program. Eighty-six percent of TCU students complete their programs, while fewer than 10 percent of Native American students who go to mainstream colleges and universities directly from reservation high schools earn a bachelor's degree (The College Fund website). By providing higher educational opportunity within the students' familiar tribal community, TCUs offer an alternative higher education opportunity for Native Americans and a better chance of success for Native Americans who struggle in a mainstream college environment.

Biographies of Notable Figures

Ned Hatathli (1923–1972)

Ned Hatathli (1923–1972) was a Navajo educator and modern leader who became the first member of his tribe to earn a PhD. He served as the first Navajo president of Navajo Community College (now Diné College) from 1969 to 1972.

On October 11, 1923, Hatathli was born at Coalmine Mesa, near Tuba City, Arizona, on the Navajo Reservation as one of ten children. He grew up in a traditional Navajo home until adolescence, when a relative encouraged him to go to school. He attended a BIA boarding school in Tuba City, Arizona, graduating in the late 1930s as a valedictorian of Tuba City High School. Hatathli decided to enroll at Haskell Institute in Lawrence, Kansas. He left Haskell before graduation to volunteer for the Navy at the outbreak of World War II, serving until the end of the war in 1945.

After leaving the military, he returned home to attend the Arizona State Teachers College (now Northern Arizona University) in Flagstaff. Upon completion of his education degrees in 1950, Hatathli moved back to the Navajo Reservation and assumed leadership of the Navajos' movement toward greater social and economic opportunity, including the tribal college movement.

Hatathli helped to establish the Navajo Arts and Crafts Guild in Window Rock, as he strongly believed that art was an essential aspect of the Navajo way of life. During the 1950s, he established standards for Navajo silversmithing and weaving to improve their quality. He also developed the raised design characteristic of Coalmine Mesa weaving.

His work in Navajo politics started after he left the Navajo Arts and Crafts Guild. In 1955, Hatathli was elected to the Navajo Tribal Council. He later resigned from the Council to become Director of Tribal Resources of the Navajo Nation. He believed that people were as important a resource as oil, uranium, coal, natural gas, or timber that existed on the Navajo Reservation. He also made sure that Navajos could benefit fully from natural resource development on their reservation.

In the mid-1960s, the Navajo Tribal Council decided to improve educational opportunity for tribal members. With two other college-educated leaders, Dillon Platero and Allan Yazzie, Hatathli pushed for the establishment of and the Rough Rock Demonstration School, and later the Navajo Community College. Earlier in life, Hatathli had believed that the primary goal of Indian education should be to advance Indians' entry into the dominant society. As he became more involved in Indian education, Hatathli came to value and learn more about traditional Navajo beliefs and traditions.

In 1966, Hatathli became the president of a group of three Navajo leaders called DINE (Demonstration in Navajo Education). The organization directed the Rough Rock Demonstration School in the first years after its establishment in 1966. The Rough Rock Demonstration School had been the first Indian school in the nation to be solely controlled by Indian people (Carney, 106). The school had the determination and belief that Navajos themselves, even if they had little or no education, could effectively control and manage their own school. The school was jointly funded by the BIA and the Office of Economic Opportunity (OEO). Eventually, DINE was dissolved, and a local all-Navajo school board replaced it. The school project proved highly successful, and tribal representatives from all over the country visited this model school. The Rough Rock Demonstration School became the first "contract school" that was locally run with BIA funding to provide educational services.

When the Navajo Community College (NCC) opened in 1968, Hatathli was appointed as the executive vice-president. He became NCC's first Navajo president when Dr. Robert Roessell, a non-Native educator and the first president of NCC, stepped aside in 1969. Both Roessell and Hatathli envisioned a Navajo studies program as the centerpiece of NCC curriculum.

Hatathli established a Navajo college administrative council staffed by Navajos and other Natives to advise him and to promote Indian self-determination. He also announced that non-Indian employees would be replaced by educated Navajos once they became eligible. This policy, although accepted by the tribal council and the NCC staff, caused dissatisfaction among non-Indian staff who, in 1970, constituted 60 percent of all employees. Hatathli truly believed in Indian self-determination and wanted NCC to reflect that commitment (Stein, 15; Reyhner and Eder, 297). As Hatathli declared, "This is an Indian owned and an Indian operated institution, and we certainly don't want any people other than Indian to dictate to us what is good for us" (quoted in Szasz, 177–78).

In 1971, Hatathli saw Congress pass the Navajo Community College Act (P.L. 92–189) to provide federal support for the college. The law also appropriated $5.5 million for construction of the campus and funding for operations. On October 12, 1972, a day before an important conference at NCC, Hatathli accidentally shot himself to death in the chest while cleaning his gun at Many Farms, Arizona. He was survived by his wife, Florence, and their four children. In honor of his contribution to the NCC, the college (renamed Diné College in 1997) named its cultural center in Tsaile the Ned Hatathli Cultural Center and Ned Hatathli Museum.

DOCUMENT EXCERPTS

During the Congressional hearing on higher education for Native American students held in June 2014, Cheryl Crazy Bull (Sicangu Lakota), president and CEO of the College Fund and former president of AIHEC and Northwest Indian College in Washington State, made a statement regarding the current condition of TCUs and their students as well as the College Fund's future plans for the betterment of educational opportunities for Native Americans.

The mission of the fund is to support programs and operations of this nation's tribal colleges and universities and to provide scholarships for access and success for tribal college students and for a limited number of Native students attending mainstream institutions. Our support is made possible through the generous contributions of individuals, foundations and corporations, because we bring private sector resources to tribal colleges and universities and their students.

You are already aware of the significant gap in participation in higher education by Native People. A contributing factor is the funding for financial aid for these students. The average income of first-time entering students at TCUs is $15,262.

The average cost of a TCU education is $13,800. Only one in 20 of the fund scholarship applicants can afford to go to college without financial aid.

Nationally, 36 percent of students receive Pell, but at tribal colleges, the average is 80 percent and in some cases as high as 90 percent. The gap between the average cost of $13,800 and a maximum Pell award of $5,645 is $8,155 of unmet need.

I also want to note that the Pell grant participation is not a substitute for adequate Federal operational funding of the TCUs. I also want to note that only two TCUs participate in Federal loan programs. As TCUs have grown 23 percent in the last five years, this gap will continue to be a significant issue.

Our institutions are rural and technologically isolated. Transportation remains a huge concern. Fifty-nine percent of TCU students are first generation students, and our students continue to combat significant social and educational issues, such as generational poverty and unemployment.

The college fund has a major role in supporting access and success. In 2013, we provided over 6,000 scholarships averaging $1,403 through 226 different scholarship programs. In the last 25 years, we have given approximately $78 million out in nearly 100,000 scholarships.

We were recently selected, along with the American Indian Graduate Center, to administer the Cobell Education Scholarship Fund. The first meeting with the Cobell board of trustees will be next week, and we expect to begin distributing scholarships this fall.

Our road map for tribal higher education through the college fund is to support strategies that help us achieve what other national organizations and the President have supported, which is a 60 percent post-secondary credentialing or degree completion among the population served by our tribal colleges. At the American Indian College Fund, we support early childhood education in K–12 programs associated with the tribal colleges, create opportunities for access in meaningful post-secondary education experiences that support persistence and completion of our students, which leads to gainful employment.

We need our tribal colleges to remain open, to be financially viable and to grow as institutions. So we need your continued support for full funding of tribal colleges and their students, for the support of adult and remedial education, to support child care and expanded student support services, all within your domain as the Senate Committee, in order for us to have our shared dream of prosperity come true.

Road Map for the Future

As we see the numbers of Native students enrolling at tribal colleges increasing, there is a growing need for scholarships and funding for programs at the tribal colleges that impact student success—while the unmet need continues for current tribal college students.

The American Indian College Fund's plan for the future is simple: we want to educate 60 percent of American Indian and Alaska Native People served by our tribal colleges and universities by 2025. With an educated American Indian and Alaska Native citizenry dedicated to working for change in their communities, we can transform Indian Country from a landscape of desperation to places of aspiration, inspiration, and imagination. This transformation contributes to a better America, one where equity and social justice thrive, and where diversity and identity are valued.

The American Indian College Fund will implement a four-step plan to provide students with financial access to a post-secondary education and to support tribal college programs and initiatives focused on student support so tribal college students succeed to positively impact their families and their communities. In the past 25 years the American Indian College Fund has distributed approximately $76,000,000 to support TCU capacity-building and student success efforts at the tribal colleges. Funding is also needed in this arena to ensure student success.

Step one of the plan includes funding the following programs to prepare students for future success. Students in grades kindergarten-fifth grade: early childhood education; Science, Technology, Education, and Mathematics (STEM) programs and initiatives; literacy; and Native language and cultural immersion. Students in sixth-twelfth grade: STEM programs and initiatives; leadership and mentoring; cultural education programs; learning labs; tutoring, study skills, and career planning; and bridge programs including early college programs.

Step two of the plan includes providing access to post-secondary education, including career and skills advising; GED preparation; college readiness and academic preparedness; financial support to make postsecondary education affordable; and building partnerships with high schools and community resources.

Step three is to provide meaningful higher learning opportunities, including academic, career, and technical education programs for a variety of career paths and skill levels; integrating technology as a resource for student learning and institutional advancement of student success; cultural integration and place-based educational strategies, including Native language; apprenticeships and internships; initiatives to support student adaptation to higher education for success; mentoring programs; leadership programs; fellowships and faculty development; development of candidates for future professional education; accreditation support; and partnerships and collaboration with private entities for supportive, cutting-edge learning opportunities.

Step four is to provide support for meaningful employment for tribal college graduates. Programs include counseling and support for new or first-time employment; career advancement planning; career centers; job search workshops and support; leadership programs; mentoring; and follow-up with tribal college alumni to assess program impact.

As we move forward into our next 25 years, the College Fund will strategically bring private sector dollars to the tribal colleges and their students to support all areas of institutional development and community outreach. The trust responsibility of the federal government to provide equitable and high quality educational access and success for AIAN is essential. We support the goals of AIHEC and the tribal colleges to develop greater federal funding to support tribal college student success in the following areas, particularly if sequestration is re-instituted: (1) federal funding for TCU operations so they can remain open and keep tuition low to provide student access to a higher education; (2) funding for GED/ABE programs so students can complete high school and continue their educations (on average, less than 50 percent of Native students graduate from high school each year in the seven states with the highest percentage of American Indian and Alaska Native students, according to The Civil Rights Project); (3) funding for day care centers at the TCUs (which are currently subsidized by about $250,000/year); and (4) funding for TCU student support services that directly impact student success, retention, and graduation rates.

Source: Excerpts from statement by Cheryl Crazy Bull, President/CEO, American Indian College Fund, for Indian Education Series: Examining Higher Education for American Indian Students, before the Committee on Indian Affairs, United States Senate, 113rd Congress, 2nd Session, June 11, 2014.

Further Reading

American Indian College Fund website. April 27, 2015. http://www.collegefund.org

American Indian Higher Education Consortium website. April 27, 2015 http://www.aihec.org

Carney, Cary Michael. *Native American Higher Education in the United States*. New Brunswick, NJ: Transaction Publishers, 1999.

Gipp. David M. "The Story of AIHEC," in Warner, Linda Sue, Gerald E. Gipp, eds. *Tradition and Culture in Millennium: Tribal Colleges and Culture in the Millennium*. Charlotte, NC: IAP-Information Age Publishing, 2009, 7–15.

Reyhner, Jon, and Jeanne Eder, *American Indian Education: A History*. Norman: University of Oklahoma Press, 2004.

Stein, Wayne J. *Tribally Controlled Colleges: Making Good Medicine*. New York: Peter Lang Publishing, 1992.

Szasz, Margaret. *Education and the American Indian: The Road to Self-Determination since 1928.* 2nd ed. Albuquerque: University of New Mexico Press, 1977.

The Carnegie Foundation for the Advancement of Teaching, *Tribal Colleges: Shaping the Future of Native America.* Lawrenceville, NJ: Princeton University Press, 1989.

The College Fund website. April 27, 2015. http://trends.collegeboard.org/college-pricing /figures-tables/tuition-fees-room-board-time-2004-05-2014-15

Tierney, William G. *Official Encouragement, Institutional Discouragement: Minorities in Academe—The Native American Experience.* Norwood, NJ: Ablex Publishing Corporation, 1992.

Tribal College: Journal of American Indian Higher Education.

U.S. Senate. *Hearing before the Committee on Indian Affairs, Indian Education Series: Examining Higher Education for American Indian Students.* 113th Cong. 2nd Sess. June 11, 2014.

White House Conference on Education Task Force. *The Final Report of the White House Conference on Indian Education: Executive Summary,* May 22, 1992.

White House Initiative on American Indian and Alaska Native Education, Department of Education. April 27, 2015. http://www.ed.gov/edblogs/whiaiane/tribes-tcus/tribal -colleges-and-universities

Voorhees, Richard A. "Characteristics of Tribal College and University Faculty," Voorhees Group, LLC: Littleton, CO, August, 2003. April 27, 2015. http://www.collegefund.org /userfiles/file/TCUFacultyPaper11.pdf

Native American Graves Protection and Repatriation Act, 1990

Joe Watkins

Chronology

1620	Pilgrims land from England at Plymouth Rock; eight days later, they rob an Indian grave.
1832	Samuel George Morton requests human skulls to build his collection to document the influence "race" might have on intelligence and social standing.
1846	The Smithsonian Institution is established.
1868	The last treaty with an Indian tribe (the Nez Perce) is ratified.
1887	General Allotment Act passes Congress. Communal tribal lands fractionated to individual ownership with "left over" lands open to general settlement.

1890	The Wounded Knee Massacre results in the death of Sioux Chief Big Foot and nearly 300 other Sioux men, women, and children, marking the last "battle" of the frontier.
1924	American Indians are provided citizenship.
1934	Indian Reorganization Act is passed.
1953	Passage of House Current Resolution 108 allows termination of federal trust relationship to tribes that accept it.
1964	Passage of Civil Rights Act of 1964 allows equal treatment under the law. Tribal human remains are not provided treatment equal to non-Indian burials and cemeteries.
1971	Iowa cemetery is disturbed by highway construction: remains of 26 European-American reburied; remains of Indian woman from same cemetery are sent to state museum.
1976	Iowa Burials Protection Act is passed.
1978	American Indian Religious Freedom Act is passed; federal agencies are required to report to Congress about policies that impact practice of American Indian religion.
1979	Archeological Resources Protection Act defines human skeletal remains as "archeological resources."
1985–1989	Scientific organizations study American Indian concerns about the continuing excavation, study, display, and retention of American Indian human remains and sacred objects.
1989	National Museum of the American Indian Act (P.L. 101–185) creates the National Museum of the American Indian and initiates repatriation of human remains and other cultural items to tribes.
1990	Native American Graves Protection and Repatriation Act (NAGPRA) (P.L. 101–601) requires museums and federal agencies to repatriate human remains and other cultural items to tribes.
1996	Human skeletal remains of Kennewick Man/The Ancient One (9,000 years) discovered washing out of the Columbia River in Kennewick, Washington. Court case is filed by six scientists to halt repatriation.
2004	District Court Magistrate John Jelderks determines Kennewick Man not "Native American" under NAGPRA, since there was no possibility of establishing "cultural affiliation" between a 9,000-year old skeleton and a currently existing Indian tribe.

1996–present Skeletal remains of Kennewick Man/The Ancient One are stored in climate-controlled storage cases in the University of Washington's Burke Museum in Seattle, Washington.

2014 Anzick Boy (12,600 years old) reburied in Montana after study and publication of DNA material.

2015 DNA of Kennewick Man published indicates a genetic relationship with members of the Colville tribe of the American Northwest.

Introduction

Thanksgiving is often celebrated in elementary school as a time of celebration, with stories about how the Pilgrims, starving that very first winter in America, were saved by the Indians. Squanto, the Indian who taught the Pilgrims how to plant corn kernels and to use fish as fertilizer to make the corn grow better, is held out as a hero to be memorialized. If you remember those stories, you will realize how great a role American Indians played in helping the Pilgrims to survive and flourish.

But other stories are rarely told. Some of the Pilgrim explorers, soon after arriving in their new land, dug up a grave of a man and a small child, and took along some cultural artifacts before covering up the bones again. Thus, only eight days after the Pilgrims had first anchored off Plymouth, Massachusetts, American Indian graves had been plundered for their contents.

Of course, grave robbers and looters are not the only people who are interested in the things left behind by people in North America. Scientists, among them anthropologists and archaeologists, often collect bits and pieces left behind by inhabitants as part of their research. These materials can provide information that helps us better understand the cultures that lived in North America; museums also view the preservation of objects from the past as a part of their duty because those items can be used to help teach people about all the different cultures that once existed or that currently exist in the world.

But, in spite of the utility these remains might have to science, many American Indian tribes, families, and individuals want museums to give human skeletal remains and special cultural objects back to the people to whom they once belonged so that tribes can ceremoniously rebury the human remains or reintroduce the sacred objects as part of their traditional religious practices. Their belief is that these sorts of materials are very important to tribes and to the families of the individuals who have been disturbed and placed on display like non-human animals.

The 1950s and 1960s were a time of social and political unrest, especially in the area of civil rights. During the 1960s, the "Pan-Indian" movement began. By identifying the problems of *any* American Indian group as a matter of concern for *all* living American Indian groups, it reflected a new political consciousness, and groups of non-related Indians began to work together for the benefit of all Indians.

Proponents of Native unity were seen as a threat by many anthropologists who sometimes felt the American Indians were attempting to restrict the anthropologists' freedom to carry out research. The idea that anthropologists have a moral right to access cultural material because their research is aimed at producing knowledge for the public benefit is in apparent conflict with the beliefs held by most American Indian groups. Anthropologists who once enjoyed good relationships with particular tribal groups were dismayed to find that new political groups such as the American Indian Movement (AIM) were trying to initiate changes in the way research was done. These organizations, made up of individuals from many different tribes rather than representatives of just a single tribe, used protests and other militant actions to make their points. Anthropologists were often taken aback by these tactics.

Repatriation, in its basic sense, is the act of returning something to its Native country. After wars, prisoners are "repatriated" to their home countries, usually with great fanfare. American Indian actions in the 1970s and 1980s were aimed at drawing attention to the fact that, in the Indians' belief, many important cultural items were—and still are—being held prisoner in foreign museums and that they need to be returned to their proper homes.

In 1978, Congress passed the American Indian Religious Freedom Act, a piece of legislation that required federal agencies to examine the ways their policies might impact the religious freedom of American Indians. One of the issues identified by American Indian groups was the status of human remains encountered in archaeological excavations and maintained in museum and institutional collections across the United States.

American Indian groups continued to push for the return of skeletal remains and to draw attention to the perceived inconsistency in the scientific study of American Indian human remains and the reburial of non-Indian remains encountered in projects.

Anthropologists might view human skeletal material as important to science, but American Indian concerns about human remains extend beyond the physical bones themselves. The bones represent living people, not just pieces of calcium. The Navajos, for example, have a ceremony whose sole purpose is to relieve what is called "ghost-sickness"—an illness caused by contact with spirits, ghosts, or places where ghosts are thought to reside. The importance of protecting the human remains of a culture from outsiders seems obvious, especially if tribal groups go to such extremes to protect themselves from the spirits associated with the remains.

Sidebar 1: Six Laws That Led to the Native American Graves Protection and Repatriation Act

1. The *Antiquities Act* (1906) was the first legislative attempt to protect historic and prehistoric remains on public lands. It established the principle that cultural resources, regardless of origin, were important to the cultural history of the United States and worthy of protection.

2. The *National Historic Preservation Act* (1966) established the process by which America's heritage is identified and protected. It recognized that American "progress" was destroying the fabric of America's important buildings and sites worthy of preservation, and created agencies and programs that ameliorate or mitigate the impact of federal projects on historic sites of historical, cultural, and traditional importance to all United States citizens.

3. The *National Environmental Policy Act* (1967) created policy requiring federal agencies to examine the impact of projects on United States natural and cultural environments. The law also requires the consideration of environmental justice issues on populations that bear a disproportionate impact of federal projects.

4. The *American Indian Religious Freedom Act* (1978) required the federal agencies to examine the impact their policies had on American Indians' free exercise of religion. Ten hearings on this law were held throughout the United States to accept American Indian testimony. These hearings called attention to the inconsistent application of federal policy and identified the most pressing issues of concern to tribes.

5. The *Archeological Resources Protection Act* (1979) replaced the Antiquities Act as the primary legislative remedy for illegal excavation of "objects of antiquity." It gives Indian tribes more control over archaeological excavations on their property, but its definition of human skeletal remains as an archaeological resource continues the scientific perspective on human remains and continues to be at odds with American Indian perspectives.

6. The *National Museum of the American Indian Act* (1989) created the National Museum of the American Indian, but it was also the First National legislation that required the repatriation of American Indian skeletal remains and associated funerary objects.

American Indian groups have been concerned about human remains in museum and archaeological collections for a long time. During hearings held on the American Indian Religious Freedom Act of 1978 across the United States, elected and traditional leaders of numerous tribes spoke out against the disturbance of Indian graves and cemeteries. They also spoke of their desires to have Indian skeletons reburied as close as possible to the places where they had been dug up.

Other organizations worked to have human remains removed from museums. In Kansas, for example, the Pawnee tribe worked to get a tourist attraction that exhibited Indian skeletons closed, and the skeletons reburied; in Nebraska, they worked with other legislators to get a law passed that required the reburial of Indian skeletons. Such actions by tribal groups and groups of members of different tribes to get American Indian skeletal material reburied made it easier for nationwide legislation to be proposed and passed.

The Native American Graves Protection and Repatriation Act

The Native American Graves Protection and Repatriation Act (NAGPRA) affirms the rights of lineal descendants, Indian tribes, and Native Hawaiian organizations to custody of Native American human remains, funerary objects, sacred items, and objects of cultural patrimony held in federal museums or agencies, or in museums that receive federal funds. Signed into law by President George H. W. Bush in November 1990, NAGPRA places the responsibility for compliance upon federal agencies and museums that receive federal funds. It requires all federal departments, agencies, or instrumentalities of the United States (except for the Smithsonian Institution) to complete summaries and inventories of Native American materials in their control (including those held by nongovernmental repositories). The affected organizations were also ordered to ensure compliance regarding inadvertent discoveries and intentional excavations of human remains conducted as part of activities on federal or tribal lands.

NAGPRA was not the first repatriation law passed. In 1989, Congress passed the National Museum of the American Indian Act (NMAIA) to establish a new National Museum of the American Indian. At the same time, it also required the Smithsonian Institution to inventory, document, and, if requested, repatriate culturally affiliated human remains and funerary objects to federally recognized Native groups. But NAGPRA is much more far-reaching.

NAGPRA lays out a mechanism for federal land managers, museums, and agency officials to consult with lineal descendants and tribal groups and to reach a determination regarding the proper disposition of human remains, associated funerary objects, objects of cultural patrimony, and sacred objects that might be excavated or discovered on federal or tribal lands. The processes for dealing with excavations or discoveries on federal or tribal lands are different from those for dealing with the disposition of objects within museum or federal agency collections, but the ultimate goal of NAGPRA is to return to the individual or tribe the materials under consideration.

The law required museums and federal agencies to go through all of their collections and identify items which might be subject to repatriation, giving them a three-year deadline to provide summaries of items that the museum thought might be unassociated funerary objects (known grave goods which are not associated with a particular set of human remains or where the museum does not own the human remains), sacred objects, or objects of cultural patrimony. Museums and agencies were given six years to consult with tribes to create an inventory of human remains and associated funerary objects within the possession or control of the institution.

Under NAGPRA, there are various categories of people who have the right to make a claim for the items covered under either law. The people who can make a claim vary, depending upon the item under consideration. For human remains, lineal descendants (those who can demonstrate direct ancestry to a named individual) have the first right to reclaim skeletal material. If there are no lineal descendants, or if the personal identity of the individual skeleton is unknown, then the tribe of the individual can request a return. If the tribe is not known, then the tribe on whose land the set of human remains was found may request the return of the material. Finally, if the remains were not found on tribal land, then the tribe on whose aboriginal territory the remains were found may request a return. In all of the above circumstances, any items that were thought to be placed with the remains at time of burial are subject to the same repatriation priority as the human remains.

In the case of unassociated funerary objects, the priority of claimants is similar—going to the tribe who is likely to have produced the items, the tribal group on whose land the materials were found, and then the tribal group on whose aboriginal territory the materials were found.

Finally, in the case of sacred items and objects of cultural patrimony, only the tribe that claims the artifacts may make a request. Since by their very nature, such artifacts may not be owned by individuals, only entire tribes are allowed to make requests for returns.

Native American groups hailed the passage of the NAGPRA as an opportunity to right centuries-old wrongs perpetrated against American Indian graves. NAGPRA gave American Indians some of the tools necessary to implement the changes they had demanded in the 1970s, even if the law has some inadequacies, such as the continued scientific study of human remains; the inconsistent application of repatriation statutes to extremely old material; repatriating the human remains of non-federally recognized tribes; materials found on private land; and the return of materials that are important to particular members within a tribe but are not classified as "tribal sacred items" or "items of cultural patrimony."

NAGPRA does not authorize the initiation of new scientific studies, but it does not preclude such research when a museum deems it necessary for determining the cultural affiliation of a set of human remains. Additionally, the law allows for the continuation of studies when the human remains under examination are indispensable for the completion of a specific scientific study, the outcome of which would be of major benefit to the United States. Many tribes are concerned about this, believing the law provides an apparent authorization for study prior to repatriation. Scientists and museums argue that it is often necessary for human remains to be studied so that cultural affiliation may be determined or so that repatriation to the most appropriate descendants or tribe can be carried out. Tribes want to curtail scientific studies of any kind on ancestral skeletal remains where existing documentation establishes geographic location and cultural affiliation by clear, reasonable belief, or by a preponderance of evidence.

Tribes are also concerned about scientific study on human remains that are so old that no tribe can demonstrate a clear cultural affiliation to it. In 1996, a set of human remains was found washing out of the bank of the Columbia River near Kennewick, Washington. Tribal groups were set to accept the remains for reburial when scientists sued for the right to conduct scientific research on the material, arguing that NAGPRA was not meant to apply to remains as old as those of Kennewick. They argued that such remains, by the very nature of their age, cannot be assigned to any single tribe, or, more specifically, that no single tribe can demonstrate cultural affiliation with a set of human remains so old. In 2004, the court decided that the remains did not meet the definition of "Native American" under the law, and were thus outside of the realm of NAGPRA. The discoveries of more and more ancient human remains have not alleviated this issue, and still contribute to a mistaken idea of American Indian origins in this hemisphere.

American Indian views on allowing repatriation of human remains and appropriate cultural items to non-federally recognized tribes are divided, but for differing reasons. Many Indians feel that non-federally recognized tribes are no less "Indian" than their federally recognized counterparts. Others are afraid that allowing unrecognized tribes equal standing under NAGPRA would allow such groups to bypass the tedious process of federal recognition.

Though all tribes agree that the human remains of unrecognized American Indian groups always were, and always will be, American Indian, many are concerned about extending rights to non-recognized groups under NAGPRA. While no specific remedies are defined for every case, tribes have offered suggestions for disposition in cases where the human remains are associated with a non-federally recognized tribe. The NAGPRA Review Committee (a group of seven

Gravemarkers of American Indian warriors at Little Bighorn Battlefield National Monument, 2016. The markers were added to the memorial in 1999. While American Indian burial grounds and graves have historically been treated as archeological finds, the Native American Graves Protection and Repatriation Act of 1990 has helped increase awareness regarding protecting and respecting gravesites. (A. Nadeau)

people established to monitor and review the implementation of the inventory and identification process and repatriation activities) has suggested regional consultations that might prove beneficial in situations where the human remains represent a population for which there are no present-day cultural survivors or where the present-day cultural survivors are members of non-federally recognized Indian tribes.

Another failure of the NAGPRA is its ability to protect human remains on private land. Many American Indian groups can only vaguely understand why the graves protection portion of NAGPRA was not applied to all lands within the United States rather than just federal or tribal lands. At least 34 states have burial-protection laws, and these laws typically prohibit the intentional disturbance of unmarked graves. Many of the laws also provide guidelines to protect the graves and mandate disposition of human remains in a way that guarantees reburial.

If such state laws designed to protect human remains have been upheld as constitutionally valid, it raises a question as to why NAGPRA was not applied to all lands. The National Congress of American Indians has called for changes in NAGPRA to extend protection of funerary remains and objects on *all* lands, wherever they might be located, within the exterior boundaries of the United States.

There are also certain objects within museum collections that were once the property of particular Indian individuals but that do not easily fall within the definition of "sacred" items or "objects of cultural patrimony." Some tribal individuals owned property that was important to their tribe even though they were privately owned and could be sold or given away. For example, a Kiowa war chief named Satanta had a war shield that did not have a specific role in Kiowa ceremonies, but nonetheless was given a place of honor in the last Sundance of the tribe. The shield ultimately made its way to a prominent museum in northern California, where the family eventually located it. The museum had a valid right to ownership, as indicated by the original accessions records.

The shield is not sacred, nor is it an object of cultural patrimony under NAGPRA. However, it is both sacred and an object of cultural patrimony to the Kiowa tribe and the family. It is believed to possess powers that were given it by its maker, and it was a part of the tribal cultural inventory relating to the Indian Wars of the 1860s and 1870s, as well as an important object related to one of the last war chiefs of the Kiowa. NAGPRA is not set up to handle this level of interpretation.

Repatriation for Good or Bad

Contrary to the fears of members of the scientific and museum communities, repatriation has not led to the destruction or anthropology or the wholesale gutting of museums. It has perhaps led to a series of inconveniences between the disciplines and American Indians, but it has also led to the formation of some strong partnerships that have proven beneficial to all.

Museums have been placed in a situation where financial concerns have risen by virtue of the need to inventory all of their collections to determine whether they possessed items that were covered under the NAGPRA. At the same time, these inventories have also proven to be a blessing in that they have forced museums to identify any deficiencies in their records or any gaps in their collections.

American Indians have benefited from the repatriation laws in various ways. Some tribes have been able to regain the remains of their ancestors for reburial (or, in some instances, initial burial). This has lessened the social hardships experienced by some tribes. Other tribes, such as the Zuni and the Onondaga, have been able to regain ownership and control over items of cultural importance to their people. Additionally, museums and American Indians have developed a sort of uneasy truce concerning collections and ethnographic information provided in museum displays.

There are some areas in which American Indians feel that NAGPRA is deficient. Many of those issues have already been discussed, but other issues will likely arise in the future. Those involved in repatriation hope that, through careful consideration of the history of repatriation and the ongoing struggle to find a middle ground where all interested parties can meet, repatriation will prove to be of some benefit to everyone it affects.

Biographies of Notable Figures

Maria Darlene Pearson

Maria Darlene Pearson was born on July 12, 1932, in Springfield, South Dakota, as Darlene Elvira Drappeaux. A member of the Yankton Dakota tribe, she was given the name "Hai-Mecha Eunka," which means "Running Moccasins." She married John Pearson in 1969 and spent most of her adult life in Iowa, where her actions successfully challenged the legal treatment of Native American human remains in that state. Her actions there served as one of the primary catalysts for the creation of the Native American Graves Protection and Repatriation Act (NAGPRA), leading to her being called "the Founding Mother of the modern Indian repatriation movement" and "the Rosa Parks of NAGPRA."

Pearson's involvement with repatriation issues began in 1971, when she learned from her husband, a district engineer for the Iowa highway commission, that the skeletal remains of Native Americans were treated differently from white remains. Her husband told her that both Native American and white remains were uncovered during road construction near Glenwood, Iowa. While the remains of 26 white burials were quickly reburied, the remains of a Native American mother and child were sent to a lab for study instead. After Iowa state archaeologist Marshall McKusick responded that he was required by Iowa law to study the bones until their historic significance could be determined, Pearson protested to Gov. Robert D. Ray. When Ray asked what he could do for her, Pearson is quoted as saying, "You can give me back my people's bones, and you can quit digging them up." Ray agreed that the differential treatment of the human remains was discriminatory, and the ensuing controversy led to the passage of the Iowa Burials Protection Act of 1976. The Iowa law was the first legislative act in the United States that specifically protected Native American remains and provided equal treatment of human remains under the law. Her actions are also considered to be one of the catalysts for the creation of NAGPRA.

Emboldened by her success, Pearson went on to lobby national leaders and national organizations such as the Society for American Archaeology and the American Anthropological Association. She was involved in the actions that led the World Archaeological Congress to create and pass the Vermillion Accord on Human Remains in 1989, and continued to be involved in indigenous issues. She was deeply involved with the World Archaeological Congress's actions in Barquisimeto, Venezuela, that led to the WAC Executive's adoption of the First Code of Ethics, which specifically dealt with archaeologists' responsibilities to indigenous peoples, in 1990.

Twice nominated for the Nobel Peace Prize, Maria Pearson—Running Moccasins—died in Ames, Iowa, on May 23, 2003.

Daniel K. Inouye (1924–2012)

Daniel Ken Inouye, the United States Senator from Hawaii, was deeply involved in the hearings that led to the development and passage of the Native American Graves Protection and Repatriation Act. As the chairman of the Senate Select Committee on Indian Affairs, Inouye stressed the inequitable treatment of American Indian remains during hearings on the proposed bill (Smith 2004: 140).

Inouye was born in Honolulu, Hawaii, on September 7, 1924. At the time of his birth, Hawaii was a territorial possession of the United States but not yet a state. He was 17 when Japan attacked the U.S. naval base at nearby Pearl Harbor, and as a medical aide, Inouye was among the first to treat the wounded. As a pre-med student and an Aid Station worker, he was exempt from military service, but he quit his job and dropped out of school to join the all-Nisei 442nd Regimental Combat Team. Inouye distinguished himself in basic training, and within his first year he was promoted to sergeant and platoon leader. On April 21, 1945, weeks before the fall of Berlin ended the war in Europe, Inouye led an assault on a heavily defended ridge known as Colle Musatello, near the town of Terenzo. Inouye suffered a wound to his midsection and leg, as well as a grenade wound that cost him his right arm. Inouye was awarded the Distinguished Service Cross for his heroism; he remained in the Army until 1947, when he was discharged with the rank of captain.

On his return to the States, Inouye committed himself to the cause of equal rights for all Americans, and for all residents of Hawaii as fully enfranchised American citizens. He returned to the University of Hawaii and pursued studies in government and economics. After graduating in 1950, he entered George Washington University Law School in Washington, D.C., receiving his law degree in 1952. Returning to Hawaii, Inouye was elected to the territorial legislature in 1954, where he served as leader of a new Democratic majority. In 1958, he was elected to the territory's Senate.

With Hawaii's approval for admission to the union as the 50th state, Inouye was elected to serve as Hawaii's first U.S. Representative; he took his seat in Congress on August 21, 1959, the day Hawaii became a state. He was re-elected to a full term in the House the following year. In 1962, Daniel Inouye was elected to a vacant seat in the U.S. Senate, where he was soon appointed to the Senate Armed Services Committee. In 1984, Senator Inouye assumed the chairmanship the Senate Committee on Indian Affairs, seeking justice for the descendants of America's first inhabitants. It was in this role that he sponsored and pushed through the passage of the Native American Graves Protection and Repatriation Act of 1990.

In 2000, after extensive review, the Distinguished Service Crosses awarded to Senator Inouye and 21 other Asian-American heroes of World War II were upgraded to full Medal of Honor status. For some, the honor came too late. Fifteen medals were awarded posthumously, but Senator Inouye and the other survivors were on hand to receive their Medals of Honor from President Clinton at the White House.

In 2009, Senator Inouye was appointed to chair the Senate Committee on Appropriations, widely considered the most powerful of senate committee assignments. The following year, Inouye became the Senate's senior member, and in keeping with Senate tradition was named president pro tempore of the Senate. This placed Senator Inouye third in line of succession to the presidency, following the Vice President and the Speaker of the House.

At age 88, the Senator was admitted to Walter Reed Army Medical Center for treatment of respiratory complications. His wife and son were by his side at the moment of his death on December 17, 2012. His office reported that his last word was "Aloha." After his death, Daniel Inouye, who had already received the nation's premier military decoration, was awarded its highest civilian honor, the Presidential Medal of Freedom.

Suzan Shown Harjo

Suzan Shown Harjo was born on June 2, 1945, in El Reno, Oklahoma. Her mother was Cheyenne, and her father Muscogee, and the family lived on her father's allotment near Beggs, Oklahoma, until the U.S. Army stationed her father in Naples, Italy, between her ages of 12 and 16 years. After her return to the States, she moved to New York City, where she met and married Frank Harjo.

The roots of Suzan Shown Harjo's activism date from the mid-1960s, when she co-produced *Seeing Red*, the first Indian news show in the United States at New York's WBAI FM station. She and her husband also worked on issues of protecting religious freedom for American Indians. After seeing sacred garments on display in the Museum of the American Indian in New York in 1967, she worked for repatriation to tribes of such items and for changes in museum policies.

Suzan and her husband moved to Washington, D.C., in 1974, when she started working as a legislative liaison for two law firms representing Indian rights. In 1978, President Jimmy Carter appointed Harjo as a congressional liaison for Indian affairs. Harjo worked with multiple subcommittees within Congress to advocate Native American positions in the formation of federal policy, supporting such issues as hunting and fishing rights on traditional lands, voting, and land contracts rights. Her continued lobbying related to religious freedom helped led to passage of the American Indian Religious Freedom Act (AIRFA) in 1978.

Harjo served as the Executive Director of the National Congress of American Indians (NCIA) from 1984 to 1989. The NCAI, a non-profit organization representing all Native American Indians as well as Alaska Natives, was founded in 1944. Harjo persisted in working with Congress to support Native American rights to traditional hunting and fishing. She supported gaining more funds for Native American education. The NCAI's goal was to ensure that Native American children were educated, and with her leadership they gained increased appropriations for that purpose in 1984, 1986, and 1988. Harjo pressed the congressional committee to gain access to government documents related to programs for Native Americans, and asked for continued support of Native American attempts at economic development. In the 1980s, she was concerned about declining federal support for health clinics on reservations and the adverse result of subsequent higher mortality rates among Native Americans.

During this period, Harjo continued to work on issues of repatriation of sacred items from museums to tribes, and changes in the ways researchers dealt with American Indian human remains and artifacts. Her work, together with hundreds of others, resulted in additional reforms and national legislation in 1989 and 1990.

Harjo contributed to development and passage of federal legislation protecting Native sovereignty, arts and cultures, language, and human rights. These include the 1978 American Indian Religious Freedom Act, which allowed the protection of Native Americans for practice of traditional religion and rituals; the 1989 National Museum of the American Indian Act, which authorized establishment of the museum at two sites; the 1990 Native American Graves Protection and Repatriation Act (NAGPRA), which allows tribes to reclaim their human remains and ceremonial items from publicly funded institutions; and the 1996 Executive Order on Indian Sacred Sites.

As president of the Morning Star Institute, which she founded in 1984 in memory of her late husband, Suzan Harjo promotes sacred land claims and protection for traditional cultural rights, artistic expression, and research. The MSI sponsors Just Good Sports, devoted to ending use of American Indian mascots and stereotypes by sports teams, a cause of Harjo's since the 1960s. Activism by Harjo and others has resulted in dramatic changes in the sports world since the late 20th century.

Harjo continues to be active in Indian activism but also contributes to the quality of American Indian life through her writing and poetry. During her fellowships at the School for Advanced Research in 2004, Harjo wrote poetry inspired by oral history related to her time working for land claims and repatriation laws and policies. She also is a columnist for Indian Country Today Media Network and a contributing writer for *First American Art Magazine*.

Because of the depth of her contributions not only to repatriation but also to bringing attention to contemporary American Indian issues, Suzan Shown Harjo was awarded the Presidential Medal of Freedom, the United States' highest civilian honor, on November 24, 2014.

DOCUMENT EXCERPTS

Accidental Discoveries from Indian Graves in the United States

Part of the National Graves Protection and Repatriation Act provides explicit instructions on how to deal with accidental discoveries of human remains or other sacred objects covered by NAGPRA. Here is an excerpt from the act describing what must be done.

§10.4 Inadvertent discoveries

(a) *General.* This section carries out section 3 (d) of the Act regarding the custody of human remains, funerary objects, sacred objects, or objects of cultural patrimony that are discovered inadvertently on Federal or tribal lands after November 16, 1990.

(b) *Discovery.* Any person who knows or has reason to know that he or she has discovered inadvertently human remains, funerary objects, sacred objects, or objects of cultural patrimony on Federal or tribal lands after November 16, 1990, must provide immediate telephone notification of the inadvertent discovery, with written confirmation, to the responsible Federal agency official with respect to Federal lands, and, with respect to tribal lands, to the responsible Indian tribe official. The requirements of these regulations regarding inadvertent discoveries apply whether or not an inadvertent discovery is duly reported. If written confirmation is provided by certified mail, the return receipt constitutes evidence of the receipt of the written notification by the Federal agency official or Indian tribe official.

(c) *Ceasing activity.* If the inadvertent discovery occurred in connection with an on-going activity on Federal or tribal lands, the person, in addition to providing the notice described above, must stop the activity in the area of the inadvertent discovery and make a reasonable effort to protect the human remains, funerary objects, sacred objects, or objects of cultural patrimony discovered inadvertently.

(d) *Federal lands.* (1) As soon as possible, but no later than three (3) working days after receipt of the written confirmation of notification with respect to Federal lands described in §10.4 (b), the responsible Federal agency official must:

  (i) Certify receipt of the notification;

  (ii) Take immediate steps, if necessary, to further secure and protect inadvertently discovered human remains, funerary objects, sacred objects, or objects of cultural patrimony, including, as appropriate, stabilization or covering;

  (iii) Notify any known lineal descendants of a deceased Native American individual whose human remains and associated funerary objects were discovered of such discovery, and, with respect to a discovery of human remains, associated funerary objects, unassociated funerary objects, sacred objects, or objects of cultural patrimony, notify the Indian tribes or Native Hawaiian organizations likely to be culturally affiliated with the cultural items, the Indian tribe or Native Hawaiian organization that aboriginally occupied the area, and any other Indian tribe or Native Hawaiian organization known to have a cultural relationship to the cultural items. This notification must be by telephone with written confirmation and must include information about the kinds of human remains, associated funerary objects, unassociated funerary objects, sacred objects, or objects of cultural patrimony, their condition, and the circumstances of their discovery;

  (iv) Initiate consultation on the inadvertent discovery pursuant to §10.5;

  (v) If the human remains, funerary objects, sacred objects, or objects of cultural patrimony must be excavated or removed, follow the requirements and procedures in §10.3 (b) of these regulations; and

  (vi) Ensure that disposition of all inadvertently discovered human remains, funerary objects, sacred objects, or objects of cultural patrimony is carried out following §10.6.

  (2) *Resumption of activity.* The activity that resulted in the inadvertent discovery may resume thirty (30) days after certification by the notified Federal agency of receipt of the written confirmation of notification of inadvertent discovery if the resumption of the activity is otherwise lawful. The activity may also resume, if otherwise lawful, at any time that a written, binding agreement is executed between the Federal agency and the affiliated Indian tribes or Native Hawaiian organizations that adopt a recovery plan for the excavation or removal of the human remains, funerary objects, sacred objects, or objects of cultural patrimony following §10.3

(b)(1) of these regulations. The disposition of all human remains, funerary objects, sacred objects, or objects of cultural patrimony must be carried out following §10.6.

(e) *Tribal lands.* (1) As soon as possible, but no later than three (3) working days after receipt of the written confirmation of notification with respect to tribal lands described in §10.4 (b), the responsible Indian tribe official may:

  (i) Certify receipt of the notification;

  (ii) Take immediate steps, if necessary, to further secure and protect inadvertently discovered human remains, funerary objects, sacred objects, or objects of cultural patrimony, including, as appropriate, stabilization or covering;

  (iii) If the human remains, funerary objects, sacred objects, or objects of cultural patrimony must be excavated or removed, follow the requirements and procedures in §10.3 (b) of these regulations; and

  (iv) Ensure that disposition of all inadvertently discovered human remains, funerary objects, sacred objects, or objects of cultural patrimony is carried out following §10.6.

  (2) Resumption of Activity. The activity that resulted in the inadvertent discovery may resume if otherwise lawful after thirty (30) days of the certification of the receipt of notification by the Indian tribe or Native Hawaiian organization.

(f) *Federal agency officials.* Federal agency officials should coordinate their responsibilities under this section with their emergency discovery responsibilities under section 106 of the National Historical Preservation Act (16 U.S.C. 470 (f) *et seq.*), 36 CFR 800.11 or section 3 (a) of the Archeological and Historic Preservation Act (16 U.S.C. 469 (a-c)). Compliance with these regulations does not relieve Federal agency officials of the requirement to comply with section 106 of the National Historical Preservation Act (16 U.S.C. 470 (f) *et seq.*), 36 CFR 800.11 or section 3 (a) of the Archeological and Historic Preservation Act (16 U.S.C. 469 (a-c)).

(g) *Notification requirement in authorizations.* All Federal authorizations to carry out land use activities on Federal lands or tribal lands, including all leases and permits, must include a requirement for the holder of the authorization to notify the appropriate Federal or tribal official immediately upon the discovery of human remains, funerary objects, sacred objects, or objects of cultural patrimony pursuant to §10.4 (b) of these regulations.

Source: 60 FR 62158, Dec. 4, 1995, as amended at 62 FR 41293, Aug. 1, 1997; 78 FR 27082, May 9, 2013.

Further Reading

Bray, Tamara. "Repatriation, Power Relations and the Politics of the Past." *Antiquity* 1996: 70 (268): 440–444.

"Daniel K. Inouye Biography—Academy of Achievement." Academy of Achievement. August 12, 2013. Accessed June 14, 2015. http://www.achievement.org/autodoc/page /ino0bio-1

Gradwohl, D. M., J.B. Thomson, and M.J. Perry (2005). *Still Running: A Tribute to Maria Pearson, Yankton Sioux*. Jointly published by the Iowa Archeological Society and the Office of the State Archaeologist.

Hutt, Sherry and David Tarler. Native American Graves Protection and Repatriation Act (NAGPRA): The Law Is Not an Authorization for Disinterment. U.S. Attorney's *Indian Country Issues*. 2014. Bulletin 62(4):41–51.

Midler, Aaron H. "The Spirit of NAGPRA: The Native American Graves Protection and Repatriation Act and the Regulation of Culturally Unidentifiable Remains." *Chicago-Kent Law Review* 2011: 89(3): 1331–61.

Pearson, Maria D. 2000. "Give Me Back My People's Bones: Repatriation and Reburial of American Indian Skeletal Remains in Iowa." In G. Bataille, D.M. Gradwohl, C.L.P. Silet, *Perspectives on American Indians in Iowa-An Expanded Edition*. Iowa City: University of Iowa Press. pp. 131–141.

Rennie-Tucker, Keely A. "Spirit of the Law: A Case Study in the Application of NAG-PRA to Collections from Hopewell Culture National Historical Park, a Unit of the National Park Service." Doctoral dissertation. 2005. Digital Commons@University of Nebraska-Lincoln.

Rose, Jerome C., Thomas J. Green, and Victoria D. Green. "NAGPRA Is Forever: The Future of Osteology and the Repatriation of Skeletons." *Annual Review of Anthropology* 1996 (25), pp. 81–103.

Seidemann, Ryan M. "NAGPRA at 20: What Have the States Done to Expand Human Remains Protections?" *Museum Anthropology* 2010, 33(2):199–209.

Smith, Laurajane. *Archaeological Theory and the Politics of Cultural Heritage*. Routledge, 2004.

Trope, Jack F. and Walter R. Echo-Hawk. "The Native American Graves Protection and Repatriation Act: Background and Legislative History." *Arizona State Law Journal* 1992,24(1):35–78.

Tsosie, Rebecca. "Privileging Claims to the Past: Ancient Human Remains and Contemporary Cultural Values." *Arizona State Law Journal*, 1999 31(2):583–677.

U.S. Government Accountability Office. "Native American Graves Protection And Repatriation Act: After Almost 20 Years, Key Federal Agencies Still Have Not Fully Complied with the Act." US Government Printing Office, Washington, D.C., 2010.

Watkins, Joe. "Sacred Sites and Repatriation." *Contemporary Native American Issues* series. New York: Chelsea House Publishers, 2006.

Watkins, Joe. *Indigenous Archaeology: American Indian Values and Scientific Practice*. Walnut Creek, CA: AltaMira Press, 2000.

Zimmerman, Larry. "Made radical by my own: An archaeologist learns to accept reburial." *Conflict in the Archaeology of Living Traditions.* Edited by R. Layton, pp. 60–67. London: Unwin Hyman, 1989.

Zimmerman, Larry. "Maria Pearson's Role in World Archaeology." *Journal of the Iowa Archaeological Society* 52(1):61–66, 2005.

Harjo et al. v. Pro Football, 1992

C. Richard King

Chronology

1932   The Boston Braves begin play in the National Football League (NFL).

1933   Owner George Preston Marshall moves the franchise from Braves Field to Fenway Park in Boston. He changes the team name to Redskins. He also hires William "Lone Star" Dietz, alumnus of Carlisle Indian Industrial School and veteran college coach. While many have speculated the team was named in honor Dietz, who was fraudulently passing himself off as an American Indian, Marshall stated clearly this was not the case at the time. Moreover, he fired Dietz after two seasons.

1937   Marshall moves the franchise to Washington, D.C. Over the next decade, he and his wife, Corinne Griffith, build the team brand around a stereotypical Indian motif.

1938   The team debuts a fight song, "Hail to the Redskins," and a marching band.

1962   Under pressure from the federal government, the Washington professional football team becomes the last NFL franchise to integrate.

1969   Dartmouth College, originally founded to educate American Indians, changes from the Indians to Big Green.

1970   University of Oklahoma drops Little Red mascot.

1972   Stanford University changes from Indians to Cardinals and drops Prince Lightfoot mascot.

1972   Native Americans protest the Washington Redskins name, calling for it to be changed. They meet with then-owner Edward Bennett Williams to press their case. The team makes changes to the fight song, but retains name, logo, and other traditions.

1973 Eastern Washington University changes from the Savages to the Eagles.

1991 Large protests against Washington professional football team at Super Bowl XXVI in Minneapolis.

1992 A group of seven American Indians, led by Suzan Shown Harjo, file suit against the franchise, seeking to strip it of its trademarks. This case becomes known as *Harjo et al v. Pro Football, Inc.*

1992 *Washington Post* columnists Clarence Page and Tony Kornheiser write pieces in support of the case. Kornheiser suggests that the team be known as the Pigskins.

1992 The *Oregonian* (Portland), among other newspapers, announce it will change its editorial policies related to teams with Native American mascots and names. It stops using the r-word in its coverage of the team.

1996 Miami University (Ohio) changes from Redskins to Redhawks

1998 Southern Nazarene University, a small Christian school in Bethany, Oklahoma, retires its *"Redskins"* nickname in favor of "Crimson Storm."

1999 The U.S. Patent and Trademark Office finds that the Washington team disparages American Indians and thus violates the Lanham Act. Its ruling strips the team of its trademarks. The franchise secures an injunction while it appeals the ruling.

2001 The U.S. Commission on Civil Rights calls for an end to the use of Native American images and team names by non-Native schools.

2005 The NCAA establishes a policy on the use of American Indian imagery by member institutions. It bases this decision on its findings that such imagery contributes to a hostile environment.

2005 The U.S. Court of Appeals returns case to the D.C. Circuit for review. It directs specific attention at the question of laches, a doctrine covering the fairness and timeliness of the legal action, in the suit against the team.

2006 Prompted in part by the ongoing litigation in *Harjo et al. v. Pro Football, Inc.*, a younger group of plaintiffs, to whom laches will not apply, files suit against the franchise. Led by Amanda Blackhorse, this case becomes known as *Blackhorse et al. v. Pro Football, Inc.*

2008 Following review, the court, finding that laches does apply, rules against the plaintiffs.

2009 The U.S. Supreme Court declines to hear an appeal in *Harjo et al v. Pro Football, Inc.* This decision brings the nearly two-decade-long case to a close.

2013   The National Museum of the American Indian hosts a symposium on "Racist Stereotypes and Cultural Appropriation in American Sports." Organized by Harjo, it plays a fundamental role in returning public attention to the issue.

2014   The Trademark Trial and Appeal Board rules in favor of the plaintiffs in *Blackhorse et al v. Pro Football, Inc.* It finds the team name disparaging to American Indians and strips of select trademarks.

2015   The ruling in *Blackhorse et al. v. Pro Football, Inc.* is upheld on appeal. The team plans subsequent litigation.

Introduction

Harjo et al. v. Pro Football was a legal case brought against the Washington professional football team in 1992. It sought to strip of the team of its trademarks on the grounds that the name and imagery registered with the federal government disparaged American Indians and thus did not merit legal protection. The Trademark Trial and Appeal Board (TTAB) found in favor of the plaintiffs in 1999. The franchise subsequently appealed the decision, which higher courts reversed on technical grounds. The U.S. Supreme Court declined to hear the case in 2009, bringing it to an end. Despite the legal defeat, *Harjo et al. v Pro Football* has proven decisive in the ongoing struggle against the team and its traditions, opening a new era of activism and laying the foundation for additional litigation against the franchise.

American Indian Mascots

Although currently the source of great controversy, when schools and sport teams began using names, imagery, and objects referencing Native Americans during the first half of the 20th century, most Americans embraced them enthusiastically. This is hardly a surprise as Americans at once idealized them for their bravery, bellicosity, and nobility and thought them doomed, certain to disappear. This mix of longing and lament had special attraction for a society made anxious by the changes in work, family, race, and gender wrought modern life, including urbanization, immigration, and industrialization. Wild West shows and movies had romanticized settling the frontier, while scouting and childhood games, decorating trends, and more encouraged many to incorporate Indianness in their lives. In this context, it was as if everyone had a claim on Indianness, believing in a sense they owned Native Americans. As a consequence, large number of Americans felt comfortable with cultural appropriation, taking from American Indian culture to make something meaningful for themselves. Stereotypical images of American Indians proliferated, offering deeper insights into the preoccupations and problems of white Americans than indigenous cultures and histories.

American Indian mascots linger as a prominent vestige of this era. They present flat and frozen images of Native Americans. They emphasize themes of war, conflict, and violence. They favor peoples from the Great Plains in flowing headdresses especially, but wherever they are from, they prefer the fighting brave and a proud renegade of the 19th century, at once a testament to, and trophy of, white victory and entitlement.

These caricatures, stereotypical remnants of conquest, have recently sparked much scholarship and divisive debates. While the latter remain ongoing, as the Washington professional football team and legal action against it underscore, the former have highlighted the ways in which such imagery reinforces anti-Indian racism, damages indigenous self-worth, and contributes to hostile environments. Together, this body of scholarship has found that far from innocent symbols, Native American mascots hurt indigenous people, dehumanizing them and denying them full enjoyment of basic civil rights.

The R*dskins

The Washington professional football team began in Boston before moving to the nation's capital. Founded in 1932 as the Boston Braves, the team moved to Fenway Park the following year, hired a new coach, and, in keeping with established practice at the time, also changed their name. Owner George Preston Marshall wanted to keep the Indian motif, but also wanted an identity distinct from other professional sporting franchises at the time. He chose to call the team the Redskins. While some maintain the name was chosen to honor the new coach, William "Lone Star" Dietz, who was a German American passing as a Native American, Marshall denied this at the time. A more likely explanation is that he hoped to build a brand and thought Dietz, whom most Americans took to be Lakota at the time, helped him consolidate the brand image.

In 1937, the franchise moved to Washington, D.C. Once there, Marshall and his wife elaborated on popular ideas and prevailing stereotypes about American Indians, creating a marching band, dressed in feathers, composing a fight song, "Hail to the Redskins," noteworthy for its broken English and racist projections, and, in time, fitted out the stadium with a massive teepee. In short, stereotypical renderings of American Indians allowed the team to brand itself and a context in which fans and media partners felt comfortable playing with Indianness and dressing in feathers at games, perhaps best exemplified by Chief Zee, the super fan and unofficial mascot of the team since 1978.

Sidebar 1: "Hail to the Redskins"

The hallmark of the team and its symphonic signature would debut in 1938. "Hail to the Redskins" articulated many of the reigning ideas about American Indians at the time. The song with its line "Braves on the Warpath" celebrated and claimed indigenous masculinity for the team and its fans, encoding it like the Indian head aside the teams helmet as a trophy and a totem—romantic, stoic, brave, defeated, and repossessed. To underscore the intense savagery at once desirable and detestable, it cast vanquishing the opponent as scalping and employed broken English to drive the point home ("We will take 'em big score"). The later addition asserting that the team "Fight for old Dixie" makes plain the shape and scope of whiteness. Importantly, "Hail to the Redskins" has changed over time. It has lost the racist dialect whites put in the mouths of their imagined Indians and it has long since stopped celebrating Dixie. The racial slur remains, but the reference to Dixie has faded away; the broken English has been edited, beautified much like the origin story and evolving rationale. One, of course, wonders why, if these elements can be reconfigured, the team name and associated iconography cannot. (King 2016)

The team name anchors the brand and allows for these other embellishments. While there is little debate about whether the r-word is a fighting word and slur today, its origins remain unclear. Opponents of the team have long suggested the term has its origins in the practice of putting bounties on American Indians, which were paid for each (bloody) skin, or red-skin, delivered. Supporters, in contrasts, suggest it is merely a robust slang term for American Indians. Recent research has demonstrated fairly convincingly that the word emerged in Indian country in the late 18th century as a reference to indigenous people. Later, whites adopt it with a similar meaning; however, by the mid-to-late 19th century it had become a slur, deeply embedded in anti-Indian racism and ethnic cleansing. This process of perjoration, by which a term becomes a pejorative, or term that disrespects and denigrates, is well known in linguistics, and also happened to the "n-word" in a slightly different, albeit equally racist, context.

American Indians had voiced opposition to the team name beginning in the early 1970s, pressing the franchise to change it. Their efforts largely fell on deaf ears. So too, did protests at home games in the 1980s and a massive demonstration at the Super Bowl in Minneapolis in 1991.

The Case

Against this backdrop, *Harjo et al. v. Pro Football* takes shape. Ownership unwilling to dialogue, and a public unmoved by the persistence of anti-Indian racism demanded a new strategy, which was found in an unlikely place, the registration of trademarks and the legal protections that these grant a corporation. The Lanham Act, specifically its provisions that one cannot register or receive protection for a trademark that disparages people, beliefs, or institutions and brings them into contempt or disrepute, provides an ideal means to challenge the team and its traditions. Suzan Shown Harjo (Cheyenne and Hodulgee Muscogee), Raymond D. Apodaca (Ysleta del Sur Pueblo), Vine Deloria Jr. (Lakota), Norbert S. Hill Jr. (Oneida), Mateo Romero (Cochiti Pueblo), William A. Means (Lakota), and Manley A. Begay Jr. (Navajo) filled suit against the National Football, who registered the trademarks on behalf of the team in 1992. Importantly, the case would not hinge not on whether the trademarks were disparaging in the year filed, but in the year registered, which was 1967.

The plaintiffs argued the team name and associated imagery used by the team disparaged American Indians. They further argued the r-word was a slur that brought Native Americans into contempt and disrepute. Finally, they asserted that American Indians shared this opinion. The team and the league, in turn, argued that the team name was not a slur at the time of registration, was not widely regarded by Native Americans or the American public generally as a pejorative, and that for most Americans the r-word in the context of the NFL referred to the team and its players. Both sides marshaled linguistic and historical evidence in support their claims. Shifting usage played an important role. How was the word used? When and by whom? In what contexts? So, too, did dictionary definitions, that is, when dictionaries begin to define the term as offensive.

Seven years after its filing, the TTAB ruled that the team name and associated marks were, in fact, disparaging and brought American Indians into contempt and disrepute. In essence, it found that the team did not enjoy legal protection for its trademarks because they were offensive and scandalous.

The victory was short-lived. The franchise appealed the case and received an injunction, staying the action of the TTAB. Following subsequent arguments by both sides, the district court ruled in favor of the Washington professional football team. Of special note, it ruled that the plaintiffs had not filed suit in a timely fashion, pointing to a legal principal known as "laches," which holds that fair and just adjudication requires individuals to assert their rights with due diligence. Thus, because the plaintiffs waited 25 years after the registration of the trademarks to file litigation, they had not fulfilled their legal obligations. Left unresolved in this ruling, however, was the claim of plaintiff Mateo Romero, who was only one in 1967. The U.S. Supreme Court refused to hear an appeal by the plaintiffs in 2009.

Aftermath

The refusal by the nation's highest court brought the case to a close, but it was not the end of *Harjo et al. v. Pro Football*. In fact, it lives on today, a vibrant force in efforts to change the name of the Washington professional football team. Specifically, it has reshaped activism against American Indian mascots and it has prompted further legal struggles.

The struggle against the term might be divided into four phases. The first had its roots in the broader indigenous renaissance of the 1960s, the emergence of red power, and diverse freedom struggles, particularly the civil rights movement. It was given its clearest expression in the demands for change in 1972 and prompted the organization to make minor alterations, including changes in the lyrics of the fight song. Second, after a lull, efforts quickened again in the late 1980s and early 1990s in conjunction with a resurgent push across the country to retire mascots. Protests and rallies at RFK Stadium during this period, according to Charlene Teters (Spokane), who helped organize them, were usually small, ranging from 20 to 50 demonstrators, and arguably climaxed in demonstrations at Super Bowl XXVI in Minneapolis. In the third phase, initiated in *Harjo et al. v. Pro Football* the

"We are people, not your mascot," shout American Indians participating in a protest of the name and logo of the Washington State football team before the game, 2014. Derogatory Indian mascots have been protested since the National Congress of American Indians led a national campaign in the early 1970s. (Toni L. Sandys/The Washington Post via Getty Images)

Sidebar 2: Changes in Attitudes toward Native Mascots

Even as the Washington professional football team has resisted calls for it to retire its moniker, numerous sport teams have opted for change. Over the past 40 years, many educational institutions have selected new mascots in response to pressure from the public, growing opposition in Indian country, and concerns voiced by their students. And while many professional teams have displayed intransigence, some have taken a more progressive path.

The Golden State Warriors began play in Philadelphia, initially employing symbols referencing American Indians. Even after moving to California in the 1960s, their logo featured a war bonnet, which was retired in 1969 in favor of a silhouette of the Golden Gate Bridge.

This rather quiet elimination stands in contrast to vocal movements led by Native American students on college campuses at the same time. In the late 1960s, and early 1970s, numerous universities, including Stanford University, Dartmouth College, and Marquette University, choose new mascots.

Opposition to Native American mascots flared again in the 1990s. Increased scrutiny prompted many school districts and universities to select new monikers and symbols. Miami University (Ohio) was among the most visible in this period, making the shift, amid much controversy, from Redskins to Redhawks.

More recently, a NCAA policy banning the use of Indian names and symbols has prompted change at a number of colleges and universities, including the University of North Dakota and the University of Illinois. Importantly, the policy allows for the continuation of such imagery at schools with support from local tribes. Both Florida State University and Central Michigan University have maintained historic logos under this provision.

Among the more creative responses to indigenous activism and changing public attitudes, the Spokane Indians (a minor league baseball team) worked the Spokane tribe to revision its public image. The collaboration produced a new logo and uniforms, incorporating indigenous language prominently.

movement shifted tactics to the courtroom, pushing to the end the anti-Indianism associated with the name by stripping the team of its trademarks. Finally, the most recent incarnation of activism begins with the filing of *Blackhorse et al. v. Pro Football, Inc.*, which shared arguments and objectives with the previous case, which has, in turn, opened new forms of opposition while invigorating a new generation of activists. In this more recent action, the plaintiffs, all of whom were born after 1967, have dispensed with the problem of laches. In 2014, the TTAB again found in favor of the plaintiffs, ruling the trademarks were disparaging and thus without legal standing. An appeals court decision affirmed this ruling in 2015. The franchise has indicated its intention to continue the defense of its trademarks.

The current moment of activism is arguably the most visible and has had the most impact to date, distinguished by novel media, strategies, and networks. Resistance now manifests itself on multiple fronts, in demonstration outside of games at FedEx Field and across the country, in the courtroom, in legislative action at the state, local, and federal levels, at academic conferences and political symposia, within traditional media outlets, and across social media. It is a national movement; it is pan-Indian, inter-tribal, and multi-ethnic. It has firm institutional footing across Indian country, including longtime opponent the National Congress of American Indians, the National Museum of the American Indian, and the Oneida Indian Nation. They, in turn, have encouraged and even spawned new oppositional groups, including one called Change the Mascot and another called Not Your Mascots. Together, they have anchored a more sustainable movement, which can more persistently, systematically, and effectively intervene and incite, and match the franchise organizationally in placing its message in the conventional media outlets. Arguably more importantly, the current iteration of the movement has masterfully used social media to advance the cause. It has made this virtual and viral space indigenous: it has organized online, recruiting new members, linking liked-minded individuals, and diffusing its message widely; it has pushed back with websites and Twitter storms targeting the franchise; it has raised money and consciousness; and it has created and disseminated videos, many of which have gone viral. And thanks in large part to research associated with litigation and a rising tide of scholarship, especially into the psychological, historical, and cultural dimensions, it has leveraged a powerful empirical case against the moniker that complements and extends its forceful moral argument against it. Throughout, the present phase of the movement remains committed to the ideals that gave life to opposition more than 40 years ago, challenging anti-Indianism embodied by the team and its traditions, pushing for change to alleviate it, and determined to reclaim and revalue indigeneneity.

Biographies of Notable Figures

Suzan Shown Harjo (June 2, 1945), born in El Reno, Oklahoma, to a Cheyenne mother and Muscogee father, has devoted her life to the defense of American Indians' rights, the promotion of religious freedom for indigenous peoples, and the protection of Native heritage, dignity, and identity. She has pursued these ends through art and poetry, museum work, policy advocacy, legislation, and litigation.

A descendant of Chief Bull Bear, Harjo grew up on a farmstead near Beggs, Oklahoma. "Her family's home," she recalled, "had no indoor plumbing or electricity, and her idea of wealth was to have ice cubes in her drink" (Belson). Later, during her adolescence, she moved with her family to Naples, Italy, where her father was posted by the U.S. military.

Harjo points to Clyde Warrior (Ponca) as an inspiration for her activism. Of special import to her was his activism against Little Red, a mascot at the University of Oklahoma, which was retired in 1970.

Harjo moved to New York City in the 1960s. There, she was active in the theater scene and became a producer on *Seeing Red*, a bi-weekly radio program devoted to American Indian Affairs. During this time, she found two of her important callings while visiting the Museum of the American Indian, repatriation, or the return of cultural patrimony to Native Peoples, and the protection of sacred objects and practices. While at WBAI, she met and married Frank Ray Harjo, with whom she had two children.

In 1974, Harjo relocated to Washington, D.C., where she took a position with the American Indian Press Association. After assisting with the transition of the Carter Administration, she became a legislative liaison for the Native American Rights Fund. This experience, in turn, led to her appointment as the congressional liaison for Indian affairs for the Carter administration in 1978. In this role, she played a leading role in the passage of the American Indian Religious Freedom Act.

After the election of Ronald Reagan, she remained in the nation's capital, where she sought to advance American Indian interests and issues through policy, advocacy, and legislation. Perhaps most notably, she served for as executive director of the National Council of American Indians from1984 to 1989. At the same time, following the death of her husband in 1984, she founded the Morning Star Institute, a national Native American rights organization, and has since served as its director. In these roles, she made important contributions to the passage of legislation directed at preserving indigenous heritage and promoting Native culture. Most important of these were the National Museum of the American Indian Act (1989), which established a museum dedicated to the histories and cultures of indigenous peoples on the National Mall, and the Native American Graves Protection and Repatriation Act (1990), which fostered the return of sacred objects, cultural patrimony, and human remains to Native nations, while laying out a new framework for relations between tribes and individuals and institutions that have historically studied, collected, and displayed their cultures.

Almost from the beginning of her time in Washington, D.C., Harjo has understood the team and its traditions to be problematic, referencing a particularly disturbing encounter with fans at a game in the early 1970s as what ultimately sparked her later activism against the team. In the intervening years, she has played a leading role in efforts to change the name, first through her leadership of NCAI and later as president of the Morning Star Institute. Then, in the courtroom, she first joined six other American Indians in 1992 to challenge the team and its trademarks in *Harjo et al. v. Pro Football, Inc.* and nearly a decade and a half later orchestrated *Blackhorse et al. v. Pro Football, Inc.* At the same time, her regular columns in *Indian Country Today*, moreover, have nurtured community and given hope, while encouraging scholars to ask questions about the history and significance of the moniker. Finally, she has the guiding force behind the symposium on "Racist Stereotypes and Cultural Appropriation in American Sports" held at the National Museum of the American Indian in February 2013. This gathering of activists, journalists, policymakers, and academics focused a spotlight on the team and sparked intense public interest. In fact, it is the catalyst of much of the recent push for change. All of these efforts make the description of her in *Business Insider* as the "Native American Grandmother who beat the Redskins" especially fitting (Walker).

Harjo has long had a deep affinity for art and culture. Dating back to her youth, she has written poetry. Later, she developed a love for theater, art, and museums. In addition to her impressive achievements in the realm of politics, she has also curated exhibits, staged conferences, written books, held a series of scholarly fellowships, and delivered countless lectures.

Her awards and accolades are many and much deserved. Perhaps most impressive, in 2014, Barak Obama awarded her the Presidential Medal of Freedom, the nation's highest civilian honor, for her work on behalf of American Indians. And, in 2015, she was honored with the Native Leadership Award by the National Congress of American Indians.

DOCUMENT EXCERPTS

After a lengthy hearing, the USTTAB found the trademarks registered by the Washington professional football team disparaged American Indians and hence were void.

Decision rendered by the U.S. Trademark Trial and Appeal Board in *Harjo et al. v. Pro Football, Inc.* (July 1999)As to each of the registrations subject to the petition to cancel herein, the petition to cancel under Section 2(a) of the Act is granted on the grounds that the subject marks may disparage Native Americans and may bring them into contempt or disrepute. As to each of the registrations subject to the petition to cancel herein, the petition to cancel under Section 2(a) of the Act is denied on the ground that the subject marks consist of or comprise scandalous matter. The registrations will be canceled in due course (p. 145).

Source: Harjo v. Pro-Football Inc., U.S. Patent and Trademark Office, Trademark Trial and Appeal Board, 1999, 50 U.S.P.Q. (BNA) 1705.

Statement of the U.S. Commission on Civil Rights on the Use of Native American Images and Nicknames as Sports Symbols (2001)

Building on the TTAB ruling, the U.S. Commission on Civil Rights offered a broader condemnation of American Indian mascots, underscoring their harms.

The U.S. Commission on Civil Rights calls for an end to the use of Native American images and team names by non-Native schools. The Commission deeply respects the rights of all Americans to freedom of expression under the First Amendment and in no way would attempt to prescribe how people can express themselves. However, the Commission believes that the use of Native American images and nicknames in school is insensitive and should be avoided. In addition, some Native American and civil rights advocates maintain that these mascots may violate anti-discrimination laws. These references, whether mascots and their performances, logos, or names, are disrespectful and offensive to American Indians and others who are offended by such stereotyping. They are particularly inappropriate and insensitive in light of the long history of forced assimilation that American Indian people have endured in this country.

Since the civil rights movement of the 1960s many overtly derogatory symbols and images offensive to African-Americans have been eliminated. However, many secondary schools, post-secondary institutions, and a number of professional sports teams continue to use Native American nicknames and imagery. Since the 1970s, American Indian leaders and organizations have vigorously voiced their opposition to these mascots and team names because they mock and trivialize Native American religion and culture.

It is particularly disturbing that Native American references are still to be found in educational institutions, whether elementary, secondary or post-secondary. Schools are places where diverse groups of people come together to learn not only the "Three Rs," but also how to interact respectfully with people from different cultures. The use of stereotypical images of Native Americans by educational institutions has the potential to create a racially hostile educational environment that may be intimidating to Indian students. American Indians have the lowest high school graduation rates in the nation and even lower college attendance and graduation rates. The perpetuation of harmful stereotypes may exacerbate these problems.

Source: Statement of the U.S. Commission on Civil Rights on the Use of Native American Images and Nicknames as Sports Symbols (2001). Online at http://www.usccr.gov/press /archives/2001/041601st.htm

After much study, the National Collegiate Athletic Association (NCAA) found that American Indian mascots were abusive and contributed to the creation of hostile

environments. With this policy, it sought to ban their use from events it sponsored. Importantly, it would later amend the policy to allow exceptions for schools, like Florida State University, whose mascots had tribal support.

NCAA Executive Committee Issues Guidelines for Use of Native American Mascots at Championship Events (August 5, 2005)

. . . the NCAA Executive Committee have adopted a new policy to prohibit NCAA colleges and universities from displaying hostile and abusive racial/ethnic/national origin mascots, nicknames or imagery at any of the 88 NCAA championships.

"Colleges and universities may adopt any mascot that they wish, as that is an institutional matter," said Walter Harrison, chair of the Executive Committee and president at the University of Hartford. "But as a national association, we believe that mascots, nicknames or images deemed hostile or abusive in terms of race, ethnicity or national origin should not be visible at the championship events that we control."

The policy prohibiting colleges or universities with hostile or abusive mascots, nicknames or imagery from hosting any NCAA championship competitions takes effect February 1, 2006 . . . Other elements of the policy approved Thursday require that institutions with hostile or abusive references must take reasonable steps to cover up those references at any predetermined NCAA championship . . . Institutions displaying or promoting hostile or abusive references on their mascots, cheerleaders, dance teams and band uniforms or paraphernalia are prohibited from wearing the material at NCAA championships, effective August 1, 2008.

Last, and effective immediately, institutions with student-athletes wearing uniforms or having paraphernalia with hostile or abusive references must ensure that those uniforms or paraphernalia not be worn or displayed at NCAA championship competitions.

Harrison stressed that institutions affected by the new policy can seek further review of the matter through the NCAA governing structure.

Source: NCAA Executive Committee Issues Guidelines for Use of Native American Mascots at Championship Events (August 5, 2005). Used by permission of the National Collegiate Athletic Association.

U.S. Court of Appeals Ruling in *Pro Football Inc. v. Harjo et al.* (July 15, 2005)

On appeal, the original TTAB decision was overturned. This ruling offered a more limited reading of the legal doctrine informing the original decision. It also laid the groundwork for Blackhorse et al. v. Pro Football, Inc.

The Lanham Trademark Act provides protection to trademark owners. *See generally* 15 U.S.C. §§ 1051–1127, 1141-1141n. To take advantage of many of its provisions, trademark owners must register their marks with the Patent and Trademark Office. Not all marks, however, can be registered. Under 15 U.S.C. § 1052, the PTO must deny registration to certain types of marks, including those which, in subsection (a)'s language, "may disparage or falsely suggest a connection with persons, living or dead, institutions, beliefs, or national symbols, or bring them into contempt, or disrepute."

Another section, 15 U.S.C. § 1064(3), provides that if a mark is registered in violation of section 1052(a), "any person who believes that he is or will be damaged by the registration" may file a petition "[a]t any time" with the PTO to cancel the registration. This triggers a proceeding before the TTAB, *see* 15 U.S.C. § 1067, which takes evidence and determines whether to cancel the mark. Yet another provision, 15 U.S.C. § 1069, states that "[i]n all . . . proceedings equitable principles of laches, estoppel, and acquiescence, where applicable may be considered and applied." (pp. 2–3)

. . .

Pursuant to 15 U.S.C. § 1071(b), Pro-Football filed suit in the U.S. District Court for the District of Columbia, seeking reinstatement of its registrations on the grounds that: (1) laches barred the Native Americans' petition; (2) the TTAB's finding of disparagement was unsupported by substantial evidence; and (3) section 1052(a) violates the First and Fifth Amendments to the U.S. Constitution both facially and as applied by the TTAB. (p. 4)

. . .

An equitable doctrine, "[l]aches is founded on the notion that equity aids the vigilant and not those who slumber on their rights." *NAACP v. NAACP Legal Def. & Educ. Fund, Inc.*, 753 F.2d 131, 137 (D.C. Cir. 1985). This defense, which Pro-Football has the burden of proving, *see Gull Airborne Instruments, Inc. v. Weinberger*, 694 F.2d 838, 843 (D.C. Cir. 1982), "requires proof of (1) lack of diligence by the party against whom the defense is asserted, and (2) prejudice to the party asserting the defense." *Nat'l R.R. Passenger Corp. v. Morgan*, 536 U.S. 101, 121–22 (2002) (internal quotation marks omitted). In this case, the Native Americans contend both that the statute bars the defense of laches and that even were laches an available defense, Pro-Football has failed to prove it. (p. 5)

. . .

But even if registrations of some marks would remain perpetually at risk, it is unclear why this fact authorizes—let alone requires—abandonment of equity's fundamental principle that laches attaches only to parties who have unjustifiably delayed in bringing suit. Pro-Football forgets that "laches is not, like limitation, a mere matter of time," *Holmberg v. Armbrecht*, 327 U.S. 392, 396 (1946) (internal quotation marks omitted), but rather turns on whether the party seeking relief "delayed inexcusably or unreasonably in filing suit" in a way that was "prejudicial" to the other party, *Rozen v. District of Columbia*, 702 F.2d 1202, 1203 (D.C. Cir. 1983) (per curiam). Why should equity give more favorable treatment to parties that harm expanding numbers of people (in which case, under Pro- Football's theory, laches runs from the date of harm) than it gives to parties that harm only a few people (in which case laches runs from whenever those people are free of legal disabilities)? Why should equity elevate Pro-Football's perpetual security in the unlawful registration of a trademark over the interest of a Native American who challenged this registration without lack of diligence? Why should laches bar *all* Native Americans from challenging Pro-Football's "Redskins" trademark registrations because *some* Native Americans may have slept on their rights? . . .

Source: Pro-Football, Inc. v. Harjo, 415 F.3d 44 (D.C. Cir. 2005).

Further Reading

Belson, Ken. "Redskins' Name Change Remains Activist's Unfinished Business." *New York Times,* October 9, 2013. Accessed October 10, 2013. http://www.nytimes.com/2013/10/10/sports/football/redskins-name-change-remains-her-unfinished-business.html

Handy, Bruce. "The Complex and Hidden Story Behind the Washington Redskins Trademark Decision." *Vanity Fair* June 25, 2014. Accessed June 30, 2014. http://www.vanityfair.com/news/2014/06/story-behind-washington-redskins-name

Harjo, Suzan Shown. "Fighting Name Calling: Challenging 'Redskins' in Court." In C. Richard King and Charles Freuhling Springwood, eds., *Team spirits: Essays on the history and significance of Native American mascots* (pp. 189–207). Lincoln: University of Nebraska Press, 2001.

King, C. Richard. *Redskins: Insult and Brand*. Lincoln: University of Nebraska Press, 2016.

King, C. Richard. 2014. "Looking Back to a Future End: Reflections on the Symposium on Racist Stereotypes in American Sport at the National Museum of the American Indian." *American Indian Quarterly* 38: 135–142.

King, C. Richard, ed. *The Native American Mascot Controversy: A Handbook*. Lanham, MD: Scarecrow Press, 2011.

Nunberg, Geoffrey. "When Slang Becomes a Slur." *The Atlantic* 23 June 23, 2014. Accessed June 30, 2014. http://www.theatlantic.com/entertainment/archive/2014/06/a-linguist-on-why-redskin-is-racist-patent-overturned/373198/

Stapleton, Bruce. *Redskins: Racial Slur or Symbol of Success*. Lincoln, NE: Writers Club Press, 2001.

Strong, Pauline Turner. "Trademarking Racism: Pseudo-Indian Symbols and the Business of Professional Sports." *Anthropology Now,* Sept. 2014. Accessed September 15, 2014. http://anthronow.com/print/trademarking-racism-pseudo-indian-symbols-and-the-business-of-professional-sports

Waggoner, Linda M. "On Trial—The Washington R*dskins' Wily Mascot: Coach William Lone Star Dietz." *Montana: The Magazine of Western History* 2013, 63 (1): 24–47.

Walker, Hunter. "Meet The Native American Grandmother Who Just Beat The Washington Redskins." *Business Insider* June 18, 2014. Accessed June 30, 2014. http://www.businessinsider.com/meet-the-native-american-grandmother-who-just-beat-the-redskins-2014 -6#ixzz3U6J7G1lU

Tribal Law and Order Act, 2010

Anne Luna-Gordinier

Chronology

1790 Federal jurisdiction extends to non-Indians committing crimes against Indians in Indian territory.

1817 The General Crimes Act expands federal jurisdiction over Indians and non-Indians committing crimes in Indian country, with the exception of crimes by Indians against Indians.

1825 The Assimilative Crimes Act applies state criminal laws to tribal lands in situations where there is no federal crime that is applicable.

1881 The Supreme Court holds in *United States v. McBratney* that when a non-Indian commits a crime against another non-Indian on tribal land, the state where the reservation is located has criminal jurisdiction.

1885 The Major Crimes Act extends federal jurisdiction over a list of specific violent crimes. The Act authorizes federal punishment of major crimes by Indians against Indians and offenses committed by Indians against non-Indians.

1896 The Supreme Court holds in *Talton v. Mayes* that the sovereign powers exercised by tribes did not come from the Constitution, but existed prior to the formation of the United States. As a result, tribal members could not seek constitutional protections against the actions of their tribes.

1953 Public Law 280 gives criminal and civil jurisdiction over tribes within their borders to six states. This ended tribal criminal jurisdiction for most tribes within the enumerated states. Public Law 280 also allowed any state to take over tribal jurisdiction of Indian lands within their borders by amending the state constitution or passing state law. Ten more states chose to take Public Law 280 jurisdiction over Indian country.

1968 Public Law 280 is amended so tribal consent is required before states could extend their jurisdiction. Predictably, no other tribe consented to relinquishing its jurisdiction.

The Indian Civil Rights Act imposes most of the requirements of the Bill of Rights on tribes for the exercise of jurisdiction, and limits sentences that may be imposed by tribal courts to a maximum of a $5,000 fine and one-year imprisonment for any crime.

1978 The Supreme Court holds in *Oliphant v. Suquamish Indian Tribe* that tribes lack criminal jurisdiction over non-Indians.

1990 The Supreme Court holds in *Duro v. Reina* that tribes do not have criminal jurisdiction over non-member Indians.

1991 Congress overturns *Duro*, affirming the inherent power of tribes to exercise power over all Indians.

1994 Senator Biden sponsors VAWA as part of the Violent Crime Control and Law Enforcement Act of 1994. On September 13, 1994, VAWA creates full faith and credit provisions requiring states and territories to enforce protection orders issued by other states, tribes, and territories.

1995 The Violence Against Women Grants Office (VAWGO) is created at the Department of Justice to implement grants programs for victims' services and provides police and court sensitivity training. VAWGO makes the first VAWA grants to tribes under the STOP Violence Against Indian Women (STOP VAIW) Program.

2006 President George W. Bush signs VAWA 2005 into law on January 5, 2006. It authorizes numerous new programs, with an increased emphasis on violence against Indian women, sexual assault, and youth victims. The first OVW Tribal Consultation convenes with DOJ officials and tribal leaders in Prior Lake, Minnesota.

2007 OVW makes its first awards under the Grants to Indian Tribal Governments program, a more comprehensive tribal program than was authorized by VAWA 2005, which replaces the STOP VAIW program.

2008 The Section 904 Violence Against Women in Indian Country Task Force holds its first meeting in Washington, D.C.

2010 President Barak Obama signs the Tribal Law and Order Act (TLOA) to empower tribal governments to provide public safety and reduce violent crime in Indian country. TLOA established the Indian Law and Order Commission.

2011 The Indian Law and Order Commission, an independent, all-volunteer advisory group, holds its first meeting. The purpose is to conduct a comprehensive study of law enforcement and criminal justice in tribal communities, and submit a report to the President and Congress with its findings, conclusions, and recommendations.

2012 Tribes begin implementing extended sentencing under TLOA.

2013 President Obama reauthorizes VAWA on March 17, 2013. Title IX, Safety for Indian Women includes Section 904 extending concurrent tribal criminal jurisdiction over violations of protection orders and domestic violence crimes involving non-Indians.

2014 Three tribes begin pilot projects to expand their jurisdiction and implement Section 904 provisions on February 6, 2014: Pasqua Yaqui, Tulalip, and the Confederated tribes of the Umatilla Indian Reservation.

2015 As of March 7, 2015, all federally recognized tribes may exercise special domestic violence criminal jurisdiction without permission from DOJ.

Asserting Sovereignty with the Tribal Law and Order Act

Crime is a pervasive problem in Indian country. Alarming rates of child abuse, homicide, juvenile crime, and substance abuse plague tribal homelands (DOJ 1997). Indigenous Americans are 2.4 times as likely to experience violent crimes, and at least twice as likely to experience rape or sexual assault crimes than all other races (Greenfeld and Smith 1999, iii). To some extent, this problem is due to the undermining of tribal traditions by forcing hierarchical legal and social structures onto tribal societies. Federal Indian law and policy have created complicated criminal jurisdictional issues, making it difficult for tribes to maintain law and order on their lands. In addition, the scant allocation of resources for tribal criminal justice systems makes law enforcement especially burdensome. Regardless of the causal factors, comprehensive federal legislation to support tribal criminal justice systems was needed. Congress responded to this problem by enacting the Tribal Law and Order Act (TLOA) for Indian country on July 29, 2010. TLOA acknowledges that tribal justice systems are often the most appropriate institutions for maintaining law and order in Indian country. Its purpose is to empower tribal governments to effectively provide public safety and reduce the prevalence of violent crime in Indian country. The TLOA is a step in the right direction for tribes seeking to resolve criminal justice issues on their lands. Once tribes begin to creatively utilize TLOA, they may develop various tactics and culturally appropriate remedies to promote public safety on the reservation. The approaches that are most likely to be successful are those rooted in tribal traditions and values. This will promote law and order on the reservation as well as help to further tribal sovereignty.

Evolution of Federal Indian Policy and Criminal Jurisdiction

In order to understand criminal justice issues in Indian country, it is essential to recognize the complex legal issues surrounding tribal criminal jurisdiction. Tribes once exerted full sovereignty over their land, government, and people; however, their powers were eroded over time by court decisions and acts of congress. Federal Indian policy has historically impeded tribes' ability to control their reservations in culturally compatible ways.

Criminal Jurisdiction

Congress has regularly responded to issues around criminal jurisdiction in Indian country by passing piecemeal legislation focused on specific issues. The nature of the law or policy is directed by the political climate at the time. Major laws affecting criminal jurisdiction include the General Crimes Act, the Assimilative Crimes Act, and the Major Crimes Act. Two subsequent acts that impact jurisdiction in Indian country are Public Law 280 (PL 280) and the Indian Civil Rights Act.

General Crimes Act

Congress passed the General Crimes Act in 1817, creating federal criminal jurisdiction over non-Indians for crimes they commit in Indian country (18 U.S.C.A. 1152). It also extends jurisdiction over Indians for select crimes against non-Indians. The act applies federal criminal law in its entirety to Indian country.

Assimilative Crimes Act

Congress enacted the Assimilative Crimes Act in 1825 (18 U.S.C.A. 13). The act applied state criminal law to crimes committed in Indian country when relevant federal criminal statutes were absent. The General Crimes Act failed to address which government has jurisdiction over crimes involving non-Indian victims and perpetrators on tribal land. The Supreme Court addressed the issue in 1881 in *United States v. McBratney* (104 U.S. 621 (1881)). The Court found that the state where the reservation is located has criminal jurisdiction when a non-Indian commits a crime against another non-Indian on tribal land.

Sidebar 1: Criminal Jurisdiction in Indian Country

Congress passed the General Crimes Act in 1817, creating federal criminal jurisdiction over non-Indians for crimes committed on tribal land. It also extends jurisdiction over Indians for select offenses against non-Indians. For jurisdictional purposes, Indian land is treated like a federal building, park, or military base. The act created three exceptions: It does not apply to crimes by Indians against other Indians, offenses by Indians that are punished by the tribe, or cases where a treaty gives the tribe exclusive jurisdiction over crime. The act applies federal criminal law to Indian country.

Congress realized that some acts are considered crimes by the state but are not prohibited by particular federal law. When these crimes were committed within federal enclaves, they would go unpunished. Essentially, state law had no force within federal enclaves including Indian Country. To resolve this issue, Congress enacted the Assimilative Crimes Act in 1825. The act applied state criminal law to crimes committed in federal enclaves that were not addressed by federal statutes. Given that Indian Country is considered a federal enclave under the General Crimes Act, it applies state criminal laws to tribal lands.

The General Crimes Act failed to address which sovereign had jurisdiction over crimes involving non-Indian defendants and victims on tribal land. The U.S. Supreme Court addressed the issue in 1881 in *United States v. McBratney*. It found that when a non-Indian commits a crime against another non-Indian on tribal land, the state where the reservation is located has criminal jurisdiction.

In 1885, Congress passed the Major Crimes Act to deal with Indian-on-Indian crimes that occur in Indian Country. The Act extended federal jurisdiction over seven crimes committed between Indians including: assault with intent to kill, arson, burglary, larceny, murder, manslaughter, and rape. Later amendments added another seven crimes: assault resulting in serious bodily injury, assault with a dangerous weapon, assault with intent to commit rape, felonious sexual molestation of a minor, incest, kidnapping, and robbery. The Act authorizes federal punishment of major crimes by both Indians against Indians, and offenses committed by Indians against non-Indians.

Major Crimes Act

In 1885, Congress passed the Major Crimes Act to deal with Indian-on-Indian crimes that occur in Indian country (18 U.S.C.A. 1153). The act extended federal jurisdiction over a list of specific violent crimes by Indians against Indians and offenses committed by Indians against non-Indians (*United States v. Henry*, 432 F.2d 114 (9th Cir. 1970)).

Criminal jurisdiction over misdemeanors committed by non-Indians was not addressed until *Oliphant v. Suquamish Indian Tribe* (435 U.S. 191 (1978)). The U.S. Supreme Court found that due to the domestic, dependent status of tribes, they do not have jurisdiction over non-Indians unless granted expressly by Congress. Tribal members seeking justice would have to petition the U.S. Attorney, often located hundreds of miles away, to prosecute even minor offenses in federal court.

In *Duro v. Reina*, the Court stated that the retained sovereignty of the tribes is only that needed to control their internal relations, and to preserve their customs and social order (495 U.S. 676 (1990)). The Court attempted to unify the precedents by articulating a theory of consent to government. Voluntary tribal membership and the right of participation in tribal government justify tribal criminal jurisdiction over members. This ruling removed tribal jurisdiction over non-member Indians on the reservation.

The *Duro* decision created a jurisdictional gap in Indian country because states lacked criminal jurisdiction in Indian country, and the federal government usually only prosecuted crimes under the Major Crimes Act due to funding constraints. Congress responded in 1991 by amending the ICRA to (1) recognize and affirm the inherent power of Indian tribes to exercise criminal jurisdiction over all Indians, and (2) explicitly expand the definition to include any person defined as an Indian under the Major Crimes Act to be within the criminal jurisdiction of tribal courts (25 U.S.C. 1301).

Jointly, these three acts extend exclusive federal jurisdiction over crimes committed in Indian country that involve non-Indian perpetrators against Indians, as well as Indian perpetrators of major crimes listed by the Major Crimes Act. States were given jurisdiction over crimes committed in Indian country within state borders that include non-Indian perpetrators and victims. Tribes maintain jurisdiction over misdemeanors committed by Indians in Indian country.

Public Law 280

Around 1950, federal Indian policy shifted toward the assimilation of Native Peoples. Several tribes were terminated as a result of this policy. Another tactic intended to promote assimilation was PL 280 (18 U.S.C.A. 1162). Essentially, in 1953 Congress gave criminal and civil jurisdiction to six states over Indian country within their borders. The original PL 280 states included Alaska, California, Minnesota, Nebraska, Oregon, and Wisconsin. This law ended tribal criminal jurisdiction for most tribes within the enumerated states. PL 280 also allows any state to take over tribal jurisdiction of Indian lands within their borders by amending the state constitution or passing state law. Ten additional states chose to take PL 280 jurisdiction over Indian country. As a result of great pressure from tribes, in 1968 an amendment to PL 280 was passed that required tribal consent before states could extend their jurisdiction (25 U.S.C. 1323). Predictably, no other tribe consented to relinquishing its jurisdiction. By that time, the assimilationist ideal had faded. Although there was a marked turn in policy toward self-determination for tribes, these policies had already wreaked havoc on American Indian life.

Indian Civil Rights Act

In *Talton v. Mayes*, the Supreme Court specifically held that the sovereign powers exercised by tribes did not come from the Constitution (163 U.S. 196 (1896)). As a result, tribal members could not seek constitutional protections against the actions of their tribes. As Congress was concerned that certain classes of citizens were not protected by the Constitution, it passed the ICRA of 1968 (25 U.S.C.A. 1301 et seq.).

With a few exceptions, the ICRA imposed the Bill of Rights on tribes. Under the ICRA, tribes do not have to provide legal counsel for indigent defendants, nor do they have to provide grand jury indictments in criminal cases. In addition, the act restricts tribal criminal jurisdiction over Indians to misdemeanors. The maximum penalties a tribal court may impose for misdemeanors are limited to $5,000 in fines and one year in jail per crime (25 U.S.C.A. 1301).

Given all of these restrictions on jurisdiction, tribes have found themselves unable to adequately maintain law and order on their lands. The confusion over who would exercise jurisdiction, lack of funding, and remote locations of Indian country all work to undermine public safety. In order for tribes to resolve these problems, they have had to seek new avenues for resolution. In order to succeed, tribes must balance the goals of tribal sovereignty with state and federal needs for accountability. Only with time, education, regained political power, and respect for traditional cultures can tribes re-envision themselves successfully.

Tribal Law and Order Act of 2010

In response to these jurisdictional gaps and the devastating crime rate in Indian country, Congress passed the Tribal Law and Order Act of 2010 (TLOA) (25 U.S.C. 2501). The congressional intent of TLOA is to guarantee tribal criminal justice, expand federal responsibility over Indian country, improve law enforcement on Indian lands, and enhance tribal sentencing authority. TLOA also established the Indian Law and Order Commission (ILOC), composed of nine volunteer members responsible for conducting a comprehensive study of criminal justice and law enforcement in Indian country. The ILOC is responsible for submitting a report to

---

Sidebar 2: Major Provisions of the Tribal Law and Order Act

- Requires federal prosecutors to maintain data on criminal declinations in Indian country and to share evidence to support prosecutions in tribal court.
- Increases tribal court sentencing authority from one to three years' imprisonment where certain constitutional protections are met.
- Requires federal officials working in Indian country to testify about information gained in the scope of their duties to support a prosecution in tribal court.
- Many tribal police have no access to criminal history records. The bill provides tribal police greater access to criminal history databases that provide them with critical information when detaining or arresting a suspect.
- Requires Indian Health Service (his) to standardize its sexual assault policies and protocols for handling sex crimes, interviewing witnesses, and handling evidence of domestic and sexual violence crimes in Indian country.
- Increases recruitment and retention efforts for BIA and tribal police.
- Expands training opportunities for BIA and tribal police to receive training at state police academies, and tribal, state, and local colleges.
- Enhances Special Law Enforcement Commission program to deputize officers to enforce federal laws on Indian lands.
- Authorizes appointment of Special Assistant U.S. Attorneys (SAUSAs) to prosecute reservation crimes in federal courts and encourages federal courts to hold cases in Indian country.
- Reauthorizes and improves existing programs designed to strengthen tribal courts, police departments, and corrections centers, as well as programs to prevent and treat alcohol and substance abuse, and improve opportunities for at-risk Indian youth.

---

the president and Congress with its findings, conclusions, and recommendations regarding issues such as improving services and programs to prevent juvenile crime, rehabilitating Indian youth in custody, as well as adjustments to the penal authority of tribal courts, alternatives to incarceration, and simplifying jurisdiction in Indian country.

Cooperation and Coordination

Historically, federal prosecutors have regularly declined to prosecute criminal cases in Indian country. For example, between 2005 and 2009, federal prosecutors declined

President Barack Obama, surrounded by members of his administration and Native American leaders, signs the Tribal Law and Order Act during a ceremony at the White House in Washington, DC, 2010. The act was passed to improve federally created jurisdictional issues on reservations that inhibited tribal law enforcement and courts in responding to various crimes, including domestic violence. (Saul Loeb/AFP/Getty Images)

to prosecute 40 percent of nonviolent cases and 52 percent of violent cases in Indian country (GAO 2010, 3). To make matters worse, tribes often do not receive notification of the declinations. This is problematic because while tribes wait to hear back, evidence may be lost or damaged, or federal witnesses may become unavailable. Even when a tribal court is able to hear a case, sentencing restrictions limit the penalties for serious crimes. Certainly something needed to be done in order to promote public safety in Indian country.

Section 212 of TLOA amends the ICRA and requires federal actors conducting investigations on tribal land to coordinate with tribal agencies in cases of declinations or non-referrals of criminal investigations (25 U.S.C. 2801 (2010), 25 U.S.C. 1301 (1968)). This coordination also encompasses the use of relevant evidence in tribal court as well as status updates on investigations. In addition, the U.S. Attorney's Office and the FBI are required to report to Congress about declinations of prosecution. The expectation is that the annual reporting requirement will decrease the rate of cases that go unresolved in Indian country. In addition, the U.S. Bureau of Prisons must now notify tribal law enforcement whenever a prisoner convicted of drug trafficking, a sex offense, or a violent crime is released into Indian country.

The TLOA also requires U.S. Attorney's Offices with jurisdiction in Indian country to appoint special assistant U.S. attorneys to work as tribal liaisons in order to promote the prosecution and coordination of cases. TLOA also authorizes the use of tribal prosecutors for this purpose. The goal is for increased coordination of cases and for tribal prosecutors to receive additional support and training. It is anticipated that these special prosecutors will increase the number of federal prosecutions in Indian country, resulting in enhanced public safety.

Tribal Policing, Training, and Cross-deputization

The piecemeal history of federal Indian law makes criminal jurisdiction in Indian country extremely convoluted. Law enforcement officers must unravel these tangled issues while working in dangerous situations. Their authority differs, depending upon particular circumstances. In addition, an inadequate number of law enforcement officers (3,000) work in all of Indian country (Reaves 2011, 1). These officers patrol vast areas, for example, 11 of the 25 largest law enforcement agencies serve jurisdictions covering over 1,000 square miles (Ibid.). The TLOA attempts to resolve these issues with a number of approaches.

The TLOA encourages the recruitment and retention of tribal law enforcement officers. For example, TLOA raises the hiring age for tribal officers from 37 to 47 years of age (25 U.S.C. 2501). This may encourage retired military or emergency-response personnel to become tribal officers. Given the high rate of recidivism from police forces, this also encourages committed and skilled officers to keep working in Indian country.

The TLOA provides funding and creates training protocols for tribal police. It also requires tribal police to have access to federal criminal intelligence databases, including the FBI's National Crime Information Center (NCIC). Access to such information improves the likelihood of the resolution of crimes in Indian country. This additional support may also help retain devoted tribal police officers.

TLOA emphasizes the need to end violence against Indian women. It authorizes new guidelines for tribal authorities addressing sexual assault and domestic violence crimes. It also requires the Indian Health Service (IHS) to standardize sexual assault policies and protocols for handling evidence and interviewing witnesses of domestic and sexual violence crimes in Indian country.

TLOA also requires training for all tribal judicial and law enforcement employees, and BIA personnel, about alcohol and substance abuse prevention for youth and adults. Training is also mandatory for narcotics investigations and prosecutions. Existing or newly created training programs will be provided by the administrator of the DEA, director of the FBI, secretary of the Interior, and the U.S. attorney general. Tribes would also benefit from incorporating cultural considerations into their codes, protocols, prevention, and training programs, to ensure that they are integrated into law enforcement. This, in turn, would enhance tribal sovereignty.

Another important approach, especially in PL 280 states, is cross-deputization. TLOA provides incentives through technical assistance and grants for tribal and state law enforcement agencies to enter into joint law enforcement agreements to combat crime in and near tribal lands. Importantly, TLOA expands the authority of tribal police to enforce federal laws, whatever the perpetrator's race. This makes it easier for tribes to exercise criminal jurisdiction, thus providing more protection from crime in Indian country. Through regular and enhanced training, streamlined sharing of information, and clarification of jurisdiction, TLOA should lead to more effective law enforcement in Indian country.

Enhancing Tribal Sovereignty

With the passage of TLOA, tribal courts may now prosecute felonies that federal authorities often considered not serious enough to pursue. TLOA amended the ICRA to allow prosecution of felony cases with sentencing of up to three years of imprisonment per crime and can be stacked up to nine years per case. Fines are limited to $15,000 per case (25 U.S.C. 2801 (2010), 25 U.S.C. 1301 (1968). For tribal judiciaries to be eligible, they must provide presiding judges who are licensed lawyers with sufficient legal training. In addition, defendants must be provided with a defense attorney who is licensed by the state bar. Tribes are also required to be courts of record. Although this poses an additional burden on tribes, they may benefit from sharing information as they codify culturally appropriate rules and codes.

Relatedly, TLOA allows for federal prosecution of crimes not prosecuted by PL 280 states. Tribes may ask the U.S. attorney general to approve concurrent jurisdiction among the federal government, the state, and the tribe. As the state's jurisdiction remains unchanged, PL 280 states no longer have to approve a change of status as previously required. This supports tribal sovereignty because it restores tribal jurisdiction over all misdemeanors and crimes perpetrated by Indians against Indians or non-Indians on tribal lands.

Tribes face serious obstacles for funding and developing critical infrastructure and programs. In an effort to address this, the TLOA reauthorizes funding to support and improve tribal justice systems. Given that tribal incarceration capacity is usually only short-term, a pilot program allows Indians sentenced for felonies in tribal court to be jailed in a federal facility at government expense. Alternatively, perpetrators may be imprisoned in tribal rehabilitation facilities, state facilities under contract with the tribe, or tribal facilities approved for long-term confinement by the Bureau of Indian Affairs (BIA). Tribally specific rehabilitation programs rooted in tribal traditions and values may be particularly helpful in promoting public safety and tribal sovereignty.

Looking Forward

Jurisdictional complications are still a major hurdle for tribes. There remains a confusing tangle of tribal, federal, and state jurisdictional issues that depend upon the location of the offense, the identity of the perpetrator, the identity of the victim, and the crime. TLOA does not resolve all of these issues, but it does attempt to improve criminal justice in Indian country.

As of 2016, ten of eligible tribes were exercising TLOA's new sentencing authority, and 15 were close to implementation (NCAI 2016). Ninety-six percent of tribes reported challenges due to funding limitations (GAO 2012, 3). Relatedly, two-thirds of the tribes who applied for funding in 2011 were ineligible because they did not have non-profit 501(c)(3) status (GAO 2012, 4). It is also unclear how TLOA will affect criminal prosecution of non-Indians in Indian country. On the bright side, declinations for federal prosecution went down to 34% by 2013 (DOJ 2013, 7). Although the act offers an opportunity to improve the justice systems in Indian country, implementation will require improved communication and significant coordination among federal agencies and all components of tribal justice systems.

One of the best ways for tribes to exercise sovereignty is to work within the framework of approved forms of jurisdiction while not limiting themselves to those areas. This enables tribes to demonstrate their competence in numerous areas of policy and legal development while also enhancing tribal sovereignty. Tribes must develop formal criminal justice protocol to appropriately and effectively respond to crime. They would benefit from creating legal codes that integrate local, cultural, and multidisciplinary responses to crime before they attempt to adopt and implement them.

Once tribes set about creatively utilizing TLOA, they may develop a multitude of tactics to address crime in Indian country. They must seek multiple funding sources, since they generally lack sufficient financial resources for enforcement. Coalition-building and information-sharing are also necessary. By developing and implementing their own culturally compatible legal codes to address crime, tribal governments will not only be able to protect their citizens, empower victims of violence, and hold perpetrators accountable, they will also further their sovereignty.

Biographies of Notable People

Sarah Deer (1972–)

Sarah Deer (Muskogee Creek) is an indigenous feminist legal scholar and advocate. Born in 1972, Deer is originally from Wichita, Kansas. Deer wanted to be an activist from an early age. She credits her grandfather, Isaac "Kelso" Deer, who was a teacher and served in the Kansas Legislature in the 1950s, for helping her make connections to her heritage and awareness of racial injustice. Her father, Montie Deer, taught high school, went to law school, and then served as a state court judge in Kansas and as a Muscogee Nation Supreme Court judge. Her mother, Jan, was also a teacher. The dedication of her family members was central to her decision to become a professor of law and an advocate for victims' rights.

Deer advocated for abortion rights during high school and went on to receive her B.A. in Women's Studies and Philosophy from the University of Kansas in 1995. While attending KU, she was heavily involved in abortion rights events and volunteered helping victims of sexual assault. She went on to earn her J.D. in 1999 with a Tribal Lawyer Certificate from the University of Kansas School of Law. She began to focus on American Indian women after she took her first tribal law class at KU.

After graduating from law school, Deer was a grant program specialist at the U.S. Department of Justice Office on Violence Against Women from 1999 to 2002. In 2000, Deer married Neal Axton, a fellow lawyer who is now the research librarian at William Mitchell College of Law. She was a victim-advocacy legal specialist and staff attorney at the Tribal Law and Policy Institute in Saint Paul, Minnesota from 2002 to 2008. She has been an online instructor of tribal legal studies for the UCLA Extension, and a lecturer of law, for the UCLA Law School.

Deer became a visiting professor of law at William Mitchell College of Law in Saint Paul Minnesota in 2008 and was hired as an assistant professor of law in 2009. In 2009, Deer and Colette Routel were tasked with restarting William Mitchell's Indian Law program. She currently teaches Constitutional Criminal Procedure, Constitutional Law, Professional Responsibility, Introduction to Tribal Law, and Criminal Law: Statutory Interpretation. She also teaches the Indian Law Clinic, and the Tribal Code Drafting Clinic.

Deer was one of the lead authors for Amnesty International's "Maze of Injustice" report wherein she reframed the problem of sexual violence in Indian Country as an international human rights issue. In addition, she brought Native American leaders, health specialists, and women's advocates together around the intersection between violence against women and tribal governance, thereby launching widespread efforts to reform federal policies that interfere with the ability of tribes to prosecute offenders. She was also a lead author of the U.S. Department of Justice's report entitled "Sexual Assault in Public Law 280 States."

Deer's work has been instrumental in the passage of the Tribal Law and Order Act of 2010, which increases the sentencing power of tribal courts and requires federal district attorneys to provide detailed information to tribal authorities about cases under their jurisdiction that will not be prosecuted. Her work also contributed to the 2013 reauthorization of the Violence Against Women Act, which restores some of the authority that was stripped from tribal governments by *Oliphant v. Suquamish* (1978). VAVA 2013 gives tribal courts the power to prosecute non–Native Americans who assault Native spouses or dating partners or violate a protection order on tribal lands. Deer believes that tribal courts remain the best place for Indian women to find justice. With her current focus on building tribal infrastructure and reinvigorating the rich history of Native Americans' pre-colonial criminal justice systems as a source for contemporary laws and policies, Deer is profoundly reshaping the landscape of support and protection for Native American women.

Deer is a Board Member of the ABA Commission on Domestic Violence and the National Alliance to End Sexual Violence. In 2012, she became the Chair of the Federal Advisory Committee for the National Coordination Committee on the American Indian/Alaska Native Sexual Assault Nurse Examiner-Sexual Assault Response Team (AI/AN SANE-SART) Initiative. I/AN SANE-SART was established with support from the U.S. attorney general to inform the U.S. Office for Victims of Crime and its federal, tribal, and nongovernment partners of the existing resources, challenges, and gaps related to sexual violence response.

Deer has testified before Congress, and in 2013 she became an Associate Justice of the Prairie Island Court of Appeals. She became an Appellate Judge for the White Earth Nation in 2015.

In 2014, the MacArthur Foundation named Deer a MacArthur Fellow. The "genius grants" recognize exceptionally creative people with a record of achievement and potential for significant future contributions. The grant will certainly help Deer continue her work on policies to help American Indian women who have been failed by tribal courts and federal laws.

She has co-authored four textbooks on tribal law, and written several academic articles on Native American women. In 2015, her first book, entitled *The Beginning and End of Rape: Confronting Sexual Violence in Native America,* was published. Deer's commitment to ending violence against Native American women and supporting tribal judicial systems promises to bring about a better future for all of Indian country.

Theresa M. Pouley (1960–)

The Honorable Theresa M. Pouley (Colville Confederated tribes) is an esteemed tribal judge and a national leader on tribal justice issues. Born in 1960, she is one of three daughters of Victor J. Desautel and Sheryl Rose Bean. Her father, Victor, worked off of the Colville Indian Reservation, so although her family lived outside the reservation, they regularly returned on weekends to stay with her grandparents in Inchelium.

Judge Pouley received her B.A. from Gonzaga University in 1984. It was there that she met her husband, Mark W. Pouley, who has been the Chief Judge of the Swinomish Tribal Court since 2004. She went on to earn her J.D. from Wayne State University Law School in 1987 and was admitted to the state bars of Michigan and Washington. She has been an attorney for over 20 years and in her practice has played a variety of roles, including private practice in Michigan and Washington until her appointment to the bench in 1999.

Judge Pouley was the Chief Judge of the Lummi Nation in Washington from 1999 to 2005. She was a member of the board of directors of the National Tribal Court Judges Association from 2003 to 2004 and became the president of the Northwest Tribal Court Judges Association in 2005. She was selected by the Washington State Supreme Court to sit on the "Historical Court of Justice," which reviewed and exonerated Chief Leschi in 2004. Judge Pouley was awarded the National Tribal Child Support Association's Award for Outstanding Judge in 2005.

Judge Pouley is currently the Chief Judge of the Tulalip Tribal Court and an Associate Justice of the Colville Court of Appeals. As a Judge of the Northwest Intertribal Court System, she serves as a trial judge and appellate court justice for several other Northwest tribes. Under her guidance, the Tulalip Tribal Court was awarded the Honoring Nations Award from American Indian Economic Development Project of Harvard University's Kennedy School of Government in 2006 for its focus on its therapeutic and indigenous approaches to criminal law.

In 2001, Tulalip retroceded its criminal jurisdiction from the state of Washington. The tribal court went from a once-per-month court system to 1,100 cases almost overnight. In 2005, the tribal council passed a resolution for a wellness court at the urging of the Tulalip Chief Justice. Since then, the wellness court has met once per week about their clients to address their needs with an integrative approach, including chemical dependency treatment providers, mental health providers, domestic violence counselors, and perpetrator treatment providers, as well as GED, job training, Northwest Indian College, and casino employment representatives. The innovative approach helped reduce the number of repeat offenders at Tulalip by 25 percent each year during the first two years. The third year, it went down an additional 12 percent. Additionally, 80 percent of the criminal case-load at Tulalip automatically requires current drug and alcohol evaluation. Tulalip's Alternative Sentencing Program incorporates the best values of Native culture into a modern and traditional court system.

In 2009, Judge Pouley worked with the Department of Justice as a facilitator for the "Tribal Nations Listening Session," and in 2010 she facilitated a "Focus

Group on Human Trafficking of American Indian and Alaska Native Women and Children" developed by the Office for Victims of Crime. She has also worked and lectured with the Washington State Administrative Office of the Courts on domestic violence and Indian law issues for the last several years.

Judge Pouley was a presenter to the United States Supreme Court Justices O'Connor and Breyer on "Indigenous Justice Paradigms." She also provided testimony to the United States Senate Committee on Indian Affairs on "Challenges in Law Enforcement in Indian Country" in 2000, the "Oversight Hearings on Tribal Courts" in 2007, and "Tribal Law and Order Act," one year later in 2011.

President Barack Obama appointed Judge Pouley to the Indian Law & Order Commission (ILOC) in 2011. The Tribal Law and Order Act created the ILOC, an independent, all-volunteer advisory group, to help address challenges to securing equal justice for Indians on tribal lands. The ILOC presented "A Roadmap for Making Native America Safer: Report to the President and Congress of the United States" in November 2013. The report represents one of the most comprehensive assessments ever undertaken of criminal justice systems serving Native American and Alaska Native communities.

Judge Pouley also spoke to the U.S. Attorney's Office about justice in Indian Country in 2014. The Tulalip tribes are one of three tribal entities in the country that were authorized by the United States Attorney General to set up a pilot program to prosecute domestic violence cases involving non-Native defendants in tribal court under Section 904 of the Violence Against Women Act (VAWA) of 2013. Judge Pouley noted that during the first nine months, five cases were brought as part of the pilot project, with three convictions, one dismissal, and one case scheduled for trial after the New Year.

Judge Pouley frequently lectures at local, state, and national conferences on tribal court and Indian law issues and makes regular presentations at the University of Washington's Indian Law Symposium. She teaches Indian law in the Paralegal Program at Edmonds Community College in Washington State and previously taught at Northwest Indian College. Chief Justice Pouley is blazing the trail for other tribes seeking to exercise criminal jurisdiction on their lands and thus further their sovereignty.

DOCUMENT EXCERPTS

Responding to Violence Against Indian Women, Sarah Deer (2011)

In 2011, Professor Sarah Deer testified before the U.S. Senate Committee on Indian Affairs, regarding historical causes of violence against Indian women, as well as jurisdictional complications that need to be addressed.

As other hearings have documented, it has been challenging for the legal system to respond to Native survivors of sexual violence because of jurisdictional complexities. The federal government has created a complex interrelation between federal, state and tribal jurisdictions that undermines tribal authority and often allows perpetrators to evade justice. Tribal and federal agencies responsible for providing the services necessary to ensure that survivors receive adequate care and that perpetrators are held accountable for their crimes are chronically underfunded and without the appropriate resources to uphold agency duties. Tribal governments are hampered by a complex set of laws and regulations created by the federal government that make it difficult, if not impossible, to respond to sexual assault in an effective manner.

. . .

Many of the current issues that American Indian and Alaska Native Peoples face in the United States, particularly Native women, can be traced back to the legacy of abuse and systematic assault on Native culture, land and people as a part of European/U.S. colonization of the Americas. Gender based violence against Native women was used by settlers as an integral part of conquest and colonization. The United States federal government has historically made a series of attempts to compel American Indian and Alaska Native Peoples to assimilate into the dominant Euro-American society. In the late 19th and early 20th centuries, a number of policies designed to promote assimilation contributed to the breaking up of tribal societies, damaging communal solidarity and traditional social networks.

. . .

While recent steps have been made to begin to address some of the issues that American Indian and Alaska Native populations face in the United States, it will take more than one piece of legislation to comprehensively address the impact of this significant historical legacy of discrimination and abuse. Native women need and deserve continued attention and resources from the federal level.

The United States federal government has a legal responsibility to ensure protection of the rights and wellbeing of American Indian and Alaska Native Peoples, including a responsibility to provide social, educational and medical services. The legacy of abuse, disempowerment and erosion of tribal government authority, and the chronic under-resourcing of law enforcement agencies and services which should protect indigenous women from sexual violence, must be reversed.

. . .

From prevention to response, the quality and availability of public safety, justice, and health care services for Native women in the U.S. are disproportionately and chronically underfunded and prioritized. The historical discrimination and ongoing economic, social, and cultural abuse of Native Peoples in the U.S. results in shocking levels of violence, including trafficking and sexual exploitation. It must be addressed immediately.

. . . . The Tribal Law and Order Act will begin to address the long-standing public safety and justice service disparities in Indian Country by beginning to restore to tribal governments the authority and resources to protect their citizens, particularly women and girls.

Yet, despite the strides made by Congress and the Administration to restore tribal authority, true tribal empowerment and sovereignty will not be possible without addressing the Supreme Court's 1978 ruling on Oliphant vs. Suquamish, which effectively strips tribal authorities of the power to prosecute crimes committed by non-Indian perpetrators on tribal land, and denies due process and equal protection of the law to survivors of sexual violence. We therefore urge Congress to re-recognize the concurrent jurisdiction of tribal authorities over all crimes committed on tribal lands, regardless of the Native identity of the accused, legislatively overriding the U.S. Supreme Court's decision on Oliphant vs. Suquamish.

Source: Deer, Sarah. "Native Women: Protecting, Shielding, and Safeguarding Our Sisters, Mothers, and Daughters." Testimony before the U.S. Senate Committee on Indian Affairs Oversight Hearing. Washington, D.C.: July 14, 2011.

Enhanced Sentencing Authority, Theresa M. Pouley (2011)

In 2011, the Honorable Theresa M. Pouley, Justice of the Tulalip Tribal Court spoke before the U.S. Senate Committee on Indian Affairs regarding the financial and political impacts of the Tribal Law and Order Act.

Since the Act passed I have had the opportunity to meet with many tribal leaders and federal and state government officials interested in the development of tribal justice systems. Congress should be encouraged that tribes are patiently and methodically taking measured and reasoned steps toward exercising the additional sentencing authority granted by the TLOA. It is important that we not misinterpret the tribes' lack of immediate implementation of this authority as a sign that the problems are not as bad as stated or that tribes do not care to exercise this authority. We must understand that the TLOA, while offering only an incremental step to improving tribal justice, presents tribes with a substantial change in the way they operate their courts. This change presents risks and costs that the tribes are measuring carefully before simply jumping forward.

The wisdom of the "opt in" provisions of the TLOA is evident as some tribes may judge the changes in TLOA coming at too high a cost to their sovereignty and independence. It is perceived that some of the requirements in TLOA, presumably adopted to protect defendants' due process, will push tribal courts to be more like federal courts, and this is not typically a welcomed push. At Tulalip we have had to carefully study ways to implement the provisions of TLOA while still retaining our tribal identity and balancing extended punishment philosophies with the holistic programs and methods that have been successful over the years. This has not been easy and it has required careful planning and cooperation of all the key players in our justice system.

When tribes take a realistic look at the provisions of TLOA, it is clear that exercising enhanced sentencing authority will require additional financial obligations. While the Act offers tribes a method to exercise enhanced sentencing authority, it came with no new sources of funding and failed to address the substantial economic challenges tribes are already facing in providing fundamental public services to their communities such as police and courts. Tribes that wish to build their own justice system are generally left to fund that system with only tribal resources. Like the federal and state systems, tribal resources are limited, and tribes must make balanced decisions on where and how they will invest those resources. The Committee should be encouraged by the time invested by tribes to ensure that the decisions they make are right today and right for the future of the tribe.

. . .

The Tribal Law and Order Act still leaves the tribes reliant upon federal prosecution of many crimes, and the U.S. Attorney will still decline to prosecute some major offenses. In situations where the U. S. Attorney's Office chooses not to prosecute, expanded authority gives tribal courts the capacity to more appropriately sentence violent offenders. As I acknowledged in 2008 although crimes requiring long-term jail sentences are not a common occurrence at Tulalip, in those situations where the court is faced with prosecuting serious violent crimes, it is important for the tribal court to have appropriate sentencing authority. At Tulalip, our focus is on alternatives to incarceration aimed at promoting positive personal changes, healing and preventing recidivism. There are, however, times when the tribal court is faced with violent offenders in which longer incarceration periods are necessary and vitally important. Because we are mindful that expanded sentencing authority comes with increased infrastructure demands and incarceration expenses we are carefully reviewing and amending our tribal code to apply the expanded authority to only the most serious of offenses.

The expense of incarceration may be the highest hurdle for tribal courts to clear before expanded sentencing will be imposed. The GAO Report on Indian Country Criminal Justice, published in February 2011, confirmed that detention space and the cost of detention are major issues for all surveyed tribes. Unless the incarceration costs are assumed or reimbursed by the federal government, few tribes will be able to bear that expense. Regionally, non-tribal governments spend over 70% of their general fund resources on law and justice expenses, and jails are the largest line item in that budget. Few tribes will be willing or able to divert those types of resources from funding sources desperately needed for housing, education, and healthcare. While the federal Bureau of Prisons pilot project to house tribal inmates is notable, it is unlikely to offer a viable long-term solution for all tribes to address this significant expense.

Source: Pouley, Theresa M. "The Tribal Law and Order Act One Year Later: Have We Improved Public Safety and Justice throughout Indian Country?" Testimony before the U.S. Senate Committee on Indian Affairs. Washington, D.C.: September 22, 2011.

See also: Violence Against Women Act, Title IX: Safety for Indian Women, 2013

Further Reading

Deer, Sarah. *The Beginning and End of Rape: Confronting Sexual Violence in Native America.* Minneapolis: University of Minnesota Press, 2015.

Deer, Sarah. "Native Women: Protecting, Shielding, and Safeguarding Our Sisters, Mothers, and Daughters." Testimony before the U.S. Senate Committee on Indian Affairs Oversight Hearing. Washington, D.C.: July 14, 2011. Accessed July 1, 2016. http://www.indian.senate.gov/sites/default/files/upload/files/Sarah-Deer-testimony.pdf

Government Accounting Office. "U.S. Department of Justice Declinations of Indian Country Criminal Matters," GAO-11-167R, December 2010. Accessed July 1, 2016. http://www.gao.gov/new.items/d11167r.pdf

Government Accounting Office. "Tribal Law and Order Act: None of the Surveyed tribes Reported Exercising the New Sentencing Authority, and the Department of Justice Could Clarify Tribal Eligibility for Certain Grant Funds." GAO-12-658R: May 2012. Accessed July 1, 2016. http://www.gao.gov/assets/600/591213.pdf

Greenfeld, Lawrence and Steven Smith. "American Indians and Crime." Bureau of Justice Statistics, U.S. Department of Justice, February 1999. Accessed July 1, 2016. http://www.bjs.gov/content/pub/pdf/aic.pdf

Indian Law and Order Commission. "A Roadmap for Making Native America Safer: Report to the President and Congress of the United States," November 2013. Accessed July 1, 2016. http://www.aisc.ucla.edu/iloc/report/files/A_Roadmap_For_Making_Native_America_Safer-Full.pdf

National Congress of American Indians. "Implementation Chart: VAWA Enhanced Jurisdiction and TLOA Enhanced Sentencing." April 2016. Accessed July 1, 2016. http://tloa.ncai.org/documentlibrary/2016/06/Implementing%20Tribes%206.8.16.pdf

Pouley, Theresa M. "The Tribal Law and Order Act One Year Later: Have We Improved Public Safety and Justice throughout Indian Country?" Testimony before the U.S. Senate Committee on Indian Affairs. Washington, D.C.: September 22, 2011. Accessed June 12, 2015. http://www.indian.senate.gov/sites/default/files/upload/files/Theresa-Pouley-testimony.pdf

Reaves, Brian. "Tribal Law Enforcement, 2008." Bureau of Justice Statistics, U.S. Department of Justice, June 2011. Accessed July 1, 2016. http://www.bjs.gov/content/pub/pdf/tle08.pdf

U.S. Department of Justice. "Indian Country Investigations and Prosecutions 2013." Department of Justice Report to Congress. Washington, D.C.: May 2013. Accessed July 1, 2016. http://www.justice.gov/sites/default/files/tribal/legacy/2014/08/26/icip-rpt-cy2013.pdf

Assimilative Crimes Act, 18 U.S.C.A. 13 (1825).
Duro v. Reina, 495 U.S. 676 (1990).
Federal Enclaves Act, 18 U.S.C.A. 1152 (1817).
Indian Civil Rights Act, 25 U.S.C. 1301 (1968).
Indian Self-Determination and Education Assistance Act, 25 U.S.C.A. 450a-n (1975).
Major Crimes Act, 18 U.S.C.A. 1153 (1885).
Oliphant v. Suquamish Indian Tribe, 435 U.S. 191 (1978).
Public Law 280, 18 U.S.C.A. 1162 (1953).
Talton v. Mayes, 163 U.S. 196 (1896).
Tribal Law and Order Act 25 USC 2801 (2010).
United States v. Henry, 432 F.2d 114 (9th Cir. 1970).
United States v. Mazurie, 419 U.S. 544 (1975).
United States v. McBratney, 104 U.S. 621 (1881).

8

Twenty-First Century, 2000–Present

Idle No More, 2012

Alan Lechusza Aquallo

Chronology

October 18, 2012 The Canadian Federal Government sidelines Bill C-45, its omnibus budget implementation bill. The bill contains measures that would alter key provisions of the Indian Act, removing protections for forests and waterways, notably the Navigable Waters Protection Act of 1882. Many environmentalists and First Nation groups object.

November 10, 2012 Jessica Gordon, Sylvia McAdams, Sheelah McLean, and Nina Wilson organize a conference at 20 Station West in Saskatoon, calling it "Idle No More." The women set up a Facebook page and website delineating their opposition to the provisions of Bill C-45 and the administration of Prime Minister Stephen Harper and Governor-General David Johnston.

November 17, 2012 Parallel events are held across Canada in Regina, Prince Albert, North Battleford, Saskatchewan, and Winnipeg.

December 10, 2012 A National Day of Action initiates a series of rallies, protests, and teach-ins in the various cities. Attawapiskat Chief Theresa Spence declares at a National Day of Action event in Ottawa that she will start a hunger strike December 11 to garner a meeting with Stephen Harper and David Johnston.

December 11, 2012	Chief Theresa Spence begins a hunger strike that lasts 43 days.
December 14, 2012	Bill C-45 passes, becoming law.
December 17, 2012	Protesters in Regina descend upon a shopping mall for a flash-mob style protest. A group of First Nation dancers perform a round dance at Cornwall Centre that Monday evening. Further round dances take place in London, England, Prague, Czech Republic, New York, New York, and Mall of America in Minnesota.
December 21, 2012	The Idle No More movement presents a national day of protest. More than 1,000 protesters march to Parliament Hill after meeting with Theresa Spence, who is on a hunger strike. National Assembly of First Nations Chief Shawn Atleo addresses the crowd, calling for all Canadians to support the movement. Demonstrations of Spence's cause take place in the United States.
December 30, 2012	Protesters block a major train line that runs between Toronto and Montreal, affecting thousands of passengers.
January 13, 2016	Professor and Assembly of First Nations co-leader Pamela Palmater holds interviews with the American media.
January 4, 2013	Prime Minister Stephen Harper agrees to meet with a commission of the Assembly of First Nations on January 11. Spence agrees to attend but will continue her hunger strike.
January 5, 2013	A court order shuts down a protesters blockade that was obstructing Canadian National Railway traffic between Moncton and Mirimachi.
January 6, 2013	Protesters block a Via Rail Canada Toronto-Montreal corridor, causing travel delays of up to two hours for more than 1,000 passengers.
January 7, 2013	Senator Patrick Brazeau, a former National Chief of the Congress for Aboriginal Peoples publicaly disapproves of the Idle No More movement's methods. He offers to meet with Theresa Spence, but Spence refuses.
January 9, 2013	Spence announces that she will not attend the January 11 meeting with Stephen Harper and the First Nations delegation after Governor-General David Johnston declines to attend.

January 10, 2013	Controversy over who will attend the meeting, and where it will be held, places the actual meeting in jeopardy. The confusion further causes a strain on the relationship between the federal government and the First Nations.
January 11, 2013	The meeting between Stephen Harper and the First Nations commences. The meeting itself, however, is trumped by ongoing protests outside of the prime minister's office building. Consequently, the attempt to use this meeting as a facilitator for multi-level change is a failure.
January 13, 2013	Three prominent Canadians—Maude Marlow, Naomi Klein, and Sarah Slean return their Diamond Jubilee Medals in solidarity with Theresa Spence.
January 16, 2013	A group of Cree children commence a 1,600 kilometer walk from Whapmagoostui, Quebec to Parliament Hill.
January 17, 2013	Former Canadian Prime Minister Paul Martin, who was influential in the Kelowna Accords of 2005, a series of agreements between the governor of Canada and the five aboriginal societies in Canada, states that the federal government has no understanding of aboriginal issues.
January 24, 2013	Theresa Spence ends her hunger strike after a meeting with the New Democratic Party leader Tom Mulcair and Liberal leader Bob Rae, who signed her declaration of commitments.
February 27, 2013	Idle No More supporters confront conservative pundit Tom Flanagan about changes to the Indian Act.
June 21, 2013	Movement supporters mark National Aboriginal Day with events including a march on Parliament Hill.
October 7, 2013	The Idle No More movement organizes a nationwide Day of Action.

Introduction

It's an assimilatory agenda. That's the whole basis for assimilation and colonial policies, and none of that has changed over time. They [Canadian government] have a whole suite of legislation ever since they've been in [power] that has been very nearly unanimously opposed—certainly by First Nations groups anyway . . . [a]nd they all have a very, very similar theme, focusing on individual rights, disbanding communal rights, and focusing what will benefit Canadians, as opposed to what will benefit First Nations." —*Pam Palmeter, First Nations Activist* (Poynter 2013)

History and Outline of the Idle No More Movement

The Idle No More movement has often been called "Canada's indigenous 'Occupy' movement"—equating this indigenous activist movement with the Occupy Wall Street (OWS) movement in the United States (2012)—by many news media sources since it began in the latter part of 2011. However, this indigenous movement is different from the OWS movement in that it involves peoples with shared histories, experiences, goals, and aspirations. As defined by Pam Palmeter, "Indigenous [p]eoples are all related, we all care about each other's futures and we share the same responsibility to protect our rights, cultures and identities for our seventh generation. This movement [Idle No More] has a special spiritual significance in that this was prophesied—that the seventh generation would rise and restore the strength of our Nations, bring balance and see that justice was restored to our [p]eoples" (Jan. 2013).

The Idle No More movement and its supporters march near the Ambassador Bridge in Windsor, Canada, on the National Day of Action. Idle No More was founded by First Nations women in Canada in 2012 and has inspired numerous protests throughout North America. (age fotostock/Alamy Stock Photo)

The founders of the movement, however, decided upon this slogan as a motivational tool in order to advocate for First Nations rights in light of 2011 legislation passed, specifically Bill C-45, by the Administration of Prime Minister Stephen Harper and Governor-General David Johnston, which sought to greatly limit indigenous, aboriginal, and First Nations sovereignty within Canada. The mission statement for this movement reads, "Idle No More call on all people to join in a revolution which honors and fulfills indigenous sovereignty which protects the land and water" (CBC, 2013). The first public reference of the Idle No More campaign came from a tweet on November 4, 2011, by Jessica Gordon which stated, "@shawnatleo wuts being done w #billc45 evry1 wasting time talking about Gwen Stefani wth!? #indianact #wheresthedemocracy #IdleNoMore" (CBC, 2013).

The first organized public responses toward the Harper administration and the second omnibus Bill C-45, took place in November 2012 with a "teach-in" by the four founding women in regards to the bill, a "day of action" on December 10, 2012, and a flash-mob round dance on December 17, 2012, which took place at the Cornwall Centre in Regina, Canada. A video of this event was published on YouTube and went viral overnight, solidifying the Idle No More movement (CBC, 2014). Following the success of the first "day of action," a second one was established on January 28, 2013. Further actions in response to the Harper administration and the second omnibus Bill C-45 included a protest by First Nations/indigenous chiefs during the Assembly of First Nations (AFN), a six-week hunger strike by the Chief of the Attawapiskat Chief Theresa Spence, and further flash-mob round dances, which expanded well beyond the Canadian borders, including London, England, Prague, Czech Republic, New York, New York, and the Mall of America in Minnesota.

First Nations Peoples nationally are organized within the Assembly of First Nations (AFN), made up of elected band chiefs from across Canada. There are also traditional governing bodies with hereditary chiefs in the First Nations communities, which are often not acknowledged by the Canadian government, who remain central to indigenous struggles and advocate for the rights of First Nations self-government and sovereignty. It is important to recall that First Nations consider themselves to be sovereign peoples who have historically entered into agreements, or treaties, with Canada and the British Crown. Through such treaty relationships, First Nations land is recognized and cannot be taken without indigenous consent, thereby establishing the current course of relationship between the Canadian government and its responsibilities to the First Nations. This relationship is outlined within the Indian Act, where the Canadian federal government has a controlling majority of as much as 75 percent of the fiduciary ties between the First Nations and the Crown (2013), while individual provinces—which are largely impoverished with limited self-sustaining resources—are left to bear the responsibility of providing for such vital resources as health and education. This discrepancy yields a complicated patchwork of governance and responsibilities that is viewed by many First Nations as a means to limit their approach to full and complete sovereignty.

Idle No More (http://idlenomore.ca)—which maintains the Twitter hashtag, #idlenomore—is an informal First Nations-led movement that came from online conversations among four women—Jessica Gordon, Sheelah McLean, Sylvia McAdam, and Nina Wilson—in Saskatchewan, Canada, who were concerned about the implications of the Bill C-45, introduced in Ottawa, Canada, on October 18, 2012. Bill C-45—also known as the second omnibus budget bill—is a sweeping piece of budget legislation that critics state would set into peril the protection of thousands of Canadian streams and lakes—including those on First Nations territories and reserves—and amends the Canadian Indian Act without consulting First Nations, therefore working toward the erosion of indigenous sovereignty. Bill C-45 was passed into law on December 14, 2012, and is now commonly known as the Jobs and Growth Act, 2012. This act changes the legislation contained within 64 acts or regulations. The Idle No More movement has focused upon three provisions within this act as foundational to the socio-political campaign for First Nations equity and social justice: The Indian Act, Navigation Protection Act (formerly known as Navigable Waters Protection Act), and Environmental Assessment Act.

Each change within Bill C-45 would present the following: The Indian Act—First Nations communities, with the passing of Bill C-45, are able to leave designated reserve lands if a majority attending a meeting called for such a purpose to vote to do so, regardless of the number of attendees. Previously, approval for such action required the support of a majority of eligible voters from the tribe in question. The Canadian Aboriginal Affairs Minster can call such a meeting to consider surrendering band/tribal territory. The Minster may, likewise, choose to ignore a resolution from the band/tribal council presented in opposition to this decision at a meeting. The Idle No More movement claims that such changes will now allow for easier opening of treaty lands and territory to those outside of the band/tribe.

Changes within the Navigation Protection Act allow major pipeline and powerline project advocates to operate without direct legislation oversight, therefore providing open access to navigable waters without defining any potential damage to the waterways, even those that cross reserves. The Idle No More movement claims that such an amendment will remove the protection for 99.9 percent of lakes and rivers within Canada.

The Environmental Assessment Act was previously overhauled within the first omnibus budget bill, whereas the second omnibus bill, Bill C-45, reduces further the number of projects that would require assessment under older provisions. The

Idle No More movement objects to such fast-track approval process without due and just review.

Notable Figures Involved in Idle No More

Chief Theresa Spence of the Attawapiskat First Nation in northern Ontario became a strong visible image of the Idle No More movement with her six-week liquid diet hunger strike starting on December 11, 2012, as a measure to organize a meeting between Prime Minister Stephen Harper and Governor General David Johnston to discuss legislation and treaties authorized by Her Majesty the Queen as applied to First Nations Peoples. Prime Minister Harper first announced the meeting sought by Chief Spence to take place on January 4, 2013, which would then be followed further at the Crown-First Nations Gathering on January 24, 2012. The actual meeting between the AFN and the Harper administration took place on January 11, 2013.

Elder of the Cross Lake First Nation in Manitoba, Raymond Robinson, began a similar hunger strike on December 12, 2012, demanding that Ottawa repeal parts of its budget-implemented bill that removed environmental regulations, changed fisheries rules, and, amended the Indian Act, all without consulting First Nations Peoples. Ray Robinson's hunger strike concluded along with Chief Theresa Spence.

The elected Grand Chief of the Assembly of Manitoba Chiefs (2011), Chief Derek Nepinak, is a well-respected leader who became that face of the chiefs who were opposed to the January 11, 2012, meeting between the AFN and Prime Minister Harper. As of the time of writing, Chief Nepinak is overseeing discussions between Manitoba and some Ontario, Saskatchewan, and Alberta tribes as to whether to withdraw from or amend their relationship with the AFN.

The National Chief of the AFN, Chief Shawn Atleo, became the mediator between the chiefs across Canada and the Harper administration.

Sylvia McAdam, Sheelah McLean, Jess Gordon, and Nina Wilson are the four women from Saskatchewan, Canada, who organized the first "teach-ins" regarding the second omnibus Bill C-45, which then generated the Idle No More movement.

Further Reading

Brean, Joseph. "Separate and Equal Nations: The Academic Theory behind Idle No More." January 12, 2013. *National Post*. Accessed April 13, 2015. http://news.nationalpost.com /news/canada/separate-and-equal-nations-the-academic-theory-behind-idle-no-more

Canadian Press, The. "Idle No More: First Nations activist movement grows across Canada." *Maclean's*. December 16, 2012. Accessed April 6, 2015. http://www.macleans.ca /general/idle-no-more-first-nations-activist-movement-grows-across-canada/

Hopper, Tristin. "In the beginning: A look at the causes behind Idle No More." *National Post*. January 5, 2013. Accessed April 10, 2015. http://news.nationalpost.com/news /canada/in-the-beginning-a-look-at-the-causes-behind-idle-no-more

"Idle No More Day of Action held as parliament resumes." huffingtonpost.ca. January 28, 2013. Accessed March 6, 2015. http://www.huffingtonpost.ca/2013/01/28/idle-no-more -day-of-action_n_2566874.html

"Idle No More Protest Closes Cornwall Bridge to U.S." Huffingtonpost.ca. Accessed March 6, 2015. http://www.huffingtonpost.ca/2013/01/05/idle-no-more-cornwall_n _2415777.html

"Idle No More Sees Multiple Flash Mobs and Round Dances Today." Indian Country Today Media Network. December 29, 2012. Accessed May 9, 2015. http://indiancountrytoday medianetwork.com/2012/12/29/idle-no-more-sees-multiple-flash-mobs-and-round -dances-today-146630

Jarvis, Brooke. "Idle No More: Native-Led Protest Movement Takes on Canadian Govern-ment." *Rolling Stone,* February 4, 2013. Accessed February 8, 2016. http://www.roll ingstone.com/politics/news/idle-no-more-native-led-protest-movement-takes-on-cana dian-government-20130204

Laboucan, Keith (reporter) (December 18, 2012). "Driftpile Cree Nation launched Idle No More Alberta highway blockade" (News story). Canada: Aboriginal Peoples Television Network. http://aptn.ca/news/2012/12/18/driftpile-cree-nation-launched-idle-no-more -alberta-highway-blockade/

Poynter, Bilbo. "Idle No More: Canada's Indigenous 'Occupy' Movement." *The Christian Science Monitor,* January 10, 2013. Accessed February 8, 2016. http://www.csmo nitor.com/World/Americas/2013/0110/Idle-No-More-Canada-s-indigenous-Occupy -movement

Schultz, Kylie. "Idle No More: Canada's Growing Indigenous Rights Movement, Fast Going Global." January 5, 2012. theinternational.org. Retrieved April 6, 2015.

Violence Against Women Act Title IX: Safety for Indian Women, 2013

Anne Luna-Gordinier

Chronology

1790 Federal jurisdiction extends to non-Indians committing crimes against Indians in Indian Territory.

1817 The General Crimes Act expands federal jurisdiction over Indians and non-Indians committing crimes in Indian country, with the exception of crimes by Indians against Indians.

1885 The Major Crimes Act creates federal jurisdiction over seven (eventually 13) crimes committed by Indians in Indian country regardless of whether the victim is Indian or non-Indian. This is the first systematic intrusion by the federal government into the affairs of tribes.

1968 The Indian Civil Rights Act imposes most of the Bill of Rights on tribes for the exercise of jurisdiction, and limits sentences that may be imposed by tribal courts to a maximum of a $5,000 fine and one-year imprisonment for any crime.

1976 The White Buffalo Calf Woman Society is founded at the Rosebud Sioux Reservation. It is the first non-profit organization dedicated to advocacy on behalf of American Indian women victims of violence.

1978 The U.S. Commission on Civil Rights holds a forum entitled Consultation on Battered Women in Washington, D.C.

The U.S. Supreme Court holds in *Oliphant v. Suquamish Indian Tribe* that tribes lack criminal jurisdiction over non-Indians.

1980 The White Buffalo Calf Woman Society establishes the first domestic violence shelter on an Indian reservation.

1981 The first annual Domestic Violence Awareness Week is celebrated.

1984 The U.S. Department of Justice (DOJ) Task Force on Family Violence is established and submits a report examining the scope and impact of domestic violence in America. The report provides recommendations to improve law enforcement, criminal justice, and community response to offenses previously considered "family matters." Congress passes the Family Violence Prevention Services Act—the first time federal funds are designated for programs serving battered women and their children.

1985 The U.S. Surgeon General identifies domestic violence as a public health issue that cannot be addressed by the police alone.

1988 Congress amends the Victims of Crime Act, requiring state victim-compensation programs to make awards to victims of domestic violence.

1990 U.S. Senator Biden introduces the first Violence Against Women Act (VAWA). The Supreme Court holds that tribes do not have criminal jurisdiction over non-member Indians, in *Duro v. Reina.*

1991 Congress legislatively overturns *Duro*, affirming the inherent power of tribes to exercise power over all Indians.

1993 Senator Biden and the Senate Judiciary Committee conclude a three-year investigation into the causes and effects of violence against women.

1994 Senator Biden sponsors VAWA as part of the Violent Crime Control and Law Enforcement Act of 1994. On September 13, 1994, VAWA creates full faith and credit provisions requiring states and territories to enforce protection orders issued by other states, tribes, and territories.

1995 The Violence Against Women Grants Office (VAWGO) is created at the U.S. Department of Justice to implement grants programs for victims' services and provides police- and court-sensitivity training. VAWGO makes the first VAWA grants to tribes under the STOP Violence Against Indian Women (STOP VAIW) Program. President Clinton appoints Bonnie Campbell to head the U.S. Department of Justice's new Violence Against Women Policy Office (VAWO).

2002 VAWO changes its name to the Office on Violence Against Women (OVW). Legislation makes OVW a permanent part of the Department of Justice with a presidentially appointed, Senate-confirmed director.

2006 President George W. Bush signs VAWA 2005 into law on January 5, 2006. It authorizes numerous new programs, with an increased emphasis on violence against Indian women, sexual assault, and youth victims. The first OVW Tribal Consultation convenes with DOJ officials and tribal leaders in Prior Lake, MN.

2007 OVW makes its first awards under the Grants to Indian Tribal Governments program, a more comprehensive tribal program than was authorized by VAWA 2005, which replaces the STOP VAIW program.

2008 The Section 904 Violence Against Women in Indian Country Task Force holds its first meeting in Washington, D.C.

2010 President Barak Obama signs the Tribal Law and Order Act on July 29, 2010, to empower tribal governments to provide public safety and reduce violent crime in Indian country.

2013 President Obama reauthorizes VAWA on March 17, 2013. Title IX, Safety for Indian Women includes Section 904 extending concurrent tribal criminal jurisdiction over violations of protection orders and domestic violence crimes involving non-Indians.

2014 Three tribes begin pilot projects to expand their jurisdiction and implement Section 904 provisions on February 6, 2014: Pasqua Yaqui, Tulalip, and the Confederated tribes of the Umatilla Indian Reservation.

2015 As of March 7, 2015, all federally recognized tribes may exercise special domestic violence criminal jurisdiction without permission from the DOJ.

Enhancing Tribal Sovereignty through the Violence Against Women Act

Domestic violence is a complex problem that pervades all of American society. Across all racial groups, violence against women is primarily domestic violence: 64 percent of women who reported being raped, physically assaulted, and/or stalked since age 18 were victimized by a current or former husband, cohabiting partner, boyfriend, or date (Tjaden and Thoennes 2000, iv). At least 70 percent of the perpetrators of violent crimes against American Indians are non-Indians (Greenfeld and Smith 1999, vi). American Indian/Alaskan Native women experience violent victimization at a greater rate than any other racial group (Tjaden and Thoennes 2000, 22). This is particularly troubling because prior to colonization, domestic violence was uncommon in traditional Native cultures (Murray 1998, 5). Some explanation for this disconnection lies in the understanding that the imposition of hierarchical legal and social structures tied the hands of tribes to do what is right for their own people. This distressing problem can be resolved by empowering tribes to once again create and enforce culturally appropriate modes of resolution. The Violence Against Women Act (VAWA) may be a vehicle for this end. Once tribes set about creatively utilizing VAWA, they may develop a multitude of tactics not only to address domestic violence on the reservation, but also to further tribal sovereignty. The methods that are most likely to be successful are those rooted in tribal values and traditions. Tribes should incorporate these considerations into codes, protocols, training, and prevention programs, to ensure that they play an integral part in law enforcement. This will promote law and order on the reservation as well as help to further tribal sovereignty.

Criminal Justice and Violence Against Women

In general, domestic violence presents a complex problem for victims and the criminal justice system because the behavior may consist of a series of ongoing noncriminal and criminal acts. In the case of stalking, when these noncriminal acts are taken into account together, they put the victim in a permanent state of physical and mental onslaught (Stevenson 1997, 7). Stalking and domestic violence often further victimize a person by restricting their access to usual activities such as maintaining a job or sending their children to school. This cycle of control extends to poor utilization of law enforcement as well.

According to National Violence Against Women Survey (NVAW) survey, only 55 percent of women victims reported stalking to the police (Atwell 2002, 83). In addition to the victimization resulting from domestic violence and stalking, victims are further stressed by the rigors of the criminal justice system. Stalking, like

---

Sidebar 1: A Statistical Dilemma: Violence against American Indian and Alaskan Native Women

American Indians and Alaska Natives are 2.5 times more likely to experience violent crimes, and at least two times more likely to experience rape or sexual assault crimes, compared to all other races.

Sixty-one percent of American Indian and Alaska Native women have been assaulted in their lifetimes, whereas 52 percent of African American women, 51 percent of white women, and 50 percent of Asian American women have been assaulted.

Thirty-four percent of American Indian and Alaska Native women will be raped in their lifetimes, compared to 19 percent of African American women, 18 percent of white women, and seven percent of Asian and Pacific Islander women.

Thirty-nine percent of American Indian and Alaska Native women will be subjected to violence by an intimate partner in their lifetimes, compared to 29 percent of African American women, 27 percent of white women, 21 percent of Hispanic women, and 10 percent of Asian women. (Futures Without Violence 2015)

"the gendered crimes of rape and domestic violence . . . depends on evidence of victim noncompliance with the defendant and evidence that the victim did not precipitate or encourage the defendant's behavior" (Dunn 2002, 3). The actions and character of the victim are often a focus of scrutiny leading to further frustration with law enforcement (Dunn 2002, 2). This creates a barrier to resolution even while the primary victimization continues unabated.

Few tribes have the legal codes in place to address stalking and domestic violence adequately. Perhaps this is because their cultures were forced to change rapidly to accommodate new social ills that had been kept under control through traditional means. Rather than focusing on reactionary measures to domestic violence, tribal societies were more likely to focus on prevention from the beginning. This was enforced and perpetuated by community and familial accountability. This is not to say that remedies for persistent and irredeemable behavior did not exist, however. Varying approaches to domestic regulation reflected the traditions, religious beliefs, and governmental structures of each society (Murray 1998, 8). Regardless of the approach, it is certain that tribal nations and families once successfully regulated issues of violence in their own culturally specific ways (Murray 1998, 5).

History of Federal Indian Policy

Integral to addressing the issues around violence against Indian women is an understanding of the complex legal issues surrounding tribal jurisdiction. Tribes once exerted full sovereignty over their land, government, and people, however, their powers have been whittled away over time. The history of federal Indian policy has hampered tribes from exercising control over their reservations in culturally compatible ways.

The Self-Determination era has led to renewed control over reservation resources and governance. However, the United States Supreme Court's Indian Country criminal and civil jurisdictional model radically cut back on the rights of tribes to regulate activities by non-Indians on the reservation. Treaties are no longer a respected basis for tribal sovereignty in the United States. Most areas of tribal life, including law enforcement, economic development, and governance, are affected by these decisions. In order for tribes to resolve these problems, they have had to seek new avenues for resolution.

Tribal control over reservation law and order is imperative for tribal sovereignty, and it is one of the few areas where tribal jurisdiction has been upheld. In order to succeed, tribes must balance the goals of tribal sovereignty with state and federal needs for accountability in an increasingly hostile legal environment. Only with time, education, regained political power, and respect for traditional cultures can tribes re-envision themselves successfully.

Shifting Federal Policy

In his attempt to clarify federal Indian law, Professor Felix Cohen addressed the position of tribal power within the American system of governance. Cohen concluded that the course of judicial decision followed three basic principles. First, prior to European contact, a tribe possessed "all the powers of any sovereign state" (Cohen 1982, 51). Second, the European process of "conquest" makes the tribe subject to the legislative power of the United States and, essentially, destroys the external powers of sovereignty of the tribe (Cohen 1982, 52). Finally, tribes retained internal sovereignty "subject to qualification by treaties and by express legislation of Congress" (Ibid). In this way, tribal powers generally were not "delegated powers granted by express acts of Congress" but instead are inherent powers of limited sovereignty that has not been extinguished (Ibid). In addition, provisions of Indian treaties that might undercut tribal authority were also read narrowly, based on some key assumptions: the treaty transaction was a cession of rights by the tribe rather than a granting of rights by the United States. These cessions, along with all other treaty provisions, were to be interpreted as the Indians would have understood them.

In many areas, tribes have been shackled by federal government bureaucracies. However, new avenues for cooperation have allowed tribes to take over control of many of their resources. The Indian Self-Determination and Education Assistance Act of 1975 gave tribes the authority to contract for and receive grants from the direct operation of Department of Interior and Health and Human Services programs serving their tribal members. Under the Act, tribal programs are funded by the federal government, but the programs are planned and administered by the tribes themselves. Some tribes have implemented reforms that bypass the Bureau of Indian Affairs (BIA), streamline tribal committees, and increase accountability.

One extremely important aspect of federal Indian law is that while policy has shifted, many of the statutes passed in each policy era were never overturned. Courts regularly have to interpret statutes based on congressional intent, even when a later Congress has expressly ended that policy and enacted new legislation. This puts courts in the powerful position of choosing how to direct Indian policy from a checkered past. This runs to the detriment of tribes, so tribes have sought other avenues to address their concerns.

An End to Criminal Jurisdiction Over Non-Indians

Oliphant v. Suquamish was decided against a backdrop of 150 years of federal criminal legislation that assumed an absence of tribal governmental authority to punish non-Indians who violated tribal laws (435 U.S. 191 (1978)). The case turned on whether the federal jurisdiction was exclusive or whether the tribal court had concurrent jurisdiction. The issue was important because if a tribe did not have authority, it would not be able to exercise criminal sanctions against non-Indian offenders. Tribal members seeking justice would have to petition the U.S. attorney, often located hundreds of miles away, to prosecute even minor offenses in federal court.

The Supreme Court held that "Indians do not have criminal jurisdiction over non-Indians absent affirmative delegation of such power by Congress." No treaty cession or congressional abrogation supported this conclusion. Instead, the Court fell back upon the theory of diminished tribal authority prohibiting tribes from exercising powers "inconsistent with their status" as domestic dependent nations.

Even though the Court found no statute or treaty provision that removed the Suquamish tribe's criminal jurisdiction over non-Indians, the Court held that by "implication" the Suquamish tribe's judiciary had no such jurisdiction. It even went so far as to hold that as a whole, "Indian tribes do not have inherent jurisdiction to try and punish non-Indians."

Sidebar 2: Significant Cases and Legislation Affecting Criminal Jurisdiction in Indian Country Following *Oliphant v. Suquamish Indian Tribe*

In *U.S. v. Mazurie*, the U.S. Supreme Court found that tribes have independent authority over matters that affect their internal and social relations. Tribes may pass laws with criminal implications that are enforceable through criminal prosecution in federal court. *Mazurie* did not expand tribal criminal jurisdiction via enforcement through tribal courts.

In *Duro v. Reina*, the Court stated that tribes retained the level of sovereignty needed to control their internal relations, preserve their customs, and social order. The Court attempted to unify the precedents by articulating a theory of consent to government. Voluntary tribal membership and the right of participation in tribal government justify tribal criminal jurisdiction over members. This ruling removed tribal jurisdiction over non-member Indians on the reservation.

The *Duro* decision created a jurisdictional gap in Indian country because states lacked criminal jurisdiction in Indian Country, and the federal government usually only prosecuted crimes under the Major Crimes Act due to funding constraints. Congress responded in 1991 by amending the Indian Civil Rights Act to (1) recognize and affirm the inherent power of Indian tribes to exercise criminal jurisdiction over all Indians, and (2) explicitly expand the definition to include any person defined as an Indian under the Major Crimes Act to be within the criminal jurisdiction of tribal courts.

National Farmers Union Insurance Companies v. Crow Tribe of Indians asserted that the basis of federal jurisdiction to assess tribal court authority is neither constitutional nor statutory in nature, but is grounded in federal common law. Tribal court authority was limited to those crimes occurring on reservation lands.

Congress passed the Tribal Law and Order Act (TLOA) in 2010. Its purpose is to empower tribal governments to provide public safety and reduce violent crime in Indian country. As of 2016, only ten of eligible tribes were exercising TLOA's new sentencing authority, and 15 were close to implementation. Most tribes reported challenges due to funding limitations, and it is still unclear how TLOA will affect the criminal prosecution of non-Indians in Indian Country.

Congressional Solutions to Gaps in Criminal Jurisdiction

Congress responded to concerns about gaps in jurisdiction by amending the Indian Civil Rights Act to (1) recognize and affirm the inherent power of Indian tribes to exercise criminal jurisdiction over all Indians, and (2) explicitly expand the definition to include any person defined as an Indian under the Major Crimes Act (18 U.S.C.A. §1153) to be within the criminal jurisdiction of tribal courts.

The Court decided that cases that conflict with this are exceptions to this general rule. The first exception is consensual relationships, such as marriage, contracts, licensing, or leases, which are subject to tribal jurisdiction. This exception does not include unmarried couples where one partner is non-Indian. Living within reservation boundaries does not constitute a consensual relationship. *Oliphant* could have robbed tribes of the right to try non-Indian stalkers and perpetrators of violence in tribal courts. The second exception is when tribes need to protect the political integrity, economic security, health, and welfare of the tribe. One could logically extend regulation of violent acts perpetrated by non-Indians against tribal members under the second exception.

The Violence Against Women Act

In 1994, U.S. Senator Joseph Biden sponsored the Violence Against Women Act (VAWA 1994) as part of the Violent Crime Control and Law Enforcement Act (42 U.S.C. 13701 (1994)). Signed into law on September 13, 1994, it requires a coordinated community response to domestic violence, sexual assault and stalking crimes, encouraging jurisdictions to engage multiple players to share experience and information to improve community-defined responses. VAWA 1994 also established grant programs through the Centers for Disease Control and Prevention, Department of Justice, and the Department of Health and Human Services. Specifically for Indian Country, VAWA 1994 included funding for a DOJ Services Training Officers Prosecutors Violence Against Indian Women (STOP VAIW) discretionary program. VAWA 1994 also created Tribes as States (TAS) status for creating and enforcing domestic violence and related codes. The program includes funds for training and technical assistance for tribal and state judges dealing with stalking and domestic violence cases (Stevenson 1997, 8). Of fundamental importance to Indian country, the statute requires every tribe and state to give full faith and credit to protective orders issued by other tribes and states (Ibid).

On October 28, 2000, President Bill Clinton signed the Violence Against Women Act of 2000 (VAWA 2000) into law under Division B of the Victims of Trafficking and Violence Protection Act of 2000. VAWA 2000 reauthorized essential programs, established new programs and strengthened federal laws. Critical to tribes, VAWA

2000 funded grants to tribal coalitions and expanded interstate stalking laws to include cyberstalking and added entering and leaving Indian Country to the interstate domestic violence and stalking crimes created by VAWA 1994.

The Violence Against Women Act of 2005 (VAWA 2005) was signed into law by President George W. Bush on January 5, 2006. VAWA 2005 authorized new programs and emphasized violence against Indian women, including culturally and linguistically specific services. The first DOJ Office on Violence Against Women (OVW) Tribal Consultation was convened at Prior Lake, MN with DOJ officials and tribal leaders. In 2007, the OVW made the first awards under the Grants for Tribal Governments program, which was more comprehensive than the original STOP VAIW program.

In 2008, the Section 904 Violence Against Women in Indian Country Task Force held its first meeting in Washington, D.C. On March 17, 2013, VAWA (VAWA 2013) was reauthorized with Title IX, Safety for Indian Women, including Section 904 extending concurrent tribal criminal jurisdiction over violations of protection orders and domestic violence crimes involving non-Indians. Three tribes were chosen for pilot projects to expand their jurisdiction and implement Section 904 provisions: Pasqua Yaqui, Tulalip, and Confederated tribes of the Umatilla Indian Reservation.

Support for Section 904 was strong, and numerous Native groups lobbied for the bill. Conservative lawmakers raised concerns that Section 904 might infringe defendants' constitutional rights. As a result, the final version of Section 904 was written narrowly. It only covers violations of protective orders or domestic violence that occur on federally recognized tribal land. To be prosecuted, the perpetrator must live or work on the reservation, have an intimate relationship with a tribal member, or have a substantial tie to the tribe. In cases where the defendant might be imprisoned, Section 904 adds civil rights protections for tribal courts. It requires tribes to offer judges with legal training, public defenders, a guarantee of effective assistance of counsel, and juries drawn from a cross section of the community at the tribe's expense.

The special domestic violence jurisdiction and civil rights provisions have been explored as part of the DOJ's pilot project since February 20, 2014. These experiences have exposed some jurisdictional gaps. The major hurdle is the inability to bring charges for crimes often occurring along with domestic violence, such as child abuse, sexual assault, substance abuse, property destruction, threats, and stalking. It is problematic to prosecute domestic violence and leave other charges to federal or state authorities. As a result, tribal prosecutors may find themselves deciding whether to prosecute only some of the crimes or to let go of jurisdiction and refer cases to other agencies.

As of March 7, 2015, all federally recognized tribes may exercise jurisdiction without permission from the DOJ. VAWA 2013 aims to recognize "the inherent powers of [a participating] tribe . . . to exercise special domestic violence criminal jurisdiction over all persons" (VAWA 2013). However, another provision requires tribes to give defendants "all other rights whose protection is necessary under the Constitution of the United States" (VAWA 2013). This could be interpreted as requiring tribes to provide defendants with the constitutional rights they would have in federal or state courts, even though tribes are not subject to the Constitution.

Even without a constitutional challenge, many tribes may not have the funding necessary to exercise VAWA jurisdiction. Tribes are eligible for federal funds, but they must compete for the grants, which takes a lot of work. Grants must be renewed regularly, require many administrative hours, and can be used only for specific activities. VAWA 2013 called for up to $5 million in grants for tribes implementing Section 904. Congress finally authorized $2.5 million in funds for the special domestic violence criminal jurisdiction program in 2016.

As a result, it has been difficult for tribes to develop and maintain the justice system infrastructure necessary for Section 904 jurisdiction. There is also concern that adopting Section 904 will undermine culturally specific court systems. The civil rights provisions of VAWA 2013 may even encourage some tribal justice systems to adopt a mainstream model.

Exercising Tribal Sovereignty to End Domestic Violence

One of the few areas where tribal sovereignty has been upheld is with VAWA. Divisions of the federal government have saved money and work hours by establishing government-to-government relationships with tribes so they can take over the administration of their own reservations. Tribes that do not establish these kinds of relationships with federal agencies will find it hard to maintain regulatory or legislative authority in the face of state challenges. Tribes must assert their jurisdiction wherever they can in order to prevent further destruction of their sovereignty.

The solutions to these problems are not simple. Tribes are faced with the awesome challenge of developing approaches to deal with constant change in the political and judicial climate. They should take over as many of the aspects of reservation management as they can. The easiest way is to start with areas where they have been granted TAS status. This enables tribes to demonstrate that they are competent in numerous areas of policy and regulatory development. Tribes should also focus on coalition building in order to rally support for new legislation supporting tribal sovereignty. One of the best ways for tribes to retain control over their reservations is to work within the framework of already-approved forms of jurisdiction while not limiting themselves to those areas.

Tribes would do well to create codes that integrate local, cultural, and multidisciplinary responses to violence before they attempt to adopt and implement them. They must develop formal criminal justice protocol to appropriately and effectively respond to violent crimes. They should form dedicated teams of police officers, prosecutors, court personnel, and parole and probation officers from existing domestic violence units. These teams should be trained to consistently investigate, monitor, arrest, and aggressively prosecute offenders. In addition, these teams need training in the use of federal interstate stalking and domestic violence laws as defined by VAWA. Tribes must also consider aggressively seeking multiple funding sources, since they generally lack sufficient financial resources for enforcement. Although Section 904 is a step in the right direction, multiple barriers still prevent Native victims of violence in Indian Country from seeking the safety and justice they deserve.

Once tribes set about creatively utilizing VAWA, they may develop a multitude of tactics not only to address domestic violence on the reservation, but also to further tribal sovereignty. The methods that are most likely to be successful are those rooted in tribal values and traditions. By designing, developing, and implementing their own culturally appropriate legal codes to address violent crimes against women, tribal governments not only will be able to protect their citizens, empower victims of violence and hold perpetrators accountable, they will also further their sovereignty.

Biographies of Notable Figures

Matilda (Tillie) Black Bear (Sicangu Lakota Nation/Rosebud Sioux tribe) is a nationally renowned victim's advocate often called the Grandmother of the Battered Women's Movement. Tillie was born in 1946 in St. Francis, South Dakota, to Dorothy Mousseaux and her biological father, James Black Bear. Her stepfather was Francis Crane. She was the third child of eleven with eight of her siblings born at home. Tillie is the mother three daughters, a grandmother of thirteen, and a survivor of domestic violence.

Tillie grew up speaking Lakota and learned traditional ways from her family. Her family was one of the first to bring the Sundance back to Rosebud reservation in 1960. They travelled to Washington, D.C., to get permission to practice their traditional spirituality openly. Tillie came from that rich tradition of resistance, which she credits with helping her achieve so much.

Tillie attended boarding school and graduated from St. Francis High School in 1965. She spent her first two years after high school attending the College of St. Mary's in Omaha, Nebraska. She went on to earn her Bachelor of Science in Sociology in 1971 from Northern State University in Aberdeen, South Dakota. She received a Master of the Arts in counseling from the University of South Dakota in 1974. She also completed course work for her PhD but did not complete her dissertation.

Over the years, Tillie worked as a therapist, certified school counselor, administrator, and comptroller. Tillie was director of student services from 1974 to 1977, a member of the Board of Regents from 1975–1976, and an instructor in the human services department at Sinte Gleska University in Mission, South Dakota. She also served on the St. Francis Indian School Board of Directors in St. Francis, South Dakota, and as a director of the Rosebud Sioux tribe's education department.

Tillie was a staunch advocate, inspirational voice, and respected leader of the battered women's movement since its beginnings. In 1976, Tillie organized her home community on the Rosebud reservation, serving as a founding mother to the White Buffalo Calf Woman Society (WBCWS). Formed to provide advocacy for battered American Indian women and their children, WBCWS was named for the deity who brought the Lakota the sacred pipe and who serves as a guide for proper conduct. Tillie partnered with the attorney general of the Rosebud Sioux tribe to implement a Tribal Council policy requiring mandatory arrest of perpetrators of violence against women and children. She worked to reclaim the sacredness of tribal women all over Turtle Island.

In 1978, Tillie began her national movement building by testifying at the first U.S. Commission on Civil Rights hearings on wife beating. The same year, Tillie acted as a founding mother of the National Coalition Against Domestic Violence (NCADV). She was also the first woman of color to chair NCADV. Tillie also led in building the South Dakota Coalition Against Domestic and Sexual Violence, where she sat on the board of directors.

In 1980, the WBCWS established the first Native women's shelter in the United States. Tillie maintained a guiding presence for the organization over the years. She served as executive director from 1987 to 1991 and returned to that position in 1996 for a total of fourteen years.

Tillie served on the advisory board of National Sexual Assault Resource Center, Pennsylvania and was a member of the professional advisory board of the National Domestic Violence Hotline in Austin, Texas. She was a council member for Clan Star National Technical Resource Center for VAWA Tribal Coalition grantees through the United States Department of Justice (DOJ).

For the next three decades, Tillie's leadership continued to indigenize federal legislation such as the Violence Against Women Act and the Family Violence Protection & Services Act. In 1995, after the passage of VAWA, Tillie met with the DOJ to ensure that VAWA included Indian tribes. In 2000, Tillie helped shape the VAWA tribal coalition program. In 2003, she led a Wiping of the Tears Ceremony at the Hart Senate Office Building to launch the struggle for the VAWA 2005 Safety for Indian Women Act. As part of the NCAI Task Force, Tillie met with the United Nations Special Rapporteur Rashida Manjoo in 2011 as a pathway to the VAWA 2013 victory, restoring criminal jurisdiction over non-Indians to Indian tribes. Also in

2013, Tillie again provided leadership to found the National Indigenous Women's Resource Center. Tillie also taught courses on cross-cultural ministry at Catholic Theological Union through Shalom Ministries out of Chicago for thirteen years.

Tillie's many awards and achievements include being honored twice by DOJ for her work with crime victims. She was named an Outstanding Young Woman in America in 1973 and 1977. She was a President Bush Points of Light Honoree in 1988. In 1989, her work at WBCWS was recognized with an award from DOJ's Victims of Crime Office. At the 1999 Millennium Conference on Domestic Violence in Chicago, Tillie was one of 10 individuals recognized as founders of the domestic violence movement in the United States In 2000, she received the Eleanor Roosevelt Human Rights Award from President Clinton.

In May 2003, Tillie was a recipient of the first annual LifeTime Achievement Award from LifeTime Television. She was also chosen as one of the recipients of the 21 Leaders for the 21st Century award by Women's ENews in 2004. In 2005, she received an award from the National Organization for Women. Tillie later received a 2009 Visionary Voice Award presented by the National Sexual Violence Resource Center. In 2014, she was also honored by the Native Women's Society of the Great Plains for her commitment and her contributions to the safety of women.

After a full and rewarding life, Tillie Black Bear walked on July 19, 2014. Her understanding of social change, organizing, and movement building continues to inspire advocates and policy makers to forge connections between shelter doors and Capitol Hill to end violence against women.

Eileen Luna-Firebaugh (Choctaw/Cherokee) is one of the most influential women in the field of American Indian law. She was born in 1945 in the Charlestown neighborhood of Boston, Massachusetts where she received her early public school education. She is the eldest of five children born to Glen and Mary Luna. Her family moved to Southern California on a relocation package in 1954. Like many relocatees, Glen struggled with alcoholism and related domestic violence. Glen left the family to fend for themselves on welfare when Luna-Firebaugh was 15. While attending high school in Imperial Beach California, Luna-Firebaugh worked as a babysitter to help support her family.

While on a full scholarship at the University of San Diego, Luna-Firebaugh became a political activist. As her activism cost Eileen her scholarship, she transferred to San Diego State University. There she helped establish one of the first women's studies departments in the United States, and she became active in one of the first Indian clubs. Her political involvement also included the free speech movement, the anti-war movement and extensive labor organizing. Luna-Firebaugh married Riley Gordinier in 1966. In 1969, while pregnant with her son Jeremy, her mother Mary passed, and Luna-Firebaugh and her husband took in her youngest two siblings and raised them.

After graduating from San Diego State, she immersed herself in union work and eventually attended the People's College of Law in Los Angeles. In 1976, during her second year of law school, Luna-Firebaugh had her daughter, Anne. She worked full time for the United Farm workers and later the Social Services Union.

In 1980, after receiving her J.D., and fueled by her background in social justice, she moved to Berkeley with her family to serve as the Executive Director of the Berkeley Police Review Commission (PRC). The PRC hears individual complaints and makes policy recommendations to ensure that Berkeley police officers act in a manner conforming to community standards.

In 1981, Luna-Firebaugh divorced her first husband. Subsequently, she met her second partner, Jon Read, a landscape architect, newspaper columnist, and social justice agitator. During this time, Luna-Firebaugh started the free legal clinic at Intertribal Friendship House (IFH) in Oakland. IFH serves as urban Indian homeland for American Indians in the Bay Area. From 1983 to 1994, she served on the executive board and later as the head.

In 1990, Luna-Firebaugh became the director of the Office of Civilian Complaint in San Francisco. In 1993, she began commuting to San Diego, where she launched the Citizen's Law Enforcement Review Board, the first countywide police review office in the country. The CLERB was the first civilian oversight agency to have jurisdiction over jails and probation officers. From 1992 to 1995, Luna-Firebaugh taught American Indian Studies classes at Palomar college, a community college serving the Native American community in northern San Diego County.

In 1995 she attended the Kennedy School of Government at Harvard University for a Master of Public Administration (MPA) program. After completing her MPA, Luna-Firebaugh became an assistant professor of Federal Indian Law and Policy in the American Indian Studies Program at the University of Arizona in Tucson. In 2000, Luna-Firebaugh and her partner, Read, separated.

In 2001, Luna-Firebaugh married her high school sweetheart, Dennis Firebaugh. Luna-Firebaugh soon became an associate professor and the Associate Chair of the American Indian Studies Program. Her publications focus on the development of international indigenous and tribal justice systems, tribal police, evaluation of human service programs on Indian lands, and juvenile community policing. She works on an international and tribal research project focused on the criminal justice barriers to higher education for American Indian juveniles and has undertaken an 18-month project for the U.S. Bureau of Justice Statistics to review all their materials referencing American Indians and criminal justice for consistency.

Luna-Firebaugh is the author of *Tribal Policing: Asserting Sovereignty, Seeking Justice,* published by the University of Arizona Press. She is a member of the faculty of the National Tribal Trial College, funded by the U.S. Department of Justice. In that capacity, she is a trainer of tribal judges, police, and prosecutors.

Luna-Firebaugh is a member of the Advisory Board for the Southwest Center on Law and Policy, funded by the U.S. Department of Justice, and of the Western Social Sciences Association, where she served on the executive board. She is a former associate justice of the Colorado River Indian Tribal Appellate Court, former member of the Advisory Board for the National Center for Responsible Gambling, and former member of the Advisory Board for the Harvard Medical School Division on Diversions Project on Pathological Gambling.

Luna-Firebaugh is a consultant to cities throughout the United States and to international governments seeking to reorganize their police complaint systems. She has worked with the Harvard Project on American Indian Economic Development, and tribal-level project coordinators, to evaluate the CIRCLE initiative (Comprehensive Indian Resources for Community and Law Enforcement). This U.S. Office of Justice Programs initiative provided three demonstration tribes (Northern Cheyenne tribe, Oglala Sioux tribe and Pueblo of Zuni) with the opportunity and resources needed to realign law enforcement and justice programs with tribal values and priorities. CIRCLE funded youth, victim services, law enforcement, domestic violence, tribal courts, and corrections programs. Equally important, it encouraged Indian nations to develop a linked, comprehensive strategy for using these funds.

Luna-Firebaugh was the principal investigator on a major, multi-year grant on reducing violence against women funded by the National Institute of Justice, which included over 130 tribal government programs. She was also the principal investigator for a National Institute of Health study of Australian Aboriginal family violence programs, conducted throughout Eastern and Southern Australia. In 2010, she served as a consultant for the United Nations Commission on Human Rights in Africa, the Soros Open Society Institute, and the Nigerian Police Services commission.

Luna-Firebaugh was recently awarded the Toihuarera Fellowship for research of Maori Programs aimed at developing juvenile diversion programs. In that capacity, she was a visiting professor at Victoria College of Law in Wellington, New Zealand, and was named a justice of the Rangatahi (juvenile) court.

DOCUMENT EXCERPTS

Service Provision and Funding Constraints in Indian Country, Carmen O'Leary (2011)

In 2011, Carmen O'Leary, Director of the Native Women's Society of the Great Plains, testified before the Senate Committee on Indian Affairs about the necessity of consistent program funding and accountability to secure safety for American Indian women.

I understand that numbers have been presented time and again about the need in Indian Country for increased services and accountability. And as a result of these numbers, various model programs have come and gone. But the instability and ongoing need for services remains a great problem in our communities. The funding that is available is usually discretionary and inconsistent. Too often, women in need of services find that the local DV/SA program is no longer funded or the services are no longer offered. This failure to provide services puts these women at increased risk for ongoing violence, and too often, death. To combat this, funding needs to be stabilized so the services are continuous and not just the duration of a two- or three-year grant. Funding these programs on a consistent, annual basis will directly and positively combat the problem of violence in our communities.

In addition to increasing the availability of services, we need to hold offenders accountable by increasing community accountability. How much time will it take to overcome decades of behavior that has been accepted due to offenders going unpunished and the community accepting the offender's actions as the status quo? This normalization of violence is imbedded deeply in our society today. I had the sad experience to observe one of the worst examples of this acceptance in a federal courtroom earlier this year. Thanks to the threat of increased sentencing, one pedophile plea bargained and was being sentenced. He had pled guilty; there was no jury or assumption of innocent at this point in his procedures. The victims who had courageously come forth all were current or former students at a Bureau of Indian Affairs school. The regional line officer of the Bureau of Indian Affairs and one of the principals of a local Bureau of Indian Affairs school wrote letters of support. But not for their students—for the pedophile. The principal sat behind the pedophile at the hearing, not behind the students. I am not sure any of us can understand the impact it must have had on these victims and those who love them—that the support of prominent people in their community supported the perpetrators, and dismissed the victims. Sadly, insult to injury is heaped on those strong enough to come forward. I find it completely inexcusable that federal employees, with a trust responsibility towards those they serve—namely the students—could act so egregiously.

As I travel across our region, I hear of the barriers that program advocates have to overcome simply to get help for those they serve. In some communities, there are no local services whatsoever. In others, there may be a local program, but when that program loses its vital funding, due to the end of a grant term or some other situation, there are no other local services for women in life threatening situations. In another community, the program staff may have to figure out one of four possible sites to take a sexual assault victim. Another program had to find a way to get women back from emergency services in a far off facility. There, the sexual assault victim was taken by ambulance to the emergency room sixty to hundred miles from home, and she was left to find her own way back with no resources. In all of these situations, very little effort has been made to plan for anything except the minimal medical response for victims. And it is the victims that suffer, often revictimized by the response process, or lack thereof, that they must face.

. . .

The long-term effects of violence to Indian women are well documented. We know that the damage to their quality of life endures well beyond the bruises. The fear they endure takes so much from women's lives and the lives of their families and our communities. Depression, substance abuse, and suicide are often the remnants of the violence in the lives of Native women and their children. It is hard to put a life back together after such violence. Then pile on the poverty, isolation, and blame that Native women subjected to violence must face. The outcome is crushing.

These are the barriers victims, women and children, come up against in small communities, over and over, in their hunt for safety and perhaps some sense of justice. For years, I have heard the stories of women and their children having to overcome huge barriers to be safe and survive in some overwhelming situations. Often times, the advocates who help victims are also threatened in numerous ways as they seek to help women and their children.

. . .

One important step is a return of criminal jurisdiction to Indian nations over crimes of domestic violence, stalking, dating violence and sexual assault by non-Indians. This type of jurisdictional fix is critical to enhancing the safety of Native Women. Many episodes of violence against Native women include perpetrators of another race who know that they can continue to offend without any consequences due to the unique and confusing jurisdictional rules present in Indian country. With a jurisdictional fix that restores tribal criminal jurisdiction over non-Indians for these limited crimes, the offender that goes unpunished under the current system might finally get what he deserves and his victim might finally achieve a sense of peace, knowing that justice was served.

Source: O'Leary, Carmen. "Native Women: Protecting, Shielding, and Safeguarding Our Sisters, Mothers, and Daughters," Testimony before the U.S. Senate Committee on Indian Affairs Oversight Hearing. Washington, D.C.: July 14, 2011.

Dear Colleague Letter Regarding VAWA Tribal Provisions, Senator Tom Udall (2012)

In 2012, U.S. Senators Akaka, Franken, Leahy, Murray, and Udall co-signed a "Dear Colleague" letter addressing the provisions of Section 904 of the Violence Against Women Reauthorization Act.

Under existing law, tribes have no authority to prosecute non-Indians for domestic violence crimes against their Native American spouses or partners on tribal lands. Yet over 50% of Native women are married to non-Natives and 76% of the overall population living on tribal lands are not Native Americans.

Currently, these crimes fall exclusively under federal jurisdiction. But federal prosecutors have limited resources and they may be located hours away from tribal communities. As a result, non-Indian perpetrators regularly go unpunished, their violence in allowed to continue and, all too often, it results in death for Native American women.

Section 904 of the Violence against Women Reauthorization Act provides a remedy for this serious criminal jurisdictional loophole. This tribal jurisdiction provision allows tribal courts to prosecute non-Indians in a very narrow set of cases that meet specific, reasonable conditions.

This provision does not extend tribal jurisdiction to include general crimes of violence by non-Indians, crimes between two non-Natives, or crimes between persons with no ties to the tribe. And nothing in this provision diminishes or alters the jurisdiction of any federal or state court.

Some question whether a tribal court can provide the same protections to defendants that are guaranteed in a federal or state court. The bill requires tribes to provide comprehensive protections to all criminal defendants who are prosecuted in tribal courts, whether or not the defendant is an Indian. Defendants would essentially have the same rights in tribal court as in state court.

Questions have also been raised about whether Congress has the constitutional authority to expand tribal criminal jurisdiction to cover non-Indians. This issue was carefully considered in drafting the tribal jurisdiction provision. The Indian Affairs and Judiciary Committees worked closely with the Department of Justice to ensure that the legislation is constitutional. Fifty prominent law professors sent a letter to Congress expressing their "full confidence in the constitutionality of the legislation, and in its necessity to protect the safety of Native women." Their letter provides a detailed analysis of the jurisdiction provision and concludes that "the expansion of tribal jurisdiction by Congress, as proposed in Section 904 of S. 1925, *is* constitutional."

Section 904 will create a local solution for a local problem. By allowing tribes to prosecute the crimes occurring in their own communities, they will be equipped to stop the escalation of domestic violence.

Right now, many Native women don't get the justice they deserve. We must act to eliminate a double standard in the law. Tribes are already successfully prosecuting, convicting, and sentencing Native Americans who commit crimes of domestic violence against Native American women. This bill would allow tribes to do the same when a non-Indian commits and identical crime.

Source: Udall, Tom. "VAWA Tribal Provisions" Dear Colleague letter, Washington, D.C.: April 24, 2012.

See also: *Oliphant v. Suquamish*, 1978; Tribal Law and Order Act, 2010

Further Reading

Atwell, Mary Weick. *Equal Protection of the Law? Gender and Justice in the United States.* New York: Peter Lang Publishing, Inc., 2002.

Bachman, Ronet, Heather Zaykowski, Rachel Kallmyer, Margarita Poteyeva, and Christina Lanier. "Violence Against American Indian and Alaska Native Women and the Criminal Justice Response: What is Known." *U.S. Department of Justice,* August 2008. Accessed June 10, 2015. https://www.ncjrs.gov/pdffiles1/nij/grants/223691.pdf

Cohen, Felix S. *Handbook of Federal Indian Law.* 1941. Reprint, Charlottesville: The Michie Company, 1982.

Dunn, Jennifer L. *Courting Disaster: Intimate Stalking, Culture, and Criminal Justice.* Piscataway, NJ: Aldine Transaction, 2002.

Futures Without Violence. "The Facts on Violence Against American Indian/Alaskan Native Women." Accessed June 10, 2015. https://www.futureswithoutviolence.org/userfiles/file/Violence%20Against%20AI%20AN%20Women%20Fact%20Sheet.pdf

Greenfeld, Lawrence and Steven Smith. "American Indians and Crime." Bureau of Justice Statistics, U.S. Department of Justice, February 1999. Accessed June 10, 2015. http://www.bjs.gov/content/pub/pdf/aic.pdf

Luna-Firebaugh, Eileen. *Tribal Policing: Asserting Sovereignty, Seeking Justice.* Tucson: University of Arizona Press, 2007.

Luna-Firebaugh, Eileen. "Violence Against Indian Women and the STOP VAIW Program." *Violence Against Women, an International and Interdisciplinary Journal,* Sage Publications, Inc. 12, 2 (July 2005).

Murray, Virginia H. "A Comparative Survey of the Historic, Civil, Common, and American Indian Tribal Law Responses to Domestic Violence." *Oklahoma City University Law Review* 23, 433 (Spring/Summer 1998).

O'Leary, Carmen. "Native Women: Protecting, Shielding, and Safeguarding Our Sisters, Mothers, and Daughters." Testimony before the U.S. Senate Committee on Indian Affairs Oversight Hearing, July 14, 2011. Accessed June 14, 2015. http://www.indian.senate.gov/sites/default/files/upload/files/Carmen-O-Leary-testimony.pdf

Tjaden, Patricia and Nancy Thonennes. "The Prevalence, Incidence, and Consequences of Violence Against Women: Findings from the National Violence Survey Against Women." National Institute of Justice & the Centers for Disease Control & Prevention, November 2000. Accessed June 10, 2015. https://www.ncjrs.gov/pdffiles1/nij/183781.pdf

Udall, Tom. "Violence Against Women Act Tribal Provisions," Dear Colleague letter, Washington, D.C.: April 26, 2012. Accessed June 12, 2015. http://www.ncai.org/resources/testimony/senator-udall-s-dear-colleague-letter-regarding-vawa-tribal-provisions

Duro v. Reina, 495 U.S. 676 (1990).
Indian Self-Determination and Education Assistance Act, 25 U.S.C.A. 450a-n (1975).
Major Crimes Act, 18 U.S.C.A. 1153 (1885).
National Farmers Union Insurance Companies v. Crow Tribe of Indians, 471 U.S. 845 (1985).
Oliphant v. Suquamish Indian Tribe, 435 U.S. 191 (1978).
Tribal Law and Order Act, 25 USC 2801 (2010).
United States v. Mazurie, 419 U.S. 544 (1975).
Violence Against Women Act, 42 U.S.C. 13701 (1994).

Canonization of Junípero Serra, 2015

Angela D'Arcy

Chronology

Time Immemorial/ 10,000–15,000 B.C.	Indigenous peoples—the ancestors of the citizens of the nearly 200 Native nations in California today—lived in the area now known as California. Each of these nations has origin, or creation, stories about how they came to exist.
1535	California first explored by the Spanish. Hernando Cortes leads expedition to La Paz.
1542	Juan Rodriguez Cabrillo lands at Point Loma in the area now known as San Diego Bay, where he claimed the land for Spain.
1769	"Sacred Expedition" launches from Baja, California. Fr. Junípero Serra founds San Diego de Alcala, the first of 21 missions established by the Catholic Church in California.
1769–1823	Twenty-one missions founded throughout California.
1771–1824	Various Native nations and indigenous peoples throughout the state organize resistance in the form of attacks on missions and mass escapes from the missions. See Sidebar 2 for more detailed discussion of these acts of resistance.
1773	Representación signed. Some refer to this as evidence of Serra's dedication to California Indians. The Representación has been referred to as the Indian Bill of Rights. However, this claim is disputed by others who argue that the Representación was actually about consolidating power in the church rather than the state and had little or nothing to do with rights for Indians.

1784	Serra dies at Mission San Carlos Borromeo de Carmelo in what is now known as Carmel, California.
1806	Great Stone Church in San Juan Capistrano collapses due to earthquake, killing 40 Acjachemen/Juaneno Indians. Descendants hold a gathering every year to this day in honor of the lives lost that day.
1834	Missions are secularized.
1835	Around 1835, Pablo Tac, from the San Luis Rey Luiseno Indians, writes *A Record of California Mission Life: Indian Life and Customs at San Luis Rey*. This writing is significant because it represents one of the only first-hand written accounts of mission life from someone who experienced it.
1934	Priests in Monterey, California make official request to initiate the process of canonization for Serra.
1948, 1949	Hearings on Serra's candidacy for sainthood are authorized by the Vatican's Sacred Congregation for the Causes of Saints and held in Fresno, California.
1988	Serra is beatified by Pope John Paul II, furthering his path to sainthood.
January 2015	Pope Francis announces intention to canonize Junípero Serra.
January– September 2015	Native nations, indigenous organizations, churches, educational and religious institutions, and art galleries host multiple events, gatherings, art exhibits, scholarly debates, peoples' tribunals, and other events in support of, and opposition to, Pope Francis's January announcement regarding canonization of Serra.
July 2015	Pope Francis apologizes on behalf of the church to indigenous people during his visit to Bolivia.
September 23, 2015	Pope Francis holds a celebratory mass in honor of sainthood for Serra at the Basilica of the National Shrine of the Immaculate Conception in Washington, D.C.

Introduction

The lives of indigenous peoples in California were altered forever when Junípero Serra landed off the coast of San Diego in 1769 and established the first California mission. Spanish era colonialism and the introduction of the mission system have had dire consequences for the Native Peoples who have been living in the area for at least ten thousand years, according to archaeological evidence and since time immemorial according to many of the nearly 200 Native nations who called California home.

Junípero Serra's name is well known throughout the state. Streets, parks, schools, and libraries are named after Serra, and his image is equally present via sculpture, paintings, mosaics, and other forms of art up and down the coast. For many, his name and the story of his role as a founder of California are a source of pride. For others, including many California Indian people and Native nations, his life and legacy represent loss of apocalyptic proportions. Due to the recent historic visit of Pope Francis to the United States in September 2015, and his announcement of sainthood for the Franciscan priest, Serra's name and legacy are now known around the world.

In order to understand why one religion's decision to designate one of its evangelizers from over 200 years ago a saint is causing such heated debates among scholars, communities, religious leaders, and Native People today, it is important to have a working understanding of California Indian history and the internationally utilized colonizing principle set forth in the Papal Bulls of 1452 and 1493, known as the Doctrine of Discovery.

This chapter introduces the concepts of colonialism and the Doctrine of Discovery, provides an overview of California Indian history with a focus on the mission period, defines canonization and sainthood, discusses the process by which one becomes a saint under Catholic law, and provides a timeline of the canonization process for Junípero Serra. Finally, the chapter concludes with a discussion of the major areas of controversy around canonization and how those opposing and supporting sainthood have responded.

Legitimizing Colonial Endeavors

The Doctrine of Discovery (DD)

DD is based on a series of Papal Bulls from the fifteenth century (Romero Institute, 2015) and has been used by European colonial powers to justify land dispossession from indigenous peoples throughout the world since then. The 1452 Papal Bull Dum Diversas authorized Portugal to "invade, capture, vanquish, and subdue all Saracens, pagans, and other enemies of Christ, to put them into perpetual slavery, and to take away all their possessions and property." This statement of colonial doctrine was followed by the Papal Bull Romanus Pontifex in 1493, which continued support for Christian dispossession of lands from non-Christians and legitimized enslavement of non-Christians throughout the world (Rotondaro 2015).

Sidebar 1: A Timeline of Doctrine of Discovery (DD) Justification

1452–1493	Papal bulls authorize Christian monarchies to claim all non-Christian lands and "vanquish and place in perpetual slavery/servitude any heathens, pagans, Saracens, or other non-Christian peoples" (SPIN). These are Doctrines of Discovery.
1537	Established under Pope Paul III, this papal bull reaffirmed that Indians should not be deprived of liberty or property or be enslaved. (Sublimis Deus, 1537) Doctrine repeatedly ignored by colonial governments.
1542	Juan Cabrillo claims land now known as California for Spain using DD to support claim.
1769	Sacred Expedition is designed to consolidate Spanish colonial power in Alta California begins, and Serra establishes the first mission.
1823	*Johnson v. McIntosh*—U.S. Supreme Court uses DD as the basis of its decision to legitimize dispossession of land from Native nations by holding that tribes possess only a "right of occupancy" rather than title to land (Frichner 2010).
1831	*Cherokee Nation v. Georgia*—U.S. Supreme Court holds that tribes are "domestic dependent nations" and that their relationship between tribes and the U.S. government is one of ward and guardian (Hon. Wiseman).
1955	*Tee-Hit-Ton Indians v United States*—U.S. Supreme Court holds that, due in part to the Tee-Hit-Tons being in the hunter-gatherer stage of civilization, they possess only a right of occupancy to the lands they have called home since time immemorial.
2007	Declaration on the Rights of Indigenous Peoples (UNDRIP) is adopted by the General Assembly of the United Nations. Although UNDRIP recognizes rights of indigenous peoples, it does not officially repudiate DD.
2009	Resolution calling for the repudiation of DD passes during the Episcopal Church's 76th General Convention (Resolution 2009-D035).
Present	Native nations continue to assert their rights as sovereign nations, and indigenous peoples around the world continue to appeal to governments and religious institutions to officially repudiate DD.

According to a report on DD prepared by the Special Rapporteur for the United Nations in 2010, DD enabled European Nations and Christian monarchies from the fifteenth century onward to "take over and profit from their [indigenous] lands and territories. . . . Centuries of destruction and ethnocide resulted from the application of the Doctrine of Discovery and framework of dominance to indigenous peoples and to their lands, territories and resources" (Gonella Frichner 2010).

Despite the fact that the papal bulls that inspired DD were created nearly 500 years ago, the ideology that indigenous peoples retain only a right of occupancy, and not a property title to lands they have occupied since time immemorial, remains a key legal principle in colonizing nations such as the United States, Canada, Australia, and New Zealand, throughout the world. It was also a key legal principle in Spain, Mexico, and U.S. colonizing efforts throughout California.

Franciscan friar Junípero Serra led the establishment of the first nine of twenty-one Spanish missions throughout the area of Alta, California, which was then part of the Spanish Empire. Pope Francis canonized him on September 23, 2015. Many Native Californians criticized Serra for the forced labor, beatings and whipping, and premature deaths of thousands of their ancestors under his supervision. (Library of Congress)

Spanish Colonization in Alta California

Although Spain first claimed territory in Alta California in 1542 when Juan Rodriguez Cabrillo landed at Point Loma in San Diego Bay and asserted title to the area for Spain under the Doctrine of Discovery, it would be nearly 200 years before Junípero Serra began the Sacred Expedition on behalf of his government. When Serra's expedition launched in 1769, Spain was anxious to establish a more permanent presence in the region due to fears of land encroachment from Russians moving south from Alaska, and the establishment of missions throughout the state supported this goal (Miranda 2015).

While Serra specifically represented the Catholic Church as a Franciscan priest, it is important to remember that at this point in European history the church and state were extremely connected in their goals and purpose. The number of non-military or church-affiliated colonists never reached more than 3,200 in Alta California, so the missions, with their aim of converting and "civilizing" the Indians, were important to maintain Spain's political and military control over the region. Additionally, the missions produced all of the colony's cattle and grain and were therefore economically valuable to Spain as well (West Film Project 2001).

These factors are important to note because they place the entire mission project, and Serra's leadership role in the endeavor, within the broader context of the political and military strategy of the Spanish empire during that time period. The establishment of missions, and the efforts to convert and maintain an Indian presence within the mission walls, were a critical component of Spain's ability to maintain and expand empire throughout Alta California.

Overview of California Indian History and the Mission Era

Indigenous Peoples in California before Colonization

Indigenous peoples have lived in California for a very long time—for at least 10,000–15,000 years, according to archaeological records rooted in the Euro-American scientific traditions and since time immemorial, according to songs and stories passed down for generations from elders to youth in Native communities. Today, there are over 170 federally recognized and unrecognized Native nations that can trace their roots to ancestral territories located in the area now known as California. Each Native nation has its own languages, histories, cultures, and unique stories about how its people came to exist in the area where they lived at the time of first contact with Spanish soldiers and missionaries.

Realities of the Mission System for California Indians

California Indian population at the time of contact is estimated at approximately 300,000. By 1860, only 30,000 California Indians remained (WFP 2001). In less than 300 years, the population decreased by nearly 90 percent. Sixty-thousand deaths were logged at California missions between 1769 and 1834. The death rate for the sixty-six years of mission operation was 13.3 percent for children and 5.9 percent for adults (Heizer 1978). Disease, in particular sexually transmitted diseases, was a significant factor in the rapid population decline among indigenous people in California. Syphilis, which was introduced by Spanish soldiers, was a major factor in rising death rates and declining birth rates since it also caused sterility (Archibald 1978).

In terms of conversion, while proponents of the mission system often point to large numbers of Indian converts—estimates place the number at around 81,000 baptisms (Heizer 1978)—as evidence of Serra's success and therefore justification for canonization, according to Professor Jonathan Cordero, an Ohlone and Chumash Sociology professor at California Lutheran University, based on mission records, fewer than 5 percent of all baptized California Indians were voluntary converts (Miranda, 2015).

According to proponents of Serra and the mission system, conversion was voluntary. However, once an Indian had been baptized, if he or she were to try to leave the mission grounds, he or she would be hunted down by soldiers and forcibly returned to the mission, often in shackles. Corporal punishment, sanctioned by Serra on multiple occasions in his own writings, was prevalent throughout the mission system. Women and men were both placed in stocks and flogged for transgressions. Twenty-one lashes with the whip was the limit placed on punishment of this sort (Archibald 1978). According to Padre Hora, a priest upset with the treatment of Indians at the missions, "The treatment shown to the Indians is most cruel. . . . for the slightest things they receive heavy floggings, are shackled and put in the stocks and treated with so much cruelty they are kept whole days without a drink of water" (Miranda 2015).

How Saints Are Made

Canonization is the process by which one is declared a saint and is a four-step process under Catholic law. Step one is a request. At least five years after the death of a person, a formal request can be made for sainthood (Sadlier 2014). In Serra's case, the request came 150 years after his death, in 1934, from one of the missions he founded in Monterey, California (Pinsky 1986).

The second step in the process is determination, which occurs once the bishop sends a formal report and request for review of the case to Rome where the candidate's life and writings are studied to make sure they comport with Church doctrine. Once a candidate is confirmed as virtuous and heroic in their faith, they are venerated (Sadlier 2014).

From 1934 to 1948, biographical information about Serra was gathered from around the world in support of his case. In 1948 and 1949, hearings on Serra were authorized by the Vatican's Sacred Congregation for the Causes of Saints and held in Fresno, California (Pinsky 1986). California Indians who objected to canonization were not allowed to participate in the hearings.

Sidebar 2: Indigenous Resistance during California's Mission Era

Time Immemorial–1500s	Area now known as California was home to hundreds of indigenous nations with distinct cultural, spiritual, ecological, and linguistic practices.
1769–1823	First Mission is established in San Diego, and 21 are established throughout Alta California over the next 50 years.
1771	One of the first recorded instances of Indian resistance to the mission system in California: Indians attack San Gabriel Mission. Historians believe that attack was triggered by a soldier's rape of a Kumivit woman (Castillo, 75).
1775	Kumeyaay Revolt Mission San Diego. Participants set the mission on fire and kill one priest. At least 15 Kumeyaay villages participate in this resistance to colonial encroachment (Archibald 1978).
1776	Costanoan (Ohlone) Indians resist the establishment of mission at San Francisco until some are threatened with execution. Indians set fire to Mission San Luis Obispo during the same year (Castillo, 75).
1785	At least six villages as well as neophytes (baptized) Indians within the mission participate in planned revolt in Tongva territory at Mission San Gabriel (Hackel, 655).
1795—1796	Over 200 Costanoan Indians stage a mass escape from Mission Dolores. During the same year, over 280 Indians escape from the San Francisco Mission in 1795, and an additional 200 escape the following year (NAN 2014).
1805	Two hundred Indians escape San Juan Bautista Mission (NAN 2014).
1824	Chumash at La Purisma Mission Revolt. Two thousand Indians capture the mission and are joined by Indians from Santa Ynez and San Fernando Missions. After four months, the Spanish recapture the missions (Castillo, 77).
1833	The Secularization Act: The Mexican government repossesses the missions.

1835	Pablo Tac, a Luiseno Indian from San Luis Rey, *writes A Record of California Mission Life,* which remains one of the only first-hand accounts of mission life from an Indian perspective (Bean and Vane, 137).

Step three is beatification and requires evidence that a miracle has been brought about by the candidate (Sadlier 2014). In 1985, Serra was venerated, and in 1988 he was beatified by Pope John Paul II after a miracle was attributed to him. The verified miracle was the claim of a 70-year-old Franciscan nun whose lupus (diagnosed as incurable) was cured after she asked Father Serra to intervene on her behalf in prayer (Pinsky 1987).

Others remained equally committed to presenting the case against Serra. In 1987, Rupert and Jeannette Costo, both Native American, published the book *The Missions of California: A Legacy of Genocide.* Rupert Costo was a Cahuilla descendant of California Indians who had survived the mission era. Jeanette Costo was Eastern Cherokee. Despite the fact that both were practicing Catholics, they considered sainthood for Serra to be "an unforgivable moral disgrace to American Indians. . . ." (Jeanette Costo, quoted in Hirsley 1988).

The final step in the process of sainthood is canonization, which generally occurs after evidence of a second miracle attributed to the candidate has been confirmed (Sadlier 2014). Despite the fact that Serra only had a single confirmed miracle attributed to him, Pope Francis announced his intention to canonize Serra on January 15, 2015. The special mass to announce his sainthood was held in Washington, D.C., on September 23, 2015.

Controversial Sainthood for Serra

Was Sainthood Justified?

Some scholars speculate that the decision to canonize Serra has a great deal to do with the changing demographic of Catholics and the church's desire to bring more Latino converts into the fold (Manson 2015). Serra was the first saint canonized on U.S. soil. For the state and secular components of missions as historic sites, sainthood for Serra is likely to bring increased tourism and visitors to the missions, especially those with special connections to Serra.

Supporters point to a so-called Indian Bill of Rights, known as the Representación, signed on March 13, 1773, as evidence of Serra's commitment to California Indians. Others argue that this document had little to nothing to do with California

Indians, but rather was about consolidating church power over Spanish military presence in Alta California (Grabowski 2015).

Opponents of the canonization effort also point to a contradiction between the pope's stance on social justice and human rights issues as well as his direct apology to indigenous peoples in July 2015 and his decision to make Serra a saint. During his visit to Bolivia in July 2015, Pope Francis offered this historic apology:

> I say this to you with regret: Many grave sins were committed against the Native People of America in the name of God. I humbly ask forgiveness, not only for the offense of the church herself, but also for crimes committed against the Native Peoples during the so-called conquest of America. (as quoted in Yardley and Neuman 2015)

Opponents ask how he can apologize on one hand and ignore the multiple requests from California Native nations and others to deny sainthood for Serra due to the long-term negative impacts on indigenous peoples in California on the other.

Another looming issue in the controversy is education. The Catholic Church, the state of California, and secular historic preservation institutions affiliated with the California missions have been criticized by opponents of canonization for perpetuation of the "mission mythology," which paints a romanticized version of the mission era, and often sanitizes, or altogether erases, local Native perspectives from the story (Miranda 2015).

Responses to Sainthood for Serra

Responses have been artistic, spiritual, and political and include participation in the canonizing mass, gatherings, art exhibits, films, direct actions, petitions, organization of scholarly convenings, and even a 750-mile walk across the state.

Father James Nieblas, the first citizen of his nation (the Juañeno Band of Mission Indians, Acjachemen Nation (JBMI)) to be ordained as a Catholic priest, was invited to participate in the canonization mass for Serra. When he received the news, Nieblas called on his Juañeno community to support a unification mass he intended to hold prior to his trip to Washington, D.C., for the pope's historic visit. Many leaders from his nation—the same nation that passed a resolution opposing canonization and calling for a repudiation of the Doctrine of Discovery—participated in his unification mass and offered traditional cultural gifts for him to bring to Pope Francis when he met him at the historic mass (Bharath 2015).

Ohlone Andrew Galvin, curator of the Dolores Mission in San Francisco, carried a reliquary containing a relic of Serra next to the altar, and his cousin, Vincent Medina, one of the few linguists fluent in Chochenyo, the language of the Ohlone people in Northern California, read the first scripture in his indigenous language during the historic mass announcing sainthood for Serra (CNC 2015).

Indigenous peoples opposed to canonization responded quickly and in a variety of ways. While it is not possible to cover every act of discourse and resistance by indigenous peoples and allies on the issue of canonization, the events and actions listed below represent a sampling of the kinds of responses indigenous peoples engaged in collectively during the year following the pope's announcement.

- Walk for the Ancestors—Fernandeño Tataviam Band of Mission Indians citizens Caroline Ward Holland and her son Keagan Holland walked over 750 miles and visited each of the 21 missions in California as a way to raise awareness about the issues and pay respects to the ancestors who lived there.
- Community Gatherings—Native nations, in collaboration with American Indian Movement Southern California (AIM SoCal), organized peaceful gatherings and prayer vigils at the 21 missions throughout the state. Hundreds of Native and non-Native People attended these events between March and November 2015.
- Tribal Resolutions and Letters—Native nations wrote letters to the pope, governor, and others urging no sainthood for Serra. The Amah Mutsun Tribal Band presented a statement opposing canonization at the United Nations Permanent Forum on Indigenous Issues. The Pechanga Band of Luiseno Indians, Juaneno Band of Mission Indians, Acjachemen Nation, Coastal Band of the Chumash Nation, Ewiiaapaayp Band of Kumeyaay Indians, Mesa Grand, Los Coyotes Band of Indians, Mooretown Rancheria, Ohlone/Coastanoan Esslen Nation, and the Winnemem Wintu tribe all wrote letters or passed resolutions opposing canonization, and in some instances also calling for a revocation of DD. Notable individuals, including Congressional Medal of Freedom recipient and founder of the Morningstar Institute Suzan Shown Harjo, and Steven Newcomb, scholar and director of the Indigenous Law Institute, also called on the pope to abandon plans for canonization and revoke the Doctrine of Discovery.
- Community-Based Symposiums—the University of California, Riverside Center for California Native Nations, established via an endowment from Cahuilla scholar Rupert Costo, hosted a day-long event titled California Indians, Canonization of Junípero Serra, and Consequences of Colonialism, and the Barbareño Chumash Tribal Council "'Iyalmuwič," Affiliate of the Seventh Generation Fund for Indigenous Peoples, and AIM SoCal, hosted a gathering titled Disrobing Junípero Serra—Saint or Monster? to address the issue.

- Connecting Canonization and the Doctrine of Discovery—Several events and film screenings were held around the country and throughout the world, including in Lenape territory in Philadelphia and on the Salt River Reservation in O'Odham Hemackam territory, calling for a revocation of DD and connecting the issue to canonization.
- Artistic Responses—AIM SoCal also organized a guerilla street theater tribunal holding Serra on trial for crimes against humanity, the MCCLA hosted an art exhibit, The Bones of Our Ancestors: Endurance and Survival Beyond Serra's Mission, and countless memes and poster art were created in response to the canonization of Serra.
- Social Media—indigenous activists established several Facebook pages, Twitter hashtags, and online petitions encouraging people to mobilize around the issue. The petition established by a citizen of a Native nation in California garnered more than 10,000 signatures prior to the pope's visit.

Conclusion

Despite substantial difference of opinion on the issue of sainthood for Serra, something that can be agreed on is that the controversy has opened the door for deeper conversations about the realities of the mission system and its impacts on Native nations and indigenous people in California.

One quote frequently attributed to Serra is "Always forward, never back." On September 23, 2015, Pope Francis made an irrevocable decision. From that point forward, in the eyes of millions of Catholics, and countless others around the world, Junípero Serra is now a saint. The collective capacity of society to "look back" in an honest and empowering way is critical to our ability to move forward together. Hopefully, in the years following the pope's decision to canonize Serra, individuals and institutions will continue to dialogue and together create a story of California that is more representative and inclusive of all views—especially those of the people who have lived in California for thousands of years or forever, depending on one's perspective.

Biographies of Notable Figures

Junípero Serra (1713–1784)

Junípero Serra is widely considered one of the most influential figures in the history of the place now known as California. Countless buildings, parks, statues, and streets throughout the state are named after him. Even though his role as colonizer has largely been unexamined in mainstream media and education, the Catholic Church's recent decision to elevate Junípero Serra to his status as saint in 2015 sparked worldwide discussion about whether or not such a designation is appropriate. Although he was officially made a saint in 2015, his impact on California Native nations will continue to be a subject of much discussion in the future.

Early Life

Serra was the third of five children born to farmers Antonio Nadal Serra and Margarita Rose Ferrer. He was born Miguel Jose Serra on November 24, 1713, in the village of Petra on the Spanish island of Majorca. Serra attended a Franciscan primary school run by monks and was 15 years old when he decided to become a priest (USCCB 2015). He then enrolled in the Franciscan university the Convento de Jesus, where he began his educational career as a philosophy student around 1729 or 1730. He took the name Junípero after one of the first companions of St. Francis of Assisi when he joined the Franciscan order in 1731 (Weber 2015).

Historians place the date of his ordination at sometime between 1737 and 1739 (Healy, Bay Area Serra Club). Serra was an intellectually astute student who soon gained the attention of his superiors as a possible future professor. At the age of 30, he became a theology professor at Lullian University in the Majorcan capital Palma (Weber 2015). A few years later, Serra decided his true calling was as a missionary and petitioned the church to allow him to travel abroad.

Serra Travels to the "New World"

Committed to bringing his faith to non-Christians through missionary work, in 1749 Serra traveled to Mexico with a former student, Francisco Palóu, to begin his evangelical career. Upon arrival, he chose to walk the entire 250-mile journey to Mexico City. While on the trek, his leg was injured, and it would trouble him for the remainder of his life (Weber 2015). In 1751, he volunteered for the Sierra Gorda missions located in the lands of the Pame Indians. For eight years, he worked there and learned the Otomi language as a mechanism to support his evangelical conversion efforts among the Pame (USCCB 2015).

In 1767, he was appointed to the presidency of the 15 missions formerly administered by the Jesuits, and in 1769 he began his journey into Alta California, establishing missions along the coast.

California Missions, 1769–1782

For the remaining years of his life, Serra worked on behalf of the church and in collaboration with the Spanish military to establish the first nine of 21 missions in California. Missions established by Serra include: San Diego, San Carlos Borromeo, San Antonio, San Gabriel, San Luis Obispo, San Francisco, San Juan Capistrano, Santa Clara, and San Buenaventura (Weber 2015).

On August 28, 1784, Serra died at the age of 70 at Mission San Carlos, located in Carmel, California. He was buried exactly 35 years from the day he sailed for the "New World," in the floor of the sanctuary at Mission San Carlos, where he remains to this day. According to the United States Conference of Catholic Bishops, by the end of his life in 1784, Indian baptisms in California reached 6,736, and 4,646 Christianized Indians were still living within the missions established by Serra at the time of his death (USCCB 2015).

Path to Sainthood

Serra's path to sainthood began in Fresno, California, in 1934 when the Diocese of Monterey officially initiated the process. For the next 50 years, efforts were maintained, and in 1985 Serra was declared venerable, meaning he was formally recognized as having lived a life of ' "heroic virtue." In 1987, a miracle was attributed to him, and on September 25, 1988, he was beatified by Pope John Paul II (Pinsky 1986).

On September 23, 2015, Pope Francis made Serra a saint during a special mass at the Basilica of the National Shrine of the Immaculate Conception in Washington, D.C. This was the first time an individual had been canonized by the Catholic Church in the United States.

During the mass, the Pope said of Serra, "[he] sought to defend the dignity of the Native community, to protect it from those who had mistreated and abused it. Mistreatment and wrongs which today still trouble us, especially because of the hurt which they cause in the lives of many people" (O'Donnell 2015).

Many California Indians, direct descendants of the indigenous survivors of the mission legacy, were in Washington, D.C., during the Pope's visit. Some were in attendance and participated in the mass, and others were there to protest the sainthood of a man credited with founding a system widely known to have resulted in the loss of thousands and thousands of Indian lives over the course of the mission era in California.

Although popular understanding of the man and his role in history have, until recently, been largely portrayed as positive in mainstream media, for many Native nations and indigenous peoples throughout the world, he was, and remains, a symbol of a brutal era of colonization that resulted in loss of language and life and suppression of ancient cultures in the name of church and state.

Despite the efforts of Serra and his colleagues to eradicate California Native cultures in an attempt to Christianize them and consolidate power in the Spanish crown, California Native nations and cultures remain strong and vocal today—as evidenced by their voices around the issue of canonization. As one Native descendant of the survivors of the mission period said, "Our histories, cultures, and lives have survived over three centuries of colonization and genocide. Not even a miracle could stop us now" (Chilcote 2015).

Toypurina (1760 est.–1799)

Toypurina is a significant figure in California Indian history. Her life and actions provide one perspective on early relationships between the indigenous nations of California and Spanish military and missionaries responsible for the first wave of colonization to reach the indigenous peoples of the region. She was a Tongva spiritual leader and co-organized a rebellion against the Mission San Gabriel in 1785 (John 2014).

What we know of her life is largely the story of a planned indigenous uprising against the mission system coordinated across multiple villages and supported by several prominent Tongva leaders of the time. Her story therefore contributes to the discussion on the controversy around the recent canonization of Junípero Serra. This uprising remains one of the most significant markers we have today of how citizens of Native nations experienced the mission system in California. It is also significant that her story illustrates that the indigenous peoples of this land recognized and respected female leadership.

Early Life

Toypurina was a young indigenous woman from the Native nation now known as Tongva or Gabrielino—one of three Native nations with ancestral territories in present-day Los Angeles County.

Estimates place the number of California Indians as high as 300,000 at the time of first contact (Indian Country Diaries 2006) and the number of Gabrielino/ Tongva at around 5,000. Tongva territory covered about 1,500 square miles of the Los Angeles Basin and stretched west to the islands off present-day Los Angeles (Hackel, 648).

Born in the village of Japchivit, Toypurnia was from an elite family. Her father was a political figure, and at the time of the rebellion her brother was chief of the village of Japchivit, and considered "very wise" by people in the community (Hackel, 654). Her strong political ties, in addition to her reputation as a medicine woman among her people, contributed to her role as a leader in the Tongva uprising at Mission San Gabriel in 1785.

Indigenous Rebellion Mission San Gabriel, 1785

On October 25, 1785, Tongva leaders allied with as many as eight local Tongva villages and planned an attack on the mission San Gabriel. While the issue of

Toypurina's exact role in the rebellion remains debated by scholars and communities today, it is well established that she was at least one of the lead organizers of the event. She worked with neophyte Nicholas Jose and others to recruit three villages and multiple tribal leaders to participate. According to some stories, her powers as a medicine woman were thought to be so great that she was expected to immobilize the missionaries before the main attack so their followers would only have the soldiers to fight. However, the Spanish soldiers and priests were made aware of the plan prior to its implementation and were therefore able to thwart it (Welch 2006).

Evidence in the record highlights that the rebellion was likely sparked by Spanish military imposition of strict penalties for Indians engaging in traditional cultural practices such as conducting annual ceremonies. During the trial, Nicholas Jose, one of the neophyte (baptized) organizers, said that he had participated in the revolt because the padres had refused to let him perform ceremonies, in particular the annual Tongva Mourning Ceremony to honor those departed in their calendar year (Hackel, 651).

In 1782, the governor of California ordered the mission guard at San Diego to forbid baptized Indians from holding traditional dances. It is likely that the governor's mandated prohibition on traditional cultural practices was communicated to soldiers at missions throughout Alta California (Hackel, 651).

It is clear from the historical record that suppression of indigenous religious freedoms was a significant, if not the central, factor in the decision of many Tongva to support the uprising. By 1785, the year of the rebellion, one-third of the adults from Nicolás José's village and one-half of the Sibapet children baptized at Mission San Gabriel were dead (Hackel, 653). The high rates of baptism and death among people from the rebellion leaders' home villages, coupled with the recent ban on traditional ceremonies, likely both contributed to the 1785 revolt.

According to court records and translations, when asked why she had participated in the resistance, Toypurina said that she "was angry with the priests and all the others at the mission, because they were living on their land" (Hackel, 655). One can read the planning of this event and Toypurina's participation in it, as further evidence that she was defending the sovereign rights of her people to continue engaging in their traditional spiritual practices.

Post-Rebellion Life

Toypurina and the other leaders of the revolt were found guilty of insurrection at trial. Five people were sentenced to 25 lashes, and twelve were sentenced to 15 to 20 lashes. The beatings took place in public to serve as a reminder to the remaining Indians of what could happen if they were to resist Spanish mission and colonizing policies (Hackel, 657).

Toypurina was held prisoner at Mission San Gabriel for the remainder of the trial. During this time, she was also baptized and renamed Regina Josepha by a mission priest. Her husband refused baptism, and their marriage was annulled by the church (Hackel, 651). It remains unclear whether this baptism was by choice or coercion.

Toypurina's sentence included banishment to Mission San Carlos Borromeo in Carmel, California, where she eventually remarried a Spanish soldier named Manuel Montera. During their marriage, they had three children—Cesario, Juane de Dios Montero, and Maria Clementia. Toypurina, now called Regina Josepha, died at Mission San Carlos in 1799, less than 15 years after helping to plan a revolt against colonizing forces invading her Tongva homelands.

Lasting Legacy

Toypurina remains a symbol of importance to her own Native nation and to many Native nations, communities, and movements today. Known in various circles as "medicine woman," "spiritual leader," "instigator," "witch," "superstitious woman," "freedom fighter," and "wise woman," one thing remains clear; her name and stories continue to evoke powerful symbols of freedom, resistance, and resilience for the people who remember her.

Further Reading

Archibald, Robert. "Indian Labor at the California Missions: Salvation or Slavery?" *The Journal of San Diego History,* Spring 1978, Vol. 24, No. 2, available at http://www .sandiegohistory.org/journal/78spring/labor.htm

Bharath, Deepa. "Orange County and Pope Francis: Native American Priest to Meet Pope for Father Serra Canonization." *Orange County Register*, September 23, 2015, available at http://www.ocregister.com/articles/nieblas-684151-mass-jimmy.html

Castillo, Edward and Robert Howard Johnson. Chapter 4, "Resistance and Social Control." In *Indians, Franciscans, and Spanish Colonization: The Impact of the Mission System on California Indians,* Albuquerque: University of New Mexico Press, 1995.

Chilcote, Olivia, Ph.D. Candidate, Ethnic Studies, UC Berkeley, "It's Complicated: One Native Californian's Thoughts on Junípero Serra's Canonization." September 22, 2015, available at http://blogs.berkeley.edu/2015/09/22/its-complicated-one-native-californians -thoughts-on-the-canonization-of-junipero-serra

General Convention, *Journal of the General Convention of the Episcopal Church*, Anaheim, 2009 (New York: General Convention, 2009), pp. 371–72.

Gonnella Frichner, Tonya (Special Rapporteur). Preliminary study of the impact on indigenous peoples of the international legal construct known as the doctrine of discovery, Permanent Forum on Indigenous Issues, 9th Session, 2010, E/C.19/2010/13.

Grabowski, Christine. "Serra-gate: The Fabrication of a Saint." *Indian Country Today Media Network,* September 16, 2015. http://indiancountrytodaymedianetwork.com/2015/09/16 /serra-gate-fabrication-saint-161759

Hackel, Steven W. "Sources of Rebellion: Indian Testimony and the Mission San Gabriel Uprising of 1785." The American Society of Ethnohistory, 2003.

Healy, Tim, ed. Junípero Serra's Biography, Bay Area Serra Club, 2015, available at http://www.serra-bayarea.org/Serra_1/serra.htm

Heizer, Robert. "Impact of Colonization on California Native Societies." *San Diego Historical Society Quarterly*, Vol. 24, No. 1, Winter 1978.

Hirsley, Michael. "Some Argue Serra was No Saint." *Chicago Tribune,* May 22, 1988.

Indian Country Diaries. California Genocide, PBS Native American Public Telecommunications, September 2006, available at http://www.pbs.org/indiancountry/history/calif.html

John, Maria. Toypurina: A Legend Etched in the Landscape, South El Monte Arts Posse, Tropics of Meta: Historiography for the Masses, January 23, 2014, available at https://tropicsofmeta.wordpress.com/2014/01/23/toypurina-a-legend-etched-in-the-landscape/#_ftn1

Juaneño Band of Mission Indians. Acjachemen Nation, "Resolution Calling for the Repudiation of the Doctrine of Discovery and Opposing the Canonization of Junípero Serra," September 6, 2015.

Miranda, Deborah. September, 20 2015, "Canonization Fodder: California Indians and the Sainthood of Junípero Serra," and "Dear Sierra: An Open Letter to California Fourth Graders," *Bad Indians Blog*, http://badndns.blogspot.com/2015/09/canonization-fodder-california-indians.html

Native American Netroots (NAN). Indian Rebellions at the California Missions, February 27, 2014, available at http://nativeamericannetroots.net/diary/1671

O'Donnell, Noreen and Nicole Puglise. Pope Canonizes Franciscan Missionary Junípero Serra, NBC New York, September 23, 2015, available at http://www.nbcnewyork.com/news/national-international/Pope-to-Canonize-Franciscan-Missionary-Junipero-Serra—Controversy-328850191.html

Pinsky, Mark I. Major Lobbying Job: Serra on a Fast Track to Sainthood, *Los Angeles Times*, March 27, 1986.

Pope Paul III, Papal Bull Sublimis Deus, 1537.

Romero Institute. Movement to revoke doctrine of discovery gains momentum, September 24, 2015, available at https://romeroinstitute.wordpress.com/2015/09/24/movement-to-revoke-doctrine-of-discovery-gains-momentum

Rotondaro, Vinnie. Disastrous doctrine has papal roots, *National Catholic Reporter*, September 4, 2015, available at http://ncronline.org/news/peace-justice/disastrous-doctrine-had-papal-roots

Sadlier, William H. Canonization: Four Steps to Becoming a Saint, 2014, available at www.sadlierwebelieveblog.com

Saint Paul Interfaith Network: Healing Minnesota Stories (SPIN), Doctrine of Discovery: A Timeline, available at http://spinterfaith.org/uploads/pdfs/Doctrine%20of%20Discovery%20Fact%20Sheets/DD%20Timeline.pdf.

Santa Barbara Archive Library. Guide to Serrana: A Summary of the Documentation about Blessed Junípero Serra OFM, 2009.

Tac, Pablo. *Indian Life and Customs at Mission San Luis Rey: A Record of California Mission Life, in Ethnology of the Alta California Indians II: Post Contact.* Edited by Lowell John Bean and Sylvia Brake Vane. New York: Garland Publishing, Inc., 1991.

Tee-Hit-Ton Indians v. U.S., 348 U.S. 272, 75 S. Ct. 313, 99 L. Ed. 314, 1955.

The West Film Project (WFP). Junípero Serra, 2001, available at https://www.pbs.org/weta/thewest/people/s_z/serra.htm

United States Conference of Catholic Bishops (USCCB). Blessed Junípero Serra, available at http://www.usccb.org/about/leadership/holy-see/francis/papal-visit-2015/junipero-serra-biography.cfm

Weber, Msgr. Francis J. "Junípero Serra: Hero of Evangelization," Knights of Columbus, April 1, 2015, http://www.kofc.org/un/en/columbia/detail/junipero-serra-hero-evangelization.html

Welch, Rosanne. PhD Program, Department of History, Claremont Graduate University, Claremont, CA, *A Brief History of the Tongva Tribe: The Native Inhabitants of the Lands of the Puente Hills Preserve*, July 2006, available at http://tongvapeople.com/native_american_history.pdf

Wiechec, Nancy. Two members of Ohlone tribe to play prominent role in canonization Mass, Catholic News Service, September 18, 2015, available at http://cnstopstories.com/2015/09/18/two-members-of-ohlone-tribe-to-play-prominent-role-in-canonization-mass

Wiseman, Hon. Joseph J. *An Overview of Key Federal Indian Law Cases, Judicial Toolkit on Indian Law.*

Yardley, Jim and William Neuman. "In Bolivia, Pope Francis Apologizes for Church's 'Grave Sins,'" *New York Times*, July 9, 2015, available at http://www.nytimes.com/2015/07/10/world/americas/pope-francis-bolivia-catholic-church-apology.html?_r=1

Recommended Resources

Anderson, Gary Clayton. *Ethnic Cleansing and the Indian: The Crime That Should Haunt America.* Norman: University of Oklahoma Press, 2014.

Andrews, Edward E. *Native Apostles: Black and Indian Missionaries in the British Atlantic World.* Cambridge, MA: Harvard University Press, 2013.

Bettinger, Robert L. *Orderly Anarchy: Sociopolitical Evolution in Aboriginal California.* Oakland: University of California Press, 2015.

Bickman, Troy O. *Savages Within the Empire: Representations of American Indians in Eighteenth-Century Britain.* New York: Oxford University Press, 2006.

Black, Jason Edward. *American Indians and the Rhetoric of Removal and Allotment.* Jackson: University Press of Mississippi, 2015.

Blackhawk, Ned. *American Indians and the Study of U.S. History.* Washington, DC: American Historical Association, 2012.

Breen, Louise A. *Converging Worlds: Communities and Cultures in Colonial America.* New York: Routledge, 2012.

Cahill, Cathleen. *Federal Fathers and Mothers: A Social History of the United States Indian Service.* Chapel Hill: The University of North Carolina Press, 2013.

Calloway, Colin. *White People, Indians, and Highlanders: Tribal Peoples and Colonial Encounters in Scotland and America.* New York: Oxford University Press, 2015.

Calloway, Colin G. *Pen and Ink Witchcraft: Treaties and Treaty Making in American Indian History.* Oxford, UK: Oxford University Press, 2013.

Calloway, Colin Gordon. *The Victory with No Name: The Native American Defeat of the First American Army.* New York: Oxford University Press, 2015.

Carpenter, Roger M. *"Times Are Altered with Us": American Indians from First Contact to the New Republic.* West Sussex, UK: Wiley Blackwell, 2015.

Carstarphen, Meta G., and John P. Sanchez. *American Indians and Mass Media.* Norman: University of Oklahoma, 2012.

Cave, Alfred A. *Lethal Encounters: Englishmen and Indians in Colonial Virginia.* Lincoln: University of Nebraska Press, 2013.

Cobb, Daniel M. *Native Activism in Cold War America: The Struggle for Sovereignty*. Lawrence: University Press of Kansas, 2008.

Cobb, Daniel M. *Say We Are Nations: Documents of Politics and Protest in Indigenous America Since 1887*. Chapel Hill: The University of North Carolina Press, 2015.

Coleman, Michael C. *Presbyterian Missionary Attitudes Toward American Indians, 1837-1893*. Jackson: University Press of Mississippi. 2007.

Confer, Clarissa W. *Cherokee Nation in the Civil War*. Norman: University of Oklahoma Press, 2012.

Cook-Lynn, Elizabeth. *A Separate Country: Postcoloniality and American Indian Nations*. Lubbock: Texas Tech University Press, 2012.

Cowell, Andrew Cowell, Alonzo Moss, and William J. C'Hair. *Arapaho Stories, Songs, and Prayers: A Bilingual Anthology*. Norman: University of Oklahoma, 2014.

Deloria, Vine. *Custer Died for Your Sins: An Indian Manifesto*. Norman: University of Oklahoma, 1988.

Dunbar-Ortiz, Roxanne. *An Indigenous Peoples' History of the United States*. Boston: Beacon Press, 2015.

Farr, William E. *Blackfoot Redemption: A Blood Indian's Story of Murder, Confinement, and Imperfect Justice*. Norman: University of Oklahoma Press, 2012.

Fisher, Linford D. *The Indian Great Awakening: Religion and the Shaping of Native Cultures in Early America*. New York: Oxford University Press, 2012.

Fixico, Donald Lee. *Call for Change: The Medicine Way of American Indian History, Ethos, & Reality*. Lincoln: University of Nebraska Press. 2013.

Foster, Stephen. *British North America in the Seventeenth and Eighteenth Centuries*. Oxford, United Kingdom: Oxford University Press, 2013.

Fulford, Tim, and Kevin Hutchings. *Native Americans and Anglo-American Culture, 1750-1850: The Indian Atlantic*. New York: Cambridge University Press, 2013.

Gallay, Alan. *Indian Slavery in Colonial America*. Lincoln: University of Nebraska Press, 2015.

Gipp, Gerald E., Linda Sue Warner, Janine Pease, and James Shanley. *American Indian Stories of Success: New Visions of Leadership in Indian Country*. Santa Barbara, CA: Praeger, 2015.

Greene, Jerome. *American Carnage: Wounded Knee, 1890*. Norman: University of Oklahoma, 2014.

Hagan, William T., and Daniel M. Cobb. *American Indians*. Chicago: The University of Chicago Press, 2013.

Harvey, Sean. *Native Tongues: Colonialism and Race from Encounter to the Reservation*. Cambridge, MA: Harvard University Press, 2015.

Heat Moon, William Least., and James K. Wallace. *An Osage Journey to Europe, 1827-1830: Three French Accounts*. Norman: University of Oklahoma Press, 2013.

Hickey, Donald R. *The War of 1812: A Forgotten Conflict*. Urbana: University of Illinois Press, 2012.

Hightower, Michael J. *Banking in Oklahoma Before Statehood*. Norman: University of Oklahoma Press, 2013.

Hillaire, Pauline, and Gregory P. Fields. *A Totem Pole History: The Work of Lummi Carver Joe Hillaire*. Lincoln: University of Nebraska Press, 2013.

Hoffman, Elizabeth DeLaney. *American Indians and Popular Culture*. Santa Barbara, California: Praeger, 2012.

Hovens, Pieter. *American Indian Material Culture*. Lincoln: University of Nebraska, 2010.

Howard, James H. *The Canadian Sioux*. Lincoln: University of Nebraska Press, 2014.

Iverson, Peter, and Wade Davies. *"We Are Still Here": American Indians Since 1890*. New York: Wiley Blackwell, 2014.

Jacobs, Jaap, and L. H. Roper. *The Worlds of the Seventeenth-Century Hudson Valley*. Albany: SUNY Press, 2014.

Josephy, Alvin M., Marc Jaffe, and Rich Wandschneider. *The Longest Trail: Writings on American Indian History, Culture, and Politics*. New York: Vintage Books, 2015.

Kelman, Ari. *A Misplaced Massacre: Struggling Over the Memory of Sand Creek*. Cambridge, MA: Harvard University Press, 2015.

Kelton, Paul. *Cherokee Medicine, Colonial Germs: An Indigenous Nation's Fight Against Smallpox, 1518-1824*. Norman: University of Oklahoma, 2015.

Kidwell, Clara Sue. *The Choctaw Nation in Oklahoma: From Tribe to Nation, 1855–1970*. Norman: University of Oklahoma Press, 2007.

King, Richard C. *The Native American Mascot Controversy: A Handbook*. New York: Rowman and Littlefield, 2015.

Kiser, William. *Dragoons in Apacheland: Conquest and Resistance in Southern New Mexico, 1846-1861*. Norman: University of Oklahoma, 2013.

Kraft, Louis. *Ned Wynkoop and the Lonely Road from Sand Creek*. Norman: University of Oklahoma Press, 2015.

Krupat, Arnold. *That the People Might Live: Loss and Renewal in Native American Elegy*. Ithaca, NY: Cornell University Press, 2012.

LaPier, Rosalyn R., and David Beck. *City Indian: Native American Activism in Chicago, 1893-1934*. Lincoln, Nebraska: University of Nebraska Press, 2015.

Laughlin, McDonald. *American Indians and the Fight for Equal Voting Rights*. Norman: University of Oklahoma Press, 2011.

Laukaitis, John. *Community Self-Determination: American Indian Education in Chicago, 1952-2006*. Albany, NY: SUNY Press, 2015.

Lawson, Russell M. *Encyclopedia of American Indian Issues Today*. Santa Barbara, CA: Greenwood, 2013.

Maddox, Lucy. *Citizen Indians: Native American Intellectuals, Race, and Reform*. Albany, NY: Cornell University Press, 2006.

Maroukis, Constantine. *The Peyote Road: Religious Freedom and the Native American Church*. Norman: University of Oklahoma Press, 2012.

Martinez, David. *Dakota Philosopher: Charles Eastman and American Indian Thought*. Minneapolis: Minnesota Historical Society Press, 2009.

McDonnell, Michael A. *Masters of Empire: Great Lakes Indians and the Making of America*. New York: Hill and Wang, a division of Farrar, Straus and Giroux, 2015.

McKenzie-Jones, Paul R. *Clyde Warrior: Tradition, Community, and Red Power*. Norman: University of Oklahoma, 2015.

Miller, Robert J. *Reservation "Capitalism": Economic Development in Indian Country*. Santa Barbara, CA: Praeger, 2012.

Milne, George Edward. *Natchez Country: Indians, Colonists, and the Landscapes of Race in French Louisiana*. Athens: The University of Georgia Press, 2015.

Milner, George. *The Moundbuilders: Ancient Peoples of Eastern North America*. London: Thames and Hudson, 2005.

Mithlo, Nancy Marie. *For a Love of His People: The Photography of Horace Poolaw*. Washington, DC: National Museum of the American Indian, Smithsonian Institution, 2014.

Mock, Shirley Boteler. *Dreaming with the Ancestors: Black Seminole Women in Texas and Mexico*. Norman: University of Oklahoma, 2010.

Mueller, James E. 2013. *Shooting Arrows and Slinging Mud: Custer, the Press, and the Little Bighorn*. Norman: University of Oklahoma Press, 2013.

Murphree, Daniel S. *Constructing Floridians: Natives and Europeans in the Colonial Floridas, 1513-1783*. Gainesville: University Press of Florida, 2006.

Murphy, Jacqueline Shea. *The People Never Stopped Dancing: Native American Modern Dance Histories*. Minneapolis, University of Minnesota Press, 2007.

Myers, Merlin G. *Households and Families of the Longhouse Iroquois at Six Nations Reserve*. Lincoln: University of Nebraska Press, 2006.

Nichols, Roger L. *American Indians in U.S. History*. Norman: University of Oklahoma Press, 2014.

Norton-Smith, Thomas M. *The Dance of Person and Place: One Interpretation of American Indian Philosophy*. Albany: SUNY University Press, 2010.

Perea, John-Carlos. *Intertribal Native American Music in the United States: Experiencing Music, Expressing Culture*. New York: Oxford University Press, 2014.

Perry, Barbara. *Silent Victims: Hate Crimes Against Native Americans*. Tuscon: University of Arizona Press, 2008.

Piatote, Beth H. *Domestic Subjects: Gender, Citizenship, and Law in Native American Literature*. New Haven, CT: Yale University Press, 2013.

Reid, Joshua. *The Sea Is My Country: The Maritime World of the Makahs, an Indigenous Borderlands People*. New Haven, CT: Yale University Press, 2015.

Reyes, Lawney. *Bernie Whitebear: An Urban Indian's Quest for Justice*. Tuscon: University of Arizona Press, 2006.

Rose, Jennie, and Francine Gachupin. *Health and Social Issues of Native American Women*. Santa Barbara, CA: Praeger, 2012.

Rosen, Deborah. *American Indians and State Law: Sovereignty, Race, and Citizenship, 1790-1800*. Lincoln: University of Nebraska Press, 2009.

Rosier, Paul. *Serving Their Country: American Indian Politics and Patriotism in the Twentieth Century*. Cambridge, MA: Harvard University Press, 2012.

Rushing, W. Jackson, III. *Modern Spirit. The Art of George Morrison*. Norman: University of Oklahoma Press, 2013.

Russell, Steve. *Sequoyah Rising: Problems in Post-Colonial Tribal Governance*. Durham, NC: Carolina Academic Press, 2010.

Scancarelli, Janine, and Heather Hardy. *Native Languages of the Southeastern United States*. Lincoln: University of Nebraska Press, 2005.

Schmidt, Ethan A. *Native Americans in the American Revolution: How the War Divided, Devastated, and Transformed the Early American Indian World*. Santa Barbara, CA: Praeger, 2014.

Schwarz, Maureen Trudelle. *Fighting Colonialism with Hegemonic Culture: Native American Appropriation of Indian Stereotypes*. Albany: SUNY University Press, 2013.

Seelye, James E., and Steven A. Littleton. *Voices of the American Indian Experience*. Santa Barbara, CA: Greenwood, 2013.

Smith, Paul Chaat. *Everything You Know about Indians Is Wrong*. Minneapolis, University of Minnesota, 2009.

Smoak, Gregory. *Ghost Dances and Identity: Prophetic Religion and American Indian Ethnogenesis in the Nineteenth Century*. Oakland: University of California Press, 2008.

Snyder, Christina. *Slavery in Indian Country: The Changing Face of Captivity in Early America*. Cambridge, MA: Harvard University Press, 2012.

Stack, David. *Taking Back the Rock: American Indians Reclaim Alcatraz, 1969*. New Haven, CT: Yale University Press. 2009.

Stands in Timber, John, and Margot Liberty. *A Cheyenne Voice: The Complete John Stands in Timber Interviews*. Norman: University of Oklahoma, 2013.

Tayac, Gabrielle, ed. *IndiVisible: African-Native American Lives in the Americas*. Washington, DC: Smithsonian Books, 2009.

Trafzer, Clifford. *American Indians/American Presidents: A History*. Washington, DC: National Museum of the American Indian, Smithsonian, 2009.

Treuer, Anton, Susan Straight, Matt Propert, and Linda Meyerriecks. *Atlas of Indian Nations*. Washington, DC: National Geographic, 2014.

Tully, John A. *Crooked Deals and Broken Treaties: How American Indians Were Displaced by White Settlers in the Cuyahoga Valley*. New York: Monthly Review Press, 2015.

Turner, Pauline Strong. *American Indians and the American Imaginary: Cultural Representation Across the Centuries*. New York: Routledge, 2013.

Warren, Stephen. *The Worlds the Shawnees Made: Migration and Violence in Early America*. Chapel Hill: The University of North Carolina Press, 2014.

Waselkov, Gregory, Peter H. Wood, and M. Thomas Hatley. *Powhatan's Mantle: Indians in the Colonial Southwest*. Lincoln: University of Nebraska Press, 2006.

Whipple, Dorothy Dora. *Chi-mewinzha: Ojibwe Stores from Leech Lake*. Minneapolis: University of Minnesota Press, 2015

Wilkins, David E. *Hollow Justice: A History of Indigenous Claims in the United States*. New Haven, CT: Yale University Press, 2013.

Williams, Robert A. *Like a Loaded Weapon: The Rehnquist Court, Indian Rights and the Legal History of Racism in America*. Minneapolis: University of Minnesota Press, 2005.

Wray, Jacilee. *Native Peoples of the Olympic Peninsula: Who We Are*. Norman: University of Oklahoma Press, 2015.

Youngbull, Kristin M. *Brummett Echohawk: Pawnee Thunderbird and Artist*. Norman: University of Oklahoma, 2015.

About the Editors and Contributors

Editors

Donna Martinez (Cherokee), PhD, graduated magna cum laude from the University of Washington in political science. She is professor and chair of ethnic studies at the University of Colorado Denver. Donna Martinez is the author of five books, including *Urban American Indians: Reclaiming Native Space* and *Native American World*.

Jennifer L. Williams Bordeaux (Sicangu Lakota/Yankton Dakota) is an enrolled member of the Sicangu Lakota Oyate, Rosebud, South Dakota. She has a master's degree in political science. Jennifer is currently the executive assistant in the department of ethnic studies at the University of Colorado Denver.

Contributors

Terry Ahlstedt earned his PhD at the University of Nebraska with his dissertation "John Collier and Mexico in the Shaping of U.S. Indian Policy: 1934–1945." His specialty is the history of the American West and Native American history.

Katherine Brooks earned her doctorate in American Indian Studies at the University of Arizona in 2014 and has worked with Native communities in the Southwest for the past eight years. Dr. Brooks specializes in American Indian material culture, ethnography, and applied anthropology. Previous degrees include an M.A. in anthropology from New Mexico State University. Currently, Dr. Brooks works as a postdoctoral research associate at the University of Arizona, School of Anthropology, and is an associate professor of anthropology at Cochise College.

Jonathan Byrn is a PhD student in American Indian Studies at the University of Arizona, studying American Indian law and policy, indigenous governance, and historical archaeology. He holds a master's degree in history from Murray State University with research areas in American Indian and western history, cultural preservation, and cultural exchange.

Roger Carpenter is an associate professor of history at the University of Louisiana at Monroe. He is the author of *"Times Are Altered with Us": American Indians from First Contact to the New Republic* (Wiley-Blackwell, 2015) and *The Renewed, the Destroyed, and the Remade: The Three Thought Worlds of the Huron and the Iroquois, 1609–1650* (Michigan State University Press, 2004). He has also published articles in *Pennsylvania History: A Journal of Mid-Atlantic Studies, The Journal of Early American Wars and Armed Conflicts,* and the *Michigan Historical Review.* In addition, he has contributed book reviews to publications such as *The American Historical Review* and *The Canadian Journal of History.*

Menoukha R. Case is an associate professor of cultural studies at SUNY Empire State College. Her previous publications are both creative and academic. Her most recent work, *Weaving the Legacy: Remembering Paula Gunn Allen,* co-edited with Stephanie Sellers, is forthcoming from West End Press.

Amy Casselman is an adjunct professor of ethnic studies at San Francisco State University and the author of *Injustice in Indian Country: Jurisdiction, American Law, and Sexual Violence against Native Women.* Prior to her career in academia, Amy was a caseworker for the Washoe tribe of Nevada and California.

Angela D'Arcy, of the Acjachemen Nation, has been working to protect indigenous sacred lands, waters, and cultures for over 15 years. She is the Executive Director of Sacred Places Institute for Indigenous Peoples, a Los Angeles-based community organization and Affiliate of the Seventh Generation Fund for Indigenous Peoples dedicated to building the capacity of Native nations and indigenous people on social and environmental justice issues.

Christine DeLucia is assistant professor of history at Mount Holyoke College. She received her PhD in American Studies from Yale University. Her first book, on King Philip's War and its contested legacies, is under contract with Yale University Press, for the Henry Roe Cloud Series on American Indians and Modernity.

Nikki Dragone, a scholar of Lakota/Dakota descent, teaches American Indian Studies and English at Black Hills State University. Dragone completed her PhD in American Studies and her J.D. at SUNY at Buffalo. She has published articles and book chapters on Native American literature and film, indigenous rights and Haude-nosaunee history.

Angelique EagleWoman (*Wambdi A. WasteWin*) is a law professor who teaches Native American Law, tribal nation Economics and Law, and Native American Natural Resources Law at the University of Idaho College of Law. She is a citizen of the Sisseton-Wahpeton Oyate of the Lake Traverse Reservation, South Dakota.

Torivio A. Foddor (Taos Pueblo, Comanche, Kiowa, Cherokee) is the associate director of the High Plains American Indian Research Institute (HPAIRI) at the University of Wyoming. Dr. Foddor is a postdoctoral fellow in the University of Wyoming American Indian Studies Program.

Claudia J. Ford has had a global career in development and health, spanning three decades and all continents. Her research interests are in gender, traditional ecologi-cal knowledge, historical ethnobotany, and sustainable agriculture. Dr. Ford earned her BA at Columbia University, and MA and PhD at Antioch University.

Anne A. Garner, PhD, MFA, is a historian in global indigenous studies, an art historian, and a visual artist. Her recent scholarship includes an analysis of con-temporary indigenous art in North America as a statement of decolonization and sovereignty. Currently, Dr. Garner teaches at SUNY Empire State College, Cheek-towaga, New York, and at Excelsior College, Albany, New York.

Frances Holmes has a PhD in Education: Language, Literacy and Culture and an MA in Native American Studies. Of Muscogee (Creek) ancestry, Kay is currently an assistant professor at Lewis College in Durango, CO, in the Native American & Indigenous Studies Department.

C. Richard King, professor of Comparative Ethnic Studies at Washington State University, has written extensively on the Native American mascot controversy, race and popular culture, and white power. He is also the author/editor of four books, including *Team Spirits: The Native American Mascot Controversy*, a CHOICE 2001 Outstanding Academic Title, *Unsettling America: Indianness in the Contemporary World, Beyond Hate: White Power and Popular Culture*, and most recently *Red-skins: Insult and Brand*.

Katie Kirakosian received her MA ('07) and her PhD ('14) in anthropology at the University of Massachusetts, Amherst. She currently works at Kaplan University as an assistant academic chair in the School of General Education.

Alexis Kopkowski, MA, is a PhD student of American Indian studies and public health at the University of Arizona. Her research focuses on healthcare delivery, health disparities, and violence prevention among the American Indian population.

Alan Lechusza Aquallo, PhD, maintains a strong track record of multidisciplinary research and multi-media performances focused upon Native American/indigenous identity and how this complicated locus is re-presented and conceptualized through the music, expressive arts and culture, both traditional and contemporary. As a Native scholar, Dr. Lechusza Aquallo's critical research provides alternative epistemologies designed to establish new theoretical concepts for the study and sociopolitical advancement of scholarship. Dr. Lechusza Aquallo's guiding philosophy is firmly engaged toward fostering new directions of Native/indigenous research, artistic practice, and multidisciplinary methodologies that produce new knowledge for the academy and the artistic community. He is currently a tenured professor of American Indian Studies at Palomar College, San Marcos, California.

Patty Loew, PhD, is a professor in the University of Wisconsin-Madison Department of Life Sciences Communication, a documentary producer, and former broadcast journalist in public and commercial television. Loew (Bad River Ojibwe) is the award-winning author of three books: *Indian Nations of Wisconsin: Histories of Endurance and Renewal, Native People of Wisconsin*, and *Seventh Generation Earth Ethics,* a collection of biographies of Native American environmental leaders. Loew has produced more than a dozen documentaries, including the award-winning *Way of the Warrior,* which aired nationally on PBS in 2007.

Drew Lopenzina is a professor of Early American and Native American literature at Old Dominion University. He is the author of *Red Ink: Native Americans Picking up the Pen in the Colonial Period* (SUNY Press 2012). His cultural biography of Pequot activist and minister William Apess, *Through an Indian's Looking-Glass,* will appear with the University of Massachusetts Press in 2017.

Anne Luna-Gordinier (Choctaw/Cherokee) is an assistant professor in the Department of Sociology at Sacramento State. She earned a JD from the James E. Rogers College of Law and a MA in American Indian Studies from the University of Arizona. She received a PhD in sociology from Howard University.

Paul McKenzie-Jones is the author of *Clyde Warrior: Tradition, Community, and Red Power.* He received his PhD in history from the University of Oklahoma in 2012 and is currently an assistant professor of Native American studies and history at Montana State University–Northern.

Jeff Means (Enrolled Member: Oglala Sioux tribe) is an associate professor of history at the University of Wyoming. His most recent article publication is "Indians shall do things in common" in *Montana: The Magazine of Western History*. He is working on his first book, *From Bison to Beeves: Cattle and the Economic Evolution of Oglala Lakota, 1750–1920*.

K.D. Motes is associate professor of history at Rockhurst University in Kansas City, Missouri. He holds a PhD in history with a focus on Native American history from the University of California, Riverside.

Azusa Ono is an associate professor at Osaka University of Economics in Osaka, Japan, and a visiting fellow at the Institute of American Studies at Rikkyo University in Tokyo, Japan.

Selene Phillips is a member of the Lac du Flambeau Band of Lake Superior Ojibwe in Wisconsin and an assistant professor at the University of Louisville in Kentucky. She teaches journalism and Native American studies in the communication department and researches and does Chautauqua performances of Sacagawea and Mary Todd Lincoln.

Ramon Resendiz is a graduate student in the M.C. Native Voices program in documentary film at the University of Washington, which aims to decolonize the portrayal and construction of indigenous peoples across media. He is a Ronald E. McNair Fellow and graduated magna cum laude from the University of North Texas with a double major in philosophy and anthropology.

Rosalva Resendiz earned her PhD in sociology at Texas Woman's University and is an associate professor at the University of Texas-Rio Grande Valley, Department of Criminal Justice. She is the coauthor of *On the Edge of Law: Culture, Labor and Deviance on the South Texas Border* (2007) and author/editor of *Gender, Crime & Justice: Critical and Feminist Perspectives* (2015).

Daniel Winunwe Rivers is an assistant professor in the Department of History at The Ohio State University and an enrolled citizen of the Choctaw Nation of Oklahoma. His research focuses on LGBT communities in the twentieth century, Native American history, the family and sexuality, and U.S. social protest movements.

Rhianna C. Rogers is assistant professor of cultural studies at State University of New York (SUNY)-Empire State College. Her previous publications and research focus on the historical and archaeological impacts of European settlement on Native communities in the Eastern United States and Mesoamerica.

Caskey Russell, originally from Seattle, is an enrolled member of the Tlingit tribe. He received his BA and MA from Western Washington University, and his PhD from the University of Oregon. He is the Director of American Indian Studies at the University of Wyoming. His is co-author of *Critical Race Theory Matters: Education and Ideology.*

LeRoy Saiz is the current program coordinator for Jeffco Public Schools–Title VII Indian Education Program, located in Golden, Colorado, where his scholarly and professional emphasis locates the implementation of indigenous educational models not only in the field of education, but also within community development.

Alan G. Shackelford is an assistant professor of American Indian history in the American Indian Studies Department at the University of North Dakota. His research focuses on late Pre-Columbian and early colonial history of the Mississippi Valley. He received his PhD in American history from Indiana University at Bloomington.

Megan Tusler received her PhD from the University of Chicago in 2015 and currently works for the MA Program in the Humanities. Her current project is called *American Snapshot: Urban Realism from New Deal to Great Society* and argues that minor and counter-culture movements in the twentieth-century United States produce unique forms of realism in response to social crisis, particularly through the mode of the photo-text. She is a member of the Osage Nation of Oklahoma.

Mark van de Logt, assistant professor of history, Texas A&M University, Qatar, specializes in Plains Indian history and is the author of *War Party in Blue: Pawnee Scouts in the U.S. Army* (2010) and several articles in the *Journal of Military History and American Indian Quarterly.*

Kiara M. Vigil is an assistant professor of American studies at Amherst College and the author of *Indigenous Intellectuals: Sovereignty, Citizenship, and the American Imagination, 1880–1930* (Cambridge University Press, 2015). She has received fellowships from Amherst College, the Mellon Foundation, the Autry National Center, Williams College, the Newberry Library, and the University of Michigan.

Joe Watkins, a member of the Choctaw Nation of Oklahoma, is the Supervisory Anthropologist and Chief, Tribal Relations and American Cultures Program, National Park Service. Watkins's studies include the ethical practice of anthropology and anthropology's relationships with descendant communities, including American Indians, Australian Aboriginals, New Zealand Maori, and Japanese Ainu.

Index

Note: Page numbers in **bold** indicate main entries in the encyclopedia.